The Romans For Dummies®

The Roman Empire

Cheat Sheet

W9-AGJ-583

Roman Emperors from 27 BC to AD 476

The following list includes Roman emperors from 27 BC to the last emperor in the West in AD 476 – not including usurpers, rebels, and so on. The eastern Roman empire continued on for about another thousand years.

Emperor	Reign	Emperor	Reign	Emperor	Reign
Augustus (Octavian)	27 BC–AD 14	Antoninus Pius	138–161	Trajan Decius	249–251
Tiberius	14–37	Marcus Aurelius	161–180	Trebonianus	251–253
Caligula	37–41	Commodus	180–192	Valerian I	253–260
Claudius	41–54	Pertinax	193	Gallienus	253–268
Nero	54–68	Didius Julianus	193	Claudius II	268–270
Galba	68–69	Septimius Severus	193–211	Aurelian	270–275
Otho	69	Caracalla	211–217	Tacitus	275–276
Vitellius	69	Macrinus	217–218	Probus	276–282
Vespasian	69–79	Elagabalus	218–222	Carus	282–283
Titus	79–81	Severus Alexander	222–235	Numerian	283–284
Domitian	81–96	Maximimus I	235–238	Carinus	283–285
Nerva	96–98	Balbinus/Pupienus	238	Diocletian (E)	284–305
Trajan	98–117	Gordian III	238–244	Maximinus I (W)	286–305
Hadrian	117–138	Philip I	244–249	Galerius (E)	305–311

(continued)

For Dummies: Bestselling Book Series for Beginners

(continued)

Emperor	Reign	Emperor	Reign	Emperor	Reign
Constantius (W)	305–306	Gratian (W)	367–383	Avitus	455–456
Licinius (W)	308–324	Valentinian II (W)	375–392	Majorian	457–461
Constantine I	307–337	Theodosius I (E)	379–395	Severus III	461–465
Constantius II	337–361	Arcadius (E)	383–408	Anthemius	467–472
Julian II	360–363	Honorius (W)	393–423 – from here Western Emperors only listed	Olybrius	472
Jovian	363–364	Johannes	423–425	Glycerius	473–474
Valentinian I (W)	364–375	Valentinian III	425–455	Julius Nepos	474–475
Valens (E)	364–378	Petronius Maximus	455	Romulus Augustus	475–476

Great Events in Roman History

The following table lists the important events that occurred during the different periods of Roman history.

Event	Year(s)	Event	Year(s)
The foundation of Rome	753 BC	**The early Empire**	
The Age of Kings	753–509 BC	Reign of Augustus	27 BC–AD 14
The Republic		The settlements	27 and 19 BC
Expulsion of the Kings	509 BC	The other Julio-Claudian Emperors	AD 14–68
Conflict of the Orders begins	471 BC	Civil War	68–69
The Twelve Tables	450 BC	Flavian Dynasty	69–96
Invasion by the Gauls	390 BC	The Five Good Emperors	96–180
Samnite Wars	343–309 and 298–290 BC	The end of imperial expansion: Hadrian	117–138
First Punic War	264–241 BC	**The Decline**	
Second Punic War	218–202 BC	Civil War	193–197
Third Punic War	151–146 BC	The Severans	193–235
Fall of Greece	146 BC	Soldier emperors	235–284
Gracchi Politics	133–121 BC	Diocletian's Tetrarchy	293
Social Wars	90–88 BC	House of Constantine	307–361
First Triumvirate	60 BC	Christianity legitimised	313
Death of Caesar	44 BC	Decline and Fall	364–410
Second Triumvirate	43 BC – the end of the Republic	Rome sacked	410
Battle of Actium	31 BC	The last days of Rome	410–476
		The last Western emperor deposed	476
		The Byzantine Empire	to 1453

For Dummies: Bestselling Book Series for Beginners

The Romans

FOR

DUMMIES®

The Romans

FOR

DUMMIES®

by Guy de la Bédoyère

JOHN WILEY & SONS, LTD

The Romans For Dummies®

Published by
John Wiley & Sons, Ltd
The Atrium
Southern Gate
Chichester
West Sussex
PO19 8SQ
England

E-mail (for orders and customer service enquires): cs-books@wiley.co.uk

Visit our Home Page on www.wiley.com

For general information on our other products and services, please contact our Customer Care Department within the U.S. at 800-762-2974, outside the U.S. at 317-572-3993, or fax 317-572-4002.

For technical support, please visit www.wiley.com/techsupport.

Wiley also publishes its books in a variety of electronic formats. Some content that appears in print may not be available in electronic books.

British Library Cataloguing in Publication Data: A catalogue record for this book is available from the British Library

ISBN-13: 978-0-470-03077-6 (P/B)

Printed and bound in Great Britain by Bell & Bain Ltd, Glasgow.

10 9 8 7 6 5 4 3 2

WILEY

About the Author

Guy de la Bédoyère is a freelance writer and broadcaster who took a history and archaeology degree at Durham University, followed by a history degree at the University of London specialising in Roman history, with papers in US history. Next came an MA in Roman Empire archaeology at University College, London. He has written many books on his specialist field of Roman Britain and is well-known for his numerous appearances on television, especially Channel 4's *Time Team* in Britain. He has also written books on a variety of other historical subjects, including the papers of Samuel Pepys, and is a Fellow of the Royal Numismatic Society. His other interests include playing the piano, travelling in the United States, and studying genealogy. He lives in Lincolnshire, England.

Author's Acknowledgements

I can't list all the Roman experts I've met and talked to over the years who have made a difference to this book whether they know it or not, but I would like to make a special mention of Richard Reece and Neil Faulkner, both of whose idiosyncratic and original perspectives on Roman history have made me think more than they know. I'd also like to thank Daniel Mersey, Samantha Clapp, and Martin Tribe at Wiley for their comments along the way on assembling the text, and Wejdan Ismail for her help. Special mention for Tracy Barr for her editorial work in developing the text through to its final form. I'm also grateful to all those people I've worked with in television archaeology and history, and the viewers, for their comments and observations which have helped me cut through the waffle to see things more clearly. Finally to my wife who endured several fourteen-hour days tramping round Rome and Ostia during the research for this book, and who has put up with the Roman Empire for nearly thirty years.

Publisher's Acknowledgements

We're proud of this book; please send us your comments through our Dummies online registration form located at www.dummies.com/register/.

Some of the people who helped bring this book to market include the following:

*Acquisitions, Editorial, and
Media Development*

Project Editor: Daniel Mersey

Development Editor: Tracy Barr

Content Editor: Steve Edwards

Commissioning Editor: Samantha Clapp

Copy Editor: Christine Lea

Proofreader: Charlie Wilson

Technical Editor: Cassian Hall

Executive Editor: Jason Dunne

Executive Project Editor: Martin Tribe

Cover Photos: © Caesar: Bettmann/ CORBIS;
 Hadrian's Wall: The National Trust
 Photolibrary/ Alamy; gladiator: Christie's
 Images/ CORBIS; clock face: Jupiterimages;
 all other images Guy de la Bédoyère.

Cartoons: Rich Tennant (www.the5thwave.com)

Composition Services

Project Coordinator: Jennifer Theriot

Layout and Graphics: Lavonne Cook,
 Stephanie D. Jumper, Barbara Moore,
 Barry Offringa, Heather Ryan, Alicia South

Proofreaders: Jessica Kramer, Charles Spencer

Indexer: Techbooks

Brand Reviewers: Zoë Wykes, Jan Withers

Publishing and Editorial for Consumer Dummies

 Diane Graves Steele, Vice President and Publisher, Consumer Dummies

 Joyce Pepple, Acquisitions Director, Consumer Dummies

 Kristin A. Cocks, Product Development Director, Consumer Dummies

 Michael Spring, Vice President and Publisher, Travel

 Kelly Regan, Editorial Director, Travel

Publishing for Technology Dummies

 Andy Cummings, Vice President and Publisher, Dummies Technology/General User

Composition Services

 Gerry Fahey, Vice President of Production Services

 Debbie Stailey, Director of Composition Services

Contents at a Glance

Table of Contents

Part III: The Rise of Rome 165

Chapter 10: Kings? No, Maybe Not – Republicans 167

Chapter 11: This Town Isn't Big Enough for All of Us – Seizing Italy 185

Introduction

● ●

*W*hen I was about 12 years old, my father came home from work with a Roman coin he'd bought for me. It was very worn, with a barely visible profile of a Roman emperor's head on one side. But I was totally fascinated by the sudden realisation that this coin had existed for a length of time I was struggling to imagine. It belonged to a truly amazing world of emperors, vast buildings, epic wars, villains, and heroes. And I could hold a part of it in my hand!

Roman history is a hotch-potch made up from every, or indeed, any source that historians and archaeologists have been able to get their hands on. There's no one-stop ancient source of Roman history, no great Roman text-book that we can pick up and start with. Even the Romans were more than a bit hazy about how their world had come together. They had historians, but most of what got written down hasn't survived. Even the works we do have are usually incomplete. What we do know is that the further the Romans looked back into their past, the more they had to fill in the gaps with myth and hearsay.

If you think back to learning about the Romans at school or watching a documentary on TV, you'd probably have come across things that sounded really exciting, like Mount Vesuvius erupting and burying Pompeii in AD 79. But you probably also got the idea that the Romans were also dreadfully serious. Some museums don't help either because rows and rows of dusty pots aren't very inspiring, especially if you had to troop around with a question sheet while on a school trip.

But the truth is that the Roman Empire is one of the most exciting periods in all history. Not only is it packed with real people living real lives, but it also has an unending series of remarkable events that mark the rise of a little village in Italy all the way from total prehistoric obscurity into the greatest of all ancient civilisations.

The Roman world is all around us. In Europe, North Africa, and the Near East, the debris is there to see wherever you go. From the crumbling line of Hadrian's Wall in northern England all the way to the rock-cut tombs of Petra in Jordan, the Romans left their mark everywhere they went and created the world's first superstate. The very fact that it's long gone is why we should use it as a mirror for our own age. 'All Things Must Pass,' said George Harrison, and when it comes to empires, he couldn't have been more correct.

About This Book

Teaching Latin goes back right to the Middle Ages. In the nineteenth century, the Victorians loved the Romans and used them as a kind of justification for what they were doing: conquering the world, basically. So Latin and ancient history were major subjects, and things didn't change for years. Generations of schoolchildren – actually, in the 1960s I was one of them – had to learn Latin so that they could translate lines like 'Caesar attacked the enemy's fortifications'. The upshot was that the Romans looked like a rather boring master-race of generals and politicians, who did a lot of standing around in togas when they weren't massacring other people. Hardly thrilling stuff and apparently completely irrelevant to today, but thanks to archaeology, cinema, and TV, they're now enjoying something of a revival.

The story's miles more interesting than that, so the idea behind this book is to tell it like it was: a rollercoaster of a drama packed with amazing events and amazing people. Now it's easy to get the idea that all the Romans came from Rome, and it was just them who made the Roman Empire what it was while everyone else watched. Not a bit of it. The Romans were very clever at what they did. They turned being Roman into an idea, a way of life, that anyone could have – under certain conditions of course, like being prepared to accept the emperor's authority without question. The fact is that millions of people did just that. They adopted Roman names, lived the Roman way, and they did that wherever they lived. There were Syrian Romans, North African Romans, Spanish Romans, and British Romans.

I can't pretend I don't think the Romans were brilliant, but that's not the same as thinking they were all good, and I'd like to think I've acknowledged the downside to Roman life. After all, it's difficult to defend the horrors of the amphitheatre, slavery, or the brutal massacre of innocent civilians during the wars of conquest. This book is undoubtedly my spin on the Roman world, but I've tried to give a balanced account, both the good and the bad.

It also goes without saying I've had to leave a lot out, so I chose the key events and people that made Rome what it was, those things that reflect what the Roman Empire and being Roman mean to us. Of course, the events related are entirely my choice, which you might not agree with, but that's always been the historian's luxury.

Foolish Assumptions

In writing this book, I've had to make a few assumptions about you:

- ✔ You have a vague idea about the Romans from school.
- ✔ You've probably been dragged to one or two Roman places on holiday.

✔ You basically thought the Romans came from Rome.

✔ You love the idea of reading history packed with murderers, megaloma-niacs, mayhem, corruption, swindles, decadence, heroic valour, and crazy weirdo gods.

How This Book Is Organised

I could very easily have started at the beginning of Roman history and written about nothing thing else until I stopped, but where's the fun in that? The Roman Empire was an ancient civilisation, full of exciting events and interesting people. In this book, you get the best of both worlds: Information about what it meant to be Roman *and* a rundown of Roman history. The following sections show you what you can expect to find in each part.

Part I: Romans – The Big Boys of the Ancient World

The first part is all about putting the Romans into context. The Romans might be popular today, but in fact they've been pretty popular ever since ancient times. Many rulers and governments along the way spotted that the Romans were good at being in charge. This part introduces you to how and why the Romans have had such an impact on later civilisations and the legacy of some of their ideas. Of course, Romans weren't just armour-clad brutes. The Romans kept their world together through a mixture of the sword and a straightforward acceptance of the structure of their society and its laws. Part I also examines Roman society: the class system, from senator to slave; the Roman fantasy about their identity; the sheer hard practicalities of being in the army; and more. Unlike almost all other ancient civilisations in the western world, the Romans really got a handle on creating a system that actually worked, even if the man in charge was sometimes a raving lunatic.

Part II: Living The Good Life

This bit is all about daily life as a Roman in the Roman Empire. This part includes lots of things that you'll have heard of, like gladiators in the Colosseum, chariot-racing, and roads. But there's loads more besides, and the idea is that this part explains how people in the Roman Empire enjoyed themselves, how they got around, where and how they lived, and the gods they prayed to in the hope that they'd be protected from all the nasty things that nature could throw at them. It's also got a bit about the Roman economy – no, not pie charts and statistics – but the international marketplace the Romans created for themselves.

Part III: The Rise of Rome

Rome was once just one of thousands of nondescript villages in Italy, so it seems almost impossible to understand how just one of them could have become so powerful. Needless to say, it didn't happen overnight. Like many great success stories, the Roman Empire had a very rocky ride to begin with. Not only that, it also started submerged in the misty obscurity of ancient legends. This part takes you from the very earliest beginnings through the succession of wars and struggles that gradually won the Romans control of Italy. Naturally, no-one gets that powerful without others noticing, and this part also discusses the first major international wars, such as the Punic Wars when the Romans beat the Carthaginians. By the end of this part, the Romans are the most powerful people in ancient Europe, poised on the brink of total domination of the Mediterranean.

Part IV: When Romans Ruled the World

Power corrupts – we all know that – and it also breeds a sense of injustice. This part starts off with the massive struggle and crisis of the late Roman Republic when a succession of military leaders like Marius, Pompey, and Julius Caesar jockeyed for power in a conflict that climaxed in a civil war. The outcome was the Roman Empire, when for the first time one man ruled the whole show: Augustus.

Of course, nothing is ever straightforward, and the story takes us through the shenanigans of the Twelve Caesars of the first century AD and the reigns of maniacs like Caligula and Nero, with occasional bouts of sanity under the rule of Vespasian and Titus. Despite the internal problems, this was the time when the power of the Romans extended over more area than ever before. The last bit is the brilliant success of the 'Five Good Emperors' of the second century when the system worked, and it was once said this was the happiest time in human history.

Part V: Throwing the Empire Away

It's tragic, isn't it? Just when human beings start to get something right, they have to ruin it. In a way, it wasn't the Romans' fault. Other people wanted a slice of the action and wanted to invade the Empire. Unfortunately, the Roman Empire was now so big that governing and defending it was almost impossible. So Part V is all about how it started to go horribly wrong. The Romans didn't help, though, because they had a succession of military adventurers, thugs, and lunatics for rulers, most of whom died a violent death after short, turbulent reigns. But in the fourth century emperors like

Dioclectian and Constantine the Great made a good stab at holding everything together. But the other problems, like barbarians rattling at the gates, didn't go away, and the coming of Christianity cut right to the very core of Roman tradition, and changed society forever. So in the end, Rome fell, though what she stood for and what she meant clung on in the Eastern Empire for another thousand years.

Part VI: The Part of Tens

This is the bit of the book where you can find the low-down on ten points in Roman history when things changed. Because that's how it is in history. There might be long-term changes afoot, but things really change when something dramatic happens, like the Battle of Actium in 31 BC. That didn't just change the history of the Roman Empire; it changed the history of the whole world. Next, I've picked out ten unusually interesting Romans whose contribution to their world and ours has marked them out as people to be reckoned with. After them come ten bad Romans because like all villains the baddies are often the most interesting people of their times. I've also chosen ten people who gave the world's first superpower a monumental runaround. These are the anti-Romans. Finally, because I know by this stage in the book you'll be champing at the bit to go and see the Roman Empire for yourself, I've made a list of ten unmissable places that have some of the most sensational remains there are.

Icons Used in This Book

When you flick through this book, you'll notice little icons in the margins. These icons pick out certain key aspects of the Roman world:

This icon marks key decisive events, which helped define the shape of things to come. Sometimes these affected just Rome's future history, but some went on to influence directly the world we live in today.

The Romans lived in the same world we do. This icon marks out events, places or things that have come down to us directly from them.

Movie-makers have often found that the Roman world is a fertile source of great stories for epic films. This icon marks out movie versions of events.

This icon indicates quotes from the Romans, things said in their own words which we can read today.

Occasionally points pop up in the text which are important to bear in mind because of what comes next. This icon marks the most important.

Technical stuff in a Roman context includes things like the staggering dimensions of an amphitheatre, or other remarkable facts, which I've popped in along the way.

Where to Go from Here

There are several different ways you can go with this book. You can start at the beginning and work your way through to the end. Or you could remember that in 1773 Dr Samuel Johnson was asked if he had read a book from cover to cover. He replied, 'No, Sir, do you read books through?' Dr Johnson would be pleased with this book (at least I hope he would have been) because you can read any part you want when you want, and as many times as you want. So if you want to know about the emperor Nero, you can dive right in at Chapter 16, but if it's soldiers you're after then Chapter 5 will set you up, while chariot-racing is lurking in Chapter 8. There's no need to read any chapter you don't want to. And one of the nicest things of all is that you can read about any bit of the Romans you want without having to learn a single Latin verb!

Part I

Romans – The Big Boys of the Ancient World

The 5th Wave   By Rich Tennant

"Oh great – an invitation to _another_ toga party."

In this part . . .

Rome started out as nothing more than a village, but the Romans and their Empire became one of the most important – possibly the *most* important – of the ancient civilisations. The Romans made an enormous contribution to the whole meaning of power, law and order, and political thought that has affected in some way almost every country that has existed since. More than that, the Romans came up with the very letters I'm writing this down with, and even the whole idea of cities as places where people live together and expect all kinds of public services.

They created such a powerful and compelling sense of identity and protective power that neighbouring villages, then the rest of Italy, all wanted a share. Although their society was organised into a hierarchy of social divisions based on wealth, starting with senators at the top and going all the way down to the slaves at the bottom, it was a flexible and mobile system. New people could be absorbed from all round the Roman world, while others could move themselves up the social ladder.

The Romans also became powerful because of their intoxicating sense of who they were and what Rome's destiny meant to them, based on their love of their rural fantasy past.

And, of course, let's not forget the Roman army. There's no getting away from the fact that a vital part of Rome's power was her army and its incredibly systematised way of working that meant even in defeat, it always came back for more to wear its enemies down.

Chapter 1

The Romans: Shaping Their World and Ours

*O*ne of the most famous comedy sketches set in the ancient world was dreamed up by the 1970s Monty Python team in their movie *The Life of Brian* (1979). Set in ancient Judaea, a remote province of the Roman Empire, Reg, leader of the rebellious anti-Roman Peoples' Front of Judaea, is holding a morale-boosting meeting. He announces in a careworn and cynical voice, 'What have the Romans ever done for us?' His fellow rebels nod in agreement and then one after another of them pipes up:

✔ Aqueducts

✔ Sanitation

✔ Roads

✔ Irrigation

✔ Education

✔ Medicine

✔ Public order

Before long, the list is as long as your arm and Reg is forced to redraft his opening gambit by asking, 'Apart from law and order, water, roads (etc) what have the Romans ever done for us?' Silence follows until a wag adds 'Peace'.

Of course, that's a laugh and it's far too simple just to say 'oh the Romans were brilliant because they brought nice things like running water, sanitation, and nice roads'. But Reg's rebels did have a sort of point. The Romans, despite the fact that their Empire could also be brutal and oppressive, contributed a great deal to the world. Their influence was so profound, in fact, that it continued long after the Romans and their Empire had vanished. You can see evidence of this influence even today.

This chapter gives you a quick overview of who the Romans were and what they did. It also answers Reg's question, 'What have the Romans ever done for us?' from a twentieth-century perspective.

Being Roman

The key thing about the Romans is that you didn't have to come from Rome to be one. Of course, the original Romans did, but over time their Empire became made of conquered peoples who were awarded Roman status and privileges and who often fought to get them. People in the Roman Empire saw themselves as Roman, while they proudly maintained their own national and ethnic heritages. It was rather like people in the United States being proudly American and also proudly Native American, Polish, German, or Mexican, and so on. But it was the Roman bit that held them all together, just as it's the American bit that keeps the USA together now.

You can find out more information about what it meant to be Roman in the remainder of this part and in Part II.

The Roman national identity

With the Romans, it was all about image. The Romans maintained a fantasy that they were all no more than country villagers and farmers; simple hardy folk whose rural origins had given them the steely discipline and strength to win an Empire. This Empire, they believed, was their reward from the gods for being such a worthy people (for more about the gods, see Chapter 9).

This myth is true, to a point. In Rome's earliest days, around 1000 BC, it was just one of the many little villages – which were nothing more sophisticated than a collection of thatched cottages – dotted around Latium, a region in central Italy on the west coast.

Yet despite its modest origins, Rome became the biggest city in the whole of Europe and the Mediterranean area. At its climax, Rome had well over a million inhabitants. (To put this in perspective, consider that most other cities of the time would have had a struggle to find 10,000 people to call their own.) More important than its size, however, was its meaning: Rome wasn't just a place to live – it was a concept, a state of mind, as explained in more detail in Chapter 6.

The Romans never lost sight of their origins. Even though those origins were really long-lost in the mists of time, they saw themselves as peasant farmers and were constantly fantasising about returning to their roots (see Chapter 4 for more on this).

The Roman myth of destiny

The Romans very definitely believed that not only were they superior to everyone else, but that they had a preordained destiny to rule the world. They set the rules and the others had to play by them. Those who went along with this arrangement were welcome to join in. And the truth is that quite a lot of people did. All over the Roman world men and women happily called themselves Roman Spaniards, Roman Africans, Roman Gauls, and so on. This only reinforced the Romans' belief in their destiny.

The Romans believed their superior virtues had won them all this power and were very upset that all the wealth had brought decadence and corruption and lousy, violent sexual perverts for emperors and aristocrats (like Nero – see Chapter 16). This corruption of the Roman ideal flew right in the face of everything the Roman world was supposed to be: honest, law-abiding, self-disciplined. But it didn't dent the myth one bit. It only made them all the more determined.

The Golden Age

In Roman myth, Jupiter's father was the god Saturn. Romans believed that Saturn had taught the ancient peoples of Latium, whom he ruled over, how to farm. He also instructed them in liberal arts. Saturn was popular and his reign gentle, and this mythical age was called 'The Saturnian kingdoms', which is the Roman equivalent of 'The Golden Age'. That's what the Romans believed in – their Golden Age as farmers. One of the Romans' most famous poets, Virgil, popped this into one of his most well-known poems, called the *Fourth Eclogue,* an allegory about the rule of Augustus (see Chapter 16). In his poem, Virgil said 'The Saturnian kingdoms are back'. In other words, 'The Golden Age is back'. Blatant propaganda, but it sounds good.

Other ancient civilisations

Roman civilisation lasted from about 753 BC up to AD 476 in the West. That's pretty remarkable when you think about it, but where do the Romans fit into world history? After all, the Romans didn't exist in some sort of historical isolation. Although the Romans thought they were the be-all and end-all, there *were* other civilisations about. So here's a potted look at the ancient civilisations who existed before, during, and after the time of the Romans.

✔ **Egypt:** By the time the Romans got up and running, the Egyptian civilisation had been going for nearly 5,000 years. By around 2700 BC, what you and I think of as ancient Egypt really got going – that's about 2,000 years before Rome was founded. During this period, the pyramids, built by the pharaohs, first started to appear. By about 1550 BC, Egypt had the astonishing pharaoh Akhenaten, and Tutankhamun, whose tomb is for sure the most famous ancient burial ever found. This period, called the New Kingdom, was the age of the Valley of the Kings, the great temple at Karnak, and other massive monuments like Abu Simbel, built by Ramesses II, the most famous of all pharaohs. But Egypt was already past her peak: Divided by rival dynasties, Egypt was invaded, first by the Assyrians, then by the Persians, and finally by Alexander the Great who established a Macedonian dynasty of pharaohs, whose last ruler, Cleopatra VII, had affairs with Julius Caesar and Mark Antony. Antony's defeat at Actium in 31 BC brought ancient Egypt to an end and the longest-established of all civilisations ever became just another Roman province.

✔ **Mesopotamia:** Mesopotamia is the land between the rivers Tigris and Euphrates in what is now modern Iraq. The Sumerians (3500–2300 BC), who wielded their power from the cities of Ur, Eridu, and Uruk, had palaces and built temples on the top of towers called *ziggurats*. By 3000 BC, they had made a vast stride that set them apart from the hundreds of thousands of years of human development: They invented writing. After the Sumerians came the Akkadians (2300–2150 BC), who were highly skilled in bronze sculpture. But Mesopotamian civilisation came to a climax with the Assyrians (1400–600 BC), whose kings commissioned magnificent relief sculptures. Then came the Babylonians (625–538 BC), whose most famous ruler is Nebuchadnezzar II, who built the Hanging Gardens of Babylon.

✔ **The Phoenicians and Carthaginians:** Phoenicia was where the coast of Lebanon and Syria is today, at the eastern end of the Mediterranean. The Phoenicians were brilliant seafarers, which incidentally the Romans never were, and one story is that they might even have sailed right round the coast of Africa. Major traders, the Phoenicians shipped their products, which included cloth, dye, and timber, everywhere they could and set up colonies all round the Mediterranean, including Spain, Malta, and Sicily. The most important Phoenician settlement was Carthage, which became Rome's most deadly rival. Founded by the ninth century BC in what is now modern Tunisia on the north coast of Africa, Carthage's wealth and influence spread north into Sicily and Italy, providing the biggest threat Roman expansion faced. It took the three Punic Wars to wipe out Carthage, finally destroyed in 146 BC, leaving the way open to the Romans to take total control of the Mediterranean. (See Chapter 12 for information on the Punic Wars.)

✔ **The Greeks:** Greece, called Achaea in ancient times, was always the story of city-states dotted about the mainland and the various islands across the Aegean Sea. The first phase of Greek civilisation is called Minoan, after Minos, the mythical king of the island of Crete who lived at Knossos. Minoan civilisation started around 3000 BC and lasted till about 1400 BC when a natural disaster seems to have seriously damaged many settlements. Meanwhile, in Greece itself, famous strongholds like Mycenae and Tiryns had developed. On the north-west coast of Turkey was Ilium, or Troy. Somewhere around the time Minoan civilisation collapsed, the famous Trojan War took place, but no-one really knows how much of the story is myth or true. All we do know is that by 800 BC Homer's poems, the *Iliad* and the *Odyssey,* had been composed. They set the pace for Greek literature, while Greek art was being developed, too. During this time, the Greek city states like Athens and Sparta developed. By the fifth century BC, Athens had reached its climax with the development of a sophisticated democracy and political theory in the age of Pericles. Greek colonies were dotted all round the Mediterranean, including southern Italy and Sicily. But the Greek city-states were forever fighting with one another. Athens and Sparta brought each other to virtual ruin in the Peloponnesian War. Weakened, Greece was easy prey first for Philip II of Macedon (357–338 BC) and then the Romans in 146 BC (see Chapter 12). But Greek art, culture, literature, and sport remained immensely popular in the days of the Roman Empire. Today, the Greeks are still heralded as the fathers of modern democracy and civilisation.

✔ **The Etruscans:** The Etruscans lived in what is now Tuscany and Umbria in Italy. Most of what is known about them comes from the excavation of their magnificent painted tombs and the grave goods, which were designed to make the afterlife as much like home life as possible. They were particularly good sailors and traders, but to this day scholars know little about them because their language still cannot be read properly. It was thanks to the Etruscans that Rome got off to a good start. The Etruscans built Rome's first walls, its temple to Jupiter, and also the great sewer called the Cloaca Maxima. Some of Rome's first kings were Etruscans too, including the last one, Tarquinius Superbus (more on him in Chapter 10).

✔ **Macedonians and Alexander the Great:** Ancient Macedonia was just a small mountainous area of northern Greece and part of what is now Bulgaria. In 338 BC, the Macedonian king, Philip II, took control of Greece, setting the pace for things to come. In 336 BC he was succeeded by his son Alexander, who proceed to conquer a vast swathe of territory across the area of modern Turkey, Iraq, and Iran by defeating the Persian Empire and reached as far as the Indus valley on the fringes of India. He then seized Egypt and made one of his generals, called Ptolemy, pharaoh. Alexander died in 323 BC from a fever in Babylon at the height of his powers. But his empire was built totally around his own personality and with him gone it fell apart quickly, with his various generals ruling different parts of it. Along with the rest of Greece, Macedonia fell to Rome in 146 BC (see Chapter 12), with Egypt and Asia Minor following afterwards.

Roman history, blow by blow

Rome's early life was more about internal social struggles, beginning with the kings. With the kings gone, the Republic was created, and Rome gradually accumulated local allies in her bid to ensure her own security. As Rome's power grew, these allies came to want to share the same social privileges the Romans enjoyed. As she grew in power and prestige, Rome increasingly came into contact with international rivals like Carthage. A seemingly endless series of wars followed, which were far from conclusive, yet Rome prevailed simply because she constantly came back for more and ultimately wore down her opponents. By the first century BC, Rome was the most powerful state in the Mediterranean. (You can read the details about this early period in Rome's history in Part III.)

Rome then started falling apart because immensely powerful generals used their armies to pursue their own political ambitions. Decades of political chaos followed until Octavian brought the wars to an end and took over supreme power. He 'restored the Republic', so he said, but he really created himself as emperor – a spin most accepted in return for peace. Ruling as Augustus, the stability he brought made Rome even more powerful. By the early second century AD, Rome under the emperors was at her zenith, controlling the whole Mediterranean area, north-west Europe, central Europe, North Africa, Egypt, and the Middle East. (This period of Roman history is covered in Part IV.)

In the third and fourth centuries AD, with barbarians battering down the frontiers, it became impossible for one emperor to control it all. So by the fourth century, it was usually the case that at least two, and sometimes more, emperors ruled different parts of the Roman Empire. The basis of the division was between the East and the West. The Eastern Empire managed to survive until 1453 but it was a mere shadow of its former self. The Western half had really ceased to exist by the mid-400s, a thousand years earlier. (To find out about the events that led to the eventual fall of Rome, go to Part V.)

After the end of the Roman Empire in the West, Europe fragmented into numerous little kingdoms, principalities, and duchies. Imagine the United States falling apart and the governor of each state becoming the head of a local dynastic monarchy. To make things worse, each king had to constantly fight for his kingdom against rivals. Borders were always changing, and the threat of invasion was never far away. In England, for example, King Alfred of the Saxons in Wessex (AD 871–899) had to fight back the Viking invaders. In medieval Italy, even cities fought one another.

Today, what was once the Roman Empire is now dozens of independent countries. It's quite remarkable to think that an area once ruled by Roman emperors even to this day is broken up into so many parts. Only with the coming of the European Union have many European countries started co-operating again.

Discovering the Romans

You might very well wonder why anyone would need to discover the Romans, what with their ruined buildings all over the place and one medieval king after another falling all over himself trying to copy the Romans. Well, one of the reasons is the Dark Ages, when a lot of what Rome was all about was forgotten. Apart from a few exceptions, books and libraries were destroyed, and buildings fell down.

When the Renaissance came during the fifteenth century, European thinkers started to rediscover the classical world: They rediscovered Greek and Roman teachings, and printing made Greek and Roman books more widely available. Inspired by what they found, Renaissance men became interested in new forms of art, ancient books on politics and philosophy, and the whole idea of learning for learning's sake.

Even though the ancient Empire fell, it left behind ruins and literature that made the people throughout the ages – including our own – marvel at what the Romans had been able to accomplish.

Great ruins and ruined cities

All over the Roman world, great cities fell into ruin, but those ruins were so enormous that people wondered at them. In far-off Britain, a poem was written about the tumbled-down ruins of the great temple of Sulis Minerva and baths complex at Bath. The poet called the ruins the work of 'giants' because he, like most of his contemporaries in the Dark Ages, couldn't imagine who else apart from a giant could possibly have built anything like that.

Many of the mighty cities of North Africa like El Djem in what is now Tunisia were left to decay in peace. Even today they have massive ruins. El Djem has its vast Roman amphitheatre. Orange, in southern France, has a Roman theatre and an aqueduct. Athens has a vast Roman temple of Zeus and a library built by the emperor Hadrian (AD 117–138), who passed this way on his travels (see Chapter 17). Baalbek in the Lebanon has two colossal temples, and one of them – the temple of Bacchus – is still practically intact.

Rome itself remained home to some of the most enormous ruins: The Colosseum, the city's biggest amphitheatre, is still largely in one piece (see Chapter 8); the ruins of the imperial palaces still cluster across the Palatine Hill, and the baths of Caracalla look like a giant's cave complex. The Aurelian walls of Rome, built in the 270s (see Chapter 19 for information on the emperor Aurelian), still surround most of Rome.

The survival of Roman books

Roman writers were all hugely influential in different ways, but it's thanks to the survival of their texts that we know what we do about the Roman world. Consider these examples:

- **Cicero (Marcus Tullius Cicero) (106–43 BC):** Cicero was a great orator, lawyer, and statesman. Well aware of his importance, he published his speeches, treatises on government *(De Re Publica)*, duty *(De Officiis)*, the nature of gods *(De Deorum Natura)*, and also a vast collection of his private correspondence. A great deal survives and he had a huge influence on thought and literature in early modern times.

- **Caesar (Gaius Julius Caesar) (100–44 BC):** Caesar wrote his own account of his war in Gaul *(Bellum Gallicum)*, and also part of his civil war with Pompey *(Bellum Civile)*. The texts are famous for sounding objective (though they aren't at all), and for their spare, terse style, but are exceptional historical resources for the time. To find out more about Julius Caesar, go to Chapter 14.

- **Catullus (Gaius Valerius Catullus) (84–54 BC):** Catullus was a young man when he died, and his passionate poetry of a new type for the age reflects that in his choice of subjects, particularly his interest in wine, life, and women. Catullus's poems are filled with his frustrations at his relationship with Lesbia, a married woman (probably Clodia Metelli) who was believed to have murdered her husband and was denounced by Cicero as a scandalous prostitute, a woman beyond his capacity to cope with.

- **Virgil (Publius Vergilius Maro) (70–19 BC):** Virgil was the great state propaganda poet of the Augustan age. His most famous poem is the *Aeneid (Aeneis)*, modelled on Greek Homeric epic poems like the *Odyssey*, which trace the adventures of Aeneas, the legendary founder of Rome, and include prophecies about the coming of Augustus. His other surviving works, the *Eclogues (Eclogae)* and the *Georgics (Georgica)*, were designed to reinforce the Roman fantasy about their rural origins by creating an image of a world of primeval rural bliss. The *Fourth Eclogue* included a description of a messianic coming, which was, in fact, written to anticipate Augustus's dynasty, but which early Christians spotted as a possible prophecy of the coming of Christ.

- **Horace (Quintus Horatius Flaccus) (65–8 BC):** The son of an ex-slave (a freedman; see Chapter 2 for information on social classes) and a friend of the poet Virgil, Horace used his writing to support the Emperor Augustus. After Virgil's death, Horace replaced him as the poetic voice of the state. Horace's works include the *Satires (Saturae* – works of social criticism), the *Odes (Carmina* – poems about state events and everyday things), and the *Secular Song (Carmen Seculare* – which celebrated the Secular Games of 17 BC).

- **Livy (Titus Livius) (59 BC–AD 17):** Livy wrote a vast history of Rome from its foundation *(Ab Urbe Condita)*. The work took most of his adult life, and unfortunately only about a quarter has survived. Although his history relied in part on myth and legend in its early parts, Livy's an invaluable source for Rome's struggle against Carthage and other aspects of early Roman history.

✔ **Ovid (Publius Ovidius Naso) (43 BC–AD 17):** Ovid's *Metamorphoses* is one of the most popular poems to survive from antiquity. A compendium of Greek and Roman myths, it tells the whole complicated story of which god did what and when and to whom, all in one place. Ovid was also a scoundrel who loved telling good stories about picking up girls in the circus.

✔ **Pliny the Elder (Gaius Plinius Secundus) (AD 23–79):** Pliny the Elder's vast *Natural History (Historia Naturalis)* is the Roman world's equivalent to a modern one-stop encyclopedia of Everything You Ever Wanted To Know Plus A Whole Lot More. Pliny was an equestrian, the second grade of Roman top society (see Chapter 2), and served in the army. A relentless and tireless enthusiast for knowledge, Pliny described everything from geography to gemstones, and medicine to monuments. Curiosity killed the cat – Pliny was asphyxiated taking a close-up look at the eruption of Vesuvius in AD 79.

✔ **Pliny the Younger (Gaius Plinius Secundus) (*c.* AD 61–113):** Pliny the Younger was Pliny the Elder's nephew who got promoted to senatorial status. Pliny the Younger's chief value to us is as a letter-writer. Many of his letters survive, covering all sorts of fascinating aspects of life at the top in the early second century. Pliny provides an eyewitness account of the eruption of Vesuvius in AD 79, a complete description of his villa, and numerous other priceless anecdotes. The letters he exchanged with the emperor Trajan (AD 98–117 – see Chapter 17 for his reign) are the most important record of the management of a Roman province to have survived.

✔ **Suetonius (Gaius Suetonius Tranquillus) (*c.* AD69–120+):** Suetonius wrote several works, but the only one to survive in full is an all-time classic of antiquity: the *Twelve Caesars,* which is a series of potted biographies of Julius Caesar (who wasn't an emperor) and then the first 11 emperors who came next, up to AD 96. Packed with scandal, intrigue, downright salacious gossip, and priceless historical detail, the *Twelve Caesars* is still a racy read and a not-to-be-missed chance to find out about some of the most extraordinary men in human history.

✔ **Tacitus (Cornelius Tacitus) (*c.* AD 55–117):** Tacitus wrote two major works: the *Annals (Annales),* and the *Histories (Historiae),* as well as an account of the German tribes *(Germania)* and a biography of his father-in-law *(Agricola).* The *Annals* covers the period AD 14–68, which is the reigns of Tiberius, Claudius, Caligula, and Nero. Most of the work survives. The *Histories* pick up where the *Annals* left off, but only the first section exists today. Tacitus was a genius of a historian who provides an unparalleled account of the first century AD. He was undoubtedly biased, but his terse style is a model of economy and his work is filled with damning and magnificent observations.

> ✔ **Cassius Dio, or Dio Cassius (Cassius Dio Cocceianus) (*c.* AD 150–235):** Dio was a senator in Rome but came from Nicaea in Asia Minor (Turkey). He wrote a history in Greek of Rome that started with Aeneas and the Trojan War. Sadly only a chunk from the middle survives, covering the period 68 BC–AD 47. Some of the rest is made good by summaries written by later authors. But it's still vitally important.

The reason we know about any Roman authors at all is because people copied their works. The people we have most of all to thank for that are the monks in the monasteries of the Middle Ages. Thanks to their work, scholars ever since have been able to analyse some of the greatest Roman literature, poetry, philosophy, and history. Unfortunately, a huge amount has been lost and of what there is, it's sometimes obvious that the copyists made mistakes. Who wouldn't? Imagine spending your day in a freezing monastery copying out thousands of lines of a Roman epic poem!

Although various copies of the same text turn up in different monasteries, they usually all go back to just one manuscript that survived antiquity. Here's a for-instance. The Roman poet Catullus is well-known today. But his entire life's work survived in just one copy that was in Verona in Italy in the early fourteenth century. Within a few decades it was lost – forever. Fortunately, two copies were made before that date. If they hadn't been, we'd know nothing about Catullus today apart from one or two other fragments.

Bringing the Romans home: Roman artifacts

Part of the whole Renaissance experience was exploring the remains of the ancient world as part of a broader cultural education. The Grand Tour, the name given to the practice of sending out wealthy young men to explore Europe and its sights, reached its climax in the eighteenth century. A Tour could last a few months or even several years. Funded by his nobleman father or a wealthy patron, a young man toured the capitals of Europe, but the ultimate object of the exercise was always to reach Italy and see the ancient ruins of Rome. Here the young men would have been instructed to buy manuscripts, books, paintings, and antiquities to ship home to decorate their fathers' stately homes.

Some of the Grand Tour men became wildly enthusiastic collectors and today Europe's great houses and museums are packed with the results of the buying. The collections stimulated interest at home and helped encourage growing tourism into the nineteenth century.

Charlemagne and the monks

The Holy Roman Emperor Charlemagne (AD 742–814) did a lot to get the ball rolling at Aix-la-Chapelle (Aachen) where he had his palace. This became the centre of what is known as the Carolingian Renaissance. Charlemagne also encouraged the copying of ancient Roman books in his library at Aachen. The copies his men made survived long enough to be copied again by monks centuries afterwards, until printing arrived in Europe and changed everything forever. Under Charlemagne's rule, a new sort of handwriting called 'Carolingian minuscule' was developed to make copying easier. That's the basis of modern English handwritten characters today.

Roman excavations: The Pompeii sensation

On 24 August AD 79, Mount Vesuvius, near Naples, erupted catastrophically. Many settlements around the volcano were buried by falling pumice or drowned by a surge of pyroclastic mud filled with ash, rock, and pumice. The two most famous places destroyed were the towns of Pompeii and Herculaneum. Yet many of the towns' buildings, complete with their contents and in some cases even their inhabitants, were preserved pretty much as they were on the day that Vesuvius erupted. Scavengers recovered what they could, but the towns and villas in the area were simply abandoned and forgotten about.

Centuries later, in 1594, Pompeii was rediscovered when work to divert a river near Pompeii uncovered some inscriptions; unfortunately nothing was done. It wasn't until 1748 that excavation began and has continued on and off ever since.

Pompeii caused a sensation amongst scholars, collectors, and wealthy men with an interest in the ancient world. The Emperor of Austria declared in 1769 that 3,000 men should be employed to clear Pompeii of its pumice covering. Once much of the town had been cleared, people could at last walk from room to room in an original house and admire the mythological and fantasy architectural scenes painted on the walls. They could walk from the house down a Roman street and visit the amphitheatre.

Pompeii stimulated other men to look for Roman remains in their own countries. In England Samuel Lysons (1763–1819) excavated the remains of a Roman villa at Bignor and published the colourful mosaic floors in a magnificent hand-painted volume. The designs influenced decorations in the houses of the rich and famous.

The Portland Vase

The Portland Vase is just one example of many great art treasures from the Roman world. Made of blue glass and decorated with white cameo classical figures, it's believed to have been made at the end of the first century BC and survived largely intact. By 1601, it was in the collection of a church cardinal. Then an Italian family acquired it. In 1778 it was bought by Sir Alexander Hamilton, a great collector of antiquities, but he sold it to the family of the Dukes of Portland two years later. They lent it to the potter Josiah Wedgwood, and it provided the direct stimulus for a style of fine pottery that has been made by Wedgwood ever since. Unfortunately, it was broken badly in 1845 but has been repaired and is now in the British Museum.

Actually, some people believe the Portland Vase was made in the Renaissance but it's impossible to prove. It doesn't matter anyway. The point is, it was thought to be Roman and was very influential on art and design in the eighteenth century, like many other Roman artefacts at the time like sculpture, coins, jewellery, and ceramics.

What happened to the Herculaneum ruins? In the early eighteenth century, deep tunnelling near the town uncovered the perfectly preserved theatre. The tunnellers ransacked the theatre for its statues, keeping no record of exactly where they found them. They also hacked tunnels through some houses, badly damaging walls as they went. Modern excavations have opened up a small part of the town, and exposed some spectacularly well-preserved buildings. But the rest, along with the theatre, remains deeply buried to this day.

What the Romans Did for Us

Whenever we think of the Romans, we tend to think of men in togas and sometimes with a crown made of laurel wreaths. That's not at all inappropriate. On the whole, that's how Roman emperors posed on their coins and on their statues. But there was far more to the Roman image of power, and it was so successful an image it's been echoing down the ages ever since.

Yet probably the main reason the Romans had such an impact on themselves and everyone else wasn't just because they had the most efficient army. It had much more to do with language, the rule of law, and the whole concept of thinking about government and what it meant. These have all had a dramatic effect on the world since the Romans. Of course, they weren't completely original – actually, some people think that the Romans had scarcely an original thought in their heads – but they were extremely good at taking all sorts of ideas from elsewhere and putting them into practice. And in the end, it was the practice that counted.

The Roman image of power

It's as if the Romans had created the template for power: If you want to be a ruler, you have to pose as a Roman. That was the Roman genius – getting people to want to be Roman – and it worked just as well centuries after their time as it did in their own. As a result, there's a relentless parade of later European rulers who wanted to be Holy Roman Emperors, or who dressed up like an original Roman emperor for paintings and statues.

Charlemagne, the Holy Roman Emperor

Ever since the Roman Empire collapsed in the West European, rulers have often gone out of their way to model themselves on Roman emperors. The first great exponent of this was Charlemagne (AD 742–814), who became King of the Franks in what is now France in 768. He actively tried to recreate the Roman Empire by conquering parts of Italy, some of Spain, and even added Hungarian territory to his domains. Charlemagne actually tried to pretend that ever since Rome had fallen to barbarians in the year 410, the post of Roman emperor had simply been vacant and now it had passed down to him, the next in line. So he had himself crowned Holy Roman Emperor in Rome by the pope in 800.

After Charlemagne's death his kingdom was divided up amongst his three sons, so his Empire fell apart almost as soon as it had started. In 962 Pope John XII made Otto I, King of Germany (AD 936–973), a new Holy Roman Emperor even though his territory was outside the old Roman Empire. The revived Holy Roman Empire staggered on until the reign of Francis II (1792–1806).

Napoleon

Francis II gave up his title when Napoleon conquered most of Germany. Napoleon Bonaparte (1769–1821) was crowned Emperor of the French in 1804, at the climax of a military and administrative career that had gone from success to success. In paintings and on medals, Napoleon was shown as if he was a Roman emperor, complete with the laurel wreath.

The Fascists

The Nazis, under Hitler, got some of their ideas about image of empire from the Romans, while Italy's fascist dictator Benito Mussolini (1883–1945) was determined to revive Rome's ancient power. He had the ancient Forum in Rome excavated and other important sites exposed to public display as part of his propaganda campaign.

The German and Russian words for their emperors, *Kaiser* and *Czar/Tsar,* both come from the Roman word *Caesar,* the family name of the first emperors (see Chapter 16).

The Victorians

During the nineteenth century, Great Britain controlled one of the largest empires the world has ever seen. Britain's dominions included Canada, Australia, New Zealand, and South Africa. The climax of the British Empire was under Queen Victoria (reigned 1837–1901), and the Victorians looked back to the days of the Roman Empire not only as their inspiration, but also as an outright justification of using force to seize territory and then impose what they believed were superior values and customs.

That's pretty much what the Romans did. Just as the Romans left Latin behind them and all the infrastructure of their world like roads and public buildings, so the Victorians littered the Empire with railways, government buildings, and the English language. Today India has long been independent from Britain, but the language of government there is still English and the nation is dependent on the railways originally laid out by the British.

The USA today

The British Empire is long gone. These days, we often hear the term 'the American Empire' because in the twenty-first century, the United States of America is the most powerful nation on Earth. Actually, it's an Empire like no other, because the USA does not seek to conquer other territories and keep a hold on them. If that's the case, then why am I banging on about the American Empire having anything to do with the Roman Empire? Well, if you look at any piece of American coinage you'll see this phrase and this word:

> _E Pluribus Unum (Liberty)_

E Pluribus Unum is a motto of the United States. It's Latin for 'One out of many' and that means there's one nation made out of the many states (or people). So the United States uses the ancient language of the Romans to express its central identity. Liberty is the main aspiration of the constitution of the United States. And that comes from the Roman Empire, too, where Libertas was a goddess used on coins by Roman emperors to show off that that's what they were protecting.

The reason the United States has symbols of the Roman world is not because the United States want to be the Roman Empire of today, but simply because the Romans set the template for the image of power. And the ultimate symbol is the eagle, used by the Romans on their standards, and today the eagle sits proudly in the middle of the Great Seal of the United States of America, together with the motto _E Pluribus Unum_ clamped in its beak.

The European Union

Much of Europe is today organised into the European Union. Unlike the Roman Empire, the European Union is dedicated to the peaceful development of Europe's political, commercial, and social interests. But the Roman Empire was the first time Europe was governed as a single entity. So that's why, when the European Union was first created, the treaty was not only signed in 1957 in Rome but also on the very Capitoline hill itself, the spiritual centre of the Roman Empire.

Language

If you've read up to this point in the book, you've taken it for granted that you could do so. If you dropped in here right at this point, you're taking it for granted that you can read this section. Whichever you did, you've been using Roman letters. You've also been using some words that have their origins in the Latin language.

Alphabet soup

Latin comes from the ancient name for the part of the Italy where Rome lies: Latium. The earliest Latin inscription dates to around the end of the seventh century BC. The Etruscans, whose civilisation came before the rise of Rome (see the sidebar 'Other ancient civilisations'), had their own alphabet but very little is known about their language. However, it's very clear that the Latin-speaking peoples used some of the Etruscan letters and letters from Greek, to create their own alphabet, which went like this:

A B C D E F G H I K L M N O P Q R S T V X Z

And of course that's pretty much the same alphabet we use today. Latin doesn't have the letters *J, W,* or *Y.* The Romans used *I* to represent sounds we'd use *I* or *J* for, and they used *V* to represent sounds we'd use either *U* or *V* for. Otherwise, it's basically the same. Of course, we now use all sorts of different fonts for these letters, but the basic design hasn't altered.

Official languages

When the Romans conquered their Empire, they found people speaking a vast array of languages and local dialects. You can't run an empire with everyone speaking different words. That's why the British ruled their Empire by using English as the official language, and that's why English is the official language of the United States. So the Romans imposed Latin as the language of government across the Empire. Although everyone continued using local languages, in the West, Latin became everyone's second language, and in the East, Greek was used. What this all means is that the whole Roman Empire was managed with just two main languages: Latin and Greek.

Any self-respecting educated Roman would have been able to use both. Imagine if you set off on a journey from New York or London today to explore all the countries round the Mediterranean and all you needed was English and, say, Spanish. But today you'd need English, Spanish, Italian, Arabic, Turkish, and plenty of others.

Spreading a language like that had a colossal impact on local languages, and that's where you can see the effect of the Romans to this day. The so-called 'Romance' languages like French, Italian, and Spanish, owe a huge amount to the Latin of the Romans. English originally grew out of the Germanic languages, but when the early English-speaking peoples advanced south and west, they adopted Latin words which have ended up in English today. The other way Latin has found its way into English is when a new word is needed and Latin terms are used to make a new one.

Law 'n' order

The Romans had a fully-fledged legal system. They had laws, judges, lawyers, courts, and punishments. Men were tried, with the case being put for the prosecution and the case for the defence. Laws were not only written down, but the Romans also kept a record of case law which means when a law was tested before a court. It all went back to the Law of the Twelve Tables in 449 BC which first set out written law, though all it actually did was modify existing customary laws which weren't written down (see Chapter 10 for information about the Twelve Tables). This type of law is called civil law, and it has had a huge influence on European law.

In about 300 BC, Gnaeus Flavius is supposed to have published legal formulae for the first time. Until then, only priests knew them and had jealously guarded them as secrets. Gnaeus Flavius wasn't the only man who actively treated the law as something to be written about and analysed. Quintus Mutius Scaevola produced a textbook of Roman law which later lawyers made great use of. Men like these established the Roman tradition of seeing the law and its practice as a formal profession in its own right.

Over the next ten odd centuries, all sorts of new laws were passed and it became increasingly complicated. The Western Empire finally collapsed in AD 476, but the Eastern half of the Empire carried on and in AD 530 the Emperor Justinian I (527–565) had the whole lot codified into a single book of law (see Chapter 21 for information on Justinian's reign).

Justinian's book is called the *Codex Iuris Civilis,* or the *Book of Civil Law.* It became the basis of civil law throughout most of Europe right up until the end of the eighteenth century. These are some of the divisions of law it contained:

- ✔ **Citizen law:** Common laws that applied to Roman citizens

- ✔ **Law of Nations:** Common laws applied to foreigners in their dealings with Roman citizens

- ✔ **Private law:** Laws to protect private individuals

- ✔ **Public law:** Laws to protect the state

> ✔ **Singular law:** Laws covering special provisions for people in special circumstances that differ from normal situations
>
> ✔ **Unwritten laws:** Laws that had become customary over time
>
> ✔ **Written laws:** Laws made by the decisions of magistrates, the emperor's declarations, and the Senate's decisions

Civil law isn't the same as common law. In England the law is based on common law, which has been made along the way by countless decisions in courts. These decisions were made on three criteria: custom, precedent, and tradition.

Even so, English law has been influenced by Roman law, and so has law in Scotland, which is based on both common and civil law. In the United States, law also has a mixed tradition and it varies from state to state. Louisiana, for example, has laws based on the Roman civil law tradition and so does Canada. So while nowhere today has a legal system exclusively based on Roman law, almost everywhere has been affected by it to some degree.

Philosophy

This probably looks like a rather heavy, deep, and meaningful section. Well, I suppose it is, but plenty of people treat philosophy, and how it should affect the way we live and govern ourselves, as seriously today as the Romans did. The Romans took a lot of their ideas from the Greeks, and it wasn't really until the first century BC that Roman philosophy really started to get written down.

Roman philosophy came in two popular flavours: Epicureanism and Stoicism.

Epicureanism

The Epicureans were devoted to the idea of sensual pleasure with the ultimate aim being complete peace of mind. They took their name from a Greek philosopher called Epicurus (341–270 BC). It was generally believed that the Epicureans were all out for indulging in bodily pleasures, when in reality they were much more interested in pleasing their souls. Physical indulgences were favoured because they stopped the soul from being pained by denial. Epicureans also believed that matter was made up of indestructible atoms moving about in a void, controlled by natural forces: Change comes about when atoms are rearranged.

Lucretius (99–55 BC) is the most famous Roman Epicurean. He put his ideas about the soul, sensation, and thought, as well as the universe and its workings, into his massive poem called *de Rerum Natura* ('On the Nature of Things'), which has survived. Lucretius influenced many later philosophers such as Pierre Gassendi (1592–1655), a Frenchman. Gassendi accepted Lucretius's ideas about the atomic basis of matter and believed this should form the foundations of scientific research. But he also believed this should be compatible with Christianity. Much more recently the English philosopher Alfred North Whitehead (1861–1947) followed the same principles of trying to associate facts found in physics into a philosophical structure – which was pretty much exactly what Lucretius had started to do 2,000 years earlier.

Stoicism

Stoicism was much more popular than Epicureanism, and it was all about accepting things as they are – which was right up the Romans' street as there was nothing they admired more than manly virtues (which they called *virtus*) and being tough even in the worst possible circumstances. Stoics believed that only things that have a physical presence actually exist. The Stoics left a valuable legacy in their construction of a system of morality based on pure reasoning. They also anticipated the way in which the mind is thought to work today because they believed that the body and the mind must obey the laws of physics like everything else, and that, therefore, the state of mind was the result of that.

Marcus Aurelius (AD 161–80) was a Stoic Roman Emperor. He, like other Stoics, was dedicated to accepting life the way it is and responding to difficulties with self-sufficiency. Marcus Aurelius composed 12 books of Meditations, all of which have survived. Here's one of his thoughts, which gives you a good idea of his mindset:

'Consider yourself to be dead, and to have completed your life up to the present; and live the remaining time allowed you according to nature. Love only what happens to you and is spun with the thread of your destiny. For what is more suitable?'

The idea of city

Many of us today live in cities, far more than in ancient times. The Romans really established the idea, not just of a city as a place to live, but also as a place that was a centre of government with public services, security, and identity. For sure, cities had existed before the days of the Roman Empire, but on nothing like the same scale, nor were they anything like so widespread.

The very basis of the whole Roman world was the city. Where the Romans found cities, especially in places like Greece, Asia Minor (Turkey), and North Africa, they adapted them into Roman cities. In the West, they often had to build cities and link them into the infrastructure of the rest of the Roman world. Roman cities, while individually unique, were all modelled on a similar idea of what a city should be. So anyone travelling around the Roman world had a fairly good idea of what to expect wherever he or she went.

Norman architecture

The Normans, from Normandy in northern France, became the most powerful force in western Europe in the eleventh century. They understood what power was all about. Although they had nothing like the resources of the Roman Empire, they did what they could to copy the power of Roman architecture by using arches and vaults to create their castles and cathedrals. The style is called Romanesque for obvious reasons, and it heralded the great age of medieval architecture that followed.

Although the styles of cathedrals changed over later centuries, many have their origins in the massive and heavy Norman arches of the original structures. Sometimes the churches and cathedrals were built out of Roman masonry that was still lying around. Take a look at St Albans Abbey church in England if you ever get a chance. It's built out of Roman brick and tiles taken by the monks from the ruined Roman city just down the hill. At the other end of the Roman world, the Roman Christian churches in Constantinople (now Istanbul) provided a template for the later mosque builders, who were amazed at the vast church of Santa Sophia built by the sixth-century Emperor, Justinian I (AD 527–565).

Many of the major cities of Europe today are a direct legacy of the Roman Empire. Consider London, capital of the United Kingdom, for example. It must be the most remarkable of all. London sits on the river Thames in England, but until the Romans came in AD 43, there was no London at all, or any kind of settlement apart from scattered farmsteads. The Romans spotted the potential of the river and an ad hoc trading settlement sprang up around a bridgehead that they built. Within a few generations, London had grown into the biggest Roman city with the biggest public buildings north of the Alps. Although it fell into disrepair when the Romans left, by the Middle Ages it was well on the way to being one of the largest cities in all of Europe.

The Roman influence on cities goes beyond Europe. Take a look at the great buildings of Washington DC, the US capital. When Pierre L'Enfant (1754–1825) produced his plans for the city in 1791, he got some of his inspiration from the classic Roman model of a street grid system. The Supreme Court (1928) uses the architectural model of a great Roman temple. Washington's Capitol (begun 1793) uses Roman types of architecture throughout, and, of course, most of the other state capitols are modelled on Washington's. Designed by Daniel Burnham, Washington DC's Union Station (opened 1907) owes its main design to the Baths of Diocletian (built AD 298–306) and its entrance to the Arch of Constantine (built 315), both in Rome.

A Long Time Ago but Not That Far Away

The Roman Empire in the West started to fall apart permanently about 1,600 years ago. In the broader history of the world, which runs into billions of years, that's no more than a pipsqueak of time. So it's not really that surprising that the Romans have had such a substantial effect on the world we live in today because they weren't very long ago.

There have been plenty of other influences along the way, and, of course, we do things the Romans could never have imagined. It's also true that there isn't a single person around today who can reliably trace his or her family tree all the way back to the Romans. But that's just because it's too long for the records to have survived.

The truth is that lots of us, millions and millions of us, have the genes of people who lived in the world of the Romans. And if you plucked a Roman out of his world and brought him to ours in a time machine, yes sure, he'd be amazed by our technology and how many of us there are. But once our Roman had settled down, he'd recognise huge amounts of his world in ours, right from the streets we drive down to the law courts where lawyers battle it out, and even to the lettering on our buildings and books. So if the Romans ever seemed irrelevant, they shouldn't do so now, wherever you live in the world today.

Chapter 2

It's the Cash That Counts: Roman Social Classes

oman society was ultimately based on wealth – and how much you had of it – and what family you'd been born into. At rock bottom were those with nothing: the men and women who didn't even own themselves. They were the slaves, the engines that drove the Roman world, often treated like a disposable resource constantly replenished through conquest. Above them came the freed slaves (freedmen), then freeborn Roman citizens, and at the top was the two-tiered aristocracy of equestrians and senators.

This chapter explains how Roman society was divided up, and what qualified a man to be at any level within the structure. It's absolutely fundamental to understanding how Roman society worked. Another key to understanding Roman society is to remember that this was primarily a man's world. It was men who did the voting and who held the jobs. But it's important to bear in mind that these traditions grew out of the old days of the Republic. In the days of the Empire, society gradually started changing and by the fourth century many of the old ways and distinctions had fallen into decline.

First Things First: The Roman Family

The core component of Roman society was the family (*familia*). The Roman family was a private and public affair. In both respects, total loyalty from members was expected and given, though more than a few of the emperors set an appalling example – the emperor Caracalla murdered his brother Geta to make sure he had sole power (see Chapter 18).

A Roman familia was much more than a married couple and their children. It was the whole extended family, overseen by the senior male, the *pater familias* ('master of the household' – he had to be a Roman citizen), even if members were living in different houses. It also included a man's adopted sons, who were treated legally as blood members of the family. The senior male had total power over all the members of his family *(patria potestas)*, which means he made all the decisions over what happened to any one of them, including marriage and punishments, and also acted as family priest. He controlled and even legally owned all their property, and also had the power to sell his son into slavery or kill him. The family was *sub manu*, 'under his hand'. The familia also included the slaves of the household, and any freedmen, too, and were linked to other families by marriage into clans called *gentes* (singular *gens*). The clan leaders became the most important controlling members of the state (more on this in the section 'Being on Top – Upper-crust Romans').

Romans were sticklers for tradition, and tradition meant unswerving loyalty to one's family and respect for precedent and authority. Roman society was *paternalistic,* based on the principle of the head male in a family, known as pater familias.

That word *pater* is the basis of many Latin terms related to families, land, inheritances, and the state, and therefore also the word patrician:

- *Patrimonium:* An inheritance
- *Patria:* One's native land (or fatherland)
- *Patriarch:* Tribal chief
- *Pater Patriae:* 'Father of the Country', a title awarded to Augustus and his successors

A family day

Family life was reinforced by the daily routine. Roman days were divided into 12 hours, measured by a sundial. This is how a typical day panned out:

- **First hour:** light breakfast *(jentaculum)* and pater familias says the morning prayers with the household

- **Second hour:** Everyone gets about their work and the pater familias greets his clients (see below)

- **Sixth hour:** Lunch *(prandium)* followed by a siesta *(meridiatio)*

- **Eighth hour:** Back to work. Affluent men headed for the baths

- **Ninth hour (mid-afternoon) or later:** The main family meal *(cena)*

Being on Top – Upper-crust Romans

Early Roman society was made up mostly of free citizens, but there was a core group of aristocratic families. The distinction between the general free population and the aristocrats gradually became clearly defined into 'orders' known as the *plebeians* (the majority) and the *patricians* (the aristocrats). There doesn't seem to have been any ethnic basis for the division. Instead, the distinctions came about through wealth founded on land.

The original patrician families became organised into clans *(gentes)* of families tied together through marriage and by owning so much land they ended up controlling Roman society. In Rome's early days, the patricians had total control of all political privilege and all high offices including the priesthood. They achieved this out of a powerful sense of social solidarity. They were absolutely determined to hang on to their power and exclude the rest, the plebs, from sharing in it.

As you can imagine, this was an arrangement that the plebs – especially the wealthier and more educated ones – resented. A political struggle between patricians and plebs, called the Conflict of the Orders, ensued (you can read about this struggle in Chapter 10). Essentially, the plebeians fought to end the patricians' monopoly on political power and all the chief offices of state. One of the most significant changes came in 455 BC when the ban on inter-marriage between plebs and patricians was lifted. In practice what happened was that patrician families accepted marriage with wealthy pleb families because one of the key ways to keep power was to marry money. These wealthy plebs really became indistinguishable from the patricians and had little in common with the rest of the plebs.

Pets

The animal-killing frenzies that went on in the arena (Chapter 8) doesn't mean Romans were totally unsentimental about animals. Some did have pets, or at least working animals that were part of the family household. Dogs and cats were essential for the control of rodents, and dogs were useful guards. There's a fourth-century AD dog tag from Rome inscribed 'Hold me, lest I flee, and return me to my master Viventius on the estate of Callistus'. A doorway mosaic in a house at Pompeii has an inscription reading *Cave Canem,* 'beware of the dog!' A wall-painting from another house at Pompeii shows a terrier-like dog that must have been a household pet. One of the most famous relics from Pompeii is the cast of a dog, tied up and unable to flee his post as the pumice and lava rained down during the eruption of AD 79 (the dog's remains decayed, leaving a void in the packed pumice and ash which was filled with plaster by archaeologists). For a curious use of dogs, see Chapter 9.

The word *plebs* just means everyone else apart from the aristocracy. It started out meaning something like the 'majority' or 'all the rest' but came to mean the 'mob' or 'common rabble', and included everyone except those wealthy plebs who had gained a foothold in Rome's upper class. You can read about them in the section 'Ordinary Citizens'.

The old patrician families struggled for survival as intermarriage and the growing power of the wealthy plebs eroded them. By Augustus's reign (27 BC–AD 14) only about 15 patrician families were left, and by Trajan's (AD 98–117) just six. In Constantine I's time (AD 307–337) the title 'patrician' had come to mean anyone who held high office in the imperial court.

Because the patricians controlled Roman society, the rest of the population became totally dependent on them, working as labourers or tenants on their land. Out of this developed the patron-client relationship:

- The patron acted like a father figure to his clients, who were often his freedmen (former slaves): He took a personal interest in their careers, financial concerns, and any legal or business problems.
- The client had a duty of loyalty to his patron, which meant helping with money if his patron was in public office or had been fined, for example, or if he was captured in war and held to ransom, and generally offering him support.

Patrons and clients could never appear against one another in a court of law, even as witnesses. Having plenty of clients was a sign of status and especially useful to politically-ambitious nobles.

Nobles (Nobiles)

By the third century BC, the mixture of old patrician families and wealthy plebs had become the new aristocracy *(nobiles)* of rich landowners – the only respectable source of wealth for a Roman aristocrat. The nobles took no part in trade or anything commercial (at least directly). Simply because they were wealthy, they fulfilled the property qualification to enter the Senate (one million sesterces by the time of Augustus) and serve in the magistracies as aediles, praetors, and so on, because all these positions were unpaid and were regarded as a public honour *(honor)*. Noble families were regarded as those who had had consuls amongst their number and who expected later generations to follow in those footsteps, serving in the magistracies of the *cursus honorum* ('the succession of honours'), the career ladder for up-and-coming Roman politicians and statesmen. So although plebs had won the right to stand for office, in practice those without a substantial income couldn't consider it. (To find out about political positions, go to Chapter 3.)

The Toga

The toga was a piece of clothing unique to the Romans. A toga was a woollen sheet made in the form of a rather stretched semicircle around 6 metres wide. It was worn by free-born Roman males as a mark of distinction. But an incredible piece of irony is that the only women who wore togas were prostitutes, making it a badge of shame for them. A toga was worn over the left shoulder with the rest gathered up into folds around the back and then hung over the left arm. It was only suitable for special occasions because it was completely useless for any sort of action or physical effort and had become almost redundant when Augustus revived it as part of restoring Roman traditions. Domitian (AD 81–96) said anyone attending the games had to wear togas. There were several different types:

- ✔ *Toga virilis* or *toga pura:* Plain off-white toga worn by adult male citizens

- ✔ *Toga praetexta:* Off-white toga with a broad purple border, worn by magistrates of aedile or senior status (see **cursus honorum** in Chapter 3), and also by free-born boys until they were old enough to wear the *toga virilis*

- ✔ *Toga candida:* A specially whitened toga worn by nobles standing for magistracies to suggest their purity

- ✔ *Toga picta:* Purple toga decorated with gold thread worn during victory parades by generals, and by emperors on special occasions

- ✔ *Toga pulla:* A dark toga for mourning

In theory, the whole citizen body could vote for the magistrates. In the real world, though, the only people who could vote were those who were in Rome at the time. What's more, the powerful noble families used their influence over their clients, as well as bribery and other means, to make sure the magistracies only went to their own. The result was that office became as good as hereditary because the key families manipulated elections to make sure the positions were handed down from generation to generation.

Nobles wore tunics with a broad vertical purple border *(laticlavius)* on either side, and togas, a traditional piece of Roman clothing (see the sidebar on 'The Toga'), with a broad purple border. Some nobles clung to the habit of wearing an iron finger ring, as an ancient symbol of simpler times.

The nobiles families possessed the right of *ius imaginum. Ius* means 'law' or 'right'. Certain high offices allowed the holder the right to sit in public in a special chair inlaid with ivory called the *Sella Curulis*. Descendants of such men were allowed to make figures with wax faces of their ancestors *(imagines)* and display them in the public rooms of the family house for all to see. The more such figures a noble family had, the greater its esteem and dignity. Men who came from families without the ius imaginum, but had managed to obtain high office, were called 'new men' *(novi homines)* and were treated with great hostility (see Chapter 7 for the experience of Marius as a new man).

Equestrians (Equites)

Equestrians went back to the days of the kings when Roman society was divided into classes according to ability to pay for military service (see Chapter 3). The top class was made up of men who could afford to field a horse and were known as the equestrians (*equites* from *equus,* 'a horse').

Over the years, as Rome's wealth grew, there were far more men with the necessary qualification to be equestrians than were needed for war, especially as Rome came to rely on allies and provincials to do the bulk of the fighting. The equestrians became more and more involved with commerce, from which the senatorial *nobiles* were excluded. By the days of the Second Punic War (218–202 BC), government contractors were supplying the Roman army, and these must have been equestrians. After the War, anyone who had the property qualification of 400,000 sesterces was counted an equestrian. These included some municipal aristocracies in Italian cities with Roman citizen status as well as the businessmen 'financier equestrians' in Rome. In the late Republic, equestrians formed an important rival political force to the senators, especially in Rome after 122 BC, when Gaius Gracchus brought in a law that said judges in jury trials had to be equestrians.

By the first century BC, equestrians were becoming recognised in their own right *(ordo equester),* and were united as a single order in the year AD 22 under the emperor Tiberius. There was no longer any connection with military service. To mark their status and distinguish them from nobles, equestrians wore a gold finger ring and their tunics had a narrow vertical purple stripe *(angusticlavius)* on either side. Equestrians could be promoted to senatorial status en masse to bump up the Senate's numbers or as individuals.

By the days of the Empire, equestrians were used to fill lots of administrative posts, such as the financial affairs of provinces, or the governorship of lesser provinces. The most famous equestrian of all is Pontius Pilate, who became governor of Judaea. You can find more about the important role equestrians played in Roman society in Chapter 3.

Ordinary Citizens

The world of senators and equestrians was very different from the one spent by the ordinary citizens in the Roman world, who fell into various types: Roman citizens, Latin citizens, and the rest (apart from slaves). These people passed their time working desperately hard to earn a living. As they were practically ignored by historians of the time, we only know about them from their tombstone inscriptions, graffiti, and archaeological remains.

These tell us that the Roman world was heaving with all sorts of service industries like clothes dyers and launderers, teachers, civil servants, and money collectors and lenders. There were manufacturers of clothing and shoes and repairers, artisans who made metal tools, implements, architectural fittings, and furniture. There were also builders, plasterers, sculptors, carpenters, and brick-makers. Food was supplied by shippers and traders, cooks, bakers, restaurant owners, fishmongers, butchers, and farmers. Some jobs were done by both slaves and freedmen.

These people led hard, short, and dangerous lives in a world where protective health and safety legislation were non-existent. But it was also these people that the nobles entertained in the circus and amphitheatre, and were fed with the corn and oil dole. The nobles might have looked down on the Roman mob, but they knew they could not do without them.

Roman citizens

Although some of the plebs had grown wealthy and joined the ranks of the aristocracy whether as senators or equestrians, the vast majority of the Roman population were just ordinary citizens.

The important thing about being a Roman citizen was that each man had the right to vote *(suffragium)* and also had duties *(munera)* to the state, which meant paying taxes and military service (women had none of these rights or duties). People power came through the *Concilium Plebis Tributum* (Council of Plebeians arranged by tribes) and its officials: the tribunes and their assistant aediles (more about this and other assemblies in Chapter 3). A man could lose his citizenship under certain conditions, for example, if he deserted the army, mutilated himself so he could not serve, or dodged a census to evade taxation.

Roman citizens were immune from summary arrest and imprisonment. In the city of Philippi in the mid-first century AD, the future St Paul was sentenced to a flogging after having been at the centre of a riot. Paul asked the man about to whip him, 'Is it lawful for you to scourge a man that is a Roman citizen and not condemned?' The commanding officer told Paul his own citizenship had cost him a great deal of money. Paul retorted, 'I was free-born', and was promptly released.

Tribal membership

It wasn't until the time of Servius Tullius (579–535 BC) and his census (see Chapter 10) that the Roman people were divided into 30 tribes, with one tribe per region. Servius Tullius did this because, until that date, the plebs were just a confused mass of people, which made them difficult to govern. Four of the new tribal regions were in Rome (the *Tribus Urbanae*) and the other 26 (originally 16) were in the countryside around Rome *(Tribus Rusticae)*. Landowners were allocated to the tribe of the region where their land was. People without land were allocated to one of the city tribes.

What's in a name?

Roman citizens had a triple name, the *tria nomina* made up of:

✔ *praenomen* (forename)

✔ *nomen* (name of clan)

✔ *cognomen* (family surname)

Some had an *agnomen* (additional surname), too. So, Publius Cornelius Scipio Africanus was a member of the Cornelii clan, of the Scipio family, with the forename Publius. His additional name Africanus helped distinguish him from other family members with the same names.

As Rome's territory increased, more tribes were added until, by 241 BC, there were 35. Despite a short-lived plan in 90–89 BC to add 10 more, 35 was all there ever were. So any new citizens, wherever they lived in the Roman Empire, were allocated to one of the existing tribes, but, of course, unless they were close enough to Rome to vote, the privilege wasn't much use.

Universal citizenship

In the early days of Rome, to be a citizen, you had to be the child of a Roman father and mother, or of a Roman parent married to someone from an approved place. Later on, citizenship could also be held by:

✔ The adopted children of such men

✔ Those who bought citizenship or earned it through membership of a city or an auxiliary army unit privileged with a grant of citizenship

✔ Those who had been honourably discharged from an auxiliary unit of the Roman army after serving for 25 years

✔ Those granted citizenship by petition to the emperor

Being a Roman citizen was a jealously guarded privilege, at least until AD 212 when the emperor Caracalla issued his famous *Constitutio Antoniniana* which made all freeborn men of the Empire into Roman citizens (see Chapter 19).

Latin citizens

Latin rights were originally dreamed up as a sort of halfway house for some of Rome's allies in Italy during the third century BC. Men from these towns were called Latin citizens and were allowed to conduct law suits in Roman courts on the same terms *(commercium)* as a Roman citizen. If they moved to Rome, they became Roman citizens. A Latin woman could marry a Roman citizen and her sons would become Roman citizens *(conubium).*

Towns instituted with similar rights were called *municipia* with a legal status called *civitas sine suffragio* ('community without the vote'). These towns had to provide troops. After 89 BC, they got the right to vote and *municipium* came to mean any self-governing Italian town except colonies. Outside Italy, municipia with Latin rights came first, and later Roman citizen rights were created as special privileges.

To discourage people from moving en masse to Rome, a law of 150 BC made magistrates of these towns into Roman citizens. It was a handy way of easing provincials into becoming Roman citizens. In 89 BC, Transpadane Gauls were made into Latins, with full citizenship following in 49 BC. Obviously after AD 212 and the edict of universal citizenship, the distinction between Roman and Latin citizens ceased to exist.

Everyone else: Provincials

Because people moved fairly freely around the Roman Empire until Diocletian's time (AD 284–305), even in the remotest areas, a traveller would find Roman citizens in the form of soldiers and administrators, Latin citizens in the army or trading, and local citizens. These non-Roman and non-Latin citizens were known as *peregrinae* ('foreigners'), and had to fulfil all the local responsibilities of their own communities. Peregrinae had no civil rights under Roman law unless they were represented by a citizen *patronus,* couldn't exercise any political function in Roman assemblies or magistracies, and were banned from wearing togas in case they tried to enter a Roman assembly.

Any such man could be granted Roman citizenship, after the reign of Augustus, though such men still had to take care of their own local responsibilities. Sometimes units of provincial soldiers in the Roman army (see Chapter 5) were rewarded with Roman citizenship en masse for acts of valour. Normally such soldiers had to wait until their term of service was up to be made citizens.

Trading insults

There was a strict protocol in Roman society about insults. Vespasian (AD 69–79) ordered that no-one should insult a senator with foul language, but if a senator insulted an equestrian, then the victim was perfectly entitled to insult the senator back the same way. In other words, any citizen could respond to an insult from another citizen in the same way, regardless of whether they held different status.

Are You Being Served?

Slavery was endemic in the Roman world, as it was throughout antiquity. As Rome grew more powerful, the numbers of slaves increased, and Roman society became increasingly dependent on them. The slave revolt of 73–71 BC, led by Spartacus (see Chapter 14) and which had nearly devastated southern Italy, preyed on Roman minds. The Senate once considered forcing slaves to wear distinctive dress until someone pointed out that then the slaves would realise how many of them there were. But if slaves made up a huge part of the population, so also did the freedmen – ex-slaves freed by their masters.

Slaves

Anyone conquered by the Romans was liable to be enslaved, and so were rebellious provincials. Their children were automatically slaves. There were other sources of slaves, like people convicted of capital crimes.

Tiberius Sempronius Gracchus (*c.* 210–150 BC), the Roman commander in Spain 180–179 BC (see Chapter 14), crushed a rebellion in Sardinia in 177 BC. He captured so many slaves there that the Roman slave market was flooded with cheap Sardinian captives. *Sardi venales,* 'Sardinians for sale', was the cry, and it became an everyday Latin expression for any commodity available in abundance and cheap as a result – a bit like our 'Made in China'!

A slave's life

Slaves could have desperately hard lives, like those sent to work in the mines or on large agricultural estates, but educated slaves owned by rich masters often lived better than poor free people. Slave marriages existed but had no legality so either partner could be sold if his or her master decided. Female slaves were liable to be sexually abused by their masters or overseers, but they also could be freed and married by their former owners (see the sidebar 'Regina the freedwoman', later in this chapter, for just such an example). Punishments were arbitrary and down to the master or mistress's whims. Slaves were expensive to buy, clothe, and feed and that could encourage meaner masters to scrimp.

Slaves in the household of a wealthy man could have a relatively pleasant life, especially if they came from parts of the Roman world thought civilised, like Greece. Pliny the Younger mentions walking and talking with educated slaves of his. Many of his slaves might have been born in the household and were treated as part of the home.

One of the reasons for better treatment was that the smarter members of the free population realised abusing slaves was likely to backfire. Largius Macedo was a praetor around the beginning of the second century AD, but his father was a freedman. As was so often the case with men who came from lowly origins, Largius Macedo went over the top to show how upper class he was and treated his own slaves cruelly. So one day, while he was bathing at his villa, some of his slaves attacked and beat him and left him for dead. Other faithful slaves revived their master and a hunt went out for those who had escaped. Most were recaptured and punished, but Macedo died a few days later.

Slave rights

Slaves also had some rights, which were steadily increased in the days of the emperors. It became illegal to kill a slave or get rid of a slave simply because he or she was ill. There were strict laws against castrating slaves or abusing their bodies in other ways. Antoninus Pius (138–161 AD) even made it possible to prosecute the murderer of a slave.

In Egypt in the year AD 182, during the days of Marcus Aurelius, an 8-year-old slave boy called Epaphroditus rushed up to the roof of his master Plution's house to watch a procession of dancers go by. He fell off in the excitement and was killed. He might only have been a slave boy, but the papyrus document that records the disaster also records how his master's father-in-law Leonidas made arrangements for the boy's proper burial.

Slaves, wherever they lived, had no freedom. One of the ironies of the way Roman society evolved into the Dominate established by Diocletian at the beginning of the fourth century (refer to Chapter 20), is that many ordinary citizens found themselves effectively enslaved to their jobs and homes with no right to move away or change profession.

Freedmen

Slaves in the Roman world, unlike most other slave-owning societies from ancient to early modern times, could always hope they might one day be freed. There were millions of freedmen and women in the Roman Empire, found in all provinces at all times and in all walks of life. As free people, they were entitled to the privileges of citizenship and some rose to positions of high status. The emperor Claudius notoriously relied on freedmen to run the Empire for him (flick to Chapter 16 for more on this).

Freeing a slave

A slave could be freed by his master in the master's will (the most usual) or as a gift during his master's lifetime, which meant going before a magistrate who touched the slave with a rod after his master had given him a pretend slap as a symbol of his last punishment as a slave. Slaves could even save up money from casual earnings or gifts and purchase their own freedom, but that usually meant negotiating a deal with their master to compensate him for the original purchase price.

The technical term for freeing a slave is *manumission,* which comes from two Latin words: *manus* ('hand') and *emittere* ('to let go').

Even though he was now free, a freedman had a duty of obligation to his former master and that meant becoming his client and remaining tied to him in that mutually-advantageous relationship. In fact, the new client might even carry on in his old job. Refer to the earlier section 'Being on Top – Upper-crust Romans' for details of the patron-client relationship.

The advantage to the old master is pretty clear: He no longer had to feed and clothe his former slave, who now had to deal with all that for himself. An ex-slave could vote on his old master's behalf, too. If a court case blew up, then his ex-slave could now serve as a witness on his behalf. The disincentive was the tax levied on freeing each slave at 5 per cent of his or her value.

Freedmen usually took their former master's name. A centurion of the XX legion called Marcus Aufidius Maximus visited the shrine and spa centre of Bath in Britain where two of his personal freedmen, Marcus Aufidius Lemnus and Aufidius Eutuches, set up dedications on their former master's behalf as he was now their patron and they his loyal clients.

Stigma

Freedmen could never become equestrians or reach senatorial rank; they suffered the social stigma of having been slaves, and were looked down on as coarse and vulgar. But it wasn't a prejudice many Romans could afford to have because so many people were descended from slaves at some point in their ancestries, even a few emperors. The emperor Pertinax (AD 193), for example, was the son of a freedman called Helvius Successus who had made his money in the timber trade; you can read more about Pertinax in Chapter 18.

The most average freedmen could hope for was to serve in the administration of their city or on the imperial service, or become modest businessmen like merchants. If successful enough, a freedman could afford to become a member of the *seviri Augustales* ('the board of six priests in the cult of Augustus'), which was monopolised by freedmen. As Pertinax's example shows, unlike their fathers, the *sons* of freedmen could rise as high as any man from a free family, without any obligations to their father's old masters.

Regina the freedwoman

Regina (Latin for 'queen') was a slave girl from the British tribe called the Catuvellauni. She was owned by a Syrian called Barates who fell in love with her, freed her, and moved her with him to South Shields on the northern frontier in Britain. Sadly she died when only 30, in the early years of the third century AD. Barates invested in a magnificently carved tombstone to his beloved wife, which has survived. You can see it in the museum there today.

Women and Children Last!

Women and children naturally made up the bulk of the population, but in theory, they were totally subject to men. Although women could be citizens, they couldn't vote.

Women

Women could have citizenship status, but they had no formal role in Roman society. Women couldn't serve in any of the capacities men served in as magistrates, politicians, or soldiers. A woman couldn't even be an empress in her own right, though they were used for family alliances, such as when Augustus made his daughter Julia marry Marcellus, then Agrippa, and finally Tiberius (see Chapter 16) in an effort to establish a dynasty through his only descendant. If an emperor left only a daughter, then the succession passed to a male relative or another man altogether.

Women had almost no legal identity other than as a man's daughter, sister, wife, or mother. Vespasian (AD 69–79) passed a law that said any woman who had become involved with a slave man should be treated as a slave herself. Real slave women had even less of an identity, if that's possible to imagine.

Barbarian women didn't think much of Roman women. When Septimius Severus campaigned in Britain in AD 208–211, he made a treaty with the Caledonians from Scotland (refer to Chapter 18). During the negotiations, the empress Julia Domna made fun of the wife of a chieftain called Argentocoxus about how British women slept with lots of different men. Argentocoxus's wife snapped back: 'We fulfil nature's demands in a much better way than you Roman women do because we consort openly with the best men, whereas you let yourself be debauched by the vilest men in secret.'

Education

Women were generally excluded from education, which was biased towards boys. But some girls from good families were taught to read and write and were known as *doctae puellae,* 'educated girls'.

Here's an exceptional case of an educated woman in the public eye. After Caesar's assassination in 44 BC, heavy taxes were imposed by the Second Triumvirate on anyone implicated with the conspirators. A woman called Hortensia (whose father was an orator called Quintus Hortensius) made a speech to the Triumvirs in 42 BC on behalf of the wives of the men affected. It was written down and studied in later years as an example of an outstanding speech and not just because it was by a woman.

Women in the home

In the man's world of the Roman Empire, women were theoretically confined to running the home and having children. The wife of a *pater familias* was known as the *mater famiilias domina* ('mistress mother of the household'), and she was supposed to be entirely subject to her husband and, before him, her father. In general though, Roman society (which means basically men), reserved their admiration for women renowned for their upright moral virtues who were regarded as the guiding force behind teaching their sons the value of honourable behaviour in public and private life. In 215 BC, during the Second Punic War, the *lex Oppia* imposed limits on women's right to own gold, wear elaborate dresses, or ride in fine carriages. It was repealed in 195 BC much to the annoyance of moral diehards like Marcus Porcius Cato (whom you can read about in Chapter 23).

By the first century BC women's rights were improving. Those over the age of 25 could have their own property and divorce their husbands if they chose. Women could also play a more important role in society, though they were still never allowed to take on any official jobs. But women were still primarily seen as wives and mothers. Augustus penalised unmarried women and men (for example, bachelors were prevented from inheriting legacies), but he rewarded those who did marry and had children.

Even so, Roman women could be legally beaten by their husbands. In fact, it was even considered a reasonable way to treat a woman if her husband thought she had misbehaved. As a result, it was not unusual for women to bear scars on their faces from the treatment they had received. One of the most horrible cases was that of Egnatius Mecenius, who beat his wife to death for drinking wine. No-one criticised him, all thinking she had deserved it.

Women's clothing and beauty treatments

Women's clothing, like most Roman clothing, was much simpler than today's:

- Breasts were supported by a strapless band *(strophium)*.

- Instead of panties or briefs a sort of bandage *(feminalia)* was often used instead, though panties very like modern ones have been found.

- A slip *(tunica interior)* was worn over these undergarments.

- On top was a woollen gown *(stola)* tied in round the waist and perhaps a shawl *(palla)*.

Wealthy women could afford silk and a Greek woman called Pamphile invented a way to weave silk so fine that the clothing made women look nude. Bronze (or silver and gold for the rich) brooches, like our safety pins, were used to hold the clothing in place. Shoes were like open leather sandals today, sometimes elaborately decorated with patterned cut-outs. Cosmetic treatments included using ass's milk on the skin or even a jelly made by boiling a bull-calf's bone for 40 days to avoid wrinkles, antimony as an eyebrow make-up, and kaolin as a face-powder.

Women and their children

Roman women had no legal rights over their children. Unwanted children could be *exposed* (abandoned in the open air), which might mean death or enslavement, depending on where the child was found and whether the mother wanted that or not. If her husband died, then the estate passed to the son and a woman could find herself with nothing at all.

Women who kept their children faced all the worry and tragedy of a very high level of infant mortality and all the pressure to produce a healthy son who lived to adulthood and could inherit his father's estate.

Special women

Apart from being confined to special jobs like serving as Vestal Virgins (refer to Chapter 9), the limitations on women didn't affect some in powerful families from having a huge amount of influence on the men around them. Agrippina the Younger, Caligula's sister and Nero's mother, was effectively in total charge until Nero had her murdered (see Chapter 16). Some of the women of the Severan dynasty – Julia Maesa, Julia Soaemias, and Julia Mamaea – were the real power behind the thrones of Elagabalus and Severus Alexander (refer to Chapter 19). Under special circumstances, women from more modest origins could also play an important role in the lives of their communities. Here are some of them:

- **Eumachia of Pompeii** was one of the city's most important business-women in the mid-first century AD; she dedicated a building in Pompeii's forum to the corporation of dyers, weavers, and launderers. Her building was used as a wool market, and Eumachia was able to afford a substantial tomb outside the city gates but no-one knows much about her. She may have been a widow who took over her husband's businesses or she may have been wealthy in her own right.

- **Sempronia** lived around the time of the Catiline Conspiracy of 62 BC (see Chapter 14). A former prostitute, Sempronia was a supporter of Lucius Sergius Catalina. Extremely good-looking and a talented musician and dancer, she had even managed get married and have children. But she was notorious for being as bold as a man in daring and wasn't the slightest concerned about her reputation. She was lustful and would approach men directly, she'd been an accessory to murder, and was constantly in debt due to her extravagant lifestyle. But according to the historian Sallust, she was witty, charming, excellent company, and a talented poet.

- **Volumnia Cytheris** was a freedwoman actress and probable prostitute in the mid-first century BC. A poet called Cornelius Gallus wrote poetry dedicated to her. Her sexual status gave her access to relationships at the top end of Roman power politics and she found time to be Mark Antony's and Brutus's mistresses. Cicero was disgusted by how she moved in such circles. Unfortunately for women like Volumnia, age was their enemy and they could easily lose favour and disappear . . . and that's what happened to her.

Children

Children were immensely important to Roman families, not just as potential heirs or wives to make family alliances but as individuals, too. The tombstones of children show that their loss was mourned just as in all societies. Children had hard lives though, even if they were born into wealthy households. Firm discipline was routine and was thought to toughen them up for adulthood and improve their character.

Upbringing and education

The better off a family, the more likely the children would be handed over to the care of a nurse when small and then male slaves *(paedagogi)* who accompanied the child everywhere: to school, or on outings to public places like the baths and theatre. They were more than just protectors: Nurses and paedagogues had to take care of their charges' moral education, manners, and behaviour.

Education was simply a matter of family wealth, but rich or poor, it was often only boys that had any real chance of a serious education. There was no system of public education in Rome or anywhere else in the Empire, though Vespasian (AD 69–79) was the first emperor to hire teachers of rhetoric at the state's expense in Rome.

Boys from wealthy families could expect the best education, which was designed to prepare them for a career in military and public life so that they could take their place amongst the movers and shakers in the Roman world. That meant grammar, rhetoric, music, astronomy, literature, philosophy, and oratory, rather than subjects we would recognise today, though, of course, reading and writing were an essential foundation.

Educating the enemy

In order to get conquered provincials 'on side', a tried-and-trusted Roman technique was to educate the sons of local rulers at Rome so that they grew up within the Roman system and took Roman ideas and customs home with them. It's just what the British did with their Empire in places like India nearly 2,000 years later. A good example is Juba II who was educated in Rome and made client King of Mauretania in 25 BC (see Chapter 16 for more on client kings) by Augustus. Juba ruled till AD 23 and introduced all sorts of Greek and Roman customs to his part of north-west Africa. It didn't always work. See Chapter 21 for Attila the Hun, who was brought up in the court of the emperor Honorius.

Children's charities

Charity was all-important in a world with no proper social services. Alimenta worked like this: The emperor lent money at low rates of interest to farmers. The farmers paid the interest, which went into a pot to pay for the upkeep of a predetermined number of children. But charity could also be private. Pliny the Younger gave half a million sesterces (equal to the annual pay of 417 legionaries) in his lifetime for the support of girls and boys in Rome. Sometimes wealthy men would leave a capital sum in their wills, so that the interest could be used to take care of poor children. Publius Licinius Papirianus of the city of Cirta in North Africa left 1.5 million sesterces to earn 5 per cent interest annually to pay for the upkeep of 300 boys and 300 girls.

Teaching was conducted in a schoolmaster's house, apartment, or even in a public place, while the rich had their own personal tutors. Basic schooling just involved literary and familiarity with literature, myth, and law. Better schools included more in-depth study as well as a grounding in Greek, while the boys from the top families went on to be taught by a *rhetor* (a teacher of oratory) to prepare them for public life.

Some examples of writing exercises have survived, showing that children could expect to find themselves copying out passages from works by Virgil or other poets, regardless of where they lived in the Roman Empire. Most of the time the students had to listen to their teachers and memorise passages because writing materials were costly. But many children went without, and only perhaps picked up reading and writing in later life if they were lucky. It's clear from archaeological evidence of graffiti and other surviving written evidence that soldiers and veterans were on the whole more literate than most of the rest of the population.

Poor children

Poor children had far fewer opportunities, though under Nerva (AD 96–98) and Trajan (AD 98–117) the imperial system of *alimenta* was introduced to provide funds to educate poor Italian children (see below).

All this presupposes poor kids were even allowed to grow up. Poor families were used to the idea that another unwanted mouth to feed, especially a girl, would be cast out *(exposed)* in the hope that they would die or be picked up by someone else. In the East anyone who found an exposed child could enslave it until Trajan outlawed the practice. Constantine I (AD 307–337) started state assistance to prevent exposure – the Empire simply couldn't afford the loss of any additional labour, though it wasn't actually banned until 374.

Children were liable to be orphaned if their mothers died in childbirth, which meant they had to hope their fathers or other relatives would take them on. The best hope for slave children was being brought up in the household where their parents worked, as nothing stopped them being sold off. Children born with congenital ailments or other serious birth defects had little or no chance of survival.

Chapter 3

Stairway to the Stars: The Greasy Path to Power

*T*he Roman Empire was all about power: getting it, keeping it, and exercising it. In the days of the Republic, the whole system was designed with a whole series of checks and balance, such as the various assemblies and always having more than one of any magistrate, to prevent any one man having supreme power. But the Romans realised that under extreme circumstances, a man in sole charge was essential for getting out of serious scrapes, so the office of *dictator* was created. (Keep in mind that the Roman term *dictator* means a magistrate temporarily elected to supreme power in an emergency. It didn't mean what it has come to mean today, thanks to men like Hitler and Mussolini.)

Despite these safeguards, various men like Marius and Sulla showed that a general who had a loyal army at his disposal could toss the Republic's system aside (refer to Chapter 14). Then Julius Caesar was created dictator for life, and the Republic collapsed as a result (see Chapter 15). What emerged was a system in which one man – the emperor – had supreme power within the Republican system.

This chapter explains how Roman power worked: who had it, how it was exercised, and how the emperors took power for themselves. It's also about the whole career structure of the elite in the Roman world: how a man's career in power politics started and where it went.

Roman Assemblies

The Roman people had several assemblies, important at different times and with different powers. They reflected the divisions of Roman society between patricians and plebs (refer to Chapter 2). Some of these assemblies had their origins in advisory bodies under the kings, like the Senate. Once the kings had been expelled, the assemblies became the basis of government. Under the Republic, the plebs challenged the patricians' control in the Senate by creating their own assembly, the *Concilium Plebis Tributum* (described later in this chapter).

Over succeeding centuries, enormous tensions built up between the various bodies, as the plebs' representatives, the tribunes, constantly challenged the aristocrats (which now included wealthy plebs) in the Senate. This tension had a dramatic effect on Roman history, contributing to the collapse of the Republic and leading to rule by one man as an emperor. Under the emperors, the assemblies remained intact but their powers were all vastly reduced.

The Comitia Curiata ('Assembly of the Divisions')

The *Comitia Curiata* was only important in the very early days of Rome. It was an ancient assembly of Roman citizens from the three original patrician tribes (Ramnes, Tities, and Luceres). These tribes were divided into 30 *curiae* ('divisions' – ten per tribe), probably consisting of family groups in *gentes* ('clans', see Chapter 2 for families and their clan groupings). The assembly had few powers, and its main role was to ratify the choice of a king, who had already been ratified by the Senate, and the appointment of magistrates.

The Comitia Centuriata ('Assembly of the Centuries')

The *Comitia Centuriata* was the assembly of the army. The 35 tribes of the Roman people were divided into the equestrians (see Chapter 2) and five classes (*classes* – yep, our word's the same as the Roman one). Classes were organised, according to wealth and subdivided into blocks called centuries (*centuriae*) of 100 men. The centuries served as infantry, with the top class having a full set of armour, a sword, and spear. Each class that followed had less equipment, until you reached the bottom class, which had pretty much nothing at all to offer except an able-bodied man who could turn up for war.

The centuries gathered in their individual classes at the Comitia Centuriata to elect magistrates such as the consuls (see the section, 'A career ladder for senators', later in this chapter). In practice, the two top classes usually voted together and effectively out-voted the rest. This system was created in Rome's early days. By the time of the Empire, the division into tribes still existed, but it was really just a formality.

The Concilium Plebis Tributum ('Council of the Plebeians arranged by Tribes')

In 471 BC during the Conflict of the Orders (refer to Chapter 14 for more on this), the patricians were forced to accept the plebeian assembly now known as the *Concilium Plebis Tributum,* which had its origins in the *Comitia Tributa* ('tribal assembly', a plebeian counterpart to the patrician Comitia Curiata – see the earlier section). The assembly passed laws (known as *plebiscita*), elected representatives called tribunes of the plebs *(tribuni plebis)* and their assistants, the *aediles plebeii* ('plebeian aediles').

Tribunes pop up throughout Parts III and IV of this book, showing how they steadily increased their power so that eventually they could do almost anything they wanted on the pretext that they were protecting the rights of the people.

The power of the tribunes

Tribuni plebis, 'tribune of the people' (first heard of in 494 BC), could convene the Senate, but his main power came from the right to interfere on behalf of a pleb who was being oppressed by a patrician (see the sidebar, 'The tribunes' power of veto'). Because the tribune was the one to decide whether someone was being oppressed, it was a great power: Tribunes could disrupt magistrate elections, stop troops, supply levies, and even suspend Senate business. Tribunes did all these things to wear down the patrician monopoly on power, so that, for example, in 367 BC plebs were admitted to the consulship. In the late Republic, rival factions exploited tribunes and their powers, causing the political chaos of the age, helped by the fact that tribunes were usually treated as sacred and inviolable.

Under Sulla, the power of tribunes was seriously reduced until Crassus and Pompey restored it (see Chapter 14). Caesar used the excuse that the Senate had infringed the tribunes' prerogative to justify his crossing of the Rubicon and marching on Rome in 50 BC.

The tribunes' power of veto

Veto means 'I forbid (this)' in Latin. If a tribune thought a law or a magistrate was against the interests or freedoms of the plebs, he could use his veto because he had the right of interference *(ius intercessionis).* Strictly speaking there wasn't any law that gave tribunes this power. It came about simply because of the sheer force of the plebs' support for their tribunes and their sworn protection of the tribunes. In other words, the Senate couldn't afford to ignore it. So if a tribune felt inclined to obstruct a measure and use his veto, the Senate had to accept it. While we're on the subject, the tribune's power to defend the common people this way was something Augustus took advantage of when he 'restored' the Republic but, in reality, made himself supreme ruler.

Tribunes under the Empire

From Augustus's time onwards, the tribunes took care to do only what the emperor wanted. Not surprising seeing as the emperors routinely served as one of the tribunes in order to give them rights over legislation and the Senate. Not many men wanted to serve as tribune alongside an emperor, so Augustus had to have a law passed that tribunes be selected by lot from men who had served as quaestors (see the later section, 'Senatorial careers'). Even though it was really no more than just an honorific post, tribunes still existed in the fifth century at Rome and carried on even later at Constantinople.

The aediles

In the beginning, the only job the aediles had was to take care of tablets on which laws passed by the Concilium Plebis and decrees of the Senate had been written. The tablets were stored in the Temple of Ceres *(aedes* means a temple, hence the word *aedile),* and the plebs were naturally concerned that the patricians would alter the tablets without the aediles around. By the late 400s BC, aediles could arrest people and take care of administration in the city. They also had various responsibilities for using public revenue to pay for public services. See the section 'A career ladder for senators' for what aediles did under the Empire.

The Latin word *plebiscitum* (plural *plebiscita*) is made up of two words: *plebs* and *scitum* ('law' or 'ordinance'). From it, we get our word *plebiscite,* which means a vote by all electors on an important issue, like a change in the Constitution of the United States. It can also mean an expression of opinion by vote, without having the binding force of law.

The Senate

The Senate was manned by the *nobiles* (discussed in Chapter 2), mainly those who had held magistracies in the career ladder. By the reign of Augustus, a senator had to have a personal estate of at least 1 million sesterces (compared to 400,000 sesterces for an equestrian).

Origins of the Senate

The Senate had its origins as a Council of Elders (*senex*, 'an old man'), made up of the head man from each of the leading clans *(gentes)*. They were the men early kings of Rome called on for advice, and they met in the *senaculum,* an open area in the Forum. Roman tradition claimed that Romulus had created a Senate of 100 members and that by the end of Tarquinius Superbus's reign in 509 BC there were 300 senators. It's very unlikely the numbers are true, but it does suggest the Senate gradually grew in size and influence under the kings, even though in those early days it had no actual legal power. A small number of families dominated the Senate, and in the last days of the Republic, this caused a huge amount of tension when rivals started using personal armies or the plebeian assembly to jockey for power.

New recruits

Equestrians (see Chapter 2 for more on these) were the prime source of new recruits to the Senate. Sulla chose 300 equestrians to bump up the Senate's numbers after the Civil War. Caesar allowed Italians and some Gauls to enter the Senate. By 29 BC, the Senate had around 1,000 members, many of whom were former equestrians, and Augustus had to get around 190 of them to withdraw voluntarily. Individual men could seek promotion to the Senate if they could stump up the money. The future emperor Vespasian secured his own promotion that way and made himself eligible for a political career. As emperor, Vespasian promoted others and even gave them the money if they were suitable but short of cash (see Chapter 16 for more on Vespasian). Over the centuries that followed, provincials from almost all over the Empire became members. Britain is one of the places not yet known to have produced a single senator. That could have been deliberate exclusion, or it could be that the province was so poor no-one ever became wealthy enough to qualify.

The powers of the Senate

The Senate had various powers. It could:

- Approve laws passed in the assembly

- Approve treaties

- Appoint governors to provinces

- From 121 BC, declare anyone an enemy of the state and support any magistrate's action against that person: effectively martial law through the power of *Senatus Consultum Ultimum* (see Chapter 14)

A Senatorial resolution (*Senatus Consultum*, abbreviated by the Romans to SC) was not a law, but it came to be as powerful as a law. The emperor generally ruled through Senatorial resolutions. Emperors placed SC on their brass and bronze coins to make it appear the small-change coinage at least was being issued with the Senate's approval. One expression of the identity of the Roman state was *Senatus Populusque Romanus* (SPQR), meaning 'The Senate and the People of Rome'. It's still used by the present-day government of the city of Rome.

The *Curia* (Senate House) in Rome's Forum is one of the most intact Roman buildings to have survived. Built in 29 BC by Augustus, and rebuilt in AD 284 by Diocletian, it could seat about 300.

The Emperors

From the time of Augustus, emperors ruled not because they had been declared supreme rulers and a formal office of 'emperor' created, but because they possessed a unique set of qualifications, titles, and prestige within what was essentially (on paper at least) the old Republican system of magistracies, and which allowed them great power over the assemblies.

The emperor's titles

When Augustus effectively became emperor in 27 BC, he'd arranged things so that the Senate awarded him his powers. This way it didn't appear that he had taken them by force or any other means (see Chapter 16 for the details). All other emperors down to the time of Diocletian's Dominate maintained this fiction, though as time passed it became increasingly obvious that it was a formality.

Some of the titles taken by emperors included the following:

✔ *Augustus:* Octavian was given this name in 27 BC by the Senate. It means 'the Revered One' or 'the One Worthy of Honour'. The month of Sextilius was renamed August, a name, of course, it still bears today. Augustus was really a kind of religious title and conveniently elevated him from just being the former Octavian of the Second Triumvirate. Augustus became a name for any reigning emperor, but if there was a junior emperor the Augustus was the senior partner (see the next bullet).

✔ *Caesar:* This was part of the family name of the Julio-Claudians (all the emperors from Augustus to Nero) and showed their actual (or adoptive, in the case of Tiberius) descent from Julius Caesar's father.

After Nero's suicide in AD 68, the Julio-Claudians had died out, so later emperors took Caesar as part of their names to maintain the fiction of a family succession. But Caesar became a way of indicating an imperial successor – usually a son or adopted son of the Augustus. Under Diocletian and later, it became *nobilissimus Caesar,* 'most noble Caesar'.

Veni, vidi, vici...

✔ ***Imperator:*** This means 'Commander (of the army)' and has the same origins as the word *imperium* (see the next bullet), used to describe the military authority endowed on a man by the Senate. Augustus came to use this as part of his name, not as a title. Because he had, effectively, supreme control, it came to mean a broader sense of supreme power which is why it has survived as our word 'emperor'. Later emperors, mainly from Vespasian on, did use imperator as a title.

Emperors greeted the Senate with the words: 'If you and your children are in health, it is well; I and the legions are in health.' The greeting reinforced the emperor's position as the head of the armed forces and maintained the formality of respect to the Senate as the senior and traditional basis of the Roman state.

✔ ***Imperium:*** *Imperium* means 'Military Command' and 'Supreme Authority'. A holder of imperium had control of war and the law, and thus he had power over armies. In the remote past, the early kings of Rome had held this title. In later times, it was reserved for dictators and magistrates. In the Republic, the title was awarded to men like Pompey the Great. Consuls and praetors also held imperium (see the section 'A career ladder for senators', later in this chapter). Amongst magistrates, there were degrees of imperium depending on individual seniority. It was normally awarded for a restricted period. The emperors had *imperium maius* 'greater imperium', to mark them at a level above the rest.

✔ **Military titles:** Emperors adopted a variety of military titles to commemorate the wars they had taken part in. These usually named the location, like Parthicus and Dacicus for Trajan's wars in Parthia, and Dacia or Armeniacus for Marcus Aurelius's Armenian war; but the title Germanicus was a more generic military title and went back to the general Germanicus, father of Caligula, who had campaigned so brilliantly in Germany during the reign of Tiberius.

✔ ***Pater Patriae:*** Augustus was awarded this title in 2 BC. It means 'Father of the Country' and was a sort of religious patriotic term that acknowledged his pre-eminent role in making the Roman world what it was. Many later emperors held the title, too.

✔ ***Pontifex Maximus:*** This title means 'Chief Priest', a position held for life and usually conferred when an emperor came to power, though Augustus did not receive it till 13 BC (14 years after he became emperor). The holder was in supreme charge of everything to do with Roman religion and ceremony. The closest equivalent today is probably the pope, who even calls himself *Pontifex Maximus.*

✔ *Princeps:* From the Latin words *primus* and *capio,* which mean literally 'I take first place'. This title went along with another phrase – *Primus Inter Pares,* which means 'First Among Equals'. Being Princeps simply awarded Augustus the premier authority in Rome. Indeed, the sheer force of his personal influence was described as being in possession of *auctoritas* ('authority'), reinforced by the strength of his *dignitas* ('worthiness'). This was transferred to his successors, so today the Roman Empire from the reign of Augustus until the reign of Diocletian is known as the Principate. Naturally the word is the source of our 'prince' and 'principality'.

✔ *Dominus Noster*: This title means 'Our Lord'. From Diocletian's time on (AD 284–305), this title gradually supplanted imperator, and marks the transition to the Dominate.

Multitasking: The emperor's jobs

Augustus and his successors took on a number of Republican magistracies and other jobs, including the position of tribune, consul, and censor. By holding these positions, they could be seen to be working *within* the Republican system, which made their power legal. After all, Augustus's great claim was that he had *restored* the Republic, not wiped it out.

The tribunician power

An emperor's tribunician power was the most important (refer to the earlier section 'Concilium Plebis Tributum' for an explanation of what a tribune is).

Augustus made being tribune the basis of his power: He could pose as defender of the people, with powers over the Senate like being able to convene it and veto anything it did. Having tribunician power also had the value-added extra of making an emperor sacred and inviolable. So in 19 BC, Augustus became tribune for life, but it was awarded annually – just a formality, of course. All his successors did the same.

The consulship

The office of consul was held much more infrequently by the emperors, so it's covered below in the career ladder of men of senatorial rank (see the section 'Climbing to the Top', later in this chapter), along with the key qualities all Roman men of rank needed to have: dignity, authority, and virtue.

Censor

This was an old Republican magistracy. The censor was in charge of public morals and from *c.* 443 BC oversaw censuses of citizens. The position was almost redundant by the end of the Republic, but some emperors like Vespasian (AD 69–79) and his son Domitian (81–96) held it.

The line of succession

Because, in theory, there was no monarchy, there was no system of succession for the emperors. In practice, though, from the time of Augustus onwards, any emperor who could tried to nominate a suitable male heir to assume the various positions and titles he had. Wherever possible, this heir was the emperor's son, but often there wasn't one available.

The hereditary principle

Augustus had no sons or surviving (or suitable) grandsons. If he was going to establish a dynasty (see Chapter 16 for the tortuous line of descent which followed down to Nero), he totally depended on marrying his daughter Julia to a suitable male successor (Marcellus, Agrippa, and finally his stepson Tiberius). But just about all the emperors from Vespasian on maintained the dynastic principle, through the second century mainly by adoption. Thereafter emperors constantly tried to have their biological or adopted sons succeed them until the reign of Diocletian (AD 284–305). If no successor was available, then the best available man for the job would be lined up, assuming someone else hadn't already decided to appoint himself emperor.

Jumping the gun

The Romans amply proved to themselves over and over again how the power of the sword ruled because when an emperor died without a clear successor, there was usually no shortage of would-be emperors with soldiers behind each one. That's how the civil wars of AD 68–69 and 193–197 started, and it's also why the third century saw such a reckless cavalcade of soldier emperors who fought and murdered their way into power before being (usually) murdered themselves (Chapter 19 goes into detail on this period).

But even this gang of cut-throats tried to install their own sons as successors, and they invariably adopted all the titles an emperor was supposed to have. Maximinus I (AD 235–238) was a Thracian peasant who rose through the ranks until he overthrew and killed Severus Alexander (222–235). Maximinus was immediately given the power of a tribune for life, awarded the titles of Augustus, Pontifex Maximus, and Pater Patriae, and served as Consul in the second year of his reign.

The only time the succession was based purely on merit was under Diocletian's Tetrarchy (refer to Chapter 19) where two senior emperors (each an *Augustus*) appointed two junior emperors (each a *Caesar*) who would succeed them, and then appoint their own Caesars and so on. The system soon crumbled when the biological sons of some of the Tetrarchs objected to being cut out. Basically, blood is thicker than water.

Climbing to the Top

Nobles and equestrians had their own career paths to climb. By the days of the Empire, these had become fairly well-defined, being based on status, wealth, and age.

A career ladder for senators

Men from noble families of senatorial rank were expected to follow a career through a succession of magistracies, mostly elected by the assemblies, and generally held for one year each. Once a man had held the first magistracy, he could enter the Senate. The senatorial career ladder was called the *cursus honorum,* 'the succession of honours [magistracies]'.

Theoretically, all the magistracies in a career were elective. In practice, they were often sold by emperors or their associates. Vespasian (AD 69–79), who loved money, sold offices, and under Commodus, the freedman Cleander did a roaring trade (see Chapter 18), but they were far from being the only culprits.

Whatever position a Roman held in the career ladder, he was expected to have several key qualities, which also applied to the emperors. Those were:

- **Authority *(auctoritas):*** The authority to command founded on personal prestige.

- **Dignity *(dignitas):*** This means being a man of honour, trust, and reliability, which meant he was faithful *(fides)* and stuck to his guns and his principles *(constantia).*

- **Manly values *(virtus):*** A Roman man was measured by his excellence, his goodness, and his personal virtue.

The magistracies

In the first and second centuries AD, senators could take on the following roles, usually in this order, as they worked their way up:

- **Quaestors *(Quaestores):*** The most junior magistracy, quaestors took care of public finance and the treasury *(aerarium),* receiving all tax income and taking charge of public expenditure. This post was usually held between the ages of 27 and 30, often after being a military tribune attached to a legion (see Chapter 5 for information on the Roman army). After serving as quaestor, a man on the make might become tribunus plebis (for this exceptional post, see the section 'Roman Assemblies', earlier in this chapter), or aedile. Neither was a compulsory post on the career ladder, and by imperial times, being a tribune was just honorific (see the sidebar on 'Gnaeus Julius Agricola's career').

✔ **Aediles** *(Aediles):* Aediles had responsibility for the corn dole, streets, public order, water supply, weights, measures, and even aspects of religious practice. Aediles started out as assistants to each of the two tribunes of the plebs, but in 367 BC, they were increased to four and became a normal magistracy. Serving as an aedile wasn't essential for the *cursus honorum,* but it was useful because an aedile could win popularity and earned the right of *ius imaginum* for his family (see Chapter 2 for this prestigious social status).

✔ **Praetor** *(Praetores):* Praetors were mainly involved with justice. The *praetor urbanus* ('city praetor') dealt with justice in Rome, while a *praetor peregrinus* ('provincial praetor') dealt with cases involving foreigners. Praetors had *imperium* (the power of military command). By the days of the emperors, there were 12 annual praetorships, held by men who were normally at least 30 years old. Men who had served as praetors had earned propraetorian status (see the following section, 'Legionary commanders and provincial governors', for details).

✔ **Consul** *(Consules):* Consuls were the senior civil and military magistrates and were the heads of state. Like praetors, consuls had imperium, but the position was of much greater prestige. Men who had been consuls ennobled their families and descendants, making them the nobiles. The first two consuls were elected in 509 BC, when the kings were expelled. Election was by the Comitia Centuriata (see the section 'Roman Assemblies' earlier). A consul had to be at least 42 for the first time, and wait ten years for re-election (ignored by Marius, see Chapter 14). But under the emperors, all these restrictions were thrown aside, and it was the emperor who usually recommended the men to be consuls, sometimes standing as one himself annually (Domitian was consul ten times in his 16-year reign). By then, several pairs of consuls were elected annually, instead of just one pair under the Republic. The first two consuls of each year were the senior pair and were called *consules ordinarii.* Later pairs in each year were called *consules suffecti* ('substitute consuls'). By increasing the numbers this way, more qualified men became available for jobs like governing provinces.

All the senatorial posts described in the preceding list really belong to the first and second centuries AD, but had their origins in the Republic. By the third century, things were changing: Equestrians were being increasingly used for jobs senators had once done. By Diocletian's Dominate, the whole system was very different. You can find out the details of that in Chapter 20, where I explain how Diocletian reorganised the Empire.

Legionary commanders and provincial governors

Ex-praetors were eligible for jobs of *propraetorian* status (commanding legions or governing less important provinces), and ex-consuls for those of *proconsular* status (governing the most senior or militarily-demanding provinces). Because emperors had almost invariably served as consuls, they also had proconsular status. The word *pro-* meant that the holder had all the powers and status of a praetor, or a consul, in the new job.

- ✔ **Proconsul:** Governor of a senatorial province, a man who had served as consul (these were the older provinces, mostly around the Mediterranean, such as Greece).

- ✔ **Praefectus urbi:** Prefect of Rome with imperium and in charge of keeping order in Rome; usually held by a senator who had been consul.

- ✔ **Legatus Augusti pro praetore:** Governor of an imperial (the emperor's) province (mostly the frontier provinces like Britain and Germany); could be of proconsular or propraetorian status. The most troublesome provinces like Britain had the senior men, but the job was always rated propraetorian so that the governor did not have technically the same status as the emperor, for whom the governor was serving as his delegate.

- ✔ **Legatus iuridicus ('judicial legate'):** Created by Vespasian to ease the workload on governors by hearing court cases, the judicial legate could hear lawsuits and deal with any legal issues while the governor was tied up with other work like fighting wars.

- ✔ **Legatus legionis:** Commander of a legion; usually a man of propraetorian status.

Gnaeus Julius Agricola's career

Agricola (AD 40–post 97) was the historian Tacitus's father-in-law. Tacitus wrote a biography of Agricola, so we know an exceptional amount about his career (there's no equivalent account for anyone else). Agricola was born in Forum Julii (Fréjus) in the province of Gallia Narbonensis. Both his grandfathers were equestrians and served as Procurators, but his father, Julius Graecinus, was promoted to senator. Everyone's career was unique, but Agricola's gives us a good example of a man at the top of Roman society.

- ✔ Aged 20: A Military Tribune at the Governor's HQ in Britain in *c.* AD 60

- ✔ Aged 23–24: Returned to Rome, got married and became *c.* 63–64 quaestor for the proconsular governor of Asia

- ✔ Aged 24–25: A year off *c.* 64–65

- ✔ Aged 26–27: Tribunus Plebis *c.* 66–67

- ✔ Aged 27–28: Praetor *c.* 67–68

- ✔ Aged 29–30: In Britain again as Propraetorian Legatus Legionis (Commander) of the XX legion by 69–70

- ✔ Aged 33–36: Propraetorian Legatus Augusti (governor) of Gallia Aquitania *c.* 73–76

- ✔ Aged 37: Consul in Rome in 77

- ✔ Aged 37–44: Proconsular Legatus Augusti (governor) of Britain, leading a major war of conquest *c.* late 77–83/4

Following his stint as governor of Britain, Agricola should have become proconsul (governor) of Asia or Africa but for political reasons declined. He held no further office.

The status of these jobs didn't stay fixed forever. During Gallienus's reign (253–268), the command of legions was increasingly given to equestrian prefects, probably experienced soldiers who had risen up through the ranks, and reflecting the needs of the age (Chapter 19).

The equestrian career ladder

Most equestrians spent their lives working as bankers and merchants. But there was a sort of elite equestrian career ladder. This was more flexible than the senatorial ladder and didn't necessarily involve passing through a standardised series of hoops. The big difference from senatorial careers is that these elite equestrians were directly dependent on the emperor for their positions.

An equestrian might progress through the commands of a series of auxiliary army units, starting perhaps with a minor administrative job like deputy manager *(promagister)* of harbour dues, before going to be *praefectus* ('prefect', a person placed in command) of an infantry unit, and rising to command a cavalry unit before being promoted to command an arm of the Roman fleet. Next he might be made *procurator* of a province, managing its financial affairs (to prevent the governor having too much control). Another equestrian could serve in a variety of civilian procuratorships, managing imperial estates or other interests (see Chapter 4 for imperial estates and Chapter 7 for mines). By the second century, these various jobs were all rated according to a pay scale based on how important the job was.

A highly successful equestrian could rise to become any one, or in succession, all of these top jobs:

- **Praefectus aegypti:** The governor of the province of Egypt, the emperor's personal possession (usually held by a former *praefectus annonae*).

- **Praefectus annonae:** Responsible for managing the grain supply to Rome and the handouts to the mob.

- **Praefectus civitatium:** An equestrian governor of a province.

    The most famous equestrian governor today is Pontius Pilate. Pilate was an equestrian prefect who governed Judaea between AD 26–36 in the time of Christ's crucifixion. Judaea was one of several small but very annoying provinces (others were Raetia and Noricum) to which the emperor allocated equestrian governors.

- **Praefectus praetorio:** Responsible for commanding the garrison of Rome.

- **Praefectus vehiculum:** In charge of Rome's roads.

- **Praefectus vigilum:** Commander of Rome's fire brigade.

Vespasian's equestrian sponges

It was said that Vespasian (AD 69–79) used to appoint the most rapacious men to the most lucrative equestrian posts so that if he condemned them later on, he could confiscate more cash. They were called his sponges because he soaked them in money when dry and then squeezed them when they were wet.

The reason these were equestrian posts was so that the emperor could keep these immensely powerful offices out of the hands of the senatorial nobiles. Not all prefects were equestrian though, and things did change. The *praefectus urbi,* effectively the mayor of Rome, was a senatorial post. Under Severus Alexander (discussed in Chapter 19), the post of praetorian prefect became senatorial, too. Conversely, command of legions went to equestrian prefects under Commodus (Chapter 18) and Gallienus (Chapter 19), instead of senators.

Because the ranks of the equestrians were used from the late Republic on to provide new recruits to the Senate, it's no surprise that many senators and even emperors, such as Agricola and Vespasian respectively, had equestrian ancestors. By Commodus's reign, some legionary commanders were equestrians, and the process carried on thereafter. The emperor Macrinus (AD 217–218) was still an equestrian when he made himself Emperor, which was unprecedented and did him no favours (see Chapter 19 for more on Macrinus). The division of Roman aristocratic society into senators and equestrians lasted until the reign of Constantine (Chapter 20), by which time the distinction had ceased to have any practical relevance.

Chapter 4

Rural Bliss – Roman Dreamland

*A*ll across the Roman world, from remote parts of Gaul to the Rhine frontier, North Africa, and by the Black Sea, untold millions of farmers and peasants toiled for their whole lives on the land, producing the vast quantities of produce that were transported to Rome to feed the mob and the populations of the Empire's cities. But to the Romans, agriculture was more than a business enterprise. Despite the fact that Roman power and identity were tied up in Rome the city, the Romans always felt that living in and off the countryside was the only means to find inner peace. Even when they couldn't be in the countryside, they adorned the walls of their townhouses with mythical pastoral scenes. The works of Roman poets and writers include literary descriptions of rustic topics, which were seen as patriotic symbols of Roman austerity, restraint, and hard work: the very qualities that had turned Rome into a powerful city with a vast Empire. Even conquered provincials started buying into the same fantasy. In short, if the heart of the Roman world was the city (see Chapter 6), its soul – at least to the Romans themselves – was the countryside.

This chapter is all about the Romans' fanciful image of the countryside, the authors who helped create and promote that idea, and the way rich Romans tried to live out their rural dream in country villas. But it's also about the everyday reality of living in a townhouse or apartment block, or eking out a life as an estate worker supporting the Roman rural dream.

The Roman Fantasy Self-image: We're Farmers at Heart

Even though the Empire only functioned because of the army, cities, communications, assemblies, magistracies, and the way the emperors ruled, the Romans permanently fantasised about an idyllic Italian rural past. Romans believed that Rome had become so powerful because of their origins as peasant farmers with the hard work and discipline that involved.

The great textbooks on Roman rural life were written by three stalwarts of the tradition: Cato (234–149 BC), Varro (116–27 BC), and Columella (first century AD). These men were very influential in their own time, mainly amongst educated men (it's unlikely the average farmer even knew the books existed, let alone had the opportunity to read or own a copy). But what matters more than that is what they tell us about the Roman self-image and the value Roman thinkers attributed to farming.

The Roman scholar Cato (full name Marcus Porcius Cato) grew up on his father's farm near the Sabine town of Reate (modern Rieti) about 60 kilometres (40 miles) north-east of Rome. He came to love the soil for its purity and the simple, straightforward life of a farmer and saw the farming life as the ultimate gesture of Roman patriotism. In his *De Agri Cultura* ('On the Cultivation of Fields'), which was supposed to be a farmer's handbook, Cato conveys the sense that farming is the only honest way to earn a living. Money-lending and trade might offer a chance of more cash, but according to Cato, they were dishonourable and full of hazards. Cato also claimed that the 'bravest and sturdiest' soldiers came from farming stock. In his work, Cato helped to reinforce the Roman tradition that the Empire was the reward and fruit of an army whose origins lay in tilling the fields.

Marcus Terentius Varro was born in Reate (Rieti) and had a successful career working for Pompey the Great (discussed in Chapter 14). In later life, he spent most of his time writing. He was almost 80 when he started his *Res Rusticae* ('Country Matters'), which was supposed to be a handbook for his wife Fundania who had just bought a farm. Varro wrote his work as a series of dialogues between various characters with appropriate rustic names like Scrofa (which also means 'breeding sow') and Stolo (which means 'a shoot growing out of a plant or tree'). In addition to providing a lot of basic technical information for farmers, Varro's work also inspired the Roman poet Virgil's *Georgics,* poems that celebrated rural idealism and were used by Augustus and later emperors to reinforce Roman self-belief.

Lucius Junius Moderatus Columella came from Spain but lived and farmed in Italy. He wrote his *Rei Rusticae* ('On Agriculture') in about AD 60–65 to encourage agriculture. He was very worried about what he considered the decline of Italian agriculture due to absentee landlords who had no interest in promoting farming. As Italy became more and more dependent on imported food, Columella was desperate to encourage landowners to take more interest, but he knew only hard graft would turn things around. The point of *Res Rusticae,* which discussed the farm buildings, crops, fruit, animals, staff duties, and trees, was to provide the essential information to work from and to make a farm a successful and profitable investment.

Life in the City; Dreams in the Country

London, Washington, and New York are full of people from every social tier. The movers and shakers at the top come to the city for business reasons, for government, to be part of the action. Other people come because of the availability of work, and the security and convenience of a city. Rome was just the same. It was the centre of power and commerce, and it attracted people like a magnet. But one of the great paradoxes of city life is that city dwellers spend a lot of time wishing they lived somewhere else.

As the Romans became more dependent on the advantages of urban life and a cosmopolitan economy, they agonised over what they had lost, just as we do. Cities are noisy, busy, dirty places, and plenty of Romans yearned for the wide open spaces away from the crowds. Educated Romans read Virgil's *Georgics* poems to dream of a past paradise, as we go and watch movies of Jane Austen novels filmed in soft focus on eighteenth-century country estates and moan about the loss of our countryside to motorways, interstates, car parks, and shopping malls.

Escaping the city

Everyone knows what happens when human beings live in close proximity, especially those who live in cities. The poet Juvenal, who lived in Rome in the early second century AD, slated city life for the horrendous noise of traffic that kept him awake at night. When he tried to move around, he found his way barred by traffic jams, accidents, crowds of people, and he dodged falling roof tiles, drunks fighting, and muggers.

For the average super-rich Roman, then, a country estate offered a blissful escape from Rome's public life and stinking racket. Rich Romans needing to escape the city raced off to extravagant country houses they called *villae* ('farms'). In exceptional cases, villas were like villages or small towns, manned by small armies of slaves, where their owners pretended they were 'downshifting' to a country lifestyle. You can read more about Roman villas in the section 'Villas: Bedrock of Roman Agriculture', later in this chapter.

IN THEIR WORDS
'Veni, vidi, vici...'

Happy Horace and others

In 39 BC the poet Horace was given a farm by his friend and patron, Maecenas. Horace was delighted, and you can see from his excitement how much it meant to him:

> 'It's just what I had been praying for: a modest-sized plot of land, where there might be a garden, and not far from the house a spring with a ceaseless flow of water, and above these a small piece of woodland. The gods have given me all this but more of it and even better. I am happy. Mercury, I ask nothing more from you except that you ensure these blessings last the rest of my life.'

Seneca (5 BC–AD 65), Nero's tutor, got sick one day and decided to escape to his country estate, desperate to get out of Rome. He wrote to a friend to rave about the experience. He sounds like someone who's managed to escape from Manchester or Chicago for the weekend:

> 'As soon as I had left behind that crushing air in Rome and that stink of smoky cooking hearths which belch out, along with all the ashes, all the poisonous fumes they've stored inside whenever they're fired up, than I noticed an immediate improvement in my condition. You can just imagine how invigorated I felt when I reached my vineyards. I ploughed into my dinner – you might as well be talking about cattle sent out into spring pastures!'

Buying and investing in land

For a noble Roman, which mean the senatorial class (refer to Chapter 2), owning land and storing wealth in land was the only acceptable way to earn a living. So a noble villa owner would always be on the lookout to increase his land holding, which meant buying up neighbouring estates if they came on the market. (Trade was regarded as vulgar, a snobbery that made it easy for the equestrians to corner the commercial markets, often earning enough to buy their own villas.)

Buying more land meant thinking about all sorts of considerations: Was the villa house in good repair? Did it even need to be kept or could it be demolished? Was the land productive and good quality? How had it been run in the past? Were the tenants reliable and well looked after? Would more slaves be needed to get the estate up to scratch and turn a good profit? If the harvest was bad, would the rents need to be put down for the tenants?

For wealthy aristocratic Romans, these were the primary considerations in life – we know they were because they wrote about them. A large and healthy estate enriched such men and their immediate families but also, and perhaps more importantly, became what they could leave to their heirs and descendants, which was a huge matter of prestige as well as security. Of course, the more prestigious the villa, the more attractive it was to bad or resentful emperors who looked for excuses to confiscate the wealthiest estates (for example, Constantius II did quite a business in this regard; see Chapter 20); so the very thing that made a Roman secure – wealth – also put him at risk.

IN THEIR WORDS

'Veni, vidi, vici...'

Tour du jour: Pliny the Younger's villa

Pliny the Younger (c. AD 61–113) (full name, Gaius Plinius Caecilius Secundus) was a Senator from Comum (Como) who became Governor of the province of Bithynia and Pontus under Trajan (98–117). He's famous for the letters he sent to friends and colleagues. One of the best-known is his description of his Laurentine villa about 25 kilometres (15 miles) from Rome in a letter he wrote in the late first century AD. It's so important and so vivid the best thing I can do is let Pliny tell you about it himself with some excerpts I've picked out. Bear in mind his villa was a luxury home despite his claims about its modesty. Now over to Pliny to take us round his place:

✔ **Entering the villa:** 'My villa is the right size for me but inexpensive to maintain. The front hall is plain, without being mean, through which you come to D-shaped colonnades which enclose a small and cheerful intermediate courtyard . . . [which] leads through to a well-lit and pleasing inner hall. From there it leads into an elegant dining room which runs down to the seashore, so that when the wind blows from the south-west it is gently splashed by the waves which work themselves out at its base.

'On every side of this dining room there are folding doors or windows of a similar size through which you have a view of three different seas, as it were, from the front and the two sides. From the back you can see through to the inner hall, the courtyards and the colonnades and from the entrance hall through to the distant woods and mountains.

'To the left of this dining room, a bit farther back from the sea, is a large bedroom and beyond that another one, but smaller, which has one window facing the rising sun, and another the setting sun. This room also has a view of the sea, but from a safer distance. In the angle formed between this bedroom and the dining room is a corner where the sun's warmth is retained and concentrated. This forms the household's winter quarters and the gymnasium because it is sheltered from all the winds except the one which brings rain and it can still be used after the weather has broken.'

✔ **The library and accommodation for slaves and guests:** 'Joining this angle is an apsidal room, with windows so arranged that the sun shines in all day. One wall is fitted with bookcases containing the works of authors I never grow tired of. Next to this is a bedroom opposite a corridor fitted with a raised floor fitted with pipes which take in hot steam and circulate it at a fixed temperature. The other rooms on this side of the villa are set aside for my slaves and freedmen but the majority of these are smart enough to put guests in.'

✔ **The baths and sea views:** 'Next comes the bath suite's cold bath. This is large and roomy and has two curved baths built into opposite walls which are quite sufficient considering that the sea is so close. Next is the oil and massage room, the furnace chamber, the boiler room, then two sanctuaries which are tasteful and very sumptuous. This leads to the hot swimming pool from which bathers survey the sea. Near

(continued)

(continued)

this is the ball-court which the sun warms as it goes down. From here you go up to a tower which is a two-up, two-down, arrangement of rooms, as well as a dining room which has a panoramic view of the sea, the coast, and all the beautiful villas along the shore. At the other end is a second tower with a room lit by the sun as it rises and as it sets. Behind here there is a large wine cellar and granary, and underneath a roomy dining room where the sea can only just be heard, even when it is rough. It looks out across the garden and the drive.'

✔ **The garden:** 'The drive is marked out with a box hedge, or rosemary where the box has gaps, because box grows very well if the buildings give it shelter but withers when exposed to the wind or sea spray, even from some distance. The inner part of the drive has a shady vine pergola where the path is so soft and forgiving that you can walk on it barefoot. The garden is mainly planted with mulberries and figs, which this soil favours as much as it repels everything else. Over here there is a dining room which despite being away from the sea has a garden view which is equally pleasant. Two rooms run round the back part of it, through the windows of which the villa entrance and a fine kitchen garden can be seen.'

In another letter Pliny tells us about what he did at his villa. As you'll see, he doesn't seem to have spent any of his time farming. Despite what men like Cato wanted Romans to do, the truth is that wealthy Romans regarded getting hands dirty as something for their tenants and slaves:

'I get up when I feel like it, normally when the sun rises, and often before that but never later. The shutters stay closed because the darkness and peace help me meditate. Freed from all those external distractions I am left to my own thoughts and my eyes don't make my mind wander. With nothing to see, my eyes are controlled by my imagination.

'Anything I am working on can be sorted out, chosen, and corrected, in my head. What I get done depends on how well I can concentrate and remember. Then I call my secretary, open the shutters, and dictate to him what I have knocked into shape. Then I send him away, call him back, and send him away again. At the fourth or fifth hour after sunrise (I don't stick to an exact time) I take a walk on the terrace or portico where I carry on thinking about or dictating whatever is outstanding on the topic I am working on. Once that's done, I go for a drive where I carry on as before when I was in my study or walking. I find the change of scene revives me and helps me concentrate.

'When I get home I have a rest and then a walk. Then I read out loud a Greek or Latin passage with proper enunciation. The reason is more for my digestion than for the good of my voice, though both are improved by the activity. Another walk follows before I am oiled, do my exercises, and have a bath. If I dine alone with my wife, or with a few friends, we have a reading during the meal. Once we have eaten we either listen to music or a comedy. When that's over I take a walk with members of the household, several of whom are well educated. So, the evenings pass with all sorts of conversations and even when the days are at their longest, they end very pleasantly.'

Villas: Bedrock of Roman Agriculture

The bedrock of the Roman agricultural world was the villa estate. *Villa* means farm, and the term was applied to almost everything from a fairly reasonable farmhouse right up to vast palatial country estates that looked as much like a farm as the White House does Abraham Lincoln's (so-called) wooden hut birthplace in Kentucky. But that didn't stop the owners pretending they were farmers in the best Roman tradition. They were encouraged by writers like Cato, who told his readers to build a villa they'd want to go and stay in often so the farm could benefit from the attention and interest. That's key: Roman villa owners rarely lived in villas the whole time; they usually split their time between a place in town and the country villa. Sometimes they even had several villas.

Rome's grain supply, and the grain used by towns and forts all over the Empire, was grown on these vast agricultural estates (for the grain supply and trade, see Chapter 7). In reality, villas were like agricultural factories, mass-producing food to make their owners wealthier.

Here a villa, there a villa . . .

Villas have been found all over the Roman world, usually on the best land, evidence for farming on an industrial scale. The biggest estates included not just thousands of slaves but whole villages of tenanted communities working vast expanses of land. Many very rich villa owners had several villas, visiting them only occasionally, and normally used resident staff like a bailiff and slaves to run the farm. It's quite possible that modest villas were parts of huge estates owned by big landlords and lived in only by tenants.

As Rome's power and influence spread across the Roman Empire, the villa tradition and the Roman love of simpler rural origins spread, too. Rome's great genius had always been to make others want to 'be Roman', rather than regarding themselves as conquered subject peoples. These villa owners picked up the Roman literary tradition as well and absorbed it into their ideas of who they were.

Imperial and giant estates

The most important landowner of all was the emperor, who had more land than anyone else thanks to his inheritances, what he had conquered himself, and what had been confiscated from his enemies. These were the imperial estates, and they were managed by imperial procurators (usually freedmen) who rented land to tenant farmers *(coloni)* or sublet it to lessees. The tenants had to hand over some of their produce (as much as one third) to the landlord, lessee, or the procurator.

Houses in the Roman Empire

There were two main types of Roman house: the country *villa,* and the townhouse *(domus).* Villas tended to sprawl out with various wings surrounding courtyards, while townhouses were compact, inward-looking buildings where the rooms faced enclosed gardens (as can best be seen at Pompeii in Italy today). Townhouses and villas were similar in having public rooms for receiving guests, clients, and business visitors, and private family rooms. These are the main ones:

- ✔ *Prothryum:* Entrance corridor.

- ✔ *Atrium:* Entrance hall with a central opening in the roof and below it a small rain-catching pool called the *impluvium.* This was the public reception hall and it also held the household shrine (*lararium* – see Chapter 9).

- ✔ *Tablinum:* A corridor room connecting the atrium to the peristylium.

- ✔ *Peristylium:* A garden surrounded by a covered walkway supported by a colonnade.

- ✔ *Oecus:* Reception room opening off the peristylium.

- ✔ *Cubicula:* Bedrooms, opening off the atrium and peristylium.

- ✔ *Triclinium:* Dining room, also usually opening off the atrium or peristylium, and often more than one, designed for summer and winter use.

- ✔ *Xystus:* A bigger enclosed garden.

- ✔ **Others:** Other rooms were used for storage, kitchens, or perhaps a library. Some street-facing rooms or suites were sublet as self-contained shops to tenants (perhaps the owner's freedmen and their families). Some townhouses had an upstairs level but these rarely survived, even at Pompeii and Herculaneum.

Needless to say only people with money could afford villas or townhouses with all these facilities.

The walls in affluent Roman villas and townhouses were painted in panels and borders of bright colours, including pictures of mythological scenes and fantasy architecture. The floors in the best rooms would have had mosaic pavements featuring geometric designs, pictures of mythological beasts, gods, and heroes, as well as a variety of rural everyday activities like hunting. The quality of the flooring and wall painting always reflected the owner's tastes, pocket, and the date. Rich people could also afford glass windows instead of an iron grille, but they were small by our standards and made of an opaque greeny-blue glass. The constant increase in luxury and extravagance in wealthy townhouses in Rome was considered by Pliny the Elder to be a mark of how excessive Roman culture had become. The smartest house in Rome in 78 BC wasn't even in the top 100 by 43 BC and by Pliny's time they'd all been surpassed by houses elsewhere.

Meanwhile, ordinary people in towns had to make do with renting rooms in apartment blocks (sometimes several storeys high) or as self-contained parts of the rich houses let out to rent. In the countryside, simple stone farmhouses might be all a peasant farmer could afford, and in remoter provinces like Britain, thatched roundhouses of an ancient Iron Age design were still used by the poorest people.

Giant villa estates weren't much different, merely that the owner was a private landlord. In Nero's time (AD 54–68), just six landlords owned half of the province of Africa, which most of them managed by constantly buying up neighbouring land. These vast slave-operated estates were called *latifundia* ('extended estates'), and by the days of the Empire, smallholdings on them were increasingly let out to free tenants, who provided additional seasonal labour.

Melania the Younger was a hyper-wealthy Christian heiress in the year AD 404. She had estates in Italy, Sicily, North Africa, Spain, and Britain. We know about her because as part of her faith she toured her property, giving it away, but it shows how the super-rich of the Roman world were truly international millionaires, despite belonging to a culture that thought it was maintaining the simple country life.

Villas in the later years of the Empire

By the fourth and fifth centuries AD, the world of Pliny the Younger and his villa seems a very long way back in the past. Some provinces had been overrun with barbarians. When Britain was abandoned in 410, the collapse of a financial system, provincial government, and a trading and communications infrastructure, as well as barbarian raids, soon saw her villas falling into ruin by the early fifth century. But in other provinces, the wealthy landowners carried on as if nothing had changed. Ausonius (AD 310–395), the Gallo-Roman poet and tutor to the emperor Gratian (367–383), wrote many poems, but one of his best-known was about the river Moselle near where he had grown up. Copying the style of Roman classical poetry from writers like Virgil, Ausonius described the Moselle as a rural paradise of abundant produce including fish, and peopled it with ancient Roman gods.

Even Gaius Sidonius Apollinaris (AD 430–*post* 475), who became Bishop of Auvergne and helped lead the Gaulish resistance against the Visigoths, wrote about his villa and rural life almost as if he was personal friend of Virgil's and had lived 500 years before his own time. Sidonius also talks about his friends' villas, showing that fifth-century southern Gaul still had plenty of senatorial aristocrats who enjoyed traditional Roman villa life.

Living in villas meant being dependent on a colossal amount of tied labour, safe and reliable communications to ship supplies in and produce out, and access to reliable markets in towns. In the Eastern Empire, this system lasted a lot longer, but in the Western Empire, as order collapsed and as provinces were lost, it became impossible to maintain villa estates and the Roman fantasy rural way of life.

A Quick Rural Reality Check

Don't be fooled by the Romans' self-image. The reality for most people in the Roman Empire was a life of endless toil in the fields, coming back from war to find your smallholding had been absorbed into a huge slave-run estate, struggling against natural disasters, bad weather, pests, tax collectors, and the economic chaos caused in the third and fourth centuries by civil war and barbarian invasions, or scraping a living in a crowded apartment block in a city. Many of these people worked as slaves or tenants on vast villa or imperial estates and had no chance at all of ever experiencing the kind of villa life men like Pliny the Younger and Ausonius banged on about.

But it's also true that the rich villa owners set the social standard for top-class living and less-well-off people did whatever they could to copy them. That's why archaeologists dig up small and modest villas with maybe just a couple of mosaic floors laid by a second-rate mosaicist, because to the less-well-off villa owner, a bad mosaic was better than no mosaic at all – a bit like people today buying cheap copies of designer clothing worn by film stars. As ever, people are pretty much the same whatever time or place you look at!

Chapter 5

When We Were Soldiers

*I*f you ask someone to describe a Roman, the first thing that'll come to mind is a Roman soldier, and most probably a Hollywood-style Roman soldier complete with extravagant breastplate, plumed helmet, red cloak, and waving an enormous sword. It's not entirely inappropriate because in much of the world conquered by the Romans the first thing local populations saw was the Roman army.

The Roman army was the driving force of Roman power. In Chapter 4, I mention the Roman writer Cato who said that it was Roman farming stock that produced the best soldiers. These were men with staying power, and it's certainly true that throughout the wars that won the Romans their Empire (see Parts III and IV of this book), it was the ability of the Roman army to cope with defeat, to be adaptable, and to keep coming back for more that wore the Romans' enemies down. So this chapter is all about the Roman army: how it worked, who fought in it, and what a soldier's life was like.

Mastering the Universe: The Fighting Men

There wasn't really 'a Roman army' with a high command nerve centre in Rome and generals gathered round a map of the Roman world directing their troops. Roman armies were put together as the need arose for different campaigns, and they were under the local command of their individual generals. That went right back to Rome's early days when citizens were classified according to what they could provide for military service.

In the days of the late Republic, armies could be official or unofficial, because they were created simply by the sheer force of circumstance. It all boiled down to the prestige and power of generals like Marius, Sulla, Pompey, and Caesar. Awarded *imperium* by the Senate to defend the state's interests, these men, unlike earlier generals, created their own armies and also pursued their own political ambitions. Unlike the earlier armies, these armies were loyal to their generals first and Rome only second. After those days, the commander-in-chief was the emperor.

Army units were stationed all round the Roman Empire, mainly in the most troublesome places. Perhaps the most remarkable thing at all, however, is that in total the Roman army probably didn't amount to more than 300,000–350,000 troops at its climax, which is an amazingly small total given the vast amount of territory the army controlled. To put it into perspective, consider this: At the outbreak of the First World War in 1914, Britain had 740,000 soldiers (including reservists and others), while France and Germany had armies of nearly 1 million troops each, making a combined total around nine times the entire Roman army. Yet most of these troops were fighting in a far smaller area than the Roman army controlled (though to be fair, the population of Europe in 1914 was much higher than in Roman times).

As a very rough estimate, around half the Roman soldiers were citizen infantry soldiers who fought in *legiones* (singular: *legio,* a legion made up of just under 5,500 soldiers). The rest were called the *auxilia* ('assistant' or 'auxiliary troops'): hired provincials who were divided up into infantry, cavalry, and mixed units sometimes with specialised forms of warfare.

It took a long time for the Roman army to evolve into the system I describe in this section; see Chapter 14 for a little more detail about how the early army operated. From its relatively humble origins as a Roman citizen army, made up of men from Rome and Latium, the Roman army grew into a large force spread out across the Roman world. It was made up of men from every last province: citizens who entered the legions, and provincials who entered the auxiliary units. It also included men from beyond the frontiers, 'barbarians' by any other name, who played an increasingly important role in the Empire's defence.

Legions and legionaries

The Roman historian Tacitus, writing around the end of the first century AD, listed 27 legions dispersed around the Roman Empire for the year AD 23. By Trajan's reign (98–117), there were about 30 legions. At the beginning of the third century, there were only 19. The number of legions fluctuated as new ones were formed and others were lost, or cashiered. Legions were stationed where they were most needed. As a result the Rhine – one of the most dangerous frontiers – had eight legions, while the whole of North Africa and Egypt had only four between them. Britain, one of the smallest provinces but one of the most troublesome, never had less than three legions.

Legionaries had to be Roman citizens. In AD 92, a soldier in the III Legion Cyrenaica was accused of not being a citizen and faced instant dismissal. The man had to call three witnesses, two soldiers and a veteran, to testify that he was a citizen.

Organising a legion

Back in the Republic, around the time of the Third Punic War (151–146 BC), a legion varied in number from 4,200 to 5,000 infantry, depending on circumstances, with 300 cavalry. The legion was divided into *maniples,* each of which was made up from two centuries of troops. Maniples of young men made up the front line. Behind them came slightly older troops and at the back were the old, experienced soldiers.

A century used to mean what it sounds like, literally 100 soldiers. Over time, however, the term became less precise, and in practice a century had 80 soldiers. Those 80 soldiers were divided up into ten 'tent parties' *(contubernia)* of eight men each. Each tent party was garrisoned together in the permanent fort, and on campaign they marched together, bringing their tent and equipment on their allocated mule.

The legions went through a lot of changes, but by the late first century AD, they'd reached the form in which they existed for most of the great years of the Roman Empire: one legion totalling 5,120 infantry Roman citizen soldiers. The legion was made up like this:

Men	Total
6 centuries of 80 men	480 (one cohort)
10 cohorts made up a legion thus:	
9 cohorts of 480 men	4,320 men

The first cohort was double-sized and made up of ten centuries of 800 men.

$$800 + 4,320 = 5,120 \text{ men}$$

That wasn't all. Each century had a *centurion* to command it, and his assistant called an *optio.* There were about 128 of these, bringing the total to 5,248.

A legion in the days of the Empire had just 120 cavalrymen used as scouts and couriers, making the final total (not including officers) of 5,368. To that you can add other ad hoc staff like doctors.

Don't imagine if you turned up to a legionary base you'd only see soldiers. Officers and some centurions could afford servants, freedmen, and slaves, and there were also sometimes officers' families, and the unofficial families of soldiers (who lived outside the fortress in the civilian settlement). When the general in Germany called Quinctilius Varus set off to his doom in AD 9 (see Chapter 16), his three legions went out on campaign with women, children, and servants, who all helped slow him down.

Legionary emblems

Various standard-bearers carried emblems on parade and into battle:

✔ **Aquila:** A gold eagle, only carried when the whole legion was on the march

✔ **Imago:** An image of the emperor or a member of his family

✔ **Signa:** A standard for an individual century

✔ **Vexilla:** A flag on a pole naming the legion or a detachment *(vexillatio)*

The loss of standards was the worst thing that could happen to the Roman army. The general Crassus was killed and lost his at Carrhae in 53 BC (Chapter 14). Varus lost his in AD 9 (Chapter 16).

The command structure

A legion was usually commanded by *legatus legionis* ('commander of the legion'), a man of senatorial rank who had served as a praetor (refer to Chapter 3). He had six military tribunes to assist him. The most senior (*tribunus laticlavius*, 'tribune with a broad purple stripe', meaning a man of senatorial rank) was one who would one day command a legion himself. The other five (*tribuni angusticlavii*, 'tribunes with narrow purple stripes') were equestrians and had usually already commanded auxiliaries and might go on to command auxiliary cavalry units.

Then there was the *praefectus castrorum* ('prefect of the camp') who was normally a former senior centurion who had risen through the ranks. Unlike the officers, he had a lifetime's experience in the army. The senior centurion in each cohort commanded his cohort. The senior centurion in the first cohort was called *primus pilus* (probably meaning 'the first spear'). He was the legion's top centurion and had the position all the junior centurions hoped to reach one day. But the truth is no-one knows exactly how the centurions' promotion system worked.

If this all sounds jolly neat and organised, you can forget it. For a start, we know that legions were often split into detachments called *vexillationes* ('wings'). Centurions were frequently sent off to command auxiliary units. We also know that legions, like every other collection of human beings since the world began, were prone to sickness and desertion, quite apart from soldiers legitimately being away from base (see the section following this to find out what duties, military and otherwise, legionaries performed).

Jack-of-all-trades: Legionary duties

Legionaries were used by the Roman state for a whole variety of tasks from putting up fortresses, forts, and civilian public buildings to building bridges, mending roads, collecting taxes, and acting as policemen. In a new province, especially one in the West like Spain or Britain, Roman soldiers would be the only men with all the necessary skills to establish Roman civilization. Their architects, engineers, carpenters, masons, and blacksmiths were invaluable and played a huge part in developing these areas.

One of our sources is a duty roster for the III Legion Cyrenaica in Egypt in the late first century AD. The duties listed include being on guard duty at the local market, road patrol, road cleaning, latrine detail, and detachment to the harbour.

By imperial times, legionaries served for about 25 years, but plenty carried on for longer. They could hope for a grant of land from the emperor on discharge, perhaps in or around a Roman colony of other veterans, and run a business or farm. Augustus claimed that he personally settled 300,000 veterans. At an uncertain later date, a legionary called Vitalinius Felix served in the I Legion Minervia on the Rhine frontier. When retired, he moved to Lugdunum (Lyons) in Gaul where he sold pottery until he died at the age of 59 years, 5 months, and 10 days.

The auxiliaries

The idea of auxiliaries was to add muscle to the Roman army by using the provincials the Romans had once fought. By tapping into their fighting skills, the Romans formed units of Gauls, Spaniards, Thracian cavalry, Sarmatian archers (from an area north of the Black Sea), and a host of others. The auxiliaries were mostly divided into infantry, cavalry, or mixed units. Even if originally hired in one province, new soldiers were often later recruited from places where units were stationed, but the unit's original ethnic title was kept. Here are some examples of auxiliaries:

- ✔ The First Ala (cavalry) of Thracians (northern Greece).
- ✔ The Third Ala of Arabians.
- ✔ The Eighth Ala of Palmyrenes.
- ✔ The First Thousand-strong Mounted Cohort of Vardullians (mixed infantry and cavalry). Vardullians came from Spain.
- ✔ The Fourth Cohort of Gauls (infantry).
- ✔ The First Cohort of Hamian (Syrian) Archers.

And that's only a tiny fraction of them!

There's no better description of the auxiliaries than that by a Roman military historian called Vegetius:

'[Auxiliaries] are hired corps of foreigners assembled from different parts of the Empire, made up of different numbers, without knowledge of one another or any tie of affection. Each nation has its own peculiar discipline, customs and manner of fighting . . . it is almost impossible for men to act in concert under such varying and unsettled circumstances. They are, however, when properly trained and disciplined, of material service and are always joined as light troops with the legions in the line. And though the legions do not place their principal dependence on them, they still look on them as a very considerable addition to their strength.'

Organising auxiliaries

Auxiliaries didn't serve in legions. They were arranged in much smaller units, based on the cohort. They were commanded by equestrian prefects or tribunes, or sometimes by legionary centurions on detachment. This is how they were divided up:

- Infantry auxiliaries were organised into cohorts of 480 or 800, divided into centuries like the legions.

- Cavalry auxiliaries were organised into wings *(alae)* of about 500 or 1000, divided up into *turmae* (squadrons) of 16 troopers each.

- There were also mixed units where blocks of 128 or 256 cavalry were added to infantry units. These were called *cohorts equitatae* ('mounted cohorts').

Fighting fodder and frontline soldiers: Auxiliaries' duties

Auxiliaries marched alongside the legionaries and even camped with them, but were paid less. Crucially, auxiliaries always bore the brunt of the fighting. The idea was that it was much better to lose provincials than Roman citizens. So in most set-piece battles, the auxiliaries would be thrown in first. Sometimes the legionaries just stood and watched.

The reason auxiliaries put up with such a raw deal was that they could earn citizenship that way, not just for themselves but for their families. Citizenship was awarded after 25 years' service (in theory – often they were kept hanging on). Yet again, Rome had an advantage because other people wanted to be Roman, too. Of course, after AD 212 and the grant of universal citizenship under Caracalla (see Chapter 18), this distinction ceased to mean anything anyway.

The Romans also hired an unending series of more casual ad hoc auxiliaries, often from barbarian tribes on or near the frontier, who were even less well paid and who had no chance of citizenship. Handy for propping up the borders, these units were treated as totally disposable and were much more loosely organised and much more unreliable as a result. These units, sometimes generally referred to as *foederati* (federates), played an increasingly important and sometimes decisive part in Rome's later history.

The Praetorian Guard: Rome's garrison

The prefect of the Praetorian Guard constantly pops up in the history of the Roman Empire (see Chapters 16 through to 19). The Praetorians were the garrison of Rome, so they were right on hand to influence the imperial succession.

The origins of the Guard went back to the days of Publius Cornelius Scipio Aemilianus Africanus the Younger (*c.* 184–129 BC) who took a personal bodyguard of 500 troops to Spain with him in the Third Punic War (151–146 BC) because the soldiers in Spain were unreliable.

Under Augustus, the Praetorians were organised into nine cohorts of about 500 men, three of which were based in barracks outside Rome and the rest in various Italian cities. Praetorians were commanded by the equestrian *praefectus praetorio* (refer to Chapter 3), were paid more than legionaries, and served for much less time (16 years only). They occasionally took part in military campaigns, could be promoted to be centurions in legions, and in AD 61, a few were even sent to find the source of the Nile.

The fleet: Rome's navy

Even though the Roman world was held together by lying around the Mediterranean, the Roman fleet *(classis)* or navy was really just an extension of the army. The Romans weren't natural sailors and had no great skills in navigation or seamanship, despite Italy's extensive coastline. When Julius Caesar invaded Britain in 55 and 54 BC, he lost ships on both occasions to storms and the tides, having no idea how extreme they could be.

The big naval successes for the Romans came earlier in the Punic Wars when Rome learned to sail ships in such a way that they could use them as platforms for landing soldiers (Chapters 12 and 13 explain the Punic Wars). Pompey's destruction of the Cilician pirates was a major triumph, but of course the decisive event that ended the Republic was the naval battle between Antony and Octavian in 31 BC (see Chapter 15 for that tale).

The first permanent naval bases were built at Forum Julii (Fréjus) in Gaul, and in Italy at Misenum and Ravenna by Augustus's time. They were designed to protect Italy and the grain fleets. Misenum became the main naval headquarters not far from where today the US Navy, the world's most powerful, has a major base at Naples. Various other Roman fleets were installed around the Empire, for example in Alexandria, the Black Sea, Syria, Germany, and Britain, where they protected commerce or supported invasion forces by bringing up supplies, reconnoitring the land, building advance bases, and carrying marines *(nauticus miles)*.

Fleets were generally commanded by equestrian prefects. Sailors, who came mostly from the east, turned up doing all sorts of other jobs from supplying recruits for new legions to building a granary on Hadrian's Wall. The most notorious fleet event came in Britain in 286 when the commander of the British fleet, Carausius, used his naval power to rebel against the emperors Diocletian and Maximian (see Chapter 20).

The Roman siege of Syracuse between 213–211 BC in the Second Punic War (covered in Chapter 12) was a powerhouse of ingenuity. The Roman general Claudius Marcellus doubled up eight of his war galleys so they could carry siege ladders right up to the city walls. The idea was that attackers could launch themselves off the top onto the Syracusan defenders. Unfortunately, the Syracusans had the brilliant mathematician Archimedes (287–211 BC) on hand. Amongst the defensive weapons he devised was one that used a grappling iron to lift Roman ships up by the bows till they were vertical. The bottoms of the ships were then tied up and the grappling irons let go, causing the ships to fall back and sink. A far less reliable and much later source says Archimedes told the Syracusans to reflect sunlight with hexagonal mirrors onto the wooden ships. This supposedly set them on fire, but modern experiments have suggested this would have been extremely difficult if not impossible. Either way, Claudius Marcellus abandoned the assault by sea, but with a combination of land forces and a Syracusan traitor, he fought his way in and seized the city. Archimedes was killed in the battle, even though Marcellus had ordered his capture.

Having the Right Equipment

Regardless of how the Roman army was organised, none of that would have mattered a jot if soldiers hadn't had the right gear. At its climax, the Roman army was the best equipped and best supplied force in the ancient world.

Uniforms and weapons

Until the mid-first century AD (around the reign of Claudius), the average legionary's equipment consisted of the following:

- Helmet (with cheek and neck guards) *(galea)*.
- Mail shirt *(lorica hamata)*.
- Dagger *(pugio)*.
- Sword *(gladius)*.
- Shield *(scutum)*.

✔ Spear *(pilum)*.

✔ Open leather boots with hobnails *(caligae)*. (These are the boots the young Caligula, emperor AD 37–41, wore and were how he got his name.)

After the mid-first century AD, a legionary was more likely to have armour made of overlapping strips of iron *(lorica segmentata)* and a more elaborate helmet with deeper neck-guard and bigger cheek-pieces. But it's plain from excavated examples that all this kit was liable to be handed down and used by many different soldiers over the years, so the likelihood is that any Roman army line-up would have looked distinctly ad hoc.

Not as ad hoc as the auxiliaries though, who used an almost unlimited array of weaponry and armour depending on their specialisations, where they came from, and what was available. The biggest show-offs were the auxiliary cavalry who loved fitting out their horses with decorative medallions on the harnesses. For special occasions, they had parade armour with face masks so that they could pose as mythical heroes in mock display battles.

The Roman army's tradition was as an offensive, not a defensive force. Scipio Africanus the Younger once saw a soldier showing off his shield and told him, 'It is a very fine one, my boy; but a Roman soldier must have more trust in his right arm than in his left', meaning his sword arm, of course.

Artillery

The Romans were experts at artillery, though, of course, with no gunpowder, it was all done by sheer brute force and tensioned ropes. This is some of what they had, and it was especially suitable for siege warfare:

✔ **Ballista:** Rather like a medieval crossbow, a *ballista* (or *cheiroballista*) fired iron darts.

✔ **Onager:** A catapult sitting in a frame. A throwing arm, tensioned with ropes wrapped round the axle, was pulled back and let go, hurling rocks and other ammunition at the enemy.

✔ **Aries:** The name means both a male sheep and a battering ram and is named because that's what male sheep do. So like the Romans, we use the same word for both. The Romans used rams housed in vehicles with wheels. Inside, men pulled the ram back and forth on rollers. There was also a similar vehicle housing a drill, turned by a winch.

The best possible Roman battle in the movies is in the opening few minutes of *Gladiator* (2000). You get to see authentic-looking Roman soldiers caked in grime after years of campaigning on the German frontier, complete with artillery, archers, and an axe-wielding barbarian enemy. It's amazingly realistic, though, in fact, it was filmed just outside London.

Holding the Fort

The Roman fort was like a miniature town. No matter where a Roman fort was built, or how big, it always conformed to the same basic design, though no two forts were identical. The biggest were legionary fortresses, accommodating more than 5,000 men, while the smallest full-sized forts housed auxiliary infantry cohorts of about 500 men. Even the fleet used coastal forts built to the same design. But smaller ones are known, right down to fortlets accommodating a dozen men.

The permanent fort was based on the marching camp, and the idea was to maintain discipline and organisation: Every Roman soldier should know exactly where he was supposed to be in the fort, whether the home base or an overnight marching camp. Permanent forts really came into being in the late first century AD and into the second century, once the Empire's frontiers became fairly static.

Fort defences

Forts were generally planned in playing-card shapes with curved corners, and flush gateways (one in each side, opposite one another). Even the biggest fortresses were larger versions of the same basic layout (see Figure 5-1).

Turf and timber ramparts were about 4–5 metres in height and supported a walkway with a timber parapet. Planks were inserted in the turf to strengthen it. Stone walls could be as high as 4.5 metres (15 feet), with a 1.5 metre (5 foot) parapet above, and were often built as facings to existing turf ramparts. Beyond the walls a huge V-shaped ditch *(fossa)* was dug, and if the location was especially dangerous, extra ditches were added, sometimes with sharpened stakes dug into the sides.

Gateways were the weak link, but the Romans heavily protected them with flanking gate-towers. Interval towers around the walls added additional viewpoints. A grid of streets divided up the inside into various zones. The most important bit was the central zone *(latera praetorii)* where the administrative buildings were.

A Roman fort could be built in timber and turf, or in stone, or even a combination. Turf and timber was quick, easy to obtain, and extremely effective. The labour in the form of soldiers was available anyway, so it's common for archaeologists to find several different builds of a fort, erected within a few years of each other on the same site, especially from the first century AD or earlier. After that date, forts were more usually built in stone because with settled frontiers, units were far less likely to move on from permanent bases.

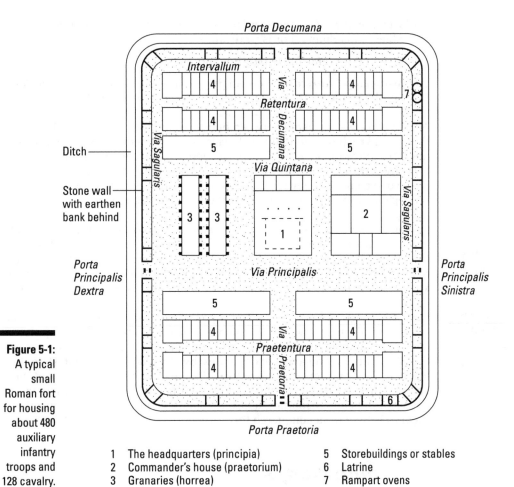

Porta Decumana

Intervallum

Retentura

Via Decumana

Via Sagularis

Ditch

Stone wall
with earthen
bank behind

Via Quintana

Via Principalis

Porta
Principalis
Dextra

Porta
Principalis
Sinistra

Praetentura

Via Praetoria

Figure 5-1:
A typical
small
Roman fort
for housing
about 480
auxiliary
infantry
troops and
128 cavalry.

Porta Praetoria

1	The headquarters (principia)	5	Storebuildings or stables
2	Commander's house (praetorium)	6	Latrine
3	Granaries (horrea)	7	Rampart ovens
4	Barracks (centuriae)		

Fort buildings

Forts had every facility necessary for daily life in the Roman army, including
armouries and workshops to make and repair everything the soldier needed,
from a humble buckle to a piece of artillery:

- **Barracks (contubernia):** Filled out most of the fort area, with one block
  for each century (80 men).

- **Commander's house (praetorium):** Next door to the headquarters.
  Legionary fortresses had houses for the tribunes nearby, too.

- **Granaries (horrea):** Usually built in pairs close to the headquarters building and heavily buttressed to withstand the pressure from settling grain.

- ✔ **Headquarters** *(principia):* The nerve centre where standards, valuables, and admin records were stored.

- ✔ **Hospital** *(valetudinarium):* Not always built.

- ✔ **Workshop** *(fabrica):* Where all the fort's needs like carpentry, blacksmithing, and clothing could be seen to (not always built).

A large gap always existed between buildings and the defences so that soldiers could rush to defend the fort walls and to protect the buildings. The only structures found around the edge were usually cooking ovens (kept away from the barracks because of the danger of fire) and latrines. Baths were such a fire risk they were often built outside the fort at some distance, but legionary fortresses usually had their baths within the walls.

Roman fort layouts are so similar that if an archaeologist finds a few key reference points by excavation, the rest of the plan can usually be worked out from that. Forts are at the heart of the Roman genius: It was all about system. Military architects could lay things out easily and quickly, and every soldier knew what he had to do and where he belonged once the fort was finished.

Sometimes legions built specialised works depots, which were industrial centres, especially useful when the legion was in a way-out place where pottery and other manufactured goods couldn't be bought in. The XX legion at Chester in Britain had a works depot nearby at a place called Holt. Here the legion made its pottery, brick, and roof tiles, amongst other things, and then shipped them downriver to their fortress at Chester. But the army had vast needs for food and resources. It also bought in goods, or simply requisitioned them as tribute from conquered territories.

Marching camps

Marching camps were simply forts built on the move, though it'd probably be better to say that forts were permanent versions of marching camps. An army on campaign obviously needed an overnight stop. A suitable place on raised ground with access to water was chosen, and the fort systematically laid out, starting with the commanding officer's tent *(praetorium)*. Once the streets were laid out with all the places for the troops, the soldiers produced their spades and dug out a ditch around 1 metre deep and used the spoil to create a rampart. Each man carried wooden stakes so an instant palisade could be set up. Troops were then allocated various details like rampart guard duty or protecting supplies. In the morning, or as soon as the army moved on, the camp was packed up and the rampart flung back into the ditch.

Hadrian's Wall

Hadrian's most famous monument was his 76-mile-long frontier in Britain. A complex of stone wall, forts, fortlets spaced at 1-mile intervals with lookout towers at one-third-mile intervals between, together with forward and rearward defensive earthworks, it created a ribbon of Roman military life across northern Britain. One Roman historian said it was 'to separate barbarians and Romans', but it's plain that crossing the Wall was allowed. Its real purpose was probably to control movement to prevent trouble and enforce taxation, rather than stop it altogether. Since Hadrian visited Britain around the time the Wall was begun, it's almost certainly the case that he helped designed it. A bronze pan, inscribed with the names of several of the Wall's forts, recently found in Britain also carries the words *Val(l)i Aeli,* which gives us the ancient name for the frontier: 'The Aelian Frontier', named after Hadrian (his full name was Publius Aelius Hadrianus). The Wall went through many repairs, restorations, and rethinks, but it remained a more or less permanent fixture until Britain was abandoned by the Empire in the early fifth century. Large stretches of the Wall can still be seen today. The Wall is studied by Roman military scholars from all over the world and visited by millions of tourists.

Keeping the enemy out: Frontier fortifications

Protecting the frontiers wasn't strictly in the Roman tradition as the Romans had generally assumed they'd be forever expanding. But by Hadrian's day (AD 117–138), the decision had been taken to stop conquering new territory (see Chapter 17). Frontiers were settled, and the Romans had to find ways of permanently protecting their troops and the borders. Wherever possible rivers, like the Rhine in Germany, or other natural boundaries were used. Watchtowers were built and acted like modern-day CCTV cameras, where troops could watch out for barbarians trying to sneak across. Warning could then be sent by beacon or mounted messenger to the nearest fort.

In some places, there just weren't the natural boundaries so the ever-practical Romans had to make their own. The most extreme and the most famous is Hadrian's Wall in Britain, but it wasn't the only one. Other frontiers joined the Rhine and Danube, for example, and out in Egypt's desert a chain of remote forts protected the Empire's richest province.

The Late Army

From the reign of Marcus Aurelius (AD 161–180) on, the Empire was under attack on the borders. Not all the time, and not everywhere, but the assaults gradually increased and got much worse in the third century during the age of short-lived 'soldier emperors' (see Chapter 19). Cavalry became especially important. Gallienus (253–268) was the first to create an independent cavalry army under its own commander and put the legions under the command of equestrians rather than senators.

The really big changes started under Diocletian (284–305) and the Tetrarchy (Chapter 20). Diocletian increased the number of legions to about 60. They were installed in pairs along the frontiers, together with cavalry units, but a few were attached directly to the mobile imperial court *(comitatus)* along with the highest grade cavalry troops.

Dividing the army

Under Constantine (307–337), the emphasis on mobility became the first priority, though the change began under Gallienus (253–268). The army now became fully divided into the following:

- *Comitatenses* (from *comes* meaning a member of the emperor's retinue): The *comitatenses* fought the wars around the Empire, and were highly trained, well-paid, quality troops based on around a dozen 500-strong cavalry units which created the core of the emperor's mobile army. These were the men who would race to confront any invading army of barbarians.

- *Limitanei* (from *limes*, 'frontier'): The mainly infantry static frontier garrisons, the *limitanei* held the restored frontier defences and were lower grade in every respect. In fact, they were frontier spear fodder, a hotch-potch of long-established auxiliary units, ad hoc bands of hired provincials, and even barbarians. As a result they were variable in their fighting ability and, even worse, in their loyalties.

Meanwhile, the legions were pulled back from the frontiers to create fortified strongholds and military centres within the Empire, which would protect civilians and military resources in the event of an invasion.

New forts for the late army

The frontier garrisons continued to occupy their old forts, but a new form of military architecture was developed that resembled medieval castles. With bigger walls and huge projecting towers and gates that supported defensive artillery, the new forts were really massive defensive compounds. The same features are often found on Roman city walls like those built by Aurelian for Rome (see Chapter 19).

The end of the Roman army in the West

The trouble is that with the army divided up into local frontier garrisons, it was easier for would-be emperors to cash in on local loyalty and rebel. There was also a huge setback in 378 when the emperor of the Eastern Empire Valens (364–378) was killed at Hadrianopolis trying to push back the Ostrogoths and Visigoths (explained in Chapter 21).

By the early fifth century, the West faced three key problems:

✔ So much territory had been lost, the West couldn't support or provide the army it needed.

✔ A succession of rebellions inside the Roman Empire had taken troops away from frontiers and allowed forts and defences to become rundown.

✔ The West became more and more dependent on hiring barbarian troops known as *foederati,* who were only loyal if they were being paid. They could turn against the Empire without warning.

Meanwhile, the East had suffered far less from invasions and was able to support the army it needed. In the end, what did it for the army in the West was simply that there weren't enough resources or money to keep it going. The very last unit from the old days recorded was the Ninth Cohort of Batavians, which nearly 400 years earlier had been responsible for some of the writing tablets found at the fort of Vindolanda in northern Britain (see Chapter 17). Some of the unit's soldiers tried to get back pay during the reign of Romulus Augustus (475–476). The troops were killed and thrown in the river. The Roman army in the West was no more.

Part II
Living the Good Life

The 5th Wave   By Rich Tennant

"Tell the emperor if he has any trouble with it,
just try jiggling the handle a little."

In this part . . .

The Roman world was a system – in fact, the first system in human history – that affected almost everyone who was part of the Roman Empire. That system included living in or visiting cities where you could marvel at Roman architectural achievements and enjoy the fruits of international trade and even on-demand running water; enjoying the first mass leisure industry the world had ever seen, complete with amphitheatres and circuses and more; and finding solace in the gods in an age of extraordinary religious tolerance.

It's important to remember that, in addition to all the wonders it offered, the Roman world was also a brutal place which enslaved untold millions of people and which made a few people very rich and powerful at the expense of the many.

The good life came at a heavy price.

Chapter 6

The Urban Jungle

The Roman Empire was an empire of cities. Rome was a city, and she used cities to run the Empire. If we look at what Rome became, we can understand a huge amount about what made the Romans tick. It's no exaggeration to say that without cities, Roman power couldn't have existed. Throughout this book, there's a constant theme: The Romans were geniuses at persuading other people that 'being Roman' was a good thing. Cities impressed people with Roman power, but they also created a sense of order, permanence, and security, and were an essential part of government and the economy.

This chapter is about getting to grips with the essence of Rome the city and its part in Roman society, the architectural techniques that made Rome's buildings possible, how those buildings functioned and what they were used for, and how all across the Roman Empire every town of consequence resembled a miniature Rome. It's also about the communications that held the Roman world of cities together: the roads.

The Idea of City

The essence of the Roman world was the city. Rome herself was often known as simply *Urbs,* 'the City'.

In the ancient Mediterranean world of the early first millennium BC, the idea of a city was already synonymous with a community. Egypt's mighty and much older civilisation was ruled from great cities like Thebes and Memphis, which were home not just to large numbers of people with their homes and businesses but which also gave over vast areas to temple complexes and royal palaces. Greece was divided up into city states where places like Athens ruled their hinterlands. The Phoenician colony of Carthage in North Africa was an important trading city, destined to become Rome's greatest rival.

Rome itself had grown out of a collection of villages that were drawn together under the early kings thanks to their shared culture and their common interest in defending themselves against enemies in the region. These early kings introduced the ideas of public services and government to the early Romans and were inspired by the cities that already existed in the Mediterranean area including the Greek colonies in Sicily and southern Italy.

The Romans also believed that their city was divinely ordained in the myth of Aeneas and his descendants Romulus and Remus (see Chapter 10 for information on the founding of Rome). So Rome wasn't just a practical facility, it was also a place with a spiritual identity whose people were destined to rule the world. This provoked an intoxicating sense of community summed up in the way the Romans portrayed the city as a female figure seated on a suit of armour, wearing a helmet, and holding a Victory (a winged goddess) in her hand.

The effect in ancient times was to create the idea that Roman urban civilisation was the bedrock of security. The natural world is dangerous and unpredictable. Cities provide man's response – it's why so many of us live in them today. For the Romans, this created a paradox: They felt that Rome and her Empire were the rewards from the gods for a superior civilisation, but that the comforts and easy living had softened them up and created a population that was no match for the hardy tough men who had founded Rome and built her up. As the pressure on Roman civilisation grew from barbarian invasions in the third century AD and later, the Romans grew absolutely terrified at the thought Rome herself might disappear. If that sounds weird, cast your mind back to 9/11 and remember how frightened New Yorkers were when it seemed their city's very existence hung in the balance.

St Jerome, a Christian teacher, wrote this in a letter of 413, just three years after the sack of Rome by Attila the Hun (Chapter 21). As a Christian, he thought it was all to do with the sins of the Roman people, echoing Tacitus's feelings three centuries before about the decadence of imperial times, but the point is Jerome thought he was witnessing the end of the world: 'Shame on us. The world is falling into ruin, but our sins still flourish. The glorious city that was once head of the Roman Empire has been devoured by one mighty fire.'

Rome: The urban template

Rome might have been just one of many cities in the Mediterranean area in antiquity, but no other ancient civilisation developed the city in quite the same way the Romans did. The city of Rome took centuries to grow into the sprawling monster she became in the days of the emperors, by which time Rome was a vast co-ordinated organism of government, public services, utilities, and communications.

Rome's power and wealth attracted people in vast quantities, who all needed governing, feeding, and entertaining. The more people, trade, and industry there was, the more prestigious were the men who controlled them. During the first century BC, a number of exceptionally powerful men (see Chapter 15) like Caesar and Pompey jockeyed for control of Rome, in part by providing public facilities and entertainments. When the emperor Augustus listed his lifetime achievements, he rattled off dozens of buildings which he had built or repaired to show his power and generosity (listed in the section 'Improving the model city', later in this chapter). These men wanted Rome to be the showcase of their own and Rome's power and divine backing. They succeeded brilliantly.

Even today Rome's magnificent history and majestic ruins give it a status above all other cities in the world. Rome has had an enormous influence on the development of cities ever since. New York's Grand Central Station and Washington DC's Union Station are modelled on Roman architecture. Liverpool's vast commercial wealth of the nineteenth century led to a suite of public buildings based directly on Roman designs.

The Romans had developed Rome into a huge template for her civilisation. In the centre were Rome's public buildings, forums for trade and commerce, basilicas for legal affairs, and temples to state religions as well as the imperial palaces. Scattered around these were the theatres, amphitheatres, and the Circus Maximus. A road network radiated from the centre through housing, while above the city, aqueducts carried water in, and below the city, sewers drained it away. Rome's system of civic magistrates from consuls down to aediles was used to govern not just Rome and her immediate environs but the whole Roman Empire. Various equestrian prefectures were created to control key services like the grain supply, the city garrison, the fire brigade, and the roads (for details of these positions, see Chapter 3). Although Rome had taken centuries to evolve, at its climax it had a number of key features:

- **Amphitheatres:** Home to gladiatorial and beast fights.
- **Basilicas:** Law courts and administration.
- **Baths:** Vast public bathing establishments provided by the state, as well as a host of private smaller concerns.
- **Circuses:** Home to chariot-racing.
- **Curia:** Senate house, where the senators met.
- **Forums:** Public piazzas for trade and politics surrounded by shops and businesses.
- **Public services:** Mainly defences, aqueducts, drains, fire service, and roads.
- **Temples and religious precincts:** Temples funded by emperors, rich citizens, or corporations to look after their interests and that of the Roman people, worshipping state, local, specialised and eastern cults.
- **Theatres:** For comedies, tragedies, and poetry-readings.

Strabo visits Rome

Strabo, a geographer, visited Rome in the days of Tiberius (AD 14–37). He wondered at the extraordinary public buildings, but he was also fascinated by the constant demolition and rebuilding that went on:

'There's a constant need for wood and stone for the endless construction work in Rome. This is caused by frequently collapsing houses, and because of the fires and house disposals which never seem to let up. These disposals are a kind of deliberate demolition, each owner knocking down his house and then rebuilding as the fancy takes him. To this end the huge number of quarries, forests, and rivers in the region which provide the materials, offer superb facilities.'

When Vespasian came to power in 69, he actively encouraged anyone to take over vacant sites caused by fires or collapse and put up new buildings, because he thought they made Rome look unsightly.

No wonder the natural historian Pliny the Elder said 'there has been no city in the world that could be compared to Rome in magnitude'. Writing about the year AD 73, he said Rome had 14 administrative regions, with roads forming 265 crossroads, and 60 miles of major roads within Rome radiating from a point in the Forum out to the 37 gates in 13 miles of defensive walls.

Improving the model city

The emperor Augustus (27 BC–AD 14) was particularly keen on making Rome into a showcase for Roman imperial power, but he was only following a trend. In the first century BC the general Pompey the Great built a massive theatre, and Julius Caesar was responsible for numerous buildings like the Basilica Julia.

Augustus used his friend Agrippa to organise much of the new work, and this is some of what they achieved (the ones you can still see today are marked with an asterisk):

- Finished off Julius Caesar's forum and basilica*
- Restored old temples and erected new ones, like the vast temple of Mars Ultor (the Avenger)* which fulfilled a vow Augustus had made before the Battle of Philippi in 42 BC, and another one to the deified Julius Caesar
- Built a new forum, the Forum Augusti*

The Forum in Rome is so ruinous that you might be forgiven for wondering whether the Romans were as good at building as is often claimed. Well, what happened is that in the year 667, the Byzantine emperor Constans II decided the bronze and iron clamps which held the stone blocks of the Forum buildings together would be far more useful to him melted down into weapons for his wars to defend the Byzantine Empire. So he had them all removed, which meant that subsequent earthquakes (not unusual in that part of the world) caused most of the buildings to collapse.

- Presided over the Altar of Augustan Peace *(Ara Pacis Augustae)**, ordered by the Senate and dedicated in 9 BC

- Built the Theatre of Marcellus* to commemorate Augustus's nephew (who died in 23 BC)

- Installed new aqueducts

- Built the original Pantheon (later rebuilt and redesigned by Hadrian)*

- Raised a vast mausoleum for Augustus and his family*

Many of the emperors who came after Augustus provided Rome with greater and more impressive public buildings. These are just some of them:

- Claudius (41–54) built an aqueduct.

- Vespasian (69–79) began the Colosseum*.

- Titus (79–81) finished the Colosseum and built public baths.

- Domitian (81–96) built a circus.

- Trajan (98–117) built more public baths and a vast new multi-level forum*.

- Hadrian (117–138) built the huge double Temple of Venus and Rome* and rebuilt the Pantheon*.

- Caracalla (211–217) built a vast bathing complex* which still dominates the southern part of Rome.

- Maximian (286–305) built the Baths of Diocletian. Enough survived of the great vaulted cold room *(frigidarium)* for it to be converted by Michelangelo (1474–1564) in the Renaissance into the Church of Santa Maria degli Angeli*, and today this is one of the great sights of Rome.

- Maxentius (306–312) built a vast vaulted basilica*, part of which towers over the Forum to this day.

The map of the city of Rome

Under Septimius Severus (AD 193–211) a vast map of Rome – the *Forma Urbis Romae* – was carved on marble and displayed in the city. Measuring 18 by 13 metres, it recorded everything from shops to mighty public buildings.

Sadly, just 10 to 15 per cent survives, broken into 1,186 pieces, but those fragments preserve vital evidence, including its plan of the Theatre of Pompey, which is still buried.

'Veni, vidi, vici...'

Civic corruption and incompetence

There were all sorts of opportunities for incompetence and corruption to ruin public building projects. In the early second century, Pliny the Younger was governor of Bithynia and Pontus in Asia Minor. He wrote to Trajan (AD 98–117) about various problems with buildings in his province including this moan:

'The Nicaeans are also rebuilding their gymnasium (which was burned down before I arrived in the province) on a much larger scale. They have already gone to considerable expense and I'm afraid it may have been for nothing. The building is irregular and badly proportioned, and the

current architect, admittedly a rival of the one who was on the project at the beginning, says that the 22-feet thick walls are not strong enough to hold up the superstructure. This is because the core is filled with rubble, and the walls have no brick facing.'

No-one knows what the outcome was. But it's plain from other excavated buildings that the Romans weren't always brilliant construction engineers, and no doubt incompetence and corruption were sometimes the reasons, just like today.

Copycat Romes

Exploring the Roman world today means visiting places like Pompeii and Ostia in Italy, Ephesus and Aspendos in Turkey, Thuburbo Majus and Dougga in Tunisia, Arles and Nîmes in Gaul, and London and Cirencester in Britain – all contain familiar Roman urban features. Every one of these towns has its own history, but in the days of the Roman Empire, they all conformed to the basic Roman urban template. The story was the same throughout the Roman Empire as provincial or regional capitals functioned like miniature Romes. Each had its own forum, basilica, temples to Capitoline Jupiter and the imperial cult, theatres, townhouses, brothels, bars, and public lavatories. Anyone from the Roman period would have recognised facilities and the layout.

But don't assume everything was copied from Rome. Rome copied ideas from elsewhere. The Romans took plenty of their ideas about classical architecture from the Greeks. In southern Italy, they found cities like Pompeii, which had a stone amphitheatre, stone theatre, and a basilica long before Rome ever did. The Roman genius was combining all these with their idea of city government to create the Roman city.

In each major city, the local civic assembly was modelled on the Roman Senate, electing its local magistrates just as Rome elected her consuls, tribunes, aediles, and quaestors. Rome had her two consuls while Pompeii, like many other cities in the Empire, had her two annually elected magistrates called the *duoviri* ('the two men'). Those magistrates were often responsible for commissioning and paying for public buildings. Doing so made them and their cities look good and was a way of buying votes, so the magistrates competed with one another to be the most generous. In a tiny town in northern Britain called Brough-on-Humber, for example, there was an aedile called Marcus Ulpius Januarius who supplied the town's theatre with a stage during the reign of Antoninus Pius (AD 138–161).

In the Eastern Empire, urban life was already well-established, and cities of Greek origin like Ephesus in Asia Minor found themselves embellished with Roman additions. In the Western Empire, urban life was more of a novelty, especially in Britain and northern Gaul. Towns had to be founded by the Romans and built to conform to a general Roman theme. In remoter areas, it was probably the emperor who had to order and pay for public buildings, rather than the local bigwigs.

Two Brilliant Ideas

The Romans weren't the most original architects. Many of their designs were borrowed from the Greeks and the Etruscans. But they made exceptional use of two fundamental techniques: concrete and the arch.

Concrete

Concrete was the miracle of Roman building, called by them *opus caementicium,* and by us 'Roman concrete' (and this is the source of our word 'cement'). It had just four components:

- ✔ Water
- ✔ Lime
- ✔ Pozzolana (sandy volcanic ash, originally found near Pozzuoli near Naples in Italy)
- ✔ Aggregate (brick chips or fragments of stone)

The brilliant thing about concrete is that it can be mixed on-site from easily found ingredients and poured into moulds or shapes to create just about any sort of structure. It's also extremely strong and very durable. The Romans built walls with concrete cores and faced them with brick or stone. It allowed large and complex buildings to be erected quickly, because it was very nearly as strong as modern concrete. Concrete was in use in Rome by the second century BC at the latest.

By varying the aggregate according to requirements, this simple concrete could form the cores of massive walls or vaults (see the following section, 'Arches and vaults') and is found everywhere in the Roman Empire. In its most advanced form, Roman concrete was good enough to be the sole material used in a vault, created by pouring it into wooden moulds. This was concrete's most dramatic impact because it meant flat wooden or stone ceilings could be done away with. This discovery lay behind most distinctive Roman architecture. All across the Roman world, concrete was used to manufacture major buildings and even modest houses. Concrete used with arches, vaults, and domes made a perfect partnership.

The ultimate example of Roman concrete building is the Pantheon, built in its present form by Hadrian (AD 117–138) (see Chapter 17 for his reign), and still completely intact in Rome today. The Pantheon's main feature is a massive dome 43 metres (141 feet) wide, sitting on top of a circular drum with a total height the same as the dome's width. The secret was lightness and strength, so the dome gets thinner from bottom to top, starting at 6 metres (20 feet) where the dome meets the drum and dropping to just 1.5 metres (5 feet) at the top with decorative recesses (coffers) reducing the weight further. The materials used also got lighter towards the top, finishing with lightweight volcanic tufa. Vast wooden moulds were used to hold the dome in place while the concrete set. It's actually the biggest masonry dome ever built, and architects from all round the world have been fascinated by it ever since.

Arches and vaults

Arches and vaults were used in almost all major Roman buildings. They relieve weight, save stone, and increase a building's strength.

The Etruscans introduced the Romans to the arch, but it was the Romans who truly mastered the arch and its close relation, the barrel vault. The ideas came from a long way beyond Italy though. Arches and vaults had been used by the mud-brick builders of Assyria and Babylonia. The Greeks picked up the designs, which then found their way to Italy. By the third century BC magnificent arched and vaulted gateways were being built in Italy like the Porta Rosa at Velia (modern Elia), south of Naples.

How arches work

Arches aren't just a way of providing an entrance or a doorway that is far stronger than one with a flat top. In rows, they're the best possible way of making a whole wall lighter. Because it's curved, an arch transmits all the force from the building above down past it and through the piers that support the arch. A vault is simply a long arch and makes massive buildings far more stable and stronger than solid masses of masonry. Barrel vaults were a key part of Roman bathhouses – they were extremely strong and, unlike timber roofs, resistant to rot from hot, damp air.

Nero's palace (Domus Aurea, 'Golden House') in Rome partly survives because its vast vaulted chambers and passageways were used by Trajan (98–117) as the substructure for his baths. Incredibly, as a result, you can still walk around the very rooms Nero strutted in more then 19 centuries ago.

Using arches and vaults

The Romans used arches together with all the components of Greek architecture like columns, capitals, architraves, and pediments and created a brilliant style of architecture that made cities, villas, palaces, public buildings, forts, and all sorts of public services like sewers and aqueducts possible. I simply can't stress enough how much this changed the world, and the impact is all around today in modern architecture.

The Romans developed the whole idea of the arch and vault so brilliantly that before long they were able to erect the most extraordinary buildings. The Colosseum, built by Vespasian and Titus (69–81), is built out of multiple tiers of arches on the outside and radial barrel vaults within. The only reason it's in ruins today is because it was robbed for stone in the Middle Ages, not because it fell down. The Basilica of Maxentius in the Forum had a 35-metre-high vaulted nave, flanked by barrel-vaulted aisles. It survived until a 1349 earthquake that left just one aisle standing.

Arches just for show

Arches and vaults were beautiful and functional, but perhaps the most striking use was the triumphal arch. Emperors erected these ceremonial arches to celebrate great military victories and triumphs. Domitian (AD 81–96) was especially fond of them. Some are single arches, some have a pair of smaller arches on either side of a big one, and some were four-way arches. But they were all decorated with carved reliefs of triumphant emperors and inscriptions recording their mighty deeds. Today in Rome, the Arches of Titus (79–81), shown in Figure 6-1, Septimius Severus (193–211), and Constantine I (307–337) all survive, but there are lots of other examples all round the Roman world.

The most famous architect – Vitruvius

Marcus Vitruvius Pollio was a professional architect who took part in Augustus's reconstruction of Rome. By 27 BC, he'd already written ten books gathered together under the title *De Architectura* ('On Architecture'), dedicated to Augustus. Those ten books are packed with detail on building materials, techniques, designs, and specifications. This work was used as a standard textbook in Roman times and survived to be copied in a monastery in northern England in the eighth century AD. In the Renaissance, Vitruvius became very influential and was read by all the architects from the fifteenth to eighteenth centuries and is still available today.

Figure 6-1:
The Arch
of Titus,
dedicated in
Rome's
Forum in
AD 71
during his
father
Vespasian's
reign,
now part-
restored.

All Roads Lead to Rome

If there's one thing the Romans are known for, it's for building long, straight roads. That's a misconception. They certainly built roads, but they often laid them on top of existing prehistoric tracks, and while Roman roads had long straight stretches, they also had corners and changed direction when appropriate.

Until the invention of railways and petrol engines, it was usually cheaper to go by sea, and the Mediterranean – a sort of watery super motorway or interstate – played a vital role in the transport of goods. But Roman roads were still extremely important. The quality of Roman road construction vastly improved their freight-carrying capacity. They linked cities and provinces into a vast network, which saw a continual traffic in men and goods. It really was true that all roads led to Rome.

Via Appia

The Via Appia (Appian Way) is today the most famous and best-preserved of Roman roads. Appius Claudius built the first part in 312 BC as a result of the experience of the Samnite Wars (explained in Chapter 11) – this metalled road created the Roman version of a high-speed communications link between Rome and Capua, down which troops could move quickly. It acted as the template for all the great Roman roads of the Empire to come. Originally just joining Rome to Capua, the Via Appia was later extended to Beneventum (modern Benevento) and finally by 191 BC to Brundisium (Brindisi). The Roman poet Horace wrote an account of a journey on the Appian Way, saying it was 'less tiring if you go slowly' and how he was nearly burned to death by an innkeeper who set his place on fire when roasting thrushes. The most famous user was St Paul, who came up the road from Appii-Forum (Foro Appio) to Rome in AD 61 – it's the only Roman landmark mentioned in the Bible (*Acts of the Apostles* xxviii.15–16).

Strabo, the Roman geographer, said: 'The Romans have built roads throughout the countryside, slicing through hills and filling in dips, so that now their wagons can carry the same-sized loads as boats.'

Road-building basics

The Romans weren't the first to build roads, and they weren't the first to make roads with metalled surfaces. But they were the first to build a very large number of roads, which meant that for the first time in European history many places were linked together.

Laying out a road

Laying out a road meant choosing solid ground and the shortest possible route from A to B. As the Romans loved system and order, straight lines were preferred but not always possible. Gradients were measured, and if the slope was more than about 10 per cent, then the road would have to zigzag up the incline. Some roads had curves to go round hills or followed terraces cut into higher ground. If absolutely essential, tunnels were sometimes cut to carry the road through a hill.

Roman surveyors used a groma to lay out lines. A *groma* had a central post and on top four arms at right angles, each with a plumb line. Two opposite arms could be used to sight a straight line with the help of an assistant standing at a distance and holding a staff. When building streets in a new town or fort, the four arms of a groma helped create neat right-angled junctions so that a grid based on squares (*insulae,* here meaning 'blocks') could be laid out.

Superstitious traffic control

Recent analysis of the deep ruts in Pompeii's streets show Roman traffic had to drive on the right to avoid jams. Romans were highly superstitious and feared anything to do with the left, which is why their words for left and left-hand, *sinister* and *sinistra,* have given us the modern meaning of 'sinister' as something frightening and evil.

Making a road

The real graft came with making the road. Sometimes army legionaries managed the work, but they also used slaves as well as forced local labour in provinces. The road had to remain solid in all weathers, and drain. So a raised bank *(agger)* was created by ramming wooden piles into soft ground (if necessary) followed by foundation layers of stone, gravel, chippings, clay, and then the cobbled road surface, which was built in a curved profile so that rainwater would run off into the drains on either side.

Being endlessly pragmatic, the Romans used whatever materials were to hand to build roads with. In Pompeii, huge slabs of volcanic lava were used for the road surface. In areas where iron ore was abundant, chunks of ore were used to make the surface. The iron rusted and created a rock-hard road surface.

Helping travellers: Road maps, itineraries, and more

The only way a Roman road system could be of much use was if people could plan their journeys. So the Romans had road maps – not accurate maps like today but more like the kind of schematic plans we use for city metro systems. They also had itineraries: lists of places on a particular road with distances between them. As some of the surviving manuscripts were copied in the Middle Ages, we have their texts.

The Antonine Itinerary *(Itinerarium Provinciarum Antonini Augusti)* was an itinerary probably compiled for Caracalla (211–217), though it was added to under later emperors. It's a whole series of 225 tailor-made specific road journeys throughout the Empire with a start and end point and total mileage for each. For archaeologists and historians these routes are extremely useful for finding out the ancient names of towns.

Bridges

Of course, roads can't go everywhere. Rivers and ravines get in the way. But since the Romans had mastered concrete and arches, rivers weren't much of an obstacle, though in more remote places wooden bridges were often built. Some of Rome's bridges are still intact and in use today. The Pons Fabricius was built over the Tiber in 62 BC out of volcanic tufa blocks and faced with marble. Its two main spars are 24 metres (80 feet) across.

One of the most celebrated Roman bridges ever built was put up over the Danube by Trajan (98–117) to control the Dacians beyond. It was probably designed by Apollodorus of Damascus and it's illustrated on Trajan's Column in Rome (see Chapter 17). The historian Dio described it like this:

✔ It had 20 stone piers 40 metres (150 feet) high

✔ Each pier stood 50 metres (170 feet) from its neighbours

✔ The superstructure was made of timber

Dio was exaggerating because this would make it far bigger than the 800 metre (0.5 mile) wide river, but there's no doubt it was still a mighty bridge. Hadrian (117–138) removed the superstructure to stop the Dacians entering the Empire and Dio says the piers were still standing in his own time a century later (in the early AD 200s).

Another way of helping people to get about was with milestones, which were set up alongside major and minor roads. These vary a lot, but most of the surviving ones are rough cylindrical stone pillars with carved inscriptions naming the current emperor, his titles for the year, and sometimes adding the distance to the next town in whole miles. Others were mass-produced with carved imperial titles and had the distance information painted on when they were set up.

Imperial post (cursus publicus)

Fast communications across the Empire were essential if the emperor was to have any chance of issuing edicts, having his orders obeyed, and keeping an eye on provincial governors and military commanders. Augustus introduced the imperial post system, which forced towns and settlements along roads to have carriages and horses permanently ready. They were a little like service stations on interstates or motorways today: They often had inns which provided travellers with beds, baths, and stabling.

Publicus means here 'the state': The service was only available to imperial messengers or anyone else on official business (though it wasn't unknown for officials to use it for private reasons – Pliny the Younger allowed his wife to use it to visit her aunt after her grandfather died). It was an expensive service and Nerva (96–98) transferred the cost to the government.

Chapter 7

Making the Roman Machine Work

● ●

In This Chapter

▶ Rome's ports and trade routes

▶ Roman water works: aqueducts, reservoirs, and sewers

▶ How the Romans stayed healthy

● ●

Trade and industry is essential for any city to work, because by definition the inhabitants rarely produce basics like food. So the city earns its existence by supplying goods and services the rest of the population needs.

Rome was rather different. Not only was it was the biggest city in the ancient world – with a population of more than 1 million, it was twice the size of its nearest competitors, Carthage and Alexandria, and 50 to 100 times bigger than almost all the other cities across the Roman Empire – but as the capital of a vast Empire, Rome simply took whatever resources it wanted or needed from the various regions under its control, whether that was grain from Egypt, marble from Greece, or lead from Britain. But that still meant having all the mechanisms of shipping and ports, merchants, and money, to supply not only Rome, but also the rest of the Empire and the far-flung Roman army as well.

This chapter explains how the Romans used trade routes and technology to keep the vast machinery of their Empire working. It also examines how the Romans managed urban water supplies, using their unparalleled command of hydraulics and plumbing. The water might have helped hygiene, but the Romans were endlessly preoccupied with staying fit and healthy enough to go about their daily business.

Trade Around the Empire

Aelius Aristides (AD117–181) was a Greek orator whose life spanned much of the Empire's greatest days (detailed in Chapter 17). Aristides loved Rome and wrote a eulogy singing the city's praises. He included this observation:

'Large continents lie around the Mediterranean Sea and never-ending supplies of goods flow from them to you [the Roman people]. Everything from every land and every sea is shipped to you . . . so that if anyone wanted to see all these things he would either have to travel the world or live in Rome.'

Rome managed this great influx of goods from around the Empire through its ports. This section gives you the details.

Ostia: The port of Rome

Ostia sums up Rome's commerce. Rome sits inland on the river Tiber, which is too narrow and windy to cope with all the ships and docking facilities Rome needed. From Ostia, ships could be towed upriver to Rome.

Ostia is on the coast, and by the middle of the fourth century BC, it was acting as Rome's port. In 267 BC, Ostia had its own quaestor (see Chapter 3 for details of magistracies). In 217 BC, supplies for the Roman army fighting Hannibal in Spain were shipped from Ostia. Ostia was important enough for Marius to capture the city in 87 BC, and in 67 BC, Pompey used it as his base for the fleet sent out to destroy the Cilician pirates. (You can find out about Marius and Pompey in Chapter 14.)

Ostia's Piazza of Corporations, built early in Augustus's reign (27 BC–AD 14), includes more than 70 offices that were operated by trading companies. Outside each one was a mosaic floor which tells us where the merchants came from and what they traded in, including one from the city of Sabratha (Sabart) in Libya trading in wild animals and ivory, a grain trader from Calares (Cagliari) in Spain, and Algerian traders in dates and fish.

Thanks to a freak of history, Ostia survives as a well-preserved ruin. The river Tiber silted up, leaving the port high and dry, so it was abandoned. Ostia has been excavated, and visitors can now wander round the streets of the city with its houses, shops, apartment blocks, temples, and warehouses.

International trade

Of course, Ostia wasn't the only port. All round the Roman world ports and towns developed because of the constant movement of goods. Part of being in the Roman Empire meant wanting to share in the Roman way of life, and that meant trade, whether you were in the East or the remotest corners of the north-western provinces. East Palmyra, until it was destroyed by Aurelian (AD 270–275; see Chapter 19) for getting above its station, grew into one of the wealthiest cities of antiquity on the great trade route to the Far East.

The many voyages of the Erythraean Sea

Some time in the first century AD, a merchant or seafarer who worked the trade routes between ports like Berenice on Roman Egypt's Red Sea coast to the Gulf of Arabia and India wrote down in Greek what he knew about the various ports, commodities, and routes that were available on a six-month voyage that depended on exploiting seasonal winds. It's a useful indication of the kind of knowledge traders all over the Roman Empire must have used. His account is called the *Periplus Mari Erythrae* ('The Many Voyages of the Erythraean Sea'). This is a little of what he says:

'Malao, distant a sail of about eight hundred stadia [about 100 miles]. The anchorage is an open roadstead, sheltered by a spit running out from the east . . . There are imported into this place the things already mentioned, and many tunics, cloaks from Arsinoe, dressed and dyed; drinking cups, sheets of soft copper in small quantity, iron, and gold and silver coin, not much. There are exported from these places myrrh, a little frankincense . . . the harder cinnamon, duaca, Indian copal and macir, which are imported into Arabia; and slaves, but rarely.'

And of India: 'On [the Ganges' bank is a market-town which has the same name as the river, Ganges. Through this place are brought malabathrum and Gangetic spikenard and pearls, and muslins of the finest sorts, which are called Gangetic. It is said that there are gold mines near these places, and there is a gold coin which is called *caltis*. And just opposite this river there is an island in the ocean, the last part of the inhabited world toward the cast, under the rising sun itself; it is called Chryse; and it has the best tortoiseshell of all the places on the Erythraean Sea.'

London

London today is one of the world's greatest cities and an international financial centre. Until the Romans arrived in Britain, there was nothing on the site. But the Romans spotted this was the ideal place to bridge the river Thames. So they did. As the river is tidal, ships could come up easily. Within a few years of the Roman invasion, a trading settlement had sprung up all on its own – the very way the Roman world functioned made trading centres essential. By the 70s AD, 30 years after the invasion and despite being destroyed in the Boudican rebellion of AD 60–61 (see Chapter 16), London had a heaving port with wharves and warehouses. Goods were shipped in from all over the Roman Empire into what had become the capital of the new province. Although London shrank after Roman times, it started growing again in the Middle Ages and hasn't stopped since, though it's no longer a port.

Of course, London wasn't the only big port in the Western Roman Empire. Others included Massilia (Marseilles) and Burdigala (Bordeaux) in Gaul, and Gades (Cadiz) in Spain, but only London came from nothing to be a Roman port and then evolve into what it is today.

A universal commodity

Samianware was the name given to a red-slip pottery tableware. Originally made in Arrezzo in Italy, by the mid-first century AD, factories in Gaul had taken over the industry. They made redwares, including plain dishes and cups as well as bowls decorated with figured scenes of gods, gladiators, plants, and animal chases, in unbelievably colossal numbers in vast factory potteries. Shiploads of the finished vessels were sent out from Gaul down rivers to the coast, where traders bought consignments and despatched them across the Western Roman Empire. Places as far apart as northern Britain,

the Rhine in Germany, Spain, and North Africa, all bought and used the same pottery from the first to second centuries AD. When the samian industries collapsed in the third century, new ones stepped in like the redware factories of North Africa, which copied samian forms and supplied a huge market across the Empire. Redware is a mark not just of how extensive Roman trade could be, but also how *universal* Roman culture had become. It's rather like today when places all over the world use televisions made by the same Japanese companies.

Trading posts beyond the Empire

Roman traders also went beyond the Empire's borders and set up trading posts in faraway places such as Muziris (possibly modern Kerala) in India. They made money, but it was also part of drawing in other places to a Roman way of thinking. Some of these places ended up being conquered and made into Roman provinces, and by then the local population had got used to the idea of wine from Italy, fish sauce from Spain, and fine pottery from Gaul and Italy. Roman traders and local suppliers also gathered around Roman forts and set up straggling informal settlements (called *canabae,* 'hutments') to help soldiers spend their money. Because forts usually ended up being a road junction, too, once a fort was given up (if it ever was), then these places often stayed and grew into a major settlement in their own right.

The merchants and guild system

Many merchants in Ostia and other ports were equestrians or freedmen, and they could often have personal trading interests in several different provinces – just like modern businesspeople who work in New York and London, or Paris and Munich. Marcus Aurelius Lunaris was a freedman who held office in the colonies of Lincoln and York in Britain. But he went on a business trip to Bordeaux in Gaul and set up an altar to commemorate arriving safely, which is how we know about him.

Rome's rubbish tip: Monte Testaccio

The most astonishing place in Rome isn't a ruined temple or amphitheatre, but Monte Testaccio. It's made out of nothing but millions of fragments of olive oil *amphorae* which came to Rome in the first three centuries AD from Spain and were dumped once their contents had been used. It's 35 metres (38 yards) high and 850 metres (930 yards) around the base. One estimate is that 53 million amphorae went into the hill and that these had brought 10.6 billion pints (6 billion litres) of olive oil to Rome.

Sobering isn't it? The Romans were like us because they had an international marketplace, and they were also like us because they created vast non-biodegradable rubbish dumps!

Merchants at Ostia formed themselves into guilds *(collegia),* and other such organisations turn up all over the Empire. These guilds stuck together, helped their members out, and made sacrifices to a favoured god. In some ways they were like modern Masonic lodges. Merchants themselves were known as *negotiatores* from which, of course, comes our word 'negotiate', as in 'negotiating' a deal. They were handy for the government, too. When life became more and more controlled under the Dominate (refer to Chapter 20), the government forced guilds to cap their prices and prohibited men from leaving their jobs.

Goodies from Around the World

We can find out about what the Romans traded in from their writings and some of what archaeologists find. But foodstuffs have almost always rotted away. The next best thing is the containers used to transport it, and the commonest of all are the *amphorae* (see Figure 7-1). An *amphora* is a pottery packing case, usually cylindrical or circular in shape, with a conical base and a long neck with two handles. The base made it easy to move around by the handles and made it easier to stack. All across the Roman world amphorae bear witness to the reach of Roman traders, whether in a remote desert oasis site in Egypt or as part of a cargo of a wrecked ship found at the bottom of the sea.

Amphorae were manufactured in their millions to carry around fish sauce, grain, dates, olives, wine – you name it. Sometimes factories stamped the amphorae, or the shippers painted on what the contents were. One from Antipolis (modern Antibes on the Cote D'Azur in the south of France) but found in London where it had been shipped to reads:

Liquam(en) Antipol(itanum) exc(ellens) L(uci) Tett(i)i Africani

Translation? 'Lucius Tettius Africanus's excellent fish sauce from Antipolis.'

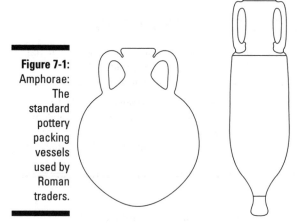

Of course, the Romans traded in more than food and drink. There were plenty of other things: textiles, glass, ceramics, spices, metals like iron, copper, tin, gold and silver, exotic stone to decorate their houses and public buildings. You name it, the Romans wanted it, and what the Romans wanted they generally got.

Food, glorious food: The grain supply

At its climax, Rome had a population of 1 million people, making it the largest city in the ancient world. Feeding all those people was a mammoth task, but Rome had the power and facilities to cope. Amongst the most important were grain ships from Egypt, North Africa, and Sicily, but alongside them came in ships with olive oil from Spain, wine from numerous places in Italy and around the Mediterranean, and also luxuries like Indian spices and Baltic amber.

Roman political leaders discovered the value of buying food for free handouts. Gaius Gracchus introduced a law that guaranteed cheap grain at a fixed price. The crooked Publius Clodius Pulcher (see Chapter 14 for his other exploits) made grain free when he was Tribune in 58 BC.

By Augustus's time (27 BC–AD 14), 200,000 people in Rome were entitled to free grain (about 20 per cent of the city's population), and providing the grain was now the emperor's personal responsibility. Dozens of officials were involved in the grain handouts, and the emperor knew that if the grain supply was disrupted, he'd have riots on his hands.

The grain dole was known as the *annona,* managed by an equestrian *praefectus* whose job was one of the most important in Rome (see Chapter 3). It also came to mean the grain tax. Soldiers used to take what they needed from populations, or make compulsory purchases, and had wages deducted to pay for it. But by Septimius Severus's time (AD 193–211), buying military loyalty included giving the troops free food so the *annona militaris* was created as a new tax on the whole Empire.

Mining for metals

As the Romans expanded their Empire, the resources they were keenest on getting hold of were mineral resources. The Empire had vast needs for metals:

- ✔ **Silver and gold** were the basis of Roman coinage, because they funded the army and the imperial bureaucrats. But they were also used for luxury goods owned by the rich and the emperors, from huge collections of plates to jewellery.

- ✔ **Iron** was vital for weapons and tools.

- ✔ **Copper, zinc, and tin** were alloyed to make bronze and brass, used in countless everyday objects like taps, brooches, furniture fittings, armour buckles, horse harnesses, small-change coinage, and cheap jewellery.

- ✔ **Lead** was the Roman Empire's plastic, being used for pipes, waterproofing roofs, and lining water tanks. It was also alloyed with tin to make pewter, a cheap substitute for silver plate, and with copper and tin to make another form of bronze. Some lead deposits produce silver as well, making them doubly attractive.

New provinces were scoured for mineral resources. Often, thanks to information from traders, the Romans knew perfectly well what was available. Both Spain and Dacia's conquests were quickly followed up by organised mining. Spain was especially attractive. Gold, silver, iron, and copper were all said to be easier to get from Spain than anywhere else. Some Spanish copper mines produced 25 per cent pure copper from every load of ore dug out; in silver mines, around 26 kilograms (57 pounds) of bullion could be dug out every three days. Britain was invaded in the year AD 43. Within six years the latest lead ingots were being shipped out of the new province. Some were used for plumbing at Pompeii, and according to Pliny the Elder, British lead was so easy to mine, a law had been passed limiting production to stop the price collapsing.

Mining was mostly done by slaves, and needless to say there wasn't the slightest concern for health and safety. With so much money to be made, new slaves could be bought as required. Under the Republic, mines were operated by government contractors, but under the emperors, equestrian procurators operated the mining settlements which were about as close to towns in the days of the Old Wild West as you can get (look at those old mining settlements in South Dakota called Silver City and Lead – it's the same story). Rough and tough, they were vicious places where the equestrian procurator was judge, sheriff, town mayor, banker, and chief employer all rolled into one. Private companies could still get a slice of the action, but they had to hand over a portion of what they mined.

Money, Money, Money

The Roman trading world depended on cash (getting metals to make money was a main reason for mining; refer to the preceding section). Roman coins survive in abundance today, a mark of how they were an everyday part of commerce.

Today the money we use is token. US dollar bills and 25-cent pieces, British £1 coins, and European Euro notes and coins aren't worth their face value in terms of the paper or metal they're made from. We accept their face value because we have to by law and because we've got used to the idea.

Roman coinage, and indeed almost any coinage until early modern times, was based on the idea of *intrinsic* value. That means the coin had to be made of metal equal to its value. To look at it another way, a coin was exchangeable at the value of the metal in it. The most important metals for ancient coinage were silver and gold, but brass and copper were used for small change.

Coinage developed in Asia Minor in the first millennium BC because it was such a handy way to store wealth. The Romans first started off using huge lumps of bronze, but by Augustus's time the system had been built round a small silver coin called a *denarius*. These are the main coin types in use until the beginning of the fourth century and the metal they were made of, starting with the lowest value (refer to Figure 7-2):

> *Quadrans* (bronze) = ½ a semis
>
> *Semis* (bronze) = ½ an as
>
> *As* (bronze) = ½ a dupondius
>
> *Dupondius* (brass) = ½ a sestertius
>
> *Sestertius* (brass) = ¼ of a denarius
>
> *Denarius* (silver) = ¹⁄₂₅ of an aureus
>
> *Aureus* (gold)

Figure 7-2: Roman coins. Top row (left to right): gold aureus, silver denarius, bronze quadrans. Middle row (l-r): brass sestertius, brass dupondius, bronze as. Bottom row (for scale): British 10-pence piece, US quarter dollar.

The important thing about the coinage system is that the coins were generally good throughout the Roman Empire. Most of it was minted at Rome and Lugdunum (Lyons) in Gaul. Egypt had its own special Roman coinage, and cities in the East were able to issue their own local bronze small change. But by and large, Roman currency was universal, and from Diocletian's reign, (284–305) mints across the Roman world produced identical issues.

Propaganda coins

In a world with no mass media, coins were a great way to publicise the emperor, his achievements, and his family. Within weeks or even just days of a new emperor taking power, coins carrying his portrait were sent out into circulation so that everyone would know who he was. Unlike today's coins, each denomination was issued in lots of versions with different reverses, depicting anything from an impressive sounding imperial virtue like *libertas* ('liberty') to pictures of great new public buildings, or commemorations of victories. Other coins might have his wife's, son's, or even mother's portrait on the obverse instead of the emperor's own. Augustus started the trend of putting his intended successor on coins to get the public used to the idea of who was coming next.

Comparative values

It's practically impossible to work out a comparison of values, but at the end of the first century AD, a legionary soldier earned a basic salary of 300 denarii a year. Half went on equipment and keep, and the rest was his. What little we know of prices suggests that ordinary labouring Romans had to work a great deal harder to buy basics than we do. A farm labourer, for example, needed to work a whole day to buy a pint (0.6 litres) of olive oil, while a pair of good quality boots could cost the equivalent of four days' work or more.

Inflation

The Romans weren't very sophisticated in their understanding of how money works. So when an Emperor like Septimius Severus (193–211) needed more silver coins to pay his troops but didn't have the bullion, he just added copper to make the silver go further. As the Empire hadn't been expanding since Trajan's time a century before, there were no new supplies of silver from conquered territory.

IN THEIR WORDS

'Veni, vidi, vici...'

Insider info, Roman style

Around the year 300, a Roman official called Dionysius in Egypt got wind that the coinage was about to be devalued by Diocletian. Before the news got out, he wrote to one of his staff on the family estate to spend all the money on goods:

Dionysius to Apio, Hail.

The divine fortune of our rulers has ordered that coinage struck in Italy shall be reduced to half the value of a nummus. Hurry and spend all the Italian cash you can and buy

any goods for me at the price you find being charged.

I'll point out from the start that if you play any tricks I'll certainly catch you out. I pray that you live long in good health, brother.

Nothing like insider information is there? Of course, the poor mugs who took the money for goods were going to wake up the next day and find it was worth a fraction of that they thought it was.

Weights and measures

Roman money generally worked because it was based on a system of weights and metal purity. This idea affected all other forms of measurement in the Roman world which were fairly consistent and enforced by law overseen by aediles (see Chapter 3 for their role). Here are some of them:

✔ **Distance** was the Roman mile, which equalled 1,536 metres or 1,680 yards, about 0.95 of a modern mile, and based on 1,000 paces of 5 Roman feet (1.48 metres each). The Romans also used the *stadium,* equal to about ⅛ mile. Subdivisions into Roman feet (*pes* = 296 millimetres or 11.65 inches)

helped the accurate design and laying out of buildings, towns, and forts.

✔ **Weights** were based on the Roman pound *(libra),* equal to 327.5 grams (11.6 ounces), and the Roman ounce *(uncia),* equal to 27.3 grams (0.96 ounces).

✔ **Dry measures** (for example, for grain) were based on the *modius,* equal to 8.67 litres or 15.2 pints.

✔ **Liquid measures** (for example, wine) were based on the *sextarius,* equal to 0.54 litres or 0.95 pint, and the *congius,* equal to 3.25 litres or 5.72 pints.

The average Roman soldier and the average Roman in the street soon spotted the difference and promptly hoarded the older, purer coin. Traders put their prices up to compensate for being paid in inferior coins and a vicious circle of debased coin and price rises followed. With one more soldier emperor after another trying to buy popularity, silver got rarer. By the 270s, the 'silver' coinage was no more than bronze with a silver wash.

With inflation out of control, Diocletian (AD 284–305) brought in all sorts of measure to try and control the problem (see Chapter 20), including introducing new denominations like the bronze *nummus.* Constantine (307–337) stabilised gold, using a new coin called the *solidus,* but silver virtually disappeared, and we know little about the bronze coins of the fourth century. Government came to depend on taxing in kind.

Turning on the Taps

Apart from roads, the other thing the Romans are famous for is their legendary ability to manage public water supplies. You might think being close to a river like the Tiber would solve all those problems. It doesn't. Rivers are mainly useful for transport and waste. Carrying and lifting water in quantity is incredibly difficult and labour-intensive.

Getting water into a city or a fort was all about gravity: finding a water source at a higher level than where it was needed and leading it there at a gentle gradient. The best thing to do is find a source at a higher level and run it in.

Getting water into cities: Aqueducts

Appius Claudius, who built the Appian Way (Via Appia) in 312 BC (see Chapter 6), also built Rome's first certain aqueduct, though one of the early kings (Ancus Martius, 642–617 BC) was supposed to have built one, too. Appius tapped a spring 16 kilometres (10 miles) from Rome and ran it through an underground tunnel most of the way. Only as it approached Rome was it run in a channel held above ground on masonry arches – which is probably what most people think of as an aqueduct.

Aqueduct just means 'water channel' and that includes buried tunnels, open surface channels, and channels suspended on vast masonry arches snaking across the countryside.

Once the water reached the city, it poured into a dividing tank *(castellum divisiorum)*. Silt and rubbish sank to the bottom. The tank relieved the pressure that built up from water running down a slope for miles and didn't overflow because the water ran straight out into separate pipes that fed:

✔ Public facilities like the amphitheatre and public baths

✔ Street fountains

✔ The houses of the rich

Because even then the pressure would have blown taps off, the water was run up into street corner cisterns suspended on towers which fed the users. These didn't overflow because the water ran off to where it was needed the whole time. It's called a *constant off-take* system. By Domitian's reign (81–96), there were about 1,350 public fountains in Rome alone.

As Rome's population grew, more aqueducts were built, bringing so much water they were, according to Strabo, like rivers. These are some of them:

✔ **Aqua Marcia:** Built 144–140 BC by Quintus Marcius Rex. It ran for 48 kilometres (30 miles) underground and 9.7 kilometres (6 miles) on masonry arches.

✔ **Aqua Vergine:** 21 kilometres (13 miles) long, it was built 19 BC by Agrippa to supply the Baths of Agrippa.

✔ **Aqua Claudia:** Built by Claudius in 52 AD to supply the imperial palaces. It was still running in the fifth century when the barbarian invaders finally wrecked it.

Pompeii's water worries

Just because the Romans had aqueducts doesn't mean the system worked the whole time. Pompeii, like other cities in the Bay of Naples, was supplied by water from the Aqua Augusta, built under Augustus (27 BC–AD 14). A network of underground tunnels and over-ground masonry arcades carried the water to all the cities in the area. Pompeii's arrived in a reservoir *(castellum)* at the highest point of town. Like all Roman public water supplies, the reservoir had three separate supplies: public baths and other public buildings, the houses of the rich, and public street fountains. A network of lead pipes fanned out to supply demand, with a system of street-corner tanks on towers by the street-corner public fountains.

The system worked until AD 62 when an earth-quake badly damaged the city, including the reservoir and the pipes. When Vesuvius erupted in AD 79 Pompeii's water service was still being fixed. Rich householders had had to give up on gushing garden pools and bubbling fountains and install tanks to collect rainwater and use wells instead. No-one knows if the street-corner fountains were working again. Today the ruins of the city preserve the best example of a Roman civic water system, even if it wasn't operational when the city was buried by pumice.

We know a lot about Rome's aqueducts because Sextus Julius Frontinus (c. AD 35–103) was put in charge of them in 97. He wrote a report on them that survives today. Amongst other things, he was worried at how people were illegally siphoning off aqueduct water into their own homes and letting trees roots damage the aqueduct structures. But he also said that the building and maintenance of the aqueducts gave 'the best testimony to the greatness of the Roman Empire *(magnitudinis Romani imperii)*'.

Wells and reservoirs

Aqueducts weren't the only solution to providing water. Sometimes chains of buckets linked together were lowered into shafts dug down to subterranean water supplies. Driven by slaves or animals, this was one way of getting water to a small baths or maybe a factory, but it would have been hopeless for anything more.

Out in more arid places, the Romans collected any rainwater they could and used underground tunnels to supply reservoirs. There's a large masonry reservoir at the city of Thuburbo Majus in modern Tunisia. A similar system in Syria at the city of Androna (Al Anderin) that included underground irrigation channels was still functioning in the 1960s until modern water systems disrupted the water table. Using all this experience in handling water, in the sixth century AD, the Byzantines built a vast subterranean reservoir (140 x 70 metres) under Constantinople's Hippodrome. Supported by 336 columns, it's still there, and you can visit it.

Baths

Bathing was fundamental to Roman life in the days of the Empire. Vast public bathing facilities were built in Rome (such as the Baths of Titus, of Trajan, of Caracalla, and of Diocletian), in every city in the Roman Empire (Pompeii had at least three public baths), and in most small settlements. Rich people could afford to install private baths in their houses and country villas.

Bathing was a daily (usually afternoon) ritual for most people and involved a series of baths, one after the other. Although bathing was mixed in some periods, for much of Roman history, baths were segregated between men and women. The bather arrived at the baths and went through a series of rooms, and as you can see, the whole set-up was rather like a modern fitness centre or sports and social club:

- *Apodyterium:* The changing room.

- *Tepidarium:* A warm room, perhaps with a warm plunge bath, where the body started sweating.

- *Caldarium:* A hot room like a Turkish bath, where bathers sat around in clouds of steam, sweating out dirt as their pores opened in the heat. Slaves used a *strigil* to scrape the skin, and oils and perfumes could be rubbed into the skin.

- *Frigidarium:* The cold bath where bathers could swim in cool water, close the pores, and relax.

- *Palaestra:* The exercise area for running, jumping, and various sports.

IN THEIR WORDS

'Veni, vidi, vici...'

Grooming and gossip

One of the best descriptions of what happened in a bath comes from Seneca, Nero's tutor (see Chapter 16 for information on Nero). Seneca lived so close to a bath, he had to put up with all the noise and complained about it in a letter to a friend:

'I hear the groans as the he-men pump iron and throw those heavy weights all over the place . . . If for instance there's a lazy chap who's satisfied with a straightforward massage I can hear the slap of a hand on his shoulder . . . If a ball player comes up and starts yelling out his score – then that's me finished. Pile on top of that the row of some

cheeky so-and-so, a thief being caught, and one of those blokes who likes singing in the bath, as well as those who dive into the pool with giant splashes of water. That's as well as those with the loud voices. Think about the skinny plucker of arm-pit hair whose yells are so resonant that everyone notices him except when he's getting on with his work and making someone else yell for him. Now add on the medley of noise from drink sellers, sausage, pastry and hot-food vendors, each hawking his goods with his own individual cry.'

Roman toilets

The Romans were sociable toilet-users. Public toilets had one-piece seating platforms all round the wall with keyhole cut-outs. People marched in and sat down next to one another (no question of individual cubicles). Meanwhile, water poured into basins where users could wash their hands and soak sponges to wipe their bottoms. The water flowed out and into a channel, boosted with extra water which ran round under the seats to carry away the waste either into a sewer or into a soakaway.

Baths weren't just a place to get clean. Baths were where business was conducted, contacts made, gossip exchanged, and dinner invitations offered. In short, they were one of the most important social centres in Roman life, and the fact that they were built all over the Empire is another reflection of the impact of Roman culture.

Bathing in huge, luxurious public facilities was something of a new fad. It seems the old Romans of the Republic were above such things. In Rome's ancient days, the Romans scarcely washed at all and were proud of how they smelled of the dirt from 'the army, of farm work, and manliness'.

Getting rid of water: Rome's sewers

Baths produced waste water, and so did public latrines, industry (like laundries and fullers), and private houses. The Romans used their skills with arches, concrete, stone, and brick to build networks of underground sewers that poured the waste into the river Tiber. The system went back at least as far as Tarquinius Superbus (535–509 BC) who built the *Cloaca Maxima*, the 'Great Sewer' (refer to Chapter 10 for his reign).

Some of the sewers in Rome were big enough for boats to sail up, which is what Agrippa did in 33 BC on a tour of inspection when he was aedile. There were so many of them, Rome was called a 'city on stilts'. Other cities had sewers, too, but the quality ranged from open-air gutters to elaborate systems like Rome's. But not all Romans benefited from sewers. Many cities relied on using the streets for open sewers. That's why Pompeii's streets have huge stepping stones, to help locals make sure they didn't step in the . . . you can guess.

Keeping Well: Medicine

Naturally the Romans got sick and suffered accidents just like we do. They knew nothing about micro-organisms like bacteria and viruses, but their love of baths, clean water, and reliable sewers did mean some or parts of their cities were a lot more hygienic than their medieval equivalents. In fact, it's broadly true to say that nowhere was as hygienic as Rome was until the Victorians started building proper sewage systems in London and other Western cities.

Incidentally, it's often said that people before modern times lived shorter lives than we do. That's only partly true. What it really means is that *average* lives were shorter. Actually, the Romans were just as capable of living into their eighties and beyond as we are; it's just that fewer of them got a chance to do so and that brings the average down. Cato the Elder was 85 when he died. The emperor Gordian I (238) was in his eighties when he committed suicide. A soldier in the XX legion in Wales reached 100 years old, and there are plenty of other examples. For most people though, disease, violence, and accidents put pay to any plans for a ripe old age. None of those things stopped the average Roman from putting his or her faith in medicine.

Medical science in the Roman era

Medicine was almost totally dominated by the Greeks, so much so that if a doctor wasn't a Greek, then he would have no credibility at all – a bit like how everyone expects acupuncturists today to be Chinese. Very few Romans practised medicine, and even if they did, it was best to publish in Greek. Greek doctors turn up all over the Roman Empire and included slaves, and freedmen. There was no formal training or system of qualifications, which meant that more or less any Greek could call himself a doctor and practise medicine.

Needless to say, the way was open to quacks who toured the Empire with patent remedies which they sold to local practitioners, like eye salves (see the later section 'Medicine for the masses'). To the smarter Romans, this was all utter nonsense.

Pliny the Elder called medicine 'the vacant words of intellectual Greeks' and reminded his readers 'not everything handed down by the Greeks deserves admiration'. Pliny pointed out that no two doctors ever produced the same diagnosis, cursing a profession that changed its claims daily (doesn't that sound familiar?!). Pliny had plenty more to say, but in the end he blamed quackery on the gullibility of people who didn't have a clue about how illness and medicine worked. No wonder so many put all their faith in healing cults, which were a big part of Roman religion (see Chapter 9).

Surgeons and doctors

Roman medicine wasn't all about quacks. Pliny the Elder was just one of a number of serious Roman scientists who were interested in what really made the world tick. Cornelius Celsus, who lived in the time of Tiberius (AD 14–37) wrote an encyclopedia on just about everything. The only part which survives is his *De Medicina* ('On Medicine'). Celsus discussed the various schools of Greek medical thought:

- ✔ **The Empiricists** who believed in the value of experience in curing people, rather than worrying about what caused diseases (they thought it was impossible to answer that, so a waste of time thinking about it).

- ✔ **The Methodics** who worked on a basis of treating diseases according to types.

- ✔ **The Dogmatics** who accepted, without question, explanations of disease handed down from ancient Greeks like Hippocrates.

Celsus showed that serious Roman doctors were very well aware of the value of a good diet and physical fitness. They knew about all sorts of diseases, which they could recognise from symptoms, and they had a good idea of a patient's prognosis. A variety of treatments were known, from treating with drugs and herbs to letting blood, which, incidentally, shows just how far off the mark Roman doctors could be. This is what Celsus says about letting blood:

> 'For a broken head, blood should be preferably let from the arm . . . blood is also at times diverted when, having burst out of one place, it is let out another.'

Despite the ideas these ancient doctors got right, they still got plenty wrong. Ironically, Pliny's own *Natural History* is just as full of nonsense as some of the medical writings he criticised. And thanks to men like Celsus, doctors were still letting blood in the belief it was a good idea until the nineteenth century.

It's a wonder the Roman population survived at all, quite apart from the risk of infection from being cut open by a doctor. No wonder the poet Martial said that he'd been fine before being examined by a doctor and his medical students, but had a fever afterwards.

Practical anatomy

Roman doctors were hampered by not knowing much about anatomy – how the body worked. It wasn't for want of trying. Celsus recommended examining a wounded gladiator whose guts were hanging out because that was an ideal way of seeing how a body worked while it was still alive, instead of relying on dead bodies.

Celsus wasn't a doctor, but Claudius Galenus (AD 129–199), a Greek from Pergamum, was. Galenus was as disgusted by the quacks as Pliny the Elder was and he ended up being chased out of Rome for being so public about his views. He wrote a book in Greek called *On the Natural Faculties,* combining his own knowledge with that of earlier doctors. He was mainly interested in clinical observation and deductive reasoning drawn from that. Unfortunately, Galenus's work was also often incorrect – for example, he thought blood went to-and-fro – and proving Galenus wrong, as did the pioneer William Harvey (1578–1657) who discovered the circulation of blood, was all part of the dawn of modern science and realising the ancients weren't perfect.

Medicine for the masses

The average Roman had little or no access to quality medical care of any sort. Of course, the Romans didn't suffer from eating the over-refined, fatty foods packed with sugar that plague our society, and they were probably a great deal fitter than we are. But for most of them, a broken limb might be set badly if at all, and for all sorts of diseases and infection, there was no reliable cure at all, even if you could afford one. For these people the only options were folk cures, cheap patent remedies sold by quacks, and a trip to the nearest healing cult centre (see Chapter 9 for information about those).

Medicines were often made in small blocks or sticks. To identify them, the makers or 'doctors' pressed engraved stone stamps into them. Some of these stamps survive like one which announces: 'Tiberius Claudius M(. . .)'s frankincense salve for every defect of the eyes. Use with egg.' Another one boasts: 'Gaius Junius Tertullus's copper oxide salve for eye-lid granulations and scars.'

Chapter 8

Entertainments: Epic and Domestic

. . . .

In This Chapter

▶ The games people watched and where they watched them

▶ The brutal life of a Roman gladiator

▶ Attacking animals, mock battles, and spectacular shows

▶ Grand Prix racing – Roman style

▶ What the Romans watched at the theatre

▶ How Romans enjoyed themselves at home

. . . .

*T*he two most famous Roman movies ever, *Spartacus* (1960) and *Gladiator* (2000), have one thing in common: the brutal world of the Roman gladiator and his short, dangerous life. They give the impression that every Roman spent his every waking hour down at the amphitheatre watching men fight to the death. Now for some Romans that might have been true, so this chapter starts with arenas and gladiators, a distinctly Italian form of entertainment with ancient origins that found a ready audience in parts of the Roman Empire.

There were also the incredible chariot races. Operated at lunatic speeds by superstar charioteers, they were the ultimate thrill for Roman boy racers. For people with politer tastes, and there were plenty of them, there were the theatres for plays and pantomimes, and little odeons for readings and poetry. And there were also the pleasures of stopping in and having dinner parties.

Introducing the Games

For most people in the Roman Empire, life was nasty, brutal, and short. In a world where war was common, where anyone could carry a lethal weapon, where appalling accidents at work happened all the time, and where people born with any kind of handicap were extremely unlikely to get medical help, physical violence and cruelty were taken for granted.

That's why most people who took part in public entertainments were slaves. If free people didn't matter much, then slaves didn't matter at all. Slaves were just a resource, and as far as the Roman authorities were concerned, one of the best ways of using them was in entertaining the mob and keeping it off the streets.

The famous phrase 'bread and circuses' *(panem et circenses)* comes from the Roman satirist Juvenal who lived *c.* AD 60–130. What he said was that the Roman people had only two interests in life: a full stomach and the action of the games. On the whole, he was probably right.

Bonding the population

Upper-class Romans originally looked down on public entertainment as a vice because games were thought undignified and nothing to do with 'proper Roman virtues' of restraint and self-discipline. So even when they put on an event in the early days, Roman aristocrats tried as hard as possible to make sure nobody enjoyed them. There weren't any seats at gladiatorial fights, for example, so everyone had to stand. When the Romans got round to putting up venues for these events to take place in, they took them apart straight-away afterwards out of a sort of shame but also because they were terrified of getting a crowd of the lower classes all together in one place.

Nevertheless, the games proved a great cultural way to bond the population, because they helped reinforce the religious connection and kept the mob out of trouble. No wonder the terrible days of the Second Punic War (discussed in Chapter 12) were when public games became more and more important.

The mob had no hang-ups about the games, so during the late Republic, men like Sulla and Caesar soon realised how putting on free games for the mob at their own personal expense could increase their popularity ratings. Later emperors followed the trend, and so did local politicians all round the Empire. A sort of free-for-all occurred, in which anyone who could afford it put on games, trying to buy political advantage and popularity. Not surprisingly, Roman historians of the day blamed the loss of 'proper Roman virtues' on all this crowd-pleasing, though they never asked themselves what the crowds would be doing if they weren't being kept busy in the arena or at the circus.

The gaming calendar

Roman public entertainments were an important part of the annual religious calendar. The *Ludi Consualia* (see the list in the next paragraph) were dedicated to Consus, another name for Neptune, god of the sea. His Greek equivalent, Poseidon, was also associated with horses. So you can see why chariot-racing might end up being associated with Neptune. Rather obscure but, as a later Roman writer called Tertullian discovered while researching the games for his book *On the Spectacles,* it was no clearer to the Romans.

By the time of the Empire, the annual religious calendar and its games were pretty well sorted out and getting on, for around half the year was allocated to religious holidays with games *(ludi).* These games included everything from chariot-racing to animal fights and gladiatorial bouts. Some, like the *Ludi Cereales,* went back to some remote part of Rome's ancient mythical past, while others were connected with politics and war. These are the main ones, but there were others – almost any excuse would do:

- ✔ **The Megalian Games** *(Ludi Megalenses):* Celebrated 4–10 April with their origins in the introduction of the Great Mother *(Magna Mater)* of the gods, Cybele, in Rome in 204 BC.

- ✔ **The Cerealian Games** *(Ludi Cereales):* Celebrated 12– 19 April in honour of Ceres, the goddess of harvests and her children, Liber and Libera, deities of planting.

- ✔ **The Floral Games** *(Ludi Florales):* Celebrated 28 April to 3 May in honour of Flora, a goddess of flowers and also associated with licentious behaviour.

- ✔ **The Apollinarian Games** *(Ludi Apollinares):* Celebrated 6–13 July and given for the first time in 212 BC to celebrate the defeat of Hannibal at Cannae. Dedicated to Apollo.

- ✔ **The Consualian Games** *(Ludi Consualia):* Celebrated twice a year, on 21 August and again on 15 December.

- ✔ **The Roman Games** *(Ludi Romani):* Celebrated 5–19 September in honour of Jupiter Optimus Maximus, the king of the gods, and the ultimate power over Roman destiny.

- ✔ **The Plebeian Games** *(Ludi Plebei):* Celebrated 4–17 November. They were started during the Second Punic War (218–202 BC) to keep up morale amongst the public (the *plebs*).

It's very unlikely whether any of the spectators screaming with excitement gave a moment's thought to the religious origins of the games. So, let's get on with the action!

The Playing Fields: Arenas and Stadiums

In the early days, almost any open area would do for putting on games. Right down to the days of Augustus, the Forum in Rome was used. Archaeologists have discovered that temporary wooden seats were erected around an area in the middle of the Forum where there were specially designed underground tunnels equipped with lifting machinery to raise weapons, scenery, and other gear for the action. When the games were over, the seats were removed and the underground chambers closed until the next time. The Colosseum (see the section 'The Colosseum', later in this chapter) later exploited this technology to the full, but made it permanent.

Rome didn't get a stone amphitheatre until 29 BC when Statilius Taurus built one in Mars Field. Funnily enough, the oldest known permanent arena, or amphitheatre, isn't in Rome but at Pompeii. It was built in 80 BC and was large enough to hold 20,000 people. Like all amphitheatres, Pompeii's had an elliptical arena surrounded by rows and rows of seats raked at an angle so that all the spectators could get a view (see Figure 8-1). In case of any danger from the gladiators or wild beasts, a high wall separated the contestants from the public.

Figure 8-1:
Pompeii's ancient amphitheatre, dating to 80 BC, and the oldest known.

Photo by the author.

Arenas could be used for several things:

- ✔ Gladiator bouts
- ✔ Animal hunts
- ✔ Re-enactments of great battles and naval events for the mob
- ✔ Displays of mock battles by army units for soldiers' entertainment
- ✔ Religious festivals

Building an arena

Arenas were usually built towards the edge of major cities or even outside the city walls. Soldiers also built them, generally just outside the walls of their forts. They also turn up sometimes at religious shrine sites in the countryside. They're generally amongst the biggest buildings put up by the Romans, but they range from colossal pieces of masonry architecture like the massive example at El-Djem in Tunisia, to ones where wooden seats were fitted to banks of earth surrounding a dug-out arena, as in Silchester in Britain. Small towns either didn't have them at all or just put up temporary wooden arenas which have left no trace.

Amphitheatres are mainly known in Italy, Gaul, parts of North Africa, Spain, and Britain, but scarcely ever appeared in the East where the Greek tradition of the theatre remained dominant. But there is the odd exception. The Romans added an amphitheatre to the great Greek city of Pergamon in Asia Minor, for instance. The most elaborate arenas had subterranean areas for storing animals, prisoners, and gladiators, and lifting gear to bring them up to ground level. They also had hydraulic equipment for flooding the arena for naval battles, and drainage systems – the water could also be used to flush out the blood and gore after the killing had finished.

Roman society was strictly hierarchical, and that was reflected in who got the best seats in the arena. The emperor, his family, and hangers-on had a kind of 'royal box'. Senators took the front rows, behind them came the equestrians, and then citizens. Their women sat behind them, and next came the lower classes in the higher rows and standing-room-only.

The Colosseum

The most famous and impressive amphitheatre of all is the Colosseum in Rome, a very large part of which still stands and dominates the middle of the city (see Figure 8-2). It was started by the emperor Vespasian (AD 69–79) who used the site of Nero's Golden Palace (see Chapter 16 for more on Nero). Since Nero (AD 54–68) had helped himself to large areas of Rome in order to build his extravagant residence, Vespasian knew that building a whopping entertainment centre on the same site was an excellent way to buy popular support.

The genius of the Colosseum was the design, and it was typical Roman: big, brash, and completely practical. Fully equipped with state-of-the-art underground chambers and hydraulics, it also had a vast sun roof that could be stretched over the crowd to keep the spectators in the shade. The underground operations took place in nine tunnel sections, with numerous workrooms branching off them. One quarter of the arena was made up of moveable flooring which acted as ceilings for the tunnels. They were pivoted at one side and were lowered by ropes and pulleys into the tunnels where scenery was prepared. Then they were raised while fighters and animals were sent up top through trap doors and elevators. Just to get an idea of the kind of killing spectacle the Colosseum could handle, as well as getting all the punters in and out in double-quick-time, under Trajan (AD 98–117), games were held to celebrate his conquest of the Dacians and an almost unbelievable 10,000 gladiators fought.

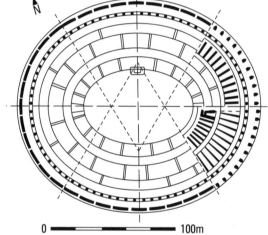

Figure 8-2:
The Colosseum, large enough to accommodate 70,000 spectators.

0 ▬▬▬ 100m

Stadiums

The stadium (or *circus*) was used for chariot-racing. A stadium had a long rectangular enclosure, curved at one end, with seats all round except at the straight end. Down the middle was the spine *(spina),* which the chariots hurtled around, lap after lap, trying to cut in front of each other.

Rome had eight chariot stadiums alone, and most other major cities either had a permanent stadium or an open field that could be set up as a temporary venue. Until very recently, far-off foggy Britain was thought to be an exception, but now one's been found at Colchester, putting it on a par with great cities of the East like Aphrodisias in Asia Minor (Turkey), which has one of the best-preserved.

Rome's greatest circus was the monumental Circus Maximus, ('The Greatest Circus'). It's one of, if not *the,* biggest buildings ever erected in world history for a spectator event. The first races were held here right back in the semi-mythical days of the kings of Rome. By the days of the emperors, it had been extended and enlarged. The Circus Maximus is still visible today in Rome, but most of the structures remain buried. One of the best-preserved is the Circus of Maxentius just outside Rome's walls by the Appian Way; Figure 8-3 shows its plan.

Colossal Colosseum fun facts

- It took 12 years to build the Colosseum out of thousands of 5-ton blocks of stone.

- Efficient use of arches and vaults meant only 9,198 cubic metres (325,000 cubic feet) of stone were used (the Empire State building used ten times as much).

- The blocks were held together by 300 tons of metal clamps.

- The Colosseum was 186 metres (611 feet) long and 154 metres (507 feet) wide and could accommodate 70,000 spectators, meaning it would still be in the Top Twenty stadiums in Europe today, beating the new Emirates Stadium for Arsenal in London by 10,000!

- There were 76 numbered entrances. Tickets were issued with specified entrances on them so the 70,000-strong crowd knew where to go and where to exit in an emergency.

- Estimated exit time for all 70,000 spectators was three minutes!

- The Colosseum wasn't finished until the reign of Vespasian's son Titus (AD 79–81) and was dedicated in AD 80.

- It got its name because a colossal bronze statue of Nero stood close by, later adapted into a Sun-God. Pliny the Elder described the statue, called the Colossus, as 32 metres high and 'breathtaking'. Because everyone knew where the statue was, it eventually became a kind of address tag for the new arena and the name stuck.

- In 217 the Colosseum was badly damaged by lightning. Repairs lasted until the reign of Gordian III (238–244).

- The last recorded animal hunts in the Colosseum were held in 523 by Eutharich, son-in-law of Theodoric the Great (go to Chapter 21 for details about him).

- The Colosseum still stands to its full height of 50 metres (163 feet) on one side.

- The gladiators' barracks were right next door to the Colosseum and a large part of them is still visible today.

Figure 8-3:
The Circus Maxentius. Smaller than the Circus Maximus, but the best-preserved at Rome (it's outside the city walls by the Appian Way).

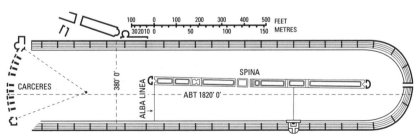

Circus Maximus fun facts

- The first stone parts were built in 174 BC.

- By the first century BC, 100,000 fans could be seated.

- By Nero's reign (AD 54–68), 250,000 fans could get in, matching today's biggest stadium: the Indianapolis Speedway (built 1909). Some believe as many as 320,000 could be crammed in later on.

- The Circus Maximus was 594 metres (1,950 feet) long and 201 metres (660 feet) wide.

- The spina down the middle had a turning post at each end.

- Each race had seven laps (about 5 miles). Seven bronze dolphins on pivots at one end of the spina and seven bronze eggs at the other were used to count them.

- Black gypsum flakes were scattered on the track to make it look bright.

- There were religious shrines along the spina.

- The spina also had obelisks shipped all the way from Egypt to show off Rome's mighty power.

- In the passageways and arches under the seats, cooks, astrologers, and prostitutes catered for the fans' other needs.

- Under Antoninus Pius (AD 138–161) overcrowding caused the deaths of more than 1,000 spectators.

- In 2006, tens of thousands of jubilant Italians gathered here once more to watch on giant screens their nation win the soccer World Cup and celebrate afterwards.

People would start gathering in the middle of the night to get the best seats. No wonder the writer Pliny the Younger looked forward to race days. He hated them, but with a quarter of a million Romans busy watching the action, it meant the streets were deserted and he could get on with his work in peace and quiet.

Fighting Men: Gladiators

Easily the best-known Roman entertainment today, gladiatorial combats were one of the most extreme forms of amusing a crowd of people in history. Specially equipped and trained fighters fought bouts in matched pairs to the death. The Etruscans probably started the idea by making prisoners fight to the death during the funerals of aristocrats, but it was the Samnites who really developed gladiator fights. They depicted bouts on their tomb walls after 400 BC. The Romans even called all gladiators 'samnites'. The first gladiator fight staged in Rome was in 264 BC when Decimus Junius Brutus made three pairs of slaves fight in honour of his dead father. It was a kind of substitute for the old human sacrifices. After that, gladiators evolved into a private form of aristocratic entertainment before becoming big-business box-office entertainment for the masses in the cities of the West and North Africa. Although amphitheatres for gladiator fights were very rare in the Eastern Empire, other venues like theatres or public squares must have been used. Ephesus in Asia Minor had no amphitheatre but the discovery of a large gladiators' cemetery (tombstone epitaphs and wounds on bones prove it) shows that even here gladiator fights were part of local entertainment.

The gladiators: Who they were

The word 'gladiator' comes from the Latin word for sword, *gladius,* so it means literally a 'swordsman'. The best way to get a man to fight to the death is to use a man who has nothing to lose, which is why slaves, criminals, and prisoners-of-war were the perfect candidates. If a man was really good, he might keep winning and get his freedom. On the whole, it was an offer he couldn't refuse even though the odds were, let's face it, not particularly good.

Slaves weren't the only gladiators, however. Some freemen volunteered, too, especially if they were down on their luck. Nero (AD 54–68), being fairly mad and with a very individual idea of what would be entertaining, once ordered that 400 senators and 600 equestrians fight as gladiators. This was a way of humiliating them, and no doubt the Roman mob thought this was extremely funny. But the most remarkable of them all was probably the emperor Commodus (AD 180–192; Chapter 18) who was a dab hand at gladiatorial fighting (not that anyone would have dared killing him). He bragged that he had fought 735 times without getting hurt and defeated 12,000 opponents.

Schools for scoundrels

There was no point in chucking just any man into the arena. Gladiatorial combat was a crowd-pleasing activity, so the action had to be good. Only men with serious fighting potential were chosen, sent to special gladiatorial schools called *ludi* that were run by businessmen called *lanistae.* The training was tough, but gladiators were well-fed and trained to the peak of physical fitness. Pompeii had a large and well-appointed gladiator school, which was buried when Mount Vesuvius erupted in AD 79. Over 60 gladiators perished there, but evidence was also found of an unexpected perk. The remains of a rich aristocratic woman were recovered – it seems she had stopped by for a 'visit' so to speak, when disaster struck. It's a reminder that successful gladiators were incredibly popular and not just for what they did in the arena.

Riot day in Pompeii

In the year AD 59, a gladiatorial contest was laid on at Pompeii by a Senator called Livineius Regulus. Rival supporters from a nearby town called Nuceria rolled up to cheer on their heroes. The locals and visitors started off by shouting at one another and then moved on to hurling stones. Soon swords were drawn, and before anyone could do anything, lots of Nucerians were being stabbed and swiped at by the Pompeians who seem to have come better equipped to cause trouble. Even women and children were cut down. The Senate in Rome was so disgusted that gladiatorial shows were banned for ten years in Pompeii as a punishment, and Regulus was forced into exile.

The fear of gladiators

Julius Caesar laid on a display of 320 gladiatorial pairs in commemoration of his dead father, but knew perfectly well it would impress people and increase his popular support. His enemies were absolutely horrified at the thought of 640 trained killers on Caesar's payroll (640 gladiators were more than a cohort of legionaries; refer to Chapter 5 for info about the Roman army) and promptly passed a law limiting the number of gladiators that could be used at any one time. The overall result was that gladiators represented a horrible, edge-of-your-seat, rabble-rousing type of glamour.

The slave revolt led by Spartacus in 73 BC started in a gladiatorial training school – remember, these boys knew how to use weapons, had nothing to lose, and terrified Italy witless (see Chapter 14 for more about the Revolt and Chapter 25 for Spartacus).

Putting on a gladiatorial show

Gladiatorial events were publicised in advance to whip up excitement to fever-pitch on the day. One painted advertisement in Pompeii announced that a total of 30 pairs of gladiators would fight each day from 8–12 April one year, together with an animal hunt. The fights were always the big event of the day. In the Colosseum, the gladiators marched in and stood before the emperor and announced *Ave Imperator, morituri te salutant* ('Hail Emperor, those about to die salute you!').

Types of gladiators

It wouldn't be much fun if all the gladiators were all the same, so the action was whizzed up by having lots of different types. This took advantage of the fact that gladiators might come from anywhere in the Roman Empire and had a whole array of specialised fighting techniques. Here are some of them:

- ✔ *Myrmillo* **(originally** *Samnis***):** Wore a fish-like helmet and had sword and large shield.

- ✔ *Retiarius:* Fought with a trident and a net.

- ✔ *Sagitarius:* Fought with a bow and arrow.

- ✔ *Secutos:* Had a shield, sword, heavy helmet, and armour on one arm. Meaning 'pursuer', the secutores were originally based on Samnite warriors.

- ✔ *Thrax:* Armed with a curved sword and small shield (the name meaning 'Thracian').

Nor was gladiator-fighting a men-only activity. From time to time women gladiators fought. Domitian (81–96) put women into the ring, but Septimius Severus (193–211) thought that was disgusting and banned women fighting. To add to the variety, even dwarf gladiators were brought on occasionally.

Gladiators all had their own personal fans who painted slogans on walls. Two at Pompeii say 'The *thrax* Celadus makes all the girls sigh' and 'The heartthrob of all the girls is Crescens the *retiarius*'.

Winner takes all

The climax of every bout was when a gladiator was down. Then it was up to the crowd. If it had been a rubbish fight, they shouted *Lugula*, 'Kill him', but if he'd fought well, they'd shout *Mitte* for 'Let him go'. The final say-so went to the man who'd put the games on. If the downed gladiator was spared, the fight continued. If not, he was killed and his body dragged off so the next bouts could take place.

Meanwhile, the lucky winner got money and a palm leaf, a symbol of victory that went back to the Greeks when men competed in sport only for the honour of taking part. If a gladiator had done especially well, he got the ultimate prize: a wooden sword, which was a symbol of his freedom. Amazingly, some gladiators earned their freedom but carried on, obviously enjoying it too much. Or perhaps they'd forgotten how to do anything else.

Fighting Animals

Wild beasts were another deadly part of Roman entertainment. There's a mosaic from a remote Roman villa in East Yorkshire in England called Rudston. It features various scenes from the amphitheatre including wild beasts. One of the lions is called *Omicida,* meaning 'man-killing' (hence our word 'homicide'). It's almost certainly a picture of a real, and famous, lion from an arena somewhere that the mosaicist or the villa-owner knew about. Mosaics like this were especially popular in North Africa so perhaps that's where he came from.

Killing wild animals was the normal way to start a day at the arena. During the Colosseum's inaugural games in AD 80, a phenomenal 5,000 animals were killed in a single day. After his conquest of Dacia, Trajan (AD 98–117) arranged in the year 107 for 11,000 animals to fight in the arena. The whole lot were killed, even though they included tame beasts. To celebrate Rome's thousandth birthday in AD 247, the emperor Philip the Arab (AD244–249) arranged for a special display that included (amongst others):

- 60 lions
- 40 wild horses
- 32 elephants
- 6 hippos
- 1 rhinoceros

Supplying animals

Of course, part of the treat was just the display of exotica, which showed off Rome's amazing control over such a wide range of territories. Lions, rhinoceroses, and giraffes had long since disappeared from Europe, but in antiquity North Africa was a good deal more fertile than it is today. Once the Romans had control of all of North Africa, they had access to wildlife that couldn't live there today even if the Romans hadn't done such a good job of wiping them out.

Expeditions were sent out to capture wild animals and bring them to ports in North Africa from where they could be shipped to Rome. Of course, it was impossible to supply every arena with a constant supply of African wildlife, so probably most of the provincial arenas had to make do with less exciting animals like hares, wolves, and wild boar.

Animals in the arena

The animals were kept in cages in the Colosseum's underground chambers and fed with cattle, or once, under Caligula, on criminals. On the day of the games, they were lifted up to the arena and sent out to do their work. Sometimes it was – literally – easy meat, especially when the entertainment on offer was the execution of criminals or other undesirables.

Although one way of having a show was simply to set animals against one another, that didn't really make for co-ordinated and organised entertainment. To warm things up and get some serious action going, specialised animal hunters were sent into the arena to thrill the crowds. Just like gladiators, they'd been selected from the ranks of criminals, slaves, and prisoners-of-war. They were called *venatores* ('hunters'), helped by *bestiarii* ('animal fighters' from *bestia,* 'wild beast'), but were nothing like as popular as the gladiators.

Julius Caesar was the first to introduce a special type of bull-killing into the arena. The hunters rode horses alongside running bulls and killed them by twisting their heads with the horns. Most unpleasant.

Epic Shows and Mock Battles

These days, we make the most of great historical events by going to watch epic movies about them. In Rome, the epics came from great tales of heroic battles and myth. The most extravagant displays in the arena came from re-enactments of these great events, or were just made up for the sake of more action. They were another way of making use of the gladiators' talents.

Julius Caesar laid on a mock battle between two armies. Each had 500 infantry, 20 elephants, and 30 cavalry. He also laid on a mock naval battle by flooding an arena and had ships brought in with two, three, and four banks of oars, each manned by a squad of soldiers. They posed as the rival fleets of Egypt and the city of Tyre. The event was so popular that people turned up from far and wide to see the spectacle, even going to the extreme of camping by the roadside to make sure of a good view on the day.

Nero staged a sea battle with mock sea monsters swimming about amongst the ships. But he had an even better idea for making himself as popular as possible. He instituted the *Ludi Maximi,* 'the Greatest Games', and organised a continuous round of free gifts all day long, ranging from 1,000 birds, food, precious metals, and jewellery right up to handing out ships, houses, and farms.

A Day at the Races – Chariot-racing

Chariot-racing was a wildly popular sport in the Roman Empire. The tradition went right back to the very beginning. Rome's mythical founder, Romulus, is supposed to have asked his neighbours, the Sabines, to pop round and enjoy an afternoon of chariot-racing back in around 753 BC. Actually, Romulus had tricked them. While the Sabines were engrossed in the action, he got his heavies to snatch the Sabine women.

Roman chariots

Roman chariots were ultra lightweight flimsy affairs with just enough room for a man to stand on and hold the reins. In an accident, the chariot would fall to pieces in an instant and hurl the charioteer out, probably into the path of another chariot. Chariots came in (mainly) three different types:

- ✔ Two-horse chariot *(biga)*
- ✔ Three-horse chariot *(triga)*
- ✔ Four-horse chariot *(quadriga)*

If you've seen the movie *Ben Hur* (1959) forget the chariots in that – they were like battleships compared to the real ones used by the Romans. But the movie is outstanding in the way it gets across the excitement and lethal danger of the chariot race, so if you haven't seen it, make sure you do.

The charioteers

Charioteers were generally slaves, freedmen, or charioteers as no self-respecting Roman citizen would demean himself by getting his hands dirty that way. Controlling a chariot required incredible skill and quick reactions. The more horses, the more difficult it got. Because the races went one way round the stadium, the slowest horse of the team was attached to the inside. One false move, and a chariot could either turn over or veer off across the track and hit the outside wall.

Charioteers rode for one of the four main teams: the Reds *(Russata),* the Whites *(Albata),* the Blues *(Veneta),* or the Greens *(Prasina).* And being a charioteer was a bit like being James Dean: You lived fast, hard, and generally not for very long.

Fans

The city mobs across the Roman world were fanatical supporters of chariot-racing. Supporters of each team took huge pleasure in putting the boot into rival supporters. They had plenty of opportunity, and soldiers were often on hand to try and keep order. The mad emperor Caligula (AD 37–41) was a fanatical supporter of the Greens, so much so that he would eat down at their stables and sometimes even spend the night there. He even gave one of the charioteers, Eutychus, a fortune in cash.

Like gladiators, charioteers were the big stars of the day: Aristocratic women swooned at the thought of a hulking charioteer, and some became international superstars, which explains why a few carried on racing even once they'd earned their freedom.

The Roman Schumacher

One of the biggest names in chariot-racing was Gaius Appuleius Diocles, who rode for several of the teams at Rome between AD 122–148. He won a fortune in prize money by coming first in 1,462 races. The total is 35 million sesterces, which, of course, is pretty meaningless today but at the time would have paid the annual wages of about six Roman legions (about 30,000 men). In other words, it was a lot of cash.

Diocles actually took part in 4,257 races which meant he took a lot of risks. His brilliant career was cut short when he was 26 and run over by a rival called Lachesis. Maybe Lachesis did it deliberately. One charioteer in North Africa cursed four of his arch rivals, begging that a demon torture and kill their horses and then crush the charioteers to death.

Chariot-racing was one of the longest-lived of all Roman sports. In the Byzantine Eastern Roman Empire capital of Constantinople, long after the fall of Rome, circus supporters were still beating the living daylights out of each other whenever they could (head to Chapter 21 for information about Constantinople).

Pantos and Plays: Roman Theatre

Along with arenas and circuses, the average Roman city had at least one theatre and sometimes more. Just like arenas and circuses, these were originally temporary affairs. It wasn't until the days of the late Republic that massive stone theatres were built. The origins of the Roman theatre lay firmly in the Greek East where many theatres had been built by the fourth century BC, like the one at Epidauros. But the Roman establishment disapproved of theatres, believing them to be a source of disturbances and immoral influence. In 209 BC, the Censor Cassius tried to build a theatre in Rome, but he was forced to stop by one of the consuls and general opposition.

Meanwhile, Greek influence was strong in southern Italy, so Pompeii had a stone theatre by the end of the third century BC, with an *odean* (a small theatre) for poetry and speeches added right next door in 80 BC. Rome's first wooden theatre was up by 179 BC. Rome's first certain stone version, the Theatre of Pompey, was built by 55 BC, but it might have replaced an earlier stone theatre which hasn't yet been found. By the time of the emperors some of these theatres were really magnificent. But theatres were much smaller than the stadiums or arenas. According to Pliny the Elder, even the enormous Theatre of Pompey held at most about 40,000 spectators (less than one-sixth of the Circus Maximus), though some modern estimates come in rather lower.

Curio's remarkable revolving theatres

Gaius Curio, a supporter of Caesar's during the Civil War in the first century BC, was determined to come up with an ingenious way to put on costly entertainments to win votes. He came up with two wooden theatres close to one another and each built on a revolving pivot. Two separate casts put on a performance of the same play to the same audience in the afternoon before the theatres suddenly revolved and were joined together to make an amphitheatre, at which point gladiator pairs replaced the actors. Pliny the Elder was fascinated by how Curio thought to win over swaying voters by making them sway dangerously from side to side in his rickety, lethal, revolving wooden theatres.

Just like arenas and circuses, the theatres put on performances that were often part of religious festivals. So one thing you often find close to a theatre is a temple. That way sacred processions could start at one and end and finish at the other.

Theatre floor plans

Roman theatres had three parts (see Figure 8-4): the stage, the orchestra, and the auditorium. The auditorium was semi-circular with concentric rows of seats rising up from the flat semicircular chorus area at the bottom. Whenever possible, the Romans built the theatre into a hillside that made for far less complicated building. If no hill was available, then the seating area was built on top of a series of archways, vaults, and walls. The stage faced the auditorium on the far side of the orchestra. In the most extravagant theatres, the stage had a huge wall behind it, decorated with all sorts of architectural features that helped form part of the scenery.

One of the most staggering and well-preserved theatres is at Aspendos in Asia Minor (Turkey), dedicated under Marcus Aurelius (AD 161–180). Its stage is 110 metres long and 24 metres high. Many other examples survive, like the wonderful remains at Dougga in Tunisia, and Orange and Arles in France. In Rome itself part of the Theatre of Marcellus, built by Augustus, still stands.

Roman music

No-one knows what Roman music really sounded like because the Romans didn't write music down in a form we can understand or which survives. But music was everywhere: in the street, in markets, in religious festivals, and in the theatres. Musical contests were used to fill out interludes in the action at the circus and arena. Roman soldiers used trumpets in battle and at ceremonial displays. Other instruments the Romans knew included:

- ✔ Small harps called *lyrae* and the more complicated *cithara*.

- ✔ Percussion instruments like castanets, cymbals, tambourines, and the Egyptian *sistrum* (a kind of rattle).

- ✔ Wind instruments such as the double pipes, bagpipes, and flutes.

- ✔ The water organ *(hydraulus),* invented by Ktesibios in the third century BC. It used a water pump to force air through the organ pipes. According to Pliny the Elder dolphins were especially enchanted by its sound!

Actors and impresarios

Rich upper-class Romans didn't think much of theatres and even less of actors. There was even a law that prohibited a senator, his son, grandson, or great-grandson from marrying a woman either of whose parents had been an actor. An actor's social rank was so low that he was listed along with gladiators, slaves, and criminals as the men a husband could kill if his wife committed adultery with any one of them.

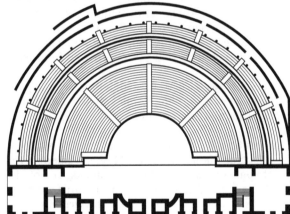

Figure 8-4: The plan of the Roman theatre at Orange in Gaul, one of the best-preserved. Most others were similar.

How to find a temple – start at the theatre

Theatres often held religious performances and were closely linked to temples. The Great Temple of Diana at Ephesus in Asia Minor (Turkey) was known to have been one of the Seven Wonders of the Ancient World but was long lost. In 1863 the British Museum sent John Turtle Wood to look for it. He started at the theatre and followed the Sacred Way from the theatre, digging it out as he went. It led all the way to the temple, now just ruined foundations in a swamp.

The only thing that was worse was an upper-class person who did like the theatre. Caligula (AD 37–41) was especially fond of an actor called Mnester and had members of the audience beaten if they made a sound while Mnester was dancing.

There was one remarkable theatre fan and impresario called Ummidia Quadratilla who died around the early second century when she was 78. Known for being on the large size even by Roman-matron standards, Ummidia owned a troupe of pantomime dancers who acted out the part of mythological characters on the stage. In her case, the dancers were freedmen, but such dancers were usually slaves. Other upper-class Romans thought her tastes were very improper for a woman of her rank. Oddly so did Ummidia, who was convinced the shows would corrupt her own grandson and prevented him from seeing them. I call that hypocrisy.

The show must go on: Performances and oratory competitions

Plays were mostly popular amongst ordinary people who were a lot less concerned about what was 'proper Roman entertainment' or not-that-snotty aristocrats. Originally there were two types of theatrical performances, called *ludi scaenici* ('plays on stage'): comedies and tragedies. The tragedies, like so much of the best of Roman culture, had been borrowed from the Greeks.

Roman comedies also borrowed ideas, and sometimes whole plots, from the Greeks but made the most of parodying Roman civilisation, especially by focusing on slaves as principal characters.

By the early second century BC the most famous comedy writer was an Italian called Titus Maccius Plautus (*c.* 254–184 BC), a failed merchant shipper. Although he got some of his ideas from the Greeks, one of his other influences was another Italian called Gnaeus Naevius. Plautus wrote at least 130 wildly popular comedies and is the only Roman playwright to have made a film in Hollywood. Well, that's not strictly true, but the famous musical and then movie *A Funny Thing Happened on the Way to the Forum* (1966), starring Zero Mostel, Phil Silvers, and Buster Keaton, was directly based on Plautus's work, as was the long-running BBC television series *Up Pompeii!*, starring Frankie Howerd as Lurcio, the slave and centre of all the action.

The Romans also enjoyed the following:

> ✔ **Action-adventures:** The performance of a play called *The Fire* during the reign of Nero was like watching an action movie being made. A house was put on stage and actually set on fire. As a reward for their performance and success in escaping the on-stage action, the actors were allowed by Nero to keep any furniture they'd rescued.

✔ **Re-enactments of myth:** These provided plenty of opportunities for displays of flesh. A Roman writer called Apuleius described a pantomime that took place in the second century AD. It was all about the Judgment of Paris (when Paris was supposed to choose the most beautiful goddess from Juno, Minerva, or Venus). The actress playing Venus arrived on stage with nothing on apart from a piece of silk around her hips and then took part in an erotic dance with other dancers.

✔ **Mimes and pantomimes:** By the end of the Republic, mime and pantomime were also performed on stage. The Romans weren't at all averse to livening up the proceedings with live violence, sex, and nudity. Oddly, mime actors did get to speak lines, but pantomime actors didn't.

✔ **Competition oratory:** One of the weirdest forms of cult entertainment for the Romans was the competition speech. Public speaking was a very important part of an educated Roman's repertoire, and Greek-speakers who modelled themselves on the great Athenian orators of the fifth century BC (known as the 'First Sophistic') were the most admired. The idea was to ask the audience for speech suggestions (which could be historical themes like the great days of Athens, or more down-to-earth themes like praising baldness), and then launch off into original, spontaneous, off-the-cuff speeches to riotous applause every time they said something especially learned or witty.

Theatrical performances don't seem to have remained very popular amongst the Romans, who preferred the violent action in the arena or the thrills in the stadium. The Theatre of Marcellus in Rome was falling into ruin by the early third century AD and in the fourth century was partly demolished to repair a bridge. Thanks to theatres being associated with religious festivals, the Empire going Christian didn't help either, though that doesn't seem to have affected the enthusiasm for the stadium.

A Night In: Entertaining at Home

The Romans didn't spend all their time at public entertainments. They had work to do and religious ceremonies to attend, but they enjoyed entertaining at home, too.

The best way to show off your house was at a dinner party. Dinner parties were especially popular, and it was quite common to throw one for guests who had spent the day at the amphitheatre. But the real purpose was to make a statement about who you were, who your friends were, and where you all stood in society. For example, patrons invited their clients (see Chapter 2 for an explanation of the patron-client relationship) as a kind of reward for their loyalty. As guests of lesser status, clients got inferior food and wine. But as it was customary for the host to give his guests a going-home present, attending might have turned out to be worth it.

Dinner and a show: The entertainment

Entertainment during the party included actors performing a scene from a popular play or panto, or a display by dancers. But in the more literary households, men would bore each other stiff, and no doubt their wives, too, by reading their own poetry, which they'd composed in the style of a famous poet like Ovid or Virgil. The whole point was to show off their technical expertise at constructing verses in various different rhythms (or *meters*). That this could be pretty tedious is obvious from the occasion when the poet Martial promised a dinner guest an especially good time by swearing that he wouldn't recite anything at all to his friend!

During dinner parties, guests lay on couches round three sides of the dining room which was called the *triclinium*, literally meaning 'three-sided table couch'. The idea was that slaves could bring the food into the centre through the open side so that everyone could reach out and help him- or herself. In the very richest houses, a summer dining room and a winter dining room were provided.

Party invite

One of the most famous pieces of writing from the Roman world was dug out of a waterlogged pit beside the ruins of a fort called Vindolanda in northern Britain. Dated to around the end of the first century AD, it's the earliest piece of writing in Latin by a woman ever found. A woman called Claudia Severa, wife of a commanding officer at another fort, wrote to Sulpicia Lepidina, wife of the commanding officer at Vindolanda, inviting her friend to come to her birthday party on 3 September:

> 'Claudia Severa to her Lepidina greetings. On the third day before the Ides of September, sister, for the day of the celebration of my birthday, I give you a warm invitation to make sure that you come to us, to make the day more enjoyable for me.'

It's an astonishing little document because right out on the wilds of the military frontier, hundreds of miles from Rome and all those aristocrats lolling about on couches at luxurious feasts, a couple of soldiers' wives (who'd probably never been to Rome) were doing their best to keep up Roman standards of entertainment and hospitality. Amazing.

Io Saturnalia!

The biggest booze-up of the year was the Saturnalia, the mid-winter festival. Starting on 17 December with a ceremony at the Temple of Saturn, it ended up lasting around a week, but for once it didn't matter who you were. People of all classes shared tables at a free banquet as part of the festivities and shouted *Io Saturnalia* as a greeting – it just means 'Wahhay Saturnalia!'. Even slaves had a day off and were served by their masters. Gifts were exchanged, and everyone tried to have a good time, which was just as well because all the usual entertainments were closed for the holiday. Does some of that sound familiar? Yes, the Christians took over the Romans' great winter festival and made it into Christmas, though I'd expect you'd find a lot of people who'd tell you it's getting a lot more like the Roman Saturnalia once again.

Tableware

The very best tableware was made of gold or silver. Cups, plates, bowls, and vast dishes were all used. The most prized were those made by designer silversmiths whose individual trademarks were their own styles of decoration. Needless to say the flashiest plate was to be found in the emperor's palace. Claudius (AD 41–54) had a slave called Drusillanus who owned a silver plate that weighed about 163 kilograms (500 pounds), and he wasn't alone. Emperors gave gold and silver plates to their favourites.

If you couldn't afford silver, *pewter* (made from tin and lead) could look like silver if it was really polished up and was a passable substitute. Then there was the pottery. Romans used loads of different types, but in a dinner-party setting, pottery was very definitely only for the lower orders, even the good stuff, which was usually a lurid red colour.

Glassware was highly prized, too, especially as it was a relatively recent innovation from Egypt. The more transparent, the more it was valued.

The menu

A collection of recipes was compiled in the fourth century and published under the name of Apicius. Many of the recipes involved adding honey, vinegar, and fish sauce, which were the main flavouring-enhancers available. But the Romans also knew about salt, pepper, mustard, and fantastically expensive spices shipped in from the Far East. Romans particularly loved a sauce called *garum*, which was made from rotten fermented fish. Legend has it that this fish sauce survives today in the form of Worcestershire sauce.

You can buy a translation of Apicius today and try the recipes yourself! These are some the dishes Roman dinner guests could look forward to: Guests might have a starter of lettuce with snails and eggs, barley soup, and wine chilled with snow lugged down from the mountains, or maybe pickled tuna. Main courses could be fish, pork, sow's udders, rabbit, stuffed poultry, dormice fattened in special pots, snails so fattened with milk they couldn't withdraw into their shells, and sea urchins.

Wine was transported in from all over the Roman world. Naturally, it was priced according to quality. Sabine wine was one of the most expensive and cost nearly four times as much as the cheapest rubbish, called 'common wine'. Wine strainers removed impurities, and it could be drunk warm or chilled.

Chapter 9

Divine Intervention

*N*ot only did the Romans believe in their divine mission to rule the world, but many also saw gods in everything, everywhere, and all the time. They believed that gods decided and controlled everything down to the last puff of wind and blade of grass. In the Roman world, places of worship existed in all shapes and sizes, from the huge temples in Rome and all other major cities, right down to tiny streetside shrines, household shrines, and even portable shrines. Even coins bore pictures of a whole array of gods and goddesses on their reverses.

Roman gods ranged from the great classical pantheon of Jupiter, Juno, and Minerva to fantastically obscure local gods (which could mean as local as being the god of the lock on your front door). They also included exotic gods from the East and strange, wild Celtic gods from the West.

The only exception was Christianity. The Romans would happily have added Christ to their list of gods (and some did), except that the Christians were having none of it. So it's remarkable that Christianity ended up as the state religion. That's also important: Religion in the Roman world was a matter of personal faith and superstition, but it was also political. Observing the state cults, including emperor worship, was part of expressing loyalty to the Empire. Anyone who refused did so at his or her peril.

Cutting a Deal: Roman Religion

Roman religion, like most ancient pagan religions, was basically about cutting a deal with a god (or gods). The average Roman wanted a service from a god, which could mean anything from support in winning a war or saving a crop, to bringing death and ruin on someone who had stolen his cloak (literally). In return for that service, the Roman promised the god a gift – usually a sacrifice or money – in return. This is how the deal worked:

- ✔ **Stage 1: The Vow.** The god was contacted and asked for a service. Depending on the god (or goddess), this could be done at a major shrine, a minor shrine, or a private shrine, often in written form on a docket which was then stored at the temple and involved specifying what was needed and what would be given in return: that's the vow *(votum)*. These are sometimes called 'curse-tablets' because they cursed the culprit and asked the god to visit violent retribution on him or her.

- ✔ **Stage 2: Fulfilling the Vow.** If the god performed the service (or was believed to have done so), the sacrifice or gift was made, and a record that the vow had been fulfilled was left at the shrine: usually a small altar of stone, earth, or wood, or a votive plaque made of bronze or silver pinned to a temple wall, which was inscribed with the person's name, the god being dedicated to, and a formula like *VSLM* which was short for *Votum Soluit Libens Merito,* 'He willingly and deservedly fulfilled the vow'.

Roman shrines ended up awash with offerings, which were buried in pits or thrown into pools. Coins were especially common, but the average Roman usually took care to throw in worn old coins of low value – well it's the thought that counts, isn't it?

Good days and bad days

A big part of religious superstition was doing things on the right day:

- ✔ **The *Kalends:*** The first day of the month was sacred to Juno.

- ✔ **The *Ides:*** The thirteenth day of short months and the fifteenth of long months were sacred to Jupiter.

- ✔ **The *Nones:*** The ninth day *before* the Ides.

Religious festivals were never held on any day before the Nones apart from an ancient one in July called *Poplifugia* (it means 'flight of the people' which might have been when everyone fled during the storm on the occasion Romulus disappeared – see Chapter 10). Similarly, religious superstition ruled when weddings could be held. The Kalends, Nones, and Ides, the first day following any of them, the whole of March, May, and the first two weeks of June were all no-nos, as were days of religious festivals.

Marriage

For most people, the marriage ceremony was a private affair starting in the bride's home with a friend presiding as *auspex* who examined entrails of a sacrificial victim to foretell the future (it's where we get our word *auspices,* meaning a forecast, from). The husband then carried his new wife into his home. Divorce was a straightforward rejection of the partner. Roman patricians had an ultra-formal wedding ceremony called *confarreatio.* The overseeing god was Jupiter Farreus, and the *pontifex maximus* ('chief priest') and *flamen dialis* ('priest of the Jupiter cult') presided. Farreus means 'made of spelt (wheat)' so a spelt cake formed a central part of the rite. Divorce for them was only possible through the ceremony of *diffarraetio.*

The key thing was ritual. Every sacrifice, every form of worship, every communication to the god had to be done exactly to a precise form of words and sequence of events. Get it wrong and the magic wouldn't work. Even if things seemed to go right, if the desired result didn't follow, then the superstitious Romans simply concluded that the ritual must have gone wrong. Less superstitious Romans, and there were plenty of them, concluded either there weren't any gods or looked around for a better one.

Divining the future

The Romans wanted to know what lay in the future. Who doesn't? But the Romans lived in a more unpredictable world than we do. Having little or no idea about impending weather catastrophes, earthquakes, disease, or their own deaths, they convinced themselves that signs must exist which foretold the future.

Omens

The Romans were obsessed with omens, good or bad. They looked out for signs of what the gods were up to. Omens counted for a lot. During the civil war of AD 68–69, the short-lived Emperor Vitellius prepared his troops to hold Italy against the approaching army of Vespasian (see Chapter 16). Vitellius got very upset by an unexpected turn of events:

- A cloud of vultures flew over and blanked out the sun.

- An ox being readied for sacrifice escaped, scattering all the ritual and sacrificial equipment, and had to be chased and killed in a non-ritual way.

Or so the story, recounted by Tacitus, went. It might have been true, but Roman historians loved being wise after the event by listing all the bad omens. Appropriately, Vitellius was defeated and killed. The Romans also saw omens of Julius Caesar's assassination (see Chapter 15). Septimius Severus concluded he was destined to be emperor, based on omens (see Chapter 18).

Being a priest was part of the official duties of men of status, which was why the emperor was also chief priest (pontifex maximus). Pliny the Younger was delighted when he was made an Omen Interpreter because (he said) it was an honour to be favoured by Trajan (AD 98–117), and also 'because the priesthood is an old-established religious office and has a particular sanctity by being held for life'.

Soothsayers

The *haruspex* was one of the specialist priests who predicted the future. There were two techniques:

- ✓ *Augurium:* The interpretation of natural phenomena like storms or animal activity
- ✓ *Extispicium:* The interpretation of the entrails of sacrificial animals

Here's an especially revolting example of soothsaying. On 15 April, special rites celebrated the sprouting seeds in the ground and the pregnancy of cows. The calves were ripped from the stomachs of their mothers, their entrails cut out for soothsaying, and the bodies burned.

Dream interpreters

Some Romans were very keen on the idea of a level of higher awareness, only reached by being profoundly intoxicated – or, basically really very, very drunk indeed. It's a similar idea to that put about by people in more modern times who believe that using mind-bending drugs gives them incredible insights to the true meaning of life (until they wake up, that is).

The lucky phallus

If you visit Pompeii today, you'll see over many of the doors into houses a representation of an erect phallus. Phalluses were connected with fertility (through Priapus, the god of procreation), but they were also symbols of good luck and were thought to ward off evil. Placing them over a door was supposed to protect the home from any evil passing in through the entrance.

Miniature phalluses were also worn as personal lucky charms as brooches or on rings. Giant phalluses were mounted in carts and wheeled around during celebrations of Bacchus. In the city of Lavinium (modern Pratica), a month was devoted to the festivities, climaxing with the phallus being displayed in the forum where matrons decorated it with flowers.

Bad day for a soothsayer

The Romans could also see the funny side of all this fortune telling and omen-reading. The poet Martial recorded what he thought was a hilarious story about a soothsayer. A billy goat was to be sacrificed to Bacchus by a Tuscan *haruspex* (soothsayer). While cutting the animal's throat, the haruspex asked a handy yokel to slice off the animal's testicles at the same time. The haruspex then concentrated on the job in hand when suddenly the yokel was shocked to see 'a huge hernia revealed, to the scandal of the rites' emerge from the goat's body – or so the yokel thought. Anxious to live up to the occasion and observe the religious requirements by removing this offensive sight, the yokel sliced off the hernia only to discover that in fact he had accidentally castrated the haruspex!

Some Roman cults grew up around this idea, with temples constructed so that the believers could drink themselves into a stupor and collapse into a drunken sleep in chambers in the temple in the presence of the god. They'd wake up the next day and recount their dreams to the resident dream interpreter who (for a fee, of course) would explain the hidden meanings. One such place was the healing shrine of a god called Mars-Nodons in Britain at a place now called Lydney. The funny thing is that the shrine was at its height when the Roman Empire was Christian, showing that some people were still keen on old pagan ideas.

Oracles

An oracle was a dedicated individual through whom a god spoke to the world. Generally oracles spoke in cryptic riddles, which needed interpreting. The most famous oracle was at Delphi in Greece, but there were many others, such as the oracle of Juno Caelestis ('Heavenly Juno') at Carthage, or the god of Carmel in Judaea. Vespasian consulted the Carmel oracle before he made a bid to become emperor in AD 69. He got a very encouraging message: Anything he wanted to, apparently, was guaranteed to happen.

Non-believers and charlatans

Not all Romans went around believing in the long-established pagan cults. Some people thought all the ritual was stuff and nonsense. Other even more cynical types spotted that fulfilling people's beliefs about religion was an excellent way of making a fast buck.

Healing cults, hot water, and dogs

The whole Greek medical tradition (refer to Chapter 7) was based on religion and went all the way back to the god Aesculapius (Greek: Asklepios). Temples of Aesculapius are found all over the Roman world and became the centres of some of the healing cults. In an age when 'real' medicine was pretty limited in its capabilities, many people put all their faith into healing cults. Hot springs were popular centres that sucked in large numbers of ailing pilgrims. They hoped for a cure in return for gifts to the presiding god or goddess. Bourbonne-les-Bains in Gaul was a major shrine and healing spring used by the Roman army, and was dedicated to a couple of local gods called Borvo and Damona.

Religious healing was big business and, until the coming of Christianity, places like this made serious money out of catering for and accommodating people desperate to get well. The most surprising element of some healing cults was the use of dogs. Dog saliva was supposed to have special healing properties, so dogs were kept at temples and encouraged to lick wounds or the eyes of blind people (eye disease was very common in antiquity).

The sceptics

Not all Romans were convinced by all this addiction to ritual, omens, and superstition:

- ✔ Cicero wondered if it didn't all amount to self-induced imprisonment, with people trapped by their fear of what omens might mean and terrified of getting ritual wrong.

- ✔ Pliny the Elder thought it was mostly superstitious self-serving nonsense and was fascinated by how people were convinced the goddess Fortuna was behind all their good luck and also responsible for their disasters and misfortune.

One of Pliny the Younger's greatest contributions to history is his letter to the historian Tacitus about the eruption of Vesuvius in AD 79. Describing the terrified crowd, he said, 'Many sought the help of the gods, but even more imagined there were no more gods left and that the universe had been plunged into permanent darkness for all eternity.'

In the motion picture *Spartacus* (1960), a politician character called Gracchus about to make a sacrifice tells the young Julius Caesar what he thought of the gods, saying, 'Privately I believe in none of them, neither do you – publicly I believe in them all.' A Hollywood script it may be, but many real Roman politicians knew how important going through the motions of belief was, regardless of what they really thought.

Religious con-artists

With so many people prepared to visit sacred shrines in search of a service from a god, it's no great surprise that there were plenty of other people interested in cashing in. A writer of the second century AD called Lucian wrote about a crook called Alexander of Abonueteichos in Bithynia and Pontus. This man cheated the credulous at his shrine by pretending to be insane and planting a goose egg in which he had placed a snake. Later he 'discovered' the egg and claimed thereby to have found the newborn Aesculapius. He also rewrote prophecies stored in the temple so he could 'prove' he'd been right all along. As far as Lucian was concerned, those who fell for this were mentally-deficient and indistinguishable from sheep. This sort of thing probably went on in a lot more places.

Roman Temples and Shrines

There were several different types of Roman temple, but in most cases the important thing to remember is that, unlike churches, pagan temples weren't places for worshippers to gather. They were sacred places to store cult statues and other cult treasures, and were only open to priests. The 'action' took place outside in the precinct, which is where altars stood for sacrifices, soothsaying, and performing ritual.

The Latin word templum for a religious precinct is now used by us just to mean the actual sacred building: that is, the temple, which the Romans called aedes or fanum.

Temples turn up in these places:

- ✔ In town centres in the forum and often near theatres because the two were closely linked in ritual. Sometimes whole towns, like Bath in Britain, grew up around a temple.

- ✔ Anywhere else in a town, often at road junctions or as part of another complex like a baths.

- ✔ At specialised rural religious centres, like a sacred tree or a sacred spring, where something special was believed to exist.

- ✔ On villa estates, tended by the villa owner for the benefit of locals.

A single precinct could have one temple, two temples, or several temples, dedicated to the same god or lots of gods in any combination. The Altbachtal sanctuary at Trier had an incredible 70 temples of various shapes and sizes. Small shrines turn up in houses, street corners, by roads, or halfway up a mountain. In short, Roman temples were everywhere and anywhere.

Classical temples

The so-called Temple of Fortuna Virilis in Rome (actually of Portumnus, the god of harbours and sea trade), shown in Figure 9-1, is what most people think of as a Roman temple: a rectangular building with columns all the way round the outside, approached up a flight of steps at the front towards columns supporting a triangular pediment filled with sculpture. At the top of the steps are one or more rows of columns before reaching a door leading into the *cella,* which makes up the bulk of the building. The cult statue stood inside the cella. Sometimes there were only columns at the front, with dummy half-columns around the walls of the cella. A few temples were circular and had columns all the way round with a central drum-shaped cella.

Classical temples could be little street-corner buildings with just four columns at the front, they could be monumental affairs, or they could be anything in between. These temples turn up all over the Roman Empire. One of the biggest was the Temple of Jupiter Heliopolitanus at Baalbek in the Roman province of Syria, now in Lebanon. Despite its vast size, the Baalbek temple was only one part of a vast religious complex of temples and courts on the site.

Figure 9-1: The so-called Temple of Fortuna Virilis, dating in this form from the first century BC. Lying close to the Tiber, it was really dedicated to Portumnus, the god of harbours.

Photo by the author.

Fun facts about the Baalbek Jupiter temple

✔ The Baalbek Jupiter temple was 49 metres (147 feet) wide and 90 metres (295 feet) long. The Lincoln Memorial in Washington is 36 metres (118 feet) wide and 57.3 metres (188 feet) long.

✔ Some of the blocks in the temple's podium are 400 cubic metres (14,000 cubic feet) in size each.

✔ These blocks each weigh nearly 1,000 tons.

✔ Each column was 19.6 metres (63 feet) high and weighed 152 tons. Six still stand today. The columns in the Lincoln Memorial are only 13.4 metres (44 feet) high.

Regional temples

Roman classical temples appear almost throughout the Roman Empire, but they picked up influences from the places they were built in, and in some provinces almost entirely gave way to local types of temple.

Egypt was always a special case in the Roman Empire. In Egypt – unlike any-where else – Roman emperors were usually portrayed in local dress, in this case as pharaohs and in Egyptian-style carvings. They turn up most often in this form on Egyptian temples, which under the Romans were built according to traditional Egyptian forms with a series of open-air courts entered through a pair of flanking pylons before reaching the main temple structure. One of the best-preserved Egyptian temples is the Temple of Hathor at Dendarah, started under Augustus and Tiberius. It's completely Egyptian, without a hint of classical Roman style in sight.

In the north-west provinces like Gaul and Britain, the Romano-Celtic temple held sway. Unlike the classical temples, these were simple square buildings with a covered corridor all the way round a central tower which formed the cella.

Basilican temples were very different. Based on the public hall design of nave and aisles, basilicas were only suitable for religions that were congregational (that is, devotees took part in the ritual inside the building). These mainly included Mithraism and Christianity.

Shrines

Shrines could take almost any form, from an outdoor bench surrounding a few altars to little covered buildings in temple form. Romans could even carry about portable shrines with a figure of the god inside.

In the movie *Gladiator* (2000), Maximus is seen early on praying to a portable set of figures he carries around with him on campaign.

In the early second century AD, Pliny the Younger wrote a description of a religious shrine complex that surrounded the springhead of the Clitumnus, a tributary of the Tiber. Clitumnus was supposed to turn cattle which drank from the water white:

> 'At the foot of a modest hill, thickly wooded with ancient cypresses, the spring gushes out into . . . a pool as clear as glass. You can count lying on the bottom glistening pebbles and coins, which have been thrown in . . . Nearby is an ancient temple in which stands a statue of the god Clitumnus, dressed in the splendid robe of a magistrate. The oracles recorded here testify to his presence and the spirit's powers of prophecy. Around about are several little shrines to named cults with their own gods.'

The Divine Mission: Roman Gods

Roman gods existed in a hierarchy that started at the top with the pantheon of major deities headed by Jupiter, the king of the gods. He had a family of associates, many of whom were identified with Greek equivalents and also had Etruscan origins, whose worship can turn up almost anywhere in the Roman Empire. But there were many other gods ranging from lesser classical gods like the Italian woodland deity Faunus and the spirit of a city like Bourdiga, the goddess of Burdigala (Bourdeaux), to the gods who represented the house and a family's ancestors, or the gods who represented a hot spring, pool, or a tree. Often Romans came across the local gods when they arrived in a region and then adopted them as their own.

Time to meet the Roman gods. I'll start with the major gods and describe more minor gods, but there were all sorts of others as well.

Public religion: Jupiter, Juno, Mars – the famous ones

The Romans saw the great gods of their classical pantheon in human form, but unlike humans, the gods were immortal and spent their time controlling the world. Jupiter was a mighty bearded old man equipped with thunderbolts. Minerva was a female warrior. Vulcan was a blacksmith. Each had a personality, particular powers, favourites, and faults – much like human beings – and some were linked by family relationships. Juno was Jupiter's wife, Mars was Juno's son, and Venus was Mars's consort, for example. They co-operated some times and rowed at others. They were shown in sculptures, on reliefs, on mosaics, and in paintings in these forms, always equipped with their identifying attributes (like Minerva's shield, or Vulcan's hammer) so that there was no doubt about who was being shown.

It was the patronage of Rome by these gods that was thought especially significant in Rome's destiny, but their essentially human traits of favouritism and squabbling add an edgy element of jeopardy and triumph over adversity: The Romans didn't take divine support for granted; it had to be sought, cajoled, and earned.

Table 9-1 lists the main Roman gods.

Table 9-1		Roman Gods
Roman God	*Greek Name*	*Description*
Jupiter	Zeus	King of the gods, also known as Jove and as Jupiter Optimus Maximus ('Jupiter the Best and Greatest') and often abbreviated to IOM on inscriptions. Husband of Juno, and father of Mercury. Worshipping Jupiter was a routine part of state and military calendars.
Juno	Hera	Queen of the gods, Jupiter's wife and mother of Mars. She was closely associated with motherly virtues. Main festivals: 1 July, 13 September.
Minerva	Athena	Inherited from the Etruscan Menrva, she was a goddess of trade and crafts as well as war (Minerva Victrix, 'the Victorious'), and is usually shown wearing a helmet and carrying a spear, with a breastplate depicting the gorgon Medusa. Main festival: 19 March.
Apollo	Apollo	The Romans adopted this Greek god and kept the name. A patron of hunting and music, he was also associated with oracles (for example at Delphi) and healing, and with the sun. Main festivals: 6–13 July (with games, see Chapter 8), and 23 September.
Ceres	Demeter	Goddess of crops (hence our word 'cereal') and natural renewal. Her festival, *Cerealia* (12–19 April), was associated with major public games (see Chapter 8).
Diana	Artemis	Goddess of hunting and the moon. Main festival: 13 August.

(continued)

Table 9-1 *(continued)*

Roman God	Greek Name	Description
Janus	(none)	The god of beginnings and doorways who rescued Saturn when he was thrown out by Jupiter. His temple was closed in times of peace, and open during war. Main festival: 17 August.
Mars	Ares	The god of war and usually shown armed. Juno's son, Mars was often associated with local gods in the north-west provinces, like hunter and warrior gods, but he was also associated with healing cults. Mars was also a god of agriculture and property boundaries. Various festivals including 1 June and 19 October.
Mercury	Hermes	Son of Jupiter and Maia (a fertility goddess). The messenger god, he also looked after trade and 'abundance'. He was extremely popular in Britain and Gaul where he was frequently associated with local gods. Main festival: 15 May.
Neptune	Poseidon	A sea god also associated with horses, so the Romans also linked him to the god of horses, Consus. Main festivals: 23 July, 1 December.
Saturn	Chronos	Father of Jupiter (Zeus). In myth Saturn ruled over a golden age and taught the Romans to farm. His name may have come from the Latin for a sower of seeds, *sator*. Saturn was thrown out by his son Jupiter and taken in by Janus. His temple in the Roman forum is one of the most ancient and best-preserved buildings there, but is a fourth-century AD reconstruction reusing bits of other buildings. Main festival: the winter solstice.
Venus	Aphrodite	Goddess of love, wife of Mars, and mythical ancestor of the Lulus clan (Julius Caesar was a member). One of her festivals was 23 April.
Vesta	Hestia	Roman goddess of the hearth fire, worshipped in every home and also in Rome itself (the latter protected by the Vestal Virgins who kept the fire going in the Temple of Vesta).
Vulcan	Hephaestus	God of fire and the smithy. Main festivals: 23 May, 23 August.

Jupiter, Juno, and Minerva form the *Capitoline Triad.* Their home temple was the Capitoline temple, the oldest temple in Rome. It was dedicated in classical form in 509 BC and restored to the same design in 76 BC. It was destroyed in AD 69 and rebuilt once more. Temples dedicated to the triad stood in the forums of most major cities of the Roman world, but these gods also had temples dedicated to them as individuals.

Household and family gods

When I say the Romans had a god for everything and everywhere, I do mean just that. If I listed them all there'd be no room for anything else in the book, so here's just a flavour.

Geniuses, Fates, and Mother goddesses

The most common of the household and family gods was the *genius,* 'guardian spirit', originally a man's guardian spirit (a little like the Christian concept of a guardian angel) but which became extended to the guardian spirit of almost anything. So the *Genius loci* was the 'Genius of the Place' which could be anything from a corner of a field to a street kerbside. There were also Geniuses of parade grounds, Geniuses of the legions, Geniuses of Our Lords (the emperors), Geniuses of any city you care to name, and Geniuses of trade guilds. Perhaps the strangest were the *Genii Cucullati,* a trio of hooded gods who have no names, recognisable facial features, or even attributes, found represented on carvings found in the north-western provinces.

Triplication was an important feature of some cults. The *Parcae* (Fates) were also worshipped in triple form, and so were the *Matres* (Mother goddesses) who were sometimes linked to the Parcae. The idea has survived into the Christian concept of the Holy Trinity.

Household gods

Every home had its resident *lares,* household guardian spirits. The head man of every household maintained a shrine for them *(lararium)* in the entrance hall *(atrium).* These gods were rather like Geniuses because there were also *lares* for road junctions and cities. Rome had lares for everyone of its 265 crossroads.

Gods for anything else

Gods could get even smaller-scale than the household gods. Believe it or not, three gods had separate protective duties over a Roman door:

- **Forculus** for the actual doors
- **Cardea** for the hinges
- **Limentinus** for the threshold

Other examples include Fabulinus, the god who helped children learn to speak. Fornax was a goddess who prevented grain being burned in driers. Robigus was the god who protected crops from mould. So you can just imagine how many gods the average household had, let alone the rest of the Roman world.

Emperor worship

Worshipping rulers as living gods was well-established in the ancient world. The whole Egyptian cycle, for example, saw the living pharaoh as the god Horus, the son of Isis and Osiris, and the dead pharaoh as the murdered Osiris, restored to life by Isis. In the Greek East, worshipping rulers as living gods had become a political fact of life. Alexander the Great asked to be worshipped as one, claiming to be the son of Ammon (Zeus).

The Romans weren't keen on the idea of living rulers being gods, and neither were most of the early emperors. Augustus (27 BC–AD 14) had to accept being worshipped in Eastern provinces because that was what the locals were used to. Tiberius wouldn't put up with it at any price. Of course, some emperors (like Elagabalus; see Chapter 19) did fancy themselves as living gods, but they usually paid for it with their lives. It's doubtful if many people seriously believed the emperor was a god, but the only ones who had a real problem with it were the Christians.

However, even Emperors like Augustus found a neat way of being associated with gods but without actually claiming to be one (until after his death). The central myth of Rome's destiny was that Aeneas was the son of Venus (see Chapter 10 for the myth surrounding the founding of Rome), one of the pantheon of classical gods. This didn't mean that her supposed descendants, the *gens* Iulus, the family of Julius Caesar, were gods. But being descended from a goddess was a thoroughly handy association and the emperors made the most of it.

This was made even more effective by making emperors into gods when they died (a process called *apotheosis,* 'to make a god of'). Cults were established in their names, like the Divus Vespasianus ('the Divine Vespasian'). What emerged for living emperors was a sort of compromise. The son of a dead emperor was thus the son of a god, and people, mainly soldiers and officials, made public displays of loyalty to the *numen* ('spirit') of the emperor and the *Domus Divina* ('the Divine Imperial House'). It was a way of treating a living emperor as if he had a kind of parallel existence as a god.

Integrating Gods from Elsewhere

The Romans were extraordinarily tolerant of religions, because they believed all gods had power, and the Romans wanted the gods to work for them and not their enemies. So they adopted cults from all over the Empire and beyond, and combined them with their own gods.

Joining Roman gods to foreign gods: Conflation

One of the reasons the Romans managed to persuade so many people that being part of the Roman Empire was a good thing was because they generally didn't try to destroy the religions of the people they came across. There were exceptions, the Jews and Christians among them, but in those situations, the problem for the Romans was mainly political, not religious.

The Romans were particularly good at creating combination-gods out of Roman ones and local ones, a process called conflation (from the Latin *conflatum,* 'a mixing together'). These are some examples:

✔ In Germany, the Romans came across a local healing god called Lenus. They conflated him with Mars at Trier and created the healing cult centre of Lenus-Mars.

✔ A Celtic god of healing called Grannus was conflated with Apollo to make Apollo-Grannus, who was worshipped in lots of places.

✔ The Ptolemaic pharaohs of Egypt joined the cults of Osiris and Apis and created Serapis, an underworld god who could perform miracles and heal people. The Romans liked Serapis – the Emperors Septimius Severus (193–211) and Caracalla (211–217) were very keen on him.

Provincials who brought their own gods with them when they joined the army or moved around the Empire were free to worship them as they pleased. That's how a German auxiliary army unit of Suebians brought their wildly-named goddess Garmangabis with them to Britain.

These are only a few examples, but you get the picture. There can't be many other times in human history when religious freedom was practised at this level.

Curiouser and curiouser: Mystery cults

Despite the vast array of gods available to the average Roman, whether he lived in Rome or in a remote part of Gaul or Syria, it seems that for many people, something was lacking. These people turned to the so-called 'mystery' cults which usually had secret rites, were only open to people who had qualified in some way through initiation, and which usually offered some sort of rebirth. The mystery cults usually came from the Eastern provinces and found their way round the Roman Empire thanks to the vast trading network and through soldiers posted to different destinations.

One of the most famous records of an initiation ceremony is the series of paintings on the walls of the Villa of the Mysteries outside Pompeii. The paintings concern a cult of Bacchus and involve ecstasy, flagellation, terror, and the triumph of overcoming the ordeals to join the sect, but little is known of their true significance. You can see the paintings there today.

In their own way, some of these cults challenged Roman religious tolerance. These are some of them, but you can also look at Chapter 19 and read about the Emperor Elagabalus and his sun cult.

The cult of Isis

Ancient Egypt was a source of endless fascination to the Romans, especially the gods and goddesses. Isis was closely linked to fertility and rebirth of the land through the annual flooding of the Nile, but her protection of marriage and navigation meant that her appeal became more universal. The cult of Isis reached the Roman port of Pozzuoli in Italy in 105 BC. A Temple of Isis was destroyed at Pompeii in the eruption of AD 79 and can still be seen today. By the third century AD, Isis was at the climax of her Roman popularity, often shown nursing her infant son Horus on her knee – a potent image taken over by the Christians. The furthest place Isis turned up in was London, and it's an amazing comment on the cosmopolitan Roman world that an ancient Egyptian goddess could be worshipped so far from her spiritual home.

The cult of Cybele

The cult of Cybele (or *Magna Mater,* the 'Great Mother') came from Phrygia in Asia Minor (Turkey). The Romans linked her to Ceres and even incorporated her into the official pantheon of gods. But the weirdest part of the cult was her male followers. Cybele's lover Atys had been unfaithful to her. Thoroughly ashamed of himself, Atys castrated himself as a punishment. So fanatical worshippers of Cybele castrated themselves, too. Even the normally tolerant Roman state found the frenzied carryings-on, including rowdy parades to the sound of cymbals and raucous horns and arm-slashing, too much. So laws were brought in to prevent public disorder.

The cult of Mithras

The men-only Persian cult of Mithras was extremely popular amongst soldiers and traders, and most Mithraic temples have been found at ports or near forts. Followers, who had to go through painful initiation ceremonies, believed Mithras had been engaged in a fight to the death with a bull created at the dawn of time. Mithras killed the bull in a cave, thus releasing the blood that contained the essence of life.

Mithraic temples had no windows in order to recreate the mystery and symbolism of the original cave. The climax of the ceremony was a ritual meal. Theatrical props, like perforated altars through which lamps cast eerie pools of light and shadow across the congregation, enhanced the sense of being in a special place.

The tolerance of pain, the significance of bloodshed as a means to eternal life, and Mithraic hymns appalled the Christians, who spotted the similarity with some of their own beliefs. In fact, Christians were the ones most likely to attack Mithraic temples that, like churches, had a nave and aisles.

The Religion that Refused to Be Assimilated: Christianity

Theoretically, Christianity was just another of the mystery cults because in its early form, and as far as the Romans were concerned, it was just another strange cult from the East that promised eternal life to believers. In fact, until Christianity became the state religion, for many Romans the idea of Christ as *another* god to add to the list of the ones they already worshipped was a perfectly good one. The emperor Severus Alexander (222–235) kept a collection of statues of gods of all types, even the Christian God, in his apartment and worshipped them all. So it's not surprising that some finds of early Christian worship show people apparently worshipping Christ in the old pagan way of making vows and leaving gifts (see the section 'Cutting a Deal: Roman Religion' at the beginning of this chapter).

But Christianity was different in key ways from the other religions that the Romans assimilated:

✔ It was open to anyone and everyone, any time and any place. This wasn't a problem for the Romans, but the next point was.

✔ Believers had to reject all other gods. If you've read this chapter up to this point, you'll realise this flew in the face of the general Roman attitude to religion.

The Roman government, therefore, got very suspicious of the Christians.

Problems with Christianity

All sorts of confused stories circulated among the Romans. When Christians consumed the bread and wine, treating them as symbolic representations of the body and blood of Christ, the word got out that they were literally practising some sort of cannibalism. Christians also made handy scapegoats for Nero (54–68) when he wanted someone to blame for the Great Fire of Rome (Chapter 16). Tacitus called Christianity a 'pernicious superstition' and said Christians were 'loathed for their vices'.

The Romans were also bewildered by the most committed followers of a cult who refused even to pay lip service to state pagan cults. Pliny the Younger, while Governor of Bithynia and Pontus under Trajan (98–117), found himself having to investigate Christians who refused to deny their beliefs and also refused to make offerings to pagan gods and to a statue of Trajan. Some actually did cave in and make the pagan offerings, but the rest refused. Pliny ordered two women deacons to be tortured to find out more, as he was very worried by Christianity's popularity. Trajan wrote to Pliny and told him not to hunt out Christians, to ignore anonymous informers, and only to punish Christians if he had to. In other words, Trajan was quite keen on the softly-softly approach.

Chi (X) and Rho (P) are the first two Greek letters of the Greek form of Christ: Χριστοζ. The two letters were placed over one another to create a symbol used by Christians on church plates, wall-paintings, and mosaics, and was also placed on coins by Christian emperors.

Persecutions

Over the next two centuries, Christianity steadily grew in popularity. Dissatisfaction with the traditional gods grew as people came to believe that all their sacrifices at temples weren't having any effect. As the Romans grew wealthier, people looked around for something with more meaning. You can see the same effect today, with people hunting around for something to believe in. Then there were the gradually increasing troubles on the frontiers. It didn't look as if the Roman system could hold up. Christianity promised a new life of eternal bliss in another world after death. It looked very attractive – except that, for the Roman state, it looked like a direct challenge to imperial authority.

Major persecutions were organised by Trajan Decius (249–251), Diocletian (284–305), and Maximian (286–305), but had been going on since Nero's time. Even Marcus Aurelius (161–180), the philosopher Emperor, authorised a persecution in 177. Persecutions took on various forms, including torture to make people give Christianity up, executions of refuseniks, confiscation of church property, banning bishops from meeting, and burning of scriptures. The persecutions had some success because some people certainly *apostatised* (gave up Christianity), but part of Christian teaching was being prepared to suffer like Christ. So the persecutors actually gave some Christians a reason to show how Christian they were by suffering under the persecution. There was even an element of competition, with Christian teachers recounting with admiration how much torture and cruelty some people had withstood without apostatising.

Tolerance and turning tables

A big change came under Constantine I (307–337). Constantine not only believed that the Christian God had been behind his own success, but he also spotted the huge political advantages of using Christianity to hold the Empire together. (You can find more about all this, and the way Christianity took hold in the Empire in Chapters 20 and 21.)

Once Christianity became legal, the church worked tirelessly to get the Romans to abandon their old customs. But as part of the job involved taking over old pagan shrines and replacing them with churches, it was tough to persuade everyone. Plenty of people decided to hedge their bets. The earliest collection of Christian silver comes from Water Newton in Cambridgeshire, England. Although covered with Chi-Rho symbols, the items include plaques exactly like those pinned to temple walls by pagans.

But paganism, or anything that smacked of it, was gradually outlawed. Even mummification in Egypt was banned. Christianity took complete hold, but if you read Chapter 21 you can see how divisions in the church rocked the Roman world to its foundations from the fourth century onwards.

Christian churches in the Roman world

Unlike pagans who worshipped their gods in specific places like shrines, Christians could worship anywhere so long as they had a priest to officiate. So early Christians often used to gather in rooms in private houses, known as house churches. One of the few to leave any traces was installed in the Roman villa at Lullingstone in Kent, England in the late fourth century. A series of rooms painted with Christian symbols served for worship and can be seen in the British Museum today. Once Christianity was legalised, the basilican hall design with its nave and aisles was used, creating the church form we know today. These were already being built in Rome by the early fourth century. Constantine (307–337) built the first Basilica of St Peter's (demolished by 1612). The best-preserved original, big Roman church is Santa Maria Maggiore, built in 366.

Burning and Burying: The Roman Way of Death

Death and burial is an appropriate way to end this chapter. The Romans lived full and extraordinary lives. It's often through the records of their lifetimes on their graves that we find out about who the Romans were and what they did. They're poignant reminders that this whole book is about real people who lived real lives. Even if we can't possibly make a direct link now, because the records don't exist, many of us can surely count them amongst our remote ancestors.

Roman afterlife: The Underworld

The spirits *(manes)* of the dead were thought by some to live in the Underworld, though the Romans also had an idea of a kind of heavenly underworld, which they called *Elysium.* (It's not very clear, and apparently the Romans weren't much clearer themselves.) According to the myth, the Underworld was ruled over by Pluto (Greek: Hades), also known as Dis, and his wife Persephone (Greek: Proserpina). To reach the Underworld, the dead were ferried across the river Styx by Charon.

Dis comes from *Dives,* 'riches', and even Pluto comes from the Greek *plouton* for rich. No-one knows why the king of the Underworld was associated with riches, unless it means the underground riches of minerals and the soil.

Cemeteries and graves

Roman funerals either involved cremation or burial of the body *(inhumation).* Cremations tended to be earlier, but burial became more and more common. By the third century AD, it was the standard practice.

Cremation

Cremations involved burning the body on a pyre, together with personal possessions, either where the body was to be buried or in a special part of the cemetery. The ashes were packed into pottery jars, glass bottles, lead urns, wooden boxes, or even just cloth. Depending on how rich the dead person was, grave goods went in, too – usually metal, glass, or pottery vessels containing food and drink for the journey to the afterlife, and coins to pay the ferryman Charon for the trip to the Underworld.

Burial (inhumation)

Inhumation involved burying the whole body. The poorest people were buried in shrouds or nothing at all, while the wealthiest could afford lead coffins or even extravagantly carved marble *sarcophagi* (large coffins; the word means 'flesh-devouring'). Burial had become the norm by the fourth century when the Roman Empire went Christian, and didn't usually involve grave goods because that was considered a pagan custom – but plenty of Christians had them anyway. Sometimes people tried to preserve the bodies by packing them with *gypsum* (calcium sulphate) to dry the body out, or in a few cases even mummifying the bodies Egyptian-style (which was still going on in Roman Egypt until it was banned in the late fourth century, even though it wasn't done anything like as well as in Ancient Egyptian times).

Cemeteries and tombs

By law, Romans had to be buried beyond a free zone *(pomerium)* outside the settled area. It was simply a matter of hygiene though; as Roman towns grew they were often built over old cemeteries. Cemeteries usually clustered along the side of roads as they exited a town. The best visible examples today are at Rome, Ostia (see the section, 'Worshipping ancestors and burial feasts', later in this chapter), and Pompeii. On opposite sides of Roman roads at these places you can still walk down roads through the city gates and past tombs of all sorts of different shapes and sizes.

Rich people could afford elaborate architectural structures with statues or carvings of the deceased, together with detailed inscriptions that tell us the names of the people buried there, how old they were, perhaps what they did, and where they came from. Poor people were lucky to have their cremated remains stuffed into an amphora buried alongside. But all tended to bury their dead in family groups unless they belonged to a guild *(collegium)*, which arranged for the burial of its members. It was common for freedmen to take care of their former master's burial.

One of the most curious tombs at Rome is the marble-faced Pyramid of Gaius Cestius, built as his tomb in 12 BC by his slaves, who were freed in his will. It's 35 metres (114 feet) high and 79 metres (260 feet) wide, and was a copy of ancient Egyptian pyramids, which had excited his imagination when he lived there for a while. It was built originally outside Rome but was incorporated into the walls built by Aurelian (AD 270–275).

Catacombs

Catacombs were subterranean cemeteries made up of multistorey tunnels with niches, chapels, and chambers cut into the side walls for burials. They became especially popular amongst Christians at Rome. The Sant'Agnese catacombs of Rome have 800 metres (half a mile) of tunnels and 8,500 tombs alone, but Rome's catacombs must originally have run into hundreds of miles.

Inscriptions on tombs

Roman tombstone inscriptions were usually formulaic and included a lot of abbreviations as well as the person's name. Not everyone could afford one, but those who could have left invaluable records for us to study. Here's a few of the abbreviations:

- ✔ **DM – *Dis Manibus*:** 'To the Spirits of the Departed'

- ✔ **HSE – *Hic situs est*:** 'Is buried here'

- ✔ **HC – *Heres curavit*:** 'His/her heir took care (of the burial)'

- ✔ **FC – *Faciendum curavit*:** 'Took care of making (the tomb)'

- ✔ **V – *Vixit*:** 'Lived' (usually followed by a number, reading, for example, 'lived 29 years')

There's a tombstone of a woman called Fasiria at the city of Makhtar in what is now Tunisia in North Africa. The Christian Chi-Rho symbol is clearly carved on the stone, but so also is the pagan DM for *Dis Manibus* ('To the Spirits of the Departed'), suggesting she believed in the Christian God but wasn't prepared to risk annoying the pagan gods.

Worshipping ancestors and burial feasts

Venerating ancestors was an important part of Roman life. In the home, the family ancestors were commemorated with busts (see also *Ius Imaginum* in Chapter 3). But the Romans also made visits to graves to hold ceremonies in which they reinforced their connection with their ancestors.

Venerating and commemorating the dead was an essential part of Roman life. Two of the biggest monuments in Rome today are the Mausoleum of Augustus and the Mausoleum of the Antonines (built by Hadrian and now the Castel Sant'Angelo).

The *Parentalia* (burial feast) was held on 13–21 February. Out of respect to the dead, temples were shut, and marriages were banned. Families got together and set off for the tombs of their ancestors outside the town walls and had private feasts. The deceased were included, too: food and drink were poured down tubes to underground burials or taken into over-ground vaults to the burials there. On the last day, there was a public ceremony. The *Rosalia* was held on 10 May when Romans decorated tombs with roses, then in full bloom.

One of the best-preserved Roman cemeteries is close to the ruins of Ostia, the ancient port of Rome, at a place called Isola Sacra ('sacred island') which is incredible because now it's only about a mile from Rome's main Fiumcino airport. It's a cluster of intact tombs, complete with dedicatory inscriptions to the deceased who once lived and worked at Ostia. You can go into the tombs and see the niches in the walls where the cremated remains of family members were stored. Outside, some the owners built copies of dining room couches for the feasts so that the family could lie down to eat with their ancestors, just like at home.

Part III
The Rise of Rome

The 5th Wave   By Rich Tennant

"Shortly after Romulus arrived, they started showing up claiming to be a relative."

In this part . . .

Imagine you live in a small village in the English countryside, with a just a couple of hundred inhabitants, a church, and maybe a pub. Or imagine you live in a small town in Wyoming with a gas station and a few shops and houses. Now imagine that same place becoming the centre of the known universe. That's what happened to Rome over the course of several centuries. The Romans always looked back fondly to those times, when their great city was just a village in and around seven small hills on the east bank of the river they called the Tiber.

Needless to say, so much time had passed that the Romans had really very little idea of the truth. But they clung to the idea that this rural past contained the secret of Rome's success. They believed that it was in Rome: the village where toil, valour, and honour had proved that the Romans were destined to rule the known world. This part of the book is about the first 600 years that made Rome what it was and took it to the brink of world domination.

Chapter 10

Kings? No, Maybe Not – Republicans

• •

In This Chapter

▶ Rome's mythical origins

▶ The establishment of the Republic

▶ The first written laws

▶ The struggle between the patricians and the plebs

• •

For a civilisation that was built around a republican system of law and government, Rome's earliest days are pretty foggy, and making sense of the first few decades is difficult. The only historical sources we have were written down much later, and the historians concerned struggled to find detailed information. But what emerged was something that the Romans would spend the rest of their days trying to prevent ever happening again: a monarchy.

Yes, that's right. Rome, the great republican state of the ancient world, had kings to begin with. But throwing the kings out for the various misdemeanours changed everything. What emerged was a class war, culminating in the rights of ordinary people (known as the *plebs*) and the first written law code in Roman history. It set the pace for the shape of things to come.

The Founding of Rome

The Romans didn't start writing history as soon as the city was founded. It wasn't until a long time afterwards that they became interested in who they were and where they'd come from. Roman historians had to hunt back through what few early records survived, and they pieced together a story that was very largely based on myth. Its most important part was linking the Romans all the way back to the gods, through the legendary hero Aeneas.

The myth

The great Roman legend about the founding of Rome goes back to the Trojan War, set in Greek Mycenaean times.

Aeneas was the mythical son of a Trojan leader called Anchises and the goddess Venus (Aphrodite is her equal in Greek mythology), and belonged to a junior branch of the Trojan royal family. According to prophecy, Aeneas would one day rule the Trojans and, according to Homer's *Iliad* (an epic poem recounting the fall of Troy), he was the only Trojan with anything to look forward to after the city was sacked by the Greeks.

After Troy fell to the Greeks, Aeneas escaped, wandered around in search of his destiny, and had grand adventures. When he finally arrived in Italy, Aeneas was greeted by King Latinus who allowed Aeneas to marry his daughter Lavinia. Aeneas founded a city called Lavinium which later became head of the Latin League, multiple cities, other than Rome, in the Latium region (see Chapter 11 for more information on the Latin League).

Aeneas's son Ascanius (who, according to one legend came with Aeneas to Italy after the fall of Troy, and in another was born after Aeneas married Lavinia) succeeded Aeneas and founded the city of Alba Longa. (Ascanius was also known as Iulus, and the family of that name claimed descent from him and thus Venus. The most famous claimant was none other than Julius Caesar, so you can see just how potent this myth was.)

Later in Alba Longa, 12 kings succeeded Aeneas's son Ascanius/Iulus. The twelfth was called Numitor, who was deposed by his brother Amulius. To make sure that Numitor's daughter Rhea Silvia wouldn't challenge him, Amulius made her into a Vestal Virgin, one of the select virgin priestesses whose main role was to guard Vesta's undying fire (which signified the permanence of Rome; Vesta was the goddess of the hearth fire). But Amulius hadn't reckoned with the god Mars, who impregnated Rhea. Rhea gave birth to the twins Romulus and Remus, who Amulius, after discovering their existence, flung into the river Tiber.

The twins were saved and suckled by a she-wolf and then brought up by a herdsman. The boys grew up to be warriors, restored their grandfather Numitor to the throne, and, in 753 BC, founded Rome. They built walls around Rome. Remus leaped over the walls, enraging his brother, who killed him. Eventually Romulus disappeared, only to reappear as the god Quirinus, a little-known ancient god who gave his name to Rome's Quirinal Hill and was once one of Rome's three principal gods along with Jupiter and Mars (he had similar powers to Mars).

How did a date as specific as 753 BC ever get assigned as the year that Rome was founded? Answer: A scholar called Marcus Terentius Varro worked back from his own time, using records, historical facts, and legend and decided that 753 BC was the date of Rome's founding. For the rest of Rome's history, 753 BC was the date from which the city's history was counted. It's a bit like Archbishop James Ussher in the seventeenth century who added up everything in the Bible and decided the world was created in 4004 BC.

The true story

Like everywhere in Europe, human history in Italy stretches back over hundreds of thousands of years, deep into the Stone Age. For millennia, early man made use of stone tools in a period called the *Palaeolithic* (the 'Old Stone Age'), a time when communities tended to move about according to the season and available resources. But around 5000 BC – which is a very approximate date – the *Neolithic* ('New Stone Age') began to spread throughout Europe. Unlike the hunter-gatherer Palaeolithic, the people of the Neolithic started establishing farms and stayed put instead of wandering about hunting.

Neolithic farmers started appearing in Italy by around 5000 BC. By about 1800 BC, some of these early Italians were making and using bronze – the Bronze Age. Meanwhile, Egypt's civilisation had already been in existence for more than a thousand years. In fact, Italy was distinctly behind the times. The Bronze Age Greeks, who had strongholds at places like Mycenae and Tiryns in Greece, were already exploring and trading around the Mediterranean. Some of these Greeks had even reached Italy and its surrounding islands.

Around 1000 BC came the Iron Age. Iron, being much stronger than bronze, was the greatest technological discovery of the era. It transformed a society's military power and made all sorts of tools possible. Iron meant far stronger weapons and equipment. Iron shovels and ploughshares lasted longer and were far more effective. Villanova, a key site in Italy, gave its name to the new culture that was making use of iron.

Early Rome: Hills with huts, and a very big sewer

Rome is famous for being on seven hills close to the river Tiber (see Figure 10-1). Those hills were called:

- ✔ Capitoline
- ✔ Palatine

- Aventine
- Esquiline
- Quirinal
- Viminal
- Caelius

Around at least 1000 BC, little farmsteads, built of *wattle and daub,* were built on some of the hills: the Palatine, Esquiline, Quirinal and Caelius. (Wattle and daub is a simple and effective way to build houses – it's a timber frame with a latticework of twigs all covered with a mixture of mud and straw.) These were no more than scattered clusters of thatched huts, just tiny villages.

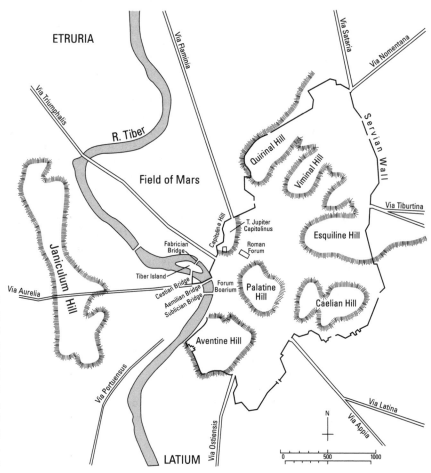

Figure 10-1:
This map shows the hills of Rome and the Servian Walls, probably built about 390 BC.

Some huts and cemeteries have been excavated, showing that by the eighth century BC the early Romans were trading with other places like Etruria and Greece, and were making their own pottery, figurines, and weapons. They grew crops like wheat and barley, raised goats and pigs, and hunted. The later Romans looked back to these simple farming times and idealised it as an era when their virtues of self-discipline, hard work, and organisation were born, and contrasted it with the riches, decadence, and indulgence of days of the Roman Empire (refer to Chapter 4 for more information on the significance of Roman myth to its rural past).

Cemeteries were dug in the marshy valleys, especially in the one that would later become the Roman Forum. The population seems to have done well because the settlements got bigger, and room soon ran out on the hills. So the marshy valleys were drained, and the settlements grew down the slopes and started to merge into one another during the seventh century BC. This was when something like a city, the earliest Rome, started to take shape.

The Romans seem to have had a folk memory of the time when Rome grew out of a collection of villages, preserved in a religious festival in which the priests and Vestal Virgins had a procession to visit shrines in the four regions of the city: the Palatine, Esquiline, Quirinal and Caelius.

During the time of the Roman kings (see the section 'The Magnificent Eight: The Kings (753–535 BC)', later in the chapter), Rome was a very primitive settlement by later standards and controlled an area of only about 150 square kilometres (60 square miles). But Rome was the most powerful state in Latium. The kings brought centralised government and organisation. Under their rule, Rome began to evolve from a cluster of villages into a city with defences, services like sewage, and religious precincts that helped foster a sense of identity.

Rome's neighbours

It's very important to remember that Rome and her inhabitants made up only one settlement of many in this part of Italy (see Figure 10-2). Some were her allies, some her rivals. Dominating this area was Rome's first step on the path to world domination.

Aequians

The ferocious Aequians lived north-east of Rome and allied themselves with the Volscians. Little is known about them because their attempts at expanding were thwarted in 431 BC. A further attempt at expanding led Rome to practically exterminate them in 304 BC.

Figure 10-2:
Rome
with her
immediate
neighbours.

Etruscans

Rome's main early rivals for control of the land between the rivers Tiber and Arno, the Etruscans lived in Tuscany and Umbria, but in the late seventh century BC, their pottery started turning up in Rome, along with their style of housing, which was more robust and had tiled roofs rather than the thatched huts the Romans had been building.

The Etruscans remain obscure because no-one has ever been able to make out more than a little of their language, which is unrelated to all the main known groups, though some words survived into Latin. But the later Roman historians recorded what they could of this period. The incredible thing is that their murky version of this remote period does seem to match the archaeology. In the end, Etruscan power was squeezed by the Gaulish Celts to the north, and Rome and the Samnites to the south. The Etruscans had considerable influence on Roman culture. The major Roman goddess Minerva (see Chapter 9) was once an Etruscan deity.

Sabines

The Sabines lived in villages in the Apennine hills to the north-east of Rome. No-one knows where they came from, but they spoke an ancient language called Oscan. Until 449 BC, they were constantly fighting the Romans, even though they had no central leadership, but it's plain from aspects of their religious belief that they had a strong influence on Roman culture. The ancient god Quirinus (see the earlier section 'The myth') was originally a Sabine deity.

Samnites

The Samnites lived in the Appenine hills well to the south of Rome. They were made up of four tribes who formed a confederation to fight their enemies. In the fourth century BC, they became important rivals when Roman power started spreading south, leading to the three Samnite Wars. Samnium stood firm against Rome and wasn't totally defeated until the early first century BC in the Social War. Pompeii is the most famous Samnite city, becoming a Roman colony in 80 BC.

Volscians

By 500 BC, the Volscians had come out of central Italy and settled south-east of Rome. They fought against Roman expansion but hadn't reckoned on Rome's allies, who defeated them in 431 BC. Not much is known about their culture because, once they had been conquered, they comprehensively adopted Roman ways.

The Magnificent Eight: The Kings (753–535 BC)

Early Rome was ruled by kings. Their story is part myth and part true – the challenge is working out which is which. The history of Rome starts off with myth but soon turns into fact, so now you have the opportunity to meet those kings, real or mythical. Three of the first four kings were Latins (with one Sabine), but the last three were Etruscans. The Etruscan kings had a tremendous effect on early Roman culture, the city's infrastructure, and Rome's early power.

Rome's kings weren't part of a hereditary monarchy, like most lines of monarchs in world history were. Rome's kings were mostly elected or chosen by the Roman people. Incidentally, don't take the dates that follow as hard fact. They're mostly approximations, at best.

Romulus (753–716 BC)

Romulus (who founded Rome along with his twin brother Remus) was the surviving grandson of Numitor. Roman tradition credited Romulus with creating various great Roman traditions such as the Senate, which was just a myth that gave the Senate an authority founded in the city's origins.

The end of Romulus

Romulus's end is another myth, which goes as follows: A storm blew up while he was sacrificing by the river, and all the people ran for shelter. Although the senators stayed with Romulus, he somehow disappeared. Only two possibilities existed regarding his disappearance, and no-one knew which one actually occurred. Either Romulus had been killed by the senators who had then cut him up and carried off the pieces hidden under their clothing, or else the gods had gathered him up to heaven.

The big story of Romulus's reign was the rape of the Sabine women. Romulus is said to have invited a neighbouring tribe called the Sabines to share in the celebrations of the god Consus (who took care of grain storage). When the Sabines turned up, the Romans stole the Sabine women (the word used was *rapere,* 'to seize'; it doesn't mean 'rape'). The Sabines attacked Rome in revenge and seized the Capitoline Hill. The Sabine women then stepped in to prevent further bloodshed, and the peace that was negotiated made the Romans and Sabines all one people with Romulus ruling jointly with the Sabine king Tatius.

The Sabine story is a myth, but because the Romans adopted Sabine words and gods, there may be some underlying truth about the Sabines and Romans coming together.

Numa Pompilius (715–673 BC)

Numa Pompilius is an even more shadowy figure than Romulus. The Sabines in Rome said it was their turn for a king, which the Romans agreed to, so long as they were allowed to choose the candidate. Numa, son of a Sabine king called Tatius, had to be persuaded to become king but eventually agreed. He was said to have set up Rome's religious cults and priests. He was also said to have invented a 12-month calendar, rather than the 10-month one, and set up Rome's boundaries. But like the story about Romulus inventing the Senate, these stories are probably just ways of firmly setting Roman customs in the most ancient tradition they could think up.

Numa founded the temple of the two-faced god Janus, who had power over beginnings and doorways. The temple's doors were open during war and closed during peace, harking back to a time when a gate *(ianua)* was opened for the army to march out to war. In the years AD 65–7 the emperor Nero (see Chapter 16) issued coins showing the temple with closed doors to commemorate a rare time of peace.

The Vestal Virgins

Numa was said to have brought the Vestal Virgins from Alba Longa to Rome. The Vestal Virgins were women priests who tended the sacred fire of Vesta, goddess of the hearth fire. The state paid for their welfare, and they lived in the Hall of Vesta near the Forum. Originally there were two, then four, and finally six. Each virgin spent 30 years in service: 10 years learning religious rituals, 10 years performing the rituals, and 10 years teaching them to the next generation. The Vestal Virgins were ruthlessly punished by being buried alive in unmarked graves if they lost their virginity (which was particularly unfair when they were raped).

Tullus Hostilius (673–641 BC)

Tullus Hostilius was chosen from the Latins. He had to fight off an invasion by the Alba Longans and destroyed Alba Longa as a punishment. He was believed to have built the Senate house – called the Curia Hostilia – in Rome. Because this Curia Hostilia house actually existed, it's likely that Hostilius was a real person (remember, distinguishing myth from history isn't clear-cut with these early kings). What certainly did happen is that Alba Longan families moved to Rome. Amongst them were the members of the Iulus clan, the ancestors of Julius Caesar's family, who claimed descent from Aeneas's son Ascanius (see the earlier section 'The myth').

Ancus Marcius (641–616 BC)

Like Tullus Hostilius, Ancus Marcius probably was a historical personality. He is said to have taken control of salt pans south of the Tiber. Marcius may have built the first bridge over the river into Rome, called the Pons Sublicius – the name means the 'wooden-piled bridge', which has an 'early' sound to it. He was also said to have built Rome's first aqueduct and founded Rome's port at Ostia. The important thing is that Ancus Marcius increased the control Rome had over territory beyond the city.

Tarquinius Priscus (616–579 BC)

This king, also known as 'Tarquin the Elder', was an Etruscan from the city of Tarquinii, 56 miles north of Rome. He was a close friend of Ancus Marcius, and had an excellent reputation for honesty, but when Marcius died, Tarquin persuaded the dead king's sons to go hunting. While they were out of town, he presented himself as a candidate for the kingship, egged on by his ambitious wife Tanaquil. Because Tarquin was so well thought of as an honest man, he got the job.

How the Romans declared war

Ancus Marcius is credited with Rome's system for declaring war. Messengers were sent to Rome's enemy to explain what Rome was angry about and to tell the enemy what compensation Rome wanted. If Rome had to declare war, specialist priests called Fetiales threw a single spear into the enemy's territory (or into a part of the Roman Forum symbolically treated as Roman territory) before command of the army was given to a general. The idea behind this process was to make sure that the gods would back the Romans, by claiming that war had been declared because the Romans had been done an injustice or an injury by their enemies first. The Fetiales priests also approved treaties at the end of war.

Tarquin introduced a proper drainage system in Rome as well as games, both of which were Etruscan interests. He was so successful that Ancius Marcius's sons were furious with jealousy. Knowing that Tarquin's children presented a dynastic threat, Marcius's sons had Tarquin murdered.

Servius Tullius (579–535 BC)

Servius was Tarquin's son-in-law and possibly even once his slave, depending on which version of the story you read. He married Tarquin's daughter, and when Tarquin was murdered, the widowed and ever-pushy Tanaquil made sure Servius became king next. What's certainly true is that his name was *plebeian* (lower-class) and is very similar to *servus* ('slave') – which means he was almost certainly a real person. A mythical king would have had a *patrician* (upper-class) name (refer to Chapter 2 for details on Roman class structure). Servius is said to have made big changes:

- ✔ He introduced a census (a national register of the population) and divided the people of Rome and the countryside into new tribes according to where they lived, rather than by what family they belonged to or how much property they had. This system automatically integrated newcomers. Eighty thousand Roman citizens who could bear arms were counted in the census; those who couldn't, including all women and children, weren't included. To create the census, two censors were appointed, usually chosen from former consuls, by the *Comitia Centuriata* (a political assembly).

- ✔ He assessed liability for military service according to wealth by dividing landholders into classes. Each class was divided into *centuries* (groups of 100 men). Men of the richest class were given funds to buy and keep a horse, while the poorest had literally no more than sticks and stones and served as the infantry.

- ✔ His new military classes were the basis of the Comitia Centuriata, in which each century submitted the majority vote of its members. The votes of the centuries from the highest class counted the most, but they also had to do most of the fighting.

- ✔ He was said to have built Rome's earliest surviving walls (although, in reality, these came after the invasion by the Gauls in 390 BC).

- ✔ He began Rome's worship of Diana, equated with Artemis, the Greek goddess of the moon, hunting, and fertility.

Whether or not Servius Tullius personally created the social hierarchy for Roman society, there's no doubt that that's what emerged from this period. The Comitia Centuriata gave the richest men the upper hand because their votes took precedence, but it also gave the poorest men a voice, too. But having a voice wasn't enough. The property-owning Roman upper classes now had a clearer idea of their power, and before long they seized their opportunity and got rid of the Etruscan kings.

Tarquinius Superbus (535–509 BC)

Tarquinius Superbus ('Tarquin the Proud') was married to Servius Tullius's ambitious daughter Tullia. Tullia persuaded her husband to kill Servius, who was now an old man. Tarquin accused Servius of being a trumped-up slave and threw him out of the Senate into the street, where he was killed. As Servius was popular, this was not a good start for Tarquin, who nevertheless had two long-lasting achievements:

- ✔ He built the Temple of Capitoline Jupiter on the Capitoline Hill. This became the central state cult of the Roman Empire.

- ✔ He built Rome's biggest sewer, the Cloaca Maxima ('Great Sewer'), which still exists today, though it wasn't covered over until *c.* 390 BC.

Tarquinius was the last King of Rome and for the rest of Rome's history, the Romans fell over themselves to prevent anybody else calling himself king.

The benefits of the Etruscan kings

The kings of Rome, regardless of whether they were mythical or real, brought in some really important changes. Rome's power originally extended over only about 60 square miles in Latium. By the end of Tarquinius Superbus's reign, Rome's power was more like six times as much. The last three Etruscan kings had done a huge amount to set Rome up for the future. They introduced political and military reforms that had started to make Rome work like clockwork.

Military reforms brought in by Servius Tullius – assessing every Roman's liability for military service according to his personal financial resources, for example – meant that the state could make the most of the resources at its disposal. The drainage of the marshy valleys, especially the one that would become the Forum, made it possible for a collection of settlements on hills to grow into a city.

The Etruscans also brought in valuable skills, such as metal-working, ceramics, and carpentry, that made trade possible. The organisation of state cults and the building of temples gave the state a spiritual identity and a sense of religious destiny. Rome was becoming known as a new force in the Mediterranean world. It's obvious from the battles with Alba Longa (see the section 'Tullus Hostilius', earlier in this chapter) that, as Rome started to flex its muscles, it would run into conflict with its neighbours.

You may get the impression that Rome was on some sort of conveyor belt to world domination and that the Etruscan kings set it in motion. In reality, by the end of the sixth century BC, Rome was becoming important, but it was no more important than anywhere else. And it was a good deal less important than some of the great cities of Greece, such as Athens, Corinth, and Sparta. At this point in its history, Rome could just as easily have disappeared without trace.

The Birth of the Roman Republic

Eventually, the Romans had had enough of being ruled by Etruscans. Tarquinius Superbus was considered to be the last word in tyranny, and the Romans decided he had to go. The traditional story is that the Rape of Lucretia was the catalyst.

The story goes like this: Sextus, son of Tarquinius Superbus, was on a campaign with other young nobles, who decided to head home and see whether their wives were behaving properly. All the wives except Lucretia, wife of Sextus's cousin, Tarquinius Collatinus, were living it up. However, Sextus was overwhelmed with desire for Lucretia. When he was round for dinner at a later date, he told Lucretia she had to sleep with him or he would rape her and arrange things to look as though she had betrayed her husband by sleeping with the slaves. Lucretia gave in but told her husband. He forgave her, but in her shame she committed suicide. The rape of Lucretia provoked total outrage amongst the Roman nobles. A conspiracy was organised by Lucius Junius Brutus (c. 545–509 BC), Tarquinius Superbus's nephew. Sextus fled but was killed, and Tarquinius Superbus was ousted from the throne.

There's no way of knowing whether any of this story is true, but it's pretty clear that Etruscan influence did start to decline, even though the decline didn't happen quickly. What's more, the Etruscans didn't give up that easily, though the story of what came next (see Chapter 11) is likely to be mostly myth.

Lucius Junius Brutus

Lucius Junius Brutus was a real toughie and the traditional founder of the Roman Republic. He was unbending and ruthlessly severe, with good reason. Tarquinius Superbus was his uncle, but he killed Brutus's father and older brother so that he could steal the family estate. Brutus got his name because everyone thought he was stupid – but it was just an act so that he could survive. Not surprisingly, Brutus loathed the kings, and he even killed his own sons for trying to have the kings reinstated. Brutus was killed in a battle between the Romans and the Tarquins in 509 BC when Tarquinius Superbus's Etrsucan allies, led by Tarquinius's son Arruns, marched on Rome.

The new constitution

With no kings around any longer, a new constitution was needed. No-one knows exactly who was responsible, but Publius Valerius Poplicola (*c.* 560–503 BC), one of the first *Consuls* (powerful magistrates who ruled Rome), went down in Roman history as one of the men involved. The constitution included the following:

- ✔ **The office of king was prohibited.** No man would ever be king of Rome again (until AD 476 anyway – see Chapter 21).

- ✔ **Two senators were to be elected annually as magistrates called *consuls* (though originally called *praetors*) by the Comitia Centuriata to run the state.** The consuls had supreme power over the law or going to war, and both consuls had the power of *veto* (the right to reject the other's decision). There's no easy modern equivalent, but the tradition survives in the way each US state has two senators.

- ✔ **Some of the king's jobs, like chief priest *(pontifex maximus)* were kept on.** The pontifex maximus was in supreme charge of everything to do with Roman religion and ceremony. The closest equivalent today of this position is the Pope or Archbishop of Canterbury.

- ✔ **The constitution allowed for a dictator in times of crisis.** If things were really bad, there was no time for two consuls to fall out over what to do. When that happened a *magister populi* (dictator) was appointed to represent both consuls and to deal with the crisis. A dictator was supposed to resign after six months at the latest.

The constitution had one very important underlying principle: In Rome's Republic no-one – and that meant no-one – was able to have permanent political power. In Part IV, you see what happened when that principle was set aside.

The fasces

The *fasces* were a bundle of rods tied up with cords with an axe in the middle. The *lictors* (assistants to magistrates) carried them. Because the bundle was very strong, the idea was to symbolise the power and unity of Rome – even though individually, the rods could be broken. However, in Rome the axe was never bundled up, a symbol of the right of appeal. The fasces first appeared in the 600s BC. Because the Italian fascists adopted the fasces as their symbol, the fasces gave their name to the fascist parties of the 1920s and 1930s.

Patricians vs. plebs

After Rome had done away with its kings, Roman society was split into two halves: the upper classes, known as the *patricians,* and the lower classes, known as the *plebs.* Great tensions existed between the two classes. Most people were plebs, and they did all the ordinary jobs. When called on, plebeian men had to serve in the army without pay. That could mean falling into debt, which could lead to financial ruin. The patricians, on the other hand, nabbed all the prestigious top jobs, like priests, and the new job of consul. (Refer to Chapter 2 for more about Roman class structure.)

The aristocrats: Consolidating power

The new constitution of the Roman Republic showed how the aristocrats were beginning to organise all the power around themselves. The Comitia Centuriata (the Assembly of the Centuries; refer to Chapter 3 for more about this group), which was made up of all men eligible to fight, may have elected the consuls, but the candidates were chosen by the senators from amongst themselves. There was no chance that a brilliant leader from a poor background was ever going to be a consul.

Also, the Senate was getting more powerful. The Senate itself was originally supposed to be just an advisory body to the kings, but after 509 BC, under the Republic, things changed. For a start, the senators were all members of the noble families. In addition, because the consuls were elected annually, no consul could get enough experience or prestige to intimidate the Senate.

The angry mob

The plebs were not particularly pleased by the new set-up at Rome. With the new constitution, it was becoming plain to them that the patricians were sewing up all the power for themselves. The situation was made worse for a variety of reasons.

FROM PAST TO PRESENT

The Temple of Saturn

The front six columns and part of the pediment of the 496 BC Temple of Saturn still stand in the Roman Forum. They form one of the best-preserved fragments of any building in the Forum, despite their great age. The annual winter festival of the Saturnalia's main celebrations were held here (Chapter 9 discusses Roman religious practices).

First, early Republican Rome plunged into an economic crisis. The clue is in the pottery. Imports of Greek pottery started to decline, but after *c.* 450 BC they nosedived. Various new temples were built between 500–450 BC, such as the Temple of Saturn in 496. But all this building work stopped when the money ran out.

Second, Rome was having trouble with its neighbours. Under the kings, Rome had got its hands on new territory, but that had stopped. Worse, attacks by neighbouring enemies disrupted farming, which led to famines. Special purchases of imported grain had to be made, and land had to be found for starving peasants.

Third, the general crisis was plunging people into debt. Ruinous rates of interest crippled families, and the severest penalty for failing to make repayments under a type of contract called a *nexum* was death. Debtors could try to clear their debts by working for their creditors, but some were sold as slaves.

Needless to say, the plebs spotted that they suffered the most during this crisis. Through the consuls, the patricians were able to impose severe punishments, often as it pleased them.

Conflict of the Orders: A Roman class war

The result of all these grievances and tensions was the so-called *Conflict of the Orders,* the name given to the class war between the patricians and the plebeians. This conflict lasted for 200 years, and the outcome set a train of events leading up to the civil war and fall of the Republic in the first century BC (covered in Chapters 14 and 15).

The plebs waded in, not with random bouts of mob violence, but in an organised way. They took some of their ideas from Greek traders in Rome who had seen how aristocrats in their own homeland had been toppled. Greek merchants were active in a trading community on the Aventine Hill in Rome, and that's where the discontented plebs first started getting together and exchanging ideas. After the rural plebs joined in, they had the strength to start getting things changed. The plebs found various ways to flex their muscles:

- They organised general strikes to withhold their military services.

- They formed an assembly called the *Concilium Plebis Tributum* (the 'Council of Plebs Arranged by Tribes') where the plebs met in their tribes to elect tribunes to represent their interests. Unlike the Comitia Centuriata, only plebs could join the Council of Plebs. (You can read in detail how these councils and their representatives worked in Chapter 3.)

- They took an oath to protect their tribunes, come what may (this helped the power of the veto, which played a big role in expanding the plebs' power through the tribunes).

The patricians were forced to accept what the plebs had done because of the sheer force of numbers and the economic power the plebs wielded. In 471 BC, a law approved the Concilium Plebis Tributum.

One law to rule them all – the Twelve Tables (450 BC)

The plebs knew the only way to protect their interests was to demand a proper code of law that set out their rights and obligations. This law would prevent the patricians making up whatever penalties they liked and setting up unwritten precedents for arbitrary punishments. This principle is key to Roman law.

The plebs turned the heat on for a code of law in 462 BC by maintaining a barrage of demands for ten years. In 451 BC, the patricians gave in and appointed ten commissioners to draw up a law code. Doing so didn't go smoothly because the commission didn't finish its work on time, and a second one had to be formed. One commissioner, Appius Claudius, rigged his re-election to the second commission and used his position to carry on ruling as a tyrant even once the commission's work was done. The plebs had to organise a general strike to force the patricians to imprison Appius and re-establish constitutional government in 449 BC.

The result of plebeian pressure was the Code of the Twelve Tables which was finished by 450 BC. Because the patricians had drawn up the Code, they naturally made sure that their interests took priority, but writing laws down at all was a radical departure from tradition and a mark of the power plebs now had. These are some of the provisions of the Code of the Twelve Tables:

✔ The rights and duties of a family and its property were defined.

✔ Traders had a right to get together for a common purpose.

✔ Burials had to take place outside the city walls.

✔ A son sold three times into slavery by his father became free.

✔ Women remained in guardianship even once they reached their majority.

✔ A common-law wife would become her own master when her husband died.

✔ Only a proper law court could order the execution of a man.

The Twelve Tables fell into disuse over the centuries that followed, but they were never repealed. A thousand years later, some of the Code's original laws were preserved in the emperor Justinian's Law Code (see Chapter 21 for info on Justinian). But the patricians had clung on to some key powers:

✔ Consuls had the last word over things like military conscription.

✔ Patricians kept secret the legal jargon to be used in civil actions so that they could control how the law was enforced and who benefited from it (which was usually them).

✔ Marriage between patricians and plebs was prohibited, thus making sure that the patrician families would never have to share their powers.

Plebs' rights – the man with the trump card

Despite the patrician's efforts to protect their power and influence, after the Twelve Tables were passed, the plebs scored some more goals in the Conflict of the Orders:

✔ Any man who harmed the plebs officers, the tribunes, and/or the *aediles* (originally temple officials), would be put to death.

✔ The aediles became assistants to the tribunes and were elected in pairs annually.

✔ In 445 BC, the law banning intermarriage between plebs and patricians was overturned, meaning that sons of pleb women could now become patricians. The repeal of the intermarriage ban was significant because tribunes had a very important power: the veto. Through their veto, they were able to obstruct anything against the interests of the plebs. You find more about this, the tribunes, and aediles in Chapter 3.

Next, thanks to the military threats Rome faced in the fifth century, the system of having two consuls was abandoned for most of the time up to 367 BC, when it was restored. In place of the consuls, three (later six) military tribunes were elected annually. Crucially, plebs were eligible for the posts. Plebs also became eligible for a new magistracy called the *quaestorship*. Quaestors helped the consuls. Eventually plebs were even entitled to be elected as one of the consuls.

A republic came into being when laws were written down, and the patricians were forced to accept plebeian institutions and offices, creating a balance of power that worked, but only just. Rome's Republican government system was all about checks and balances. It worked so long as powers like the veto weren't abused, and also because the kind of pleb who was powerful enough and rich enough to get himself elected as a tribune knew his interests were similar to the patricians.

Chapter 11

This Town Isn't Big Enough for All of Us – Seizing Italy

In This Chapter

▶ Rome's struggle with the Latin League

▶ Defeating the Gauls

▶ Rome's conquest of Italy

*B*y about 450 BC, the Romans had gone a long way to setting up a political system that would define the next four centuries of their history (refer to Chapter 10 for the birth of the Roman Republic). But for the moment, Rome still didn't matter very much to the rest of the world. In the fifth century BC, Athens was the most powerful force in the Mediterranean. So much so that centuries later in the Renaissance, learned men looked back eagerly at Athens's experiments with democracy and what had happened in Greece. Egypt was now in an advanced state of decline and Alexander the Great's Macedonian Empire was still more than a century in the future. In north-western Europe, places like Gaul and Britain, which would one day be part of the Roman Empire, were just beginning to trade with the classical world.

Most of these places knew nothing at all about Rome. By 270 BC, however, despite having to deal with their own internal political problems as well as attacks by neighbours, Rome was well on the way to controlling all of Italy. Armed with the resources of the whole of Italy, Rome was poised on the brink of seizing an international empire.

What made the difference is that Rome used every setback to regroup and return to the attack. Every victory was followed up by ruthless consolidation of the territory won. Crucially, the Romans also created settled conditions in Italy that looked attractive to many of the Italian peoples. That was one of the great secrets of Rome's success – they made being ruled by Rome into a major advantage. The Etruscans and Gauls held out for a few more years, but Rome's ruthless reprisals made them give up.

Winning Over the Latin League (493 BC)

This period is one of the most complicated phases in Roman history, and many of the key details are lost to us. What seems to have happened is that there were really three power groups involved: the Romans, the Etruscans, and the Latins. When Rome pushed out the Etruscan kings, she struck a major blow. But although Rome was turning into the biggest player around, the Latin cities weren't in a rush to accept Rome's power. Getting them to do that was a decisive moment.

Fights with the Etruscans

Tarquinius Superbus was the last of the kings of Rome who, because of his tyranny and cruelty, was rather unceremoniously ousted from power (refer to Chapter 10 for the gory details). Tarquinius, an Etruscan, was naturally infuriated by this and fought a battle against the Romans to reclaim his throne, but he was unsuccessful. Not ready to give up, he went to Lars Porsenna, another Etruscan leader (he was king of a city called Clusium), for help. Porsenna seems to have had no plans to put Tarquinius back on the throne and used the invitation to start exercising his own muscle.

According to legend, Porsenna marched on Rome but couldn't cross the bridge to capture the city, thanks to a heroic defence by Horatius Cocles (which means one-eyed), who, with only two companions, held the crucial bridge long enough for the Romans to destroy it. Once the bridge was down, Horatius leaped into the river Tiber and swam home to be greeted by the cheering Romans.

Porsenna was very impressed by Horatius's display of bravery, and also by Mucius Scaevola, who crept into the Etruscan camp planning to assassinate Porsenna and, when caught, put his right hand into a fire to show how brave he and other Romans were. It wasn't just the men of Rome, either, who were tough. A woman hostage, Cloelia, held by the Etruscans, escaped back to Rome, but out of a sense of honour, the Romans sent her back. Porsenna let her go and abandoned the siege.

Thoroughly stirring stuff, designed to prove to the Romans just how honourable and brave their ancestors had been. Another version, probably more reliable, has Porsenna taking Rome, but not staying long. It seems that Rome's resistance to Etruscan control impressed other local Latin cities, creating the foundations of the Latin League.

The creation of the Latin League

In about 506 BC, determined to throw off the Etruscans for good, the Latins organised themselves into the League. The League was made up of about 30 cities (*not* including Rome) in the Latium region, including Alba Longa, Bovillae, Lavinium, Praeneste, and Tibur. These cities shared the same gods and also realised the benefits of working together to defend themselves against external enemies, mainly the Etruscans. The Latin League seems to have grown out of an earlier League of Aricia, which Rome tended to control. But Rome was left out of the new Latin League.

In response to the creation of the Latin League, the Etruscan Porsenna sent his son Arruns to teach the League a lesson, but the League defeated him at the Battle of Aricia, cutting the Etruscans off from southern Italy and permanently weakening them. It wasn't till 359 BC that the Etruscans tried again.

Rome: At odds with the Latin League

With Arruns defeated, you'd have thought that the Latins and the Romans would have spotted they had common interests, but the problem was that there were huge tensions because the Latins resented the way Rome threw her weight about, claiming to speak for various Latin cities based on the old League of Aricia.

Although the Latins had been impressed by Roman resistance to the Etruscans, they were less impressed by the prospect of Rome's growing power. The Latins were now organised in a League that left out the Romans, largely because the newly-independent Rome now claimed control of much of Latium. This claim even featured in a treaty she signed with Carthage about this time. Galvanised by their success against the Etruscans, the Latins decided to gear up for a trial of strength against the Romans.

Doing a deal with the Latins

Rome naturally wasn't prepared to back down in the face of the Latin League's resistance. Rome fought a battle against the Latins at Lake Regillus in 496 BC. Although the battle ended in a draw, it always went down in Roman tradition as a divinely inspired victory.

In reality, the Roman 'victory' had more to do with politics than divine intervention. The Latins were having trouble with mountain tribes coming down and invading their land and were forced to come to terms with the Romans to control this threat. Rome took advantage of the Latins' vulnerability and negotiated a winning deal called the *foedus Cassianum* (a treaty named after the consul Spurius Cassius) in 493 BC. It worked like this:

- ✔ The Latin League and Rome provided equal shares of a common defensive army.
- ✔ Rome and the Latin League split any spoils of war.

Rome was now a match for the Latin League. The deal had very important implications later because the Latin cities were now being drawn into the Roman system. Rome planted colonies *(coloniae)* of Roman citizens and Latins in places where the presence of a loyal town with a defensive capability would be useful. Colonists stopped being Roman citizens and became citizens of the new city, which was made a member of the Latin League. The League, incidentally, lasted till 340 BC when Rome took the opportunity to undermine it (see the section 'Meanwhile . . . the Latins strike back' later for more detail).

Crushing the local opposition

The problems Rome and the Latins faced were the Etruscan city of Veii to the north, the Aequi people to the east, and the Volscians to the south. Tradition has it that a Roman traitor called Coriolanus led a Volscian invasion of Rome. Whether this tale is true or not, the Romans did make a treaty after the year 486 BC with a people called the Hernici who lay between the Aequi and the Volsci, effectively stopping the Aequi and the Volsci from joining forces against Rome. By the late fifth century, these two cities no longer posed a serious threat.

The Etruscan city of Veii, however, stood up to the Romans. In 426 BC, the Romans defeated the Veians, and they returned in 405 BC, determined to wipe out the city once and for all. A ten-year siege, which nearly crippled Rome thanks to Veii's impregnable location, followed. Only an assault by a Roman general called Marcus Furius Camillus, who tunnelled under the walls, won the day in 396 BC.

The Romans exacted a brutal revenge on the Veians: Camillus told his troops they could kill the Veians at will and sell any survivors into slavery. The land the Romans seized was divided up amongst its poorer citizens. This sort of revenge set the pattern of Roman world-dominating brutality in later times.

Having the Gaul to Invade – 390 BC

By the early 390s BC, Gaulish Celts found their way south into northern Italy's fertile Po Valley, called by the Romans *Cisalpine Gaul*. In 391, they threatened an Etruscan city called Clusium which appealed to Rome for help. Rome warned off the invaders, but in 390 a Gaulish army reached the river Allia ten miles north of Rome.

Gaul is roughly equivalent to modern France. The Gaulish tribes were just one small group of peoples spread across central and north-western Europe and known to the Romans as *Celts*, a very loose term that doesn't mean one common cultural group, though these days it's often treated as if it does. The Celts knew about the Mediterranean world through trading contacts.

Getting sacked

In 390 BC (or 387 according to some sources), the Romans met the Gauls in battle and were totally defeated. The Romans didn't have the equipment or the tactics to face the Gauls and their long swords. The Romans might be famous today for their highly disciplined and well-equipped professional regular army, but that belongs to a later period in Roman history. In the early days, the Roman army was drawn from the ranks of citizens on an as-needed basis, and they were often not up to the job.

Rome was saved because the Gauls failed to take advantage of the open road, which gave the Romans time to build a last stand on the Capitoline Hill. When the Gauls burst into Rome, they sacked the city and besieged the Capitoline for seven months. Eventually the Romans had to surrender and pay a ransom of gold. Amazingly at that point, the Gauls went back to northern Italy. But the damage was done.

This Gallic invasion turned out to be a curious portent of Rome's future when, in AD 410, marauding tribes would once again come from northern Europe to sack and destroy Rome.

Changes at home

The invasion by the Gauls had all sorts of serious consequences. For a start, the Gauls had done a lot of damage to farmland. It took decades for Rome to repair what she had, rather than spending time on getting hold of new territory. Military service became more essential. The upshot was another economic decline.

The Tribune's image

Many years later, the Roman historian Plutarch described how the tribunes of the plebs *(tribuni plebis)* had to dress and behave like ordinary citizens, without any of the pomp and ceremony that surrounded officials like consuls. In fact, the more ordinary a tribune appeared, the more powerful he became. Approachability was essential, so his door was never locked, day or night, and he was treated almost as if he was sacred.

Another development was the growth in Roman citizenship (see Chapter 2 for more information about the benefits of citizenship). The number of Roman citizens grew for the following reasons:

✔ Latins who came to Rome and settled there could become Roman citizens with full voting rights. Foreigners, or people from other parts of Italy, who came to Rome could become 'half-citizens' – they were called *cives sine suffragio,* which means 'citizens without the vote'. Roman citizenship became a very useful device later on, awarded to certain cities other than Rome.

✔ Another source of new citizens were the families of slaves. After a slave was freed he became a *libertus* ('freedman'). He was not allowed to vote, but his sons could do so (see Chapter 2 for information about freedmen).

✔ There were also more plebs, thanks to the practice of creating colonies and also the *municipia* (cities founded by the Romans but whose inhabitants lacked the full rights of Roman citizens), and at the same time, fewer patricians. Many patricians had been killed in the fighting, and they continued to avoid marrying plebs even though that was now legal (refer to Chapter 10).

Despite the economic decline and because of the plebs' growing numbers, the plebs were gaining the upper hand. The better-off plebeians were determined to take the opportunity to demand economic and political change. (See Chapter 10 for more on the class war, the Conflict of the Orders, between the patricians and plebs.)

Economic muscle

Part of the way the plebs showed how their power was increasing came when they demanded economic measures to stave off ruin and also wanted the end of patrician privileges. The plebs forced in new laws to help debtors. The fact that they were able to do this showed the tensions between them and the patricians, and that the patricians weren't able to stop them. This is what they achieved:

✔ Maximum interest rates were fixed.

✔ Enslavement of debtors was ended.

✔ The amount of public land anyone could hold was limited, making it possible for small parcels to be distributed amongst the poorer citizens.

Political reform

Plebeians also demanded, and got, political reform. The most important reform came in 367 BC when the plebs introduced the principle that one of the two annually elected consuls had to be a pleb. In 342 BC this came into force. Because the consulship was the senior magistracy, this meant that plebs could hold any of the magistracies. After plebs started holding the consulship, they effectively became a new plebeian aristocracy. By 300, the plebs won the right of appeal against a sentence of death. In 287 came the crowning victory: the right of the *Concilium Plebis Tributum* (the Council of Plebs arranged by Tribes; refer to Chapter 10) to pass laws which bound not just the plebs, but also the patricians.

As a result of these key reforms, the Roman magistracies evolved into a career structure with a clear hierarchy. A man began with military service and then served in each of the magistracies until he reached the consulship (see Chapter 3 for the career ladder in its mature form).

Because magistracies were short-term appointments, it was the Senate that provided the underlying long-term stability. The Senate couldn't make laws, but because senators were ex-magistrates, its resolutions had so much prestige they were generally treated as laws. Certainly no serving magistrate would risk challenging the Senate.

Throughout all these changes, the Concilium Plebis Tributum was the real winner. It started out an illegal body, but by 300 BC, although it had none of the trappings or status of a magistracy, the Concilium Plebis Tributum had the power of veto over anything any magistrate did, or over any resolution of the Senate.

A new army and a new Latin League

After being defeated by the Gauls in 390 BC, the Romans were in a seriously weakened state. After having thrown their weight around for a century, all the hard-won advantage had been lost in a trice. But being Romans, they took it on the chin and set about repairing the damage:

✔ **They built walls so that no Gauls, or anyone else, would ever capture Rome again.** The new walls were 8.9 kilometres (5.5 miles) long, 7.3 metres (24 feet) high and 3.67 metres (12 feet) thick. Some of these walls, falsely said to have been built by the Etruscan king of Rome, Servius

Tullius, still stand today and are known as the 'Servian Walls'. When the Gauls invaded again in 360, the Romans made use of their new defences. In fact, they hid behind their new walls until the Gauls went home again.

✔ **They reorganised and re-equipped the army so that the Roman forces couldn't be rushed by a high-speed barbarian attack.** Instead of fighting in a solid wall of infantry, Roman soldiers were divided up into more flexible units. Troops were equipped with javelins as well as swords. The Roman army was no longer a defensive force. It was an army capable of conquest.

✔ **They reorganised the Latin League.** The Gauls' invasion of 360 BC encouraged the Etruscans to try their hand at attacking Rome again, this time in 359. In response, Rome reorganised the Latin League so that Rome took total military control instead of sharing it. The Romans thoroughly defeated the Etruscans, and by 350 had made themselves safe against possible invasion by a neighbour.

Knocking out the Samnites

The Samnites were the tribes who lived along the Appenine Mountains in central and southern Italy. Because the Romans and Latins lived in the plains below the mountains to the west and started to make inroads on Samnite territory, and the Samnites were starting to encroach on the plains, it was plain that the Romans and Samnites would come to blows.

The Samnites lived in widely-dispersed villages and had little control over any individual community's involvement in raiding or warfare. So the Samnites earned themselves a bad reputation for causing trouble. Even so, in 354 BC, the Romans accepted an offer of a treaty from the Samnites; probably both sides fearing another Gaulish invasion. But this treaty didn't solve all the problems between the Samnites and the Romans.

The First Samnite War (343–341 BC)

In 343 BC, the Samnites started hassling the city of Capua in Campania, about 350 kilometres (220 miles) south-east of Rome. Capua appealed to Rome for help. Rome saw its chance to take control over the region of Campania and promptly threw out the Samnite treaty, even though there had never been any tradition of the Romans helping the Capuans.

The First Samnite War was short and inconclusive. To begin with, the Romans drove the Samnites out of the area around Capua. But in 342, Roman soldiers mutinied because they resented being away from home on long campaigns. That could have wrecked Rome's prestige once again, but fortunately the Samnites had to retreat to defend themselves against a Greek colony called Tarentum in the far south of Italy. The result was that in 341 BC, the Romans and Samnites renewed their treaty.

Meanwhile . . . the Latins strike back

The First Samnite War wasn't a military disaster for the Romans, but it was very nearly a political one. The Latins spotted how the army mutiny had nearly scuppered Rome's ability to hold back the Samnites and decided to try their chances at gaining back parity.

The bold bid fails

So in 340, the Latins demanded a restoration of equal rights between themselves and Rome. Naturally the Romans refused. So the Latins made an alliance with the Campanians and Rome's old enemy, the Volsci (refer to the section 'Crushing the local opposition'), which looked like a good way of overpowering Rome. Except that the Romans were smarter and now used their alliance with the Samnites to defeat the Latins and Campanians.

Dismantling the Latin League

After defeating the Latins and the Campanians, the Romans offered excellent peace terms to the Campanians, who promptly left their alliance with the Latins. Now in a position of unassailable strength, the Romans simply dismantled the Latin League and forced each city to come to terms individually with Rome in a settlement of 338 BC. The Romans introduced:

- **Municipal status:** Some of the existing Latin cities were made into municipiae, divided into two types: those whose citizens became Roman citizens with full voting rights; and those where the citizens had no voting rights but still had to supply Rome with soldiers.

- **New Roman colonies:** Rome also set up colonies *(coloniae)* of Roman citizens to guard strategic locations. The city of Antium (modern Anzio), for instance, had its fleet destroyed by the Romans. It was allowed to remain in existence, but a colony of Roman citizens was planted in its territory to guard the port. Another colony called Cales was established in 334 BC to defend Capua.

The technique the Romans used to thwart the Latin League's coup is called *divide and rule*. The Romans had used it before, and they'd use it again in the centuries to come, playing off one tribe against another. Similarly, coloniae and municipia were brilliant devices that Rome would use in the future (see Chapter 2 for more on municipia). These devices left cities with their own identities and some powers of self-government, but at the same time gave the inhabitants status within the Roman system.

The Second Samnite War (326–304 BC)

Having well and truly sorted out the Latin League to its advantage (see the preceding section), Rome decided to ignore the Samnites in her settlement of 338 BC. The last straw for the Samnites was when the Romans, always looking for a way to enhance their power and influence, made a treaty with the powerful Greek trading and manufacturing city of Tarentum in southern Italy in 334 BC, while the Tarentines were at war with the Samnites.

By 327, the Samnites had made peace with Tarentum and now started trying to expand their power westwards. They placed a force of theirs into the Greek port and colony of Neapolis (Naples). The nearby Capuans objected and asked Rome for help.

Naturally, the Romans responded and sent a force down to Naples. The Roman army besieged the Samnite garrison but offered them such excellent terms the Samnites surrendered. But the Samnites hadn't given up their scheme to conquer the western coastal plains. The next few years were a stalemate. The Romans didn't dare fight in the Samnites' mountain territory, and the Samnites were held back by Roman garrisons.

The war's first phase ended in 321 BC. Impatient for a decisive action, the Romans sent an army from Capua to attack Samnium. The Samnites trapped the Roman army in the mountains at the Caudine Forks, near Capua, and forced them into a humiliating surrender. The Samnites thought they'd won, but the Romans used the peace to regroup. As usual after a defeat, the Roman army was enlarged and tactics improved.

In 316 BC, the Romans restarted the war, but things quickly went wrong. Another Roman force was defeated, and the Capuans promptly went over to the Samnites. But in 314, the Romans won back control, forced the Capuans back on their side, and set up new colonies to control the territory.

The Samnites could see they had little chance of winning under these circumstances, and in 304 BC they made peace with Rome. The Romans were keen to end the fighting and made no attempt to conquer Samnite territory. They were secure in the knowledge that, if war broke out again, they now had the upper hand with so much more territory under their control and with colonies dotted about to keep it safe.

Try, try, and try again: The Third Samnite War (298–290 BC)

Despite Rome's advantages, the Third Samnite War was a close-run thing for them. This time round the Samnites were joined by the Etruscans and the Gauls. The Samnites, under their leader Egnatius Gellus, soundly defeated the Romans at Camerinum (modern Cameria) in 295 BC. The Romans nearly lost again that year at the Battle of Sentinum (Sassoferrato), but Roman bravery (and the withdrawal of the Etruscans) turned the potential disaster into a victory. The Samnite leader Egnatius was killed, causing the Samnites to collapse. Afterwards, the Samnites' allies made peace with Rome. That's when Rome moved in to snatch a victory. By 291, the Samnites were cut off and isolated. In 290, they gave up and accepted the status of allies of Rome, and as such were forced to contribute to Rome's army. As was so often the case, Rome appeared magnanimous but had worked everything to her advantage by not seeking revenge.

Now for the Rest of Italy

The Romans had control of much of central Italy, but there was still *Magna Graecia* ('Great Greece') to deal with. Magna Graecia was the name given to southern Italy – where the Greek colonies were in control. The most powerful Greek colony was Tarentum (modern Taranto), with a wealthy economy based on wool and pottery, which enabled the Tarentines to field a 15,000-strong army, maintain a navy, and afford mercenaries to fend off their enemies, such as the Samnites, as well as their local rivals and enemies the Lucanians, a tribe who lived in part of southern Italy called Lucania.

In 334 BC, the Tarentines hired Alexander the Great's brother-in-law, Alexander of Epirus, to help them to fight off raids by the Samnites and Lucanians. Alexander negotiated a treaty with the Romans then, in alliance with the Samnites. Under the treaty, the Romans promised not to help the Samnites fight the Tarentines. The problem for the Tarentines was that the Roman alliance might have helped them hold off the Samnites, but the Second and Third Samnite Wars saw Roman armies move into the region. That worried the Tarentines, who had also realised Alexander was more interested in conquering his own empire. So they abandoned him to be defeated and killed by the Lucanians and then started deciding what to do about the Romans.

Pyrrhus arrives to show who's who

The Tarentines became more and more worried by Rome's ambitions. Rome's power was such that she was constantly being asked for help by places that felt under threat. The Greek city of Thurii was being attacked by the Lucanians, so in 282 BC, the Thurians asked the Romans for military support. As Thurii was only a few miles down the coast from Tarentum on the Gulf of Otranto, the Tarentines were worried and annoyed at the breach of Alexander's treaty (in which Rome had agreed *not* to send any of her ships into the Gulf). So the Tarentines attacked and defeated the Roman forces.

Because the Romans were still fighting off the Etruscans and Gauls, Romans asked for compensation instead of fighting back. But the Tarentines threw that out. They were feeling confident because by then they had hired King Pyrrhus of Epirus, considered to be the number one Greek soldier of his day, to make sure they could push the Romans back and encourage Rome's allies to defect.

Pyrrhus couldn't resist the opportunity to throw his weight about, so when the Tarentines called for his help, he turned up with a force of 25,000 men – a very bad omen for the Romans.

Pyrrhus won the first round in 280 BC. The Romans brought him to battle at Heraclea, not far from Tarentum on the Gulf of Otranto in southern Italy. The Roman cavalry was routed by the arrival of Pyrrhus's army of elephants. The Samnites and Lucanians promptly joined Pyrrhus, spotting their chance for revenge on the Romans. In 279, Pyrrhus beat the Romans again, this time at Asculum, but it was a hard-won victory.

Pyrrhus decided that defeating the Romans permanently would take far too long and cost too many lives. He offered peace on the condition that the Romans abandoned southern Italy, which the Roman Senate refused to do. In 278 Rome's forces were bolstered by money and ships from the Carthaginians of North Africa who were worried Pyrrhus might attack them.

Pyrrhus's victory over the Romans in 279 BC cost him so dearly he said 'another victory like that, and we're done for'. Nowadays the term *Pyrrhic victory* means any success won at so much cost it wasn't worth it.

In fact, Pyrrhus did indeed go off to attack the Carthaginians. While he was away doing that, the Romans attacked his Samnite and Lucanian allies (these battles are sometimes called the Fourth Samnite War). In 276 BC, the Samnites begged Pyrrhus to come back and help them. He did, but was roundly defeated by the Romans near Beneventum, just south-east of Capua and dangerously close to Rome.

Pyrrhus fled home and was killed two years later when a pot thrown out of a window accidentally fell on his head, which just goes to show how history can be turned around by remarkably trivial events.

By Jove, I think we've done it

With Pyrrhus gone, the way was open for the Romans. They captured Tarentum in 272 BC, which meant they'd not only seized a hugely wealthy city, but they also had control of the Italian peninsula.

The Greek cities of the south were drawn into the Roman net and became allies *(socii)*. Unlike the Latin cities, the Greek cities provided ships rather than troops. Latin colonies were planted here and there to secure strategic locations, like Paestum. The Samnite federation was permanently broken up into units that were individually allied to Rome.

More importantly, the other players on the Mediterranean saw that there was a new kid on the block. At the same time as the Carthaginians were renewing their treaty with the Romans, far to the east, the Macedonian Pharaoh of Egypt, Ptolemy II (285–246 BC), was making a pact of friendship with Rome.

Chapter 12

Carthage and the First Two Punic Wars

. . . .

In This Chapter

▶ How Rome became the biggest player in the Mediterranean

▶ Why the first two Punic Wars nearly broke Rome

▶ How Rome clung on to its allies and finished off Italy

▶ Greece falls into Rome's lap

. . . .

*I*n 264 BC, Rome was nearly 500 years old. It had grown from an insignificant cluster of villages on a few hills by the river Tiber into a world-class state. Nevertheless, Rome's expansion hadn't been an overnight success. There were constant internal political struggles, which were still far from settled, and Rome's wars with its neighbours were rarely walkovers.

Still, by 264 BC Roman rule was widely accepted throughout Italy. Instead of having only the resources of a city and its surrounding area to work with, Rome could call on the manpower and resources of all Italy. The Romans had done this by imposing more or less the same system of government throughout Italy. Armed with this phenomenally important asset, the Romans created a solid basis for their Empire. But like the previous 500 years, the next 250 years wouldn't be plain sailing.

The Sicilian Story – the First Punic War (264–241 BC)

Carthage, where Tunisia is now, was a trading colony set up in North Africa by the Phoenicians of Tyre in 814 BC (in reality, Carthage was probably founded around the time that Rome was said to have been founded). Carthage was extremely successful. Its influence spread across the western

Mediterranean, especially in Sicily and southern Italy, and it traded for tin probably as far as Cornwall. One story going around Rome was that the Carthaginian commander Hanno had even sailed all round Africa. It was inevitable that Rome's rise would matter a very great deal to the Carthaginians, and vice versa.

In fact, Rome and Carthage had made several treaties in earlier times. Under the treaty of 348 BC, the Romans allowed the Carthaginians to trade slaves in Latium and recognised the Carthaginians' monopoly of trade across the whole western Mediterranean, including Sardinia, Corsica, and Sicily. In return, the Carthaginians agreed not to set up any permanent colonies of their own in Latium. At the time, the Romans didn't have any intention of treading on the Carthaginians' toes. Another treaty, in 278, gave the Romans support from the Carthaginians against Pyrrhus (refer to Chapter 11).

By 264 BC, Rome was in full control of Italy. With Sicily only a few yards away, the situation was completely different. The Carthaginians saw that their wealth and power was under direct threat, while Rome's relentless drive to expand its land and power meant their paths were bound to cross.

The result was a series of long, drawn-out wars called the Punic Wars. They were Rome's first massive international struggle and played a monumentally decisive role in establishing Rome's power and shaping the course of history in Europe and the whole of western civilisation. In fact, the Punic Wars were a turning-point in world history. The Romans won, but had it gone the other way, this book might have been called *Carthaginians For Dummies*. Rome would have popped up in just a few paragraphs, and you and I would never have heard of Julius Caesar.

The Latin word *Punicus* is another version of the Latin *Poenicus* which comes from the Greek *Phoinikikos* (Φοινικικοζ), a Phoenician. The word comes from the Greek for purple because the Phoenicians and Carthaginians produced a highly-prized purple dye.

The Mamertines play with fire

Rome controlled Italy, but not all Italians were in Rome's service. Campanian mercenaries (from south-west Italy) had been employed by Agathocles, tyrant of Syracuse in Sicily. In 315 BC, Agathocles captured the wealthy city of Messana, just a few miles from Rhegium in Italy. After Agathocles's death in 289 BC, the mercenaries went back on their agreement to leave Sicily and out of greed captured Messana, divided it up amongst themselves, and then changed their name to Mamertines, based on their local version of Mars, the god of war, called Mamers. Not surprisingly the Syracusans were furious and attacked the Mamertines, who asked both the Romans and Carthaginians for help.

The trouble for the Romans was that, not long before, another bunch of Campanians had seized the Italian city of Rhegium, just across the straits from Messana, massacring some of the inhabitants. The Romans were disgusted by this and recaptured Rhegium. Because the Mamertines had committed more or less the same crime, the Romans couldn't decide what to do. In the end, ever practical, they put honour on the back burner and went with what was most advantageous for them: They decided to help the Syracusans. Rome's reasoning: The Carthaginians already controlled most of western Sicily. If the Carthaginians threw out the Mamertines from Messana, Carthage might get control of the eastern part of Sicily as well, and that would mean the Carthaginians were only a short hop from Italy.

Messana isn't enough: Going for Sicily

In their efforts to stop the Carthaginians from claiming more of Sicily, the Romans got off to a good start. First, they used diplomacy to break up the alliance between the Carthaginians and the Syracusans. Next, they captured a Carthaginian city on Sicily's south coast called Agrigentum and stopped the Carthaginians from sending over a bigger army.

Something changed at this point. The Romans had fallen into the Sicilian war purely because of the Mamertines in Messana. Within a year or two, the Mamertines had been completely forgotten by the Romans and the Carthaginians. The Romans saw their chance to seize all of Sicily and went to war. So began the First Punic War.

Battles and victory at sea: Becoming a naval power

Fighting the First Punic War took the Romans to a new level of military expertise because they built a naval fleet, despite having little or no naval experience, by copying the design of a Carthaginian wreck. They put the fleet under the command of Gnaeus Cornelius Scipio Asina, who trained up his naval forces. In 260 BC, although an advance force under Asina was caught out by the Carthaginians, the rest of the Roman fleet wiped out the main Carthaginian fleet off the north coast of Sicily.

The legend of Marcus Atilius Regulus

The story of Marcus Atilius Regulus (c. 310–250 BC) is fiction, but it was dreamed up to help create an image of Roman honour and self-sacrifice. The story goes that Regulus was leading the Roman army in North Africa. In 255 BC, the Carthaginians destroyed his army and captured him. They sent Regulus back to Rome to present the Carthaginians with terms for peace, on the condition that, if the Romans refused, he was to return to Carthage. Regulus went back to Rome and gave such an inspiring speech to reject the Carthaginians' peace terms that, of course, the Romans threw the terms out. But Regulus kept his promise, returned to Carthage, and was tortured and killed. In truth, Regulus was a real man, who probably died in prison in Africa.

The Romans realised they had no idea about naval tactics. To compensate, they built portable boarding ramps, which they threw across to enemy ships; then the Roman soldiers darted across and turned what would otherwise be a naval battle into a land battle – a very successful tactic.

Attacking Sicily wasn't going to defeat the Carthaginians for good. Rome won a second naval battle, at Ecnomus, in 256 BC using the same tactics: boarding ramps and *grappling irons* (iron-clawed hooks for seizing the enemy ships). The Romans invaded Africa with a huge army but were totally defeated by the Carthaginians in 255 BC, and the Roman fleet, which came to rescue survivors, was destroyed in a storm.

The struggle between Rome and the Carthaginians went on for another 14 years. The Romans suffered another naval disaster in 253 BC when a fleet was wrecked, and again 249 BC when Claudius Appius Pulcher took a fleet to destroy the Carthaginian navy in the port at Drepana. The Carthaginians moved out of the harbour before the Romans arrived. Pulcher sent his ships in and carried on sending them in even though the first ones were trying to get out again and chase the Carthaginians. In the mayhem, 93 out of 120 Roman ships were lost.

For some bizarre reason, despite having defeated the Romans at sea, the Carthaginians decided to take their ships out of service, completely unaware that the Romans had been busy building a new fleet, paid for by voluntary loans. In fact, they'd built two – the first was wrecked in yet another storm, but they promptly set to and built another.

Faced with this sudden resurgence of Roman naval power in 242 BC, the Carthaginians were totally wrong-footed. A new Carthaginian fleet had to be thrown together in double-quick time. In March 241 BC, the Roman fleet met the Carthaginian fleet off the coast of Sicily, and the Romans totally defeated the Carthaginians and occupied Sicily. The Carthaginians executed their admiral, Hanno, and were forced to abandon their claims to Sicily and pay compensation for the war!

Setting the stage for the Second Punic War

The Romans made a lot of mistakes in the First Punic War but they won because:

- They had so much manpower they could afford losses.
- They learned new methods of warfare from their enemies.
- They kept coming back for more battle even when they had setbacks.

After defeating the Carthaginians in Sicily, the Romans realised that Carthaginian trading wealth was up for grabs. With Carthage defeated, the Romans followed the war up by capturing the islands of Sardinia and Corsica, preventing the Carthaginians from having handy bases from which to launch assaults on Italy's west coast.

The Carthaginians, having lost Sicily, decided to make up for the loss by building up their control in Spain – a decision that led directly to the Second Punic War.

Staying busy in the interim: Capturing northern Italy

With the First Punic War out of the way, and before the Second Punic War broke out, the Romans had to deal again with the Gauls of northern Italy.

The Gauls of northern Italy last invaded central Italy in 390 BC. They'd sacked Rome but went home with a huge ransom, rather than troubling themselves to take the opportunity to destroy Rome once and for all. The Gauls were a thorn in the flesh of the Romans for much of the next century, and the Gauls even took part in the Third Samnite War (refer to Chapter 11 for details about the Gauls). Major defeats of the Gauls took place in the 280s, and a Roman colony was planted on the edge of Gaulish territory near the site of modern Ancona, in northern Italy. In 279 BC, an army of Gauls was defeated by the Greeks at Delphi in Greece.

It took more than 50 years before the Gauls finally forgot about these setbacks and for a new generation of have-a-go warriors to grow up, determined to earn themselves reputations as heroic fighters. These new Gaulish warriors joined up with other tribes from farther north and sent an army of 70,000 into Italy. Big mistake. By now the Romans had the whole of Italy at their disposal and had no trouble in sending an army nearly twice as big against the Gauls.

The Gauls were soundly defeated and the Romans decided that the best thing to do was conquer northern Italy and end the chances of another Gaulish comeback. Not that that was a difficult decision to make. Just as the First Punic War opened Roman eyes to the chances of seizing the Carthaginians' wealth, so the Gaulish invasion of 225 BC made the Romans see the attraction of holding the fertile northern plains of Italy, abundant in woodland, corn, and livestock.

Unbelievably, the Romans took just three seasons of campaigning to capture the whole of northern Italy and push the Gauls back. They built new roads and set up naval bases in the region. By 220 BC, the Romans held an area almost identical to modern Italy and controlled the whole area from the Alps to the southernmost tip of Sicily.

The Second Punic War (218–202 BC)

The Carthaginians had been well and truly bruised by the First Punic War. The loss of the rich island of Sicily made a big dent in their wealth. Their damaged prestige meant other peoples under their control tried to throw them off. To bolster Carthaginian power and reputation, the Carthaginians decided to build up their control in Spain.

Hamilcar Barca, a Carthaginian general who was busy suppressing revolts in North Africa, was the ideal man for the job. He'd spent a lot of time fighting the Romans in Sicily in the First Punic War and resented the Romans from the bottom of his heart.

Hamilcar set up new Carthaginian bases in Spain, including Nova Carthago ('New Carthage' – modern Cartagena). Hamilcar's work was carried on by his son-in-law Hasdrubal, and then his son Hannibal. The Romans didn't like what Hamilcar was doing one bit and demanded that the Carthaginians stay south of the river Ebro in north-east Spain. Figure 12-1 shows the territory controlled by the Rome and Carthage in 218 BC when Hannibal crossed the Alps into Italy in the Second Punic War.

The Carthaginians did, indeed, stay south of the river Ebro. Unfortunately for the Carthaginians, in 'their' area was a coastal city called Saguntum, a Roman ally (refer to Figure 12-1). A Roman delegation was sent to New Carthage to warn the Carthaginians to leave Saguntum alone. Hannibal (Hamilcar's son) took no notice and besieged Saguntum in 219. The city fell after eight months because the Romans were too tied up with Illyrian pirates to help (see the section 'Trouble in the East: The Macedonian Wars' for that bit of history), but by 218, Rome had defeated the Illyrians and were free to deal with the situation in New Carthage.

Rome sent a deputation to Carthage to demand that Hannibal be surrendered. The Carthaginians naturally said no and told the Roman deputation to offer them peace or war. The Roman envoys offered war and the Carthaginians accepted, which was a decisive moment in history.

The amazing march of elephants

The Carthaginian forces in Spain were miles from home and the Romans controlled the sea. The Roman plan was to use their navy to send an army to fight Hannibal in Spain. Hannibal had other ideas.

Hannibal realised that, by marching into Italy overland, he could dodge the Roman navy. In 218 BC, Hannibal crossed the Alps with his army and his elephants. The Roman force turned up too late to stop him. Hannibal was immediately joined by the Gaulish tribes who were delighted at the chance to have another go at Rome, especially as it looked as if the Romans were going to lose (refer to the earlier section 'Staying busy in the interim: Capturing northern Italy' for information on the Gauls of northern Italy).

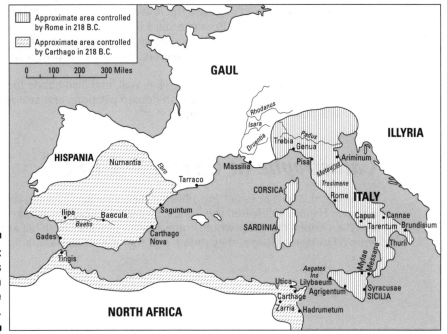

Figure 12-1:
The areas involved in all three Punic Wars.

Hannibal's march over the Alps was a logistical triumph. Hannibal sent scouts ahead to plan the route and bribe the Gauls. Crossing rivers, especially for the elephants, was a big problem. Rafts made to look like a natural bridge by covering them with earth were built to lure the elephants aboard so that they could be towed across.

There's no certainty about how big Hannibal's army was. The lowest estimate was 20,000 infantry and 6,000 cavalry as well as 21 surviving elephants, but Hannibal lost a large number of men along the way (and about 40 elephants). Some of the army had refused to make the journey, while he was said to have lost 36,000 men alone after crossing the Rhône.

The Battle of Lake Trasimene – 217 BC

Despite the losses on the way, Hannibal's army was unstoppable. He fought off a Roman army in northern Italy, and the Romans fell back. The Romans thought Hannibal would come into Italy down the main road called the Via Flaminia. He didn't – he sneaked in through an unguarded mountain pass, forcing a 25,000-strong Roman army under Caius Flaminius to chase after him. Flaminius, and a large part of his army, were promptly wiped out on the banks of Lake Trasimene.

What happened at Lake Trasimene was a classic ambush. As Flaminius's force travelled by on a narrow road, warriors hurtled down the hills on either side, while cavalry attacked from behind. The ambush happened far too quickly for Flamninius to organise the Roman troops into their battle lines – the formation in which the Roman armies fought best. Out of formation, all their careful discipline and tactics collapsed. Being taken by surprise was a catastrophe. Of the 25,000 Roman soldiers, more than half were killed.

Trasimene was a brilliant success for Hannibal, and also handy for his men, who now re-equipped themselves with Roman weapons and armour. But Hannibal's plan started to go wrong.

Catastrophe at Cannae – 216 BC

Rome's genius had been getting allies on their side and keeping them there. So when Hannibal defeated the Roman General Flamninius at Lake Trasimene and then hoped the allies would come over to him and swell his army, he was wrong. Luckily for Rome, they didn't, and that meant all Hannibal's hopes of being supplied by grateful Italian cities vanished. So Hannibal bypassed Rome and tried his luck in southern Italy. The cities of the south wouldn't help him either.

At this point in the Second Punic War, Hannibal really ought to have been defeated. He wasn't able to get the help from the Roman allies that he had counted on, and by 216 BC, he had at the most about 40,000 to 50,000 men. But the Romans made a disastrous mistake. They thought that, by having a huge army, they would crush Hannibal easily. They massed an army of 50,000 and put it under the command of two Roman consuls who had no idea of Hannibal's strategy or tactics. Worse, the two consuls constantly argued, and the army threatened mutiny. Not the best way to prepare for a battle that could cost the Romans Italy. The situation was a recipe for disaster.

The Romans found Hannibal at Cannae, about 180 miles south-east of Rome. Initially, the battle went well for the Romans. They threw their main force in on the Carthaginian centre, which was made up of Gauls and Spaniards. Then the Gauls and Spaniards fell back, and the Romans found themselves trapped between the Carthaginian wings of African infantry and cavalry.

The Carthaginian wings moved in on the now-exhausted Romans and totally defeated them. One estimate put the Romans losses at 45,500 infantry and 2,700 cavalry; another put it as high as 70,000. The point is that the Roman army was wiped out, but Hannibal only lost about 6,000 troops.

Bloody and bruised, but still swinging

It hardly needs saying that after Cannae, the Romans faced total and utter ruin. Up to this point, they'd lost possibly as many as 100,000 men in Hannibal's campaign. Now Rome's allies started to defect. Capua changed sides, lured by the prospect of Rome's collapse and the chance of becoming the chief city in Italy. Overseas, places like Sardinia, Spain, and Sicily also started simmering with rebellion. One of history's great truths is that whenever a powerful state starts to look like a loser, even the most loyal friends look to the winner.

Hannibal's gamble about the Roman allies joining him didn't pay off, and most stayed loyal to Rome. Hannibal also found that Rome's persistence – even in the face of humiliating adversity – was beyond his ability to wear down. By means of heavy taxation and military conscription, Rome now threw its resources into winning the war. That included knocking out Hieronymus of Syracuse in Sicily who thought Cannae was such a brilliant victory he was easily persuaded by the Carthaginians to join in on their side in return for half of Sicily. Even though he was soon murdered by Syracusans to prevent this, they were so horrified by Roman brutality they ended up renewing the alliance with Carthage and faced an invasion by the Roman general Claudius Marcellus. The city fell in 211 BC (see Chapter 5 for the remarkable story of its defence by Archimedes against the Roman navy).

In 211 BC, Rome recaptured Capua despite Hannibal's threat to invade Rome. Rome punished Capua by lowering its status and confiscating much of its land. In 209 BC, Rome recaptured Tarentum, another defector.

When the Carthaginians sent another army from Spain to reinforce Hannibal, the Romans put together another vast army under Caius Claudius Nero. Nero's army headed off the Carthaginian reinforcements before they joined Hannibal. In 207 BC, the new Carthaginian army was totally defeated at Metaurus and its commander, Hannibal's brother Hasdrubal, was killed. Just to add insult to injury, Roman cavalry threw Hasdrubal's severed head into Hannibal's camp, which was a double shock to Hannibal, who hadn't even known that Hasdrubal had reached Italy. The game was up for Hannibal: It was obvious that despite Trasimene and Cannae, he had completely failed to capture Rome or any other Roman cities, or defeat the Romans decisively. Amazingly, the Senate wrote Hannibal off as a spent force, and he managed to hide out in the toe of Italy for four years before escaping back to North Africa to face the Romans again.

Scipio in the nick of time

Publius Cornelius Scipio was a Roman aristocrat and brilliant soldier who'd cut his teeth in the Second Punic War. He'd certainly been at the Roman defeat at Cannae and was probably at Trasimene, too. Although he was a young man – too young to be consul – he had bucketloads of military experience.

In 210 BC, Scipio was sent with an army to fight the Carthaginians in Spain. In 209 BC, taking advantage of the fact that the Carthaginians thought the Romans were a spent force in Spain and had divided their forces, Scipio captured New Carthage, the Carthaginian capital in Spain. He followed this up with a major victory against the Carthaginians at Ilipa in southern Spain in 206. With the Carthaginians knocked out of Spain, Scipio then turned to the main event, the attack on the Carthaginian homeland itself: Africa.

Meanwhile, back home in 205 BC, Scipio became Consul, despite being technically too young (the usual minimum age was 42) and was also made governor of Sicily, the perfect launch pad for an invasion of Africa. Scipio bided his time, planned the campaign to invade Africa, and made sure he had a first-class army to deliver the final blow. Scipio invaded Africa in 204 BC and set about destroying Carthaginian armies. The Carthaginians initially sued for peace, but when Hannibal came back from Italy to fight Scipio, the peace talks were abandoned.

The Battle of Zama – 202 BC

Hannibal and Scipio met at the Battle of Zama in North Africa in 202 BC. Sheer force of numbers, especially cavalry, rather than brilliant tactics, won the day for the Romans. Even so, Scipio did exactly what Hannibal had done at Cannae: He surrounded the enemy and trapped them. Hannibal surrendered, and the peace terms left the Carthaginians powerless:

- Their navy was cut down to ten ships.
- Their ally Numidia was made independent and an ally of Rome.
- They lost their possessions outside Africa.
- They had to pay 800,000 pounds of silver to Rome over 50 years.
- They could not wage war without Rome's permission.

Nonetheless, Carthage got over its defeat and eventually became a wealthy power again. Next time round, Rome's revenge would be total and permanent (see Chapter 13).

Scipio, little more than 30 years old, returned to Rome at the peak of his fame and popularity. He had saved Rome from its greatest enemy and recovered Rome's pre-eminence in North Africa. He took the name Africanus and celebrated with great triumph (for more on Scipio see Chapter 23).

The Romans had come to see the Carthaginians as their bitterest enemy and came to call treachery *Punica fide,* 'with Carthaginian faith'. As a result, 'Carthage' became a byword for treachery in everyday Latin.

An Italian propaganda movie, made when the Fascist dictator Mussolini ruled the nation, celebrated Scipio's victory over Hannibal. Called *Scipio Africanus: The Defeat of Hannibal* (1939), this movie features a full-scale elephant charge at the height of the Battle of Zama and the elephants' gory deaths at the hands of the Roman soldiers. The film's production was supervised by Mussolini's son Vittorio, and Mussolini himself may have taken a hand in its script.

Trouble in the East: The Macedonian Wars

Until the end of the Second Punic War in 202 BC, most of Rome's attention had been focused on Italy, the Carthaginians, and Spain. The Illyrians, people in what is now Albania and the former countries of Yugoslavia, had caused trouble before the Second Punic War, but the trouble had only been a side show (you can read the tale in the section 'A bit of background: Philip V and Illyrian pirates'). After Philip V of Macedon got involved with the Carthaginians and

Seleucids, Rome could not stand by because the campaign against Philip took Rome on a punishing journey east into Greece and beyond and eventually led Rome to conquer vast tracts of territory there: so it was a decisive moment. In 500 years, the Eastern Mediterranean region (including modern Greece, Turkey, Macedonia, Bulgaria, Turkey, Syria, Israel, and Egypt) was to become the home of what was left of the Roman Empire (see Chapter 21).

A bit of background: Philip V and Illyrian pirates

Between the First and Second Punic War, the Romans found themselves facing a problem with the Illyrians (Illyria is the coast of what used to be Yugoslavia down to Greece). This bit of trouble prompted the Romans' first foray eastwards.

The Illyrian tribes were professional pirates who made an excellent living out of stealing the valuable cargoes of merchant ships in the Adriatic. Their leaders encouraged and helped organise the piracy. In 231 BC, under their King, Agron, the Illyrians had been working as mercenaries for King Philip V of Macedon and had saved the city of Medion, under siege from a force of Aetolians (from an area farther south in Greece).

Following this victory, King Agron of the Illyrians died (he literally drank himself to death while celebrating), and his queen, Teuta, got it into her head that the Illyrians could do as they pleased. She declared that all other states were enemies and that the Illyrian navy must attack anyone and everyone. The Romans decided enough was enough. In 229 BC a diplomatic mission was sent to the Teuta. One of the ambassadors was murdered, so Rome sent a fleet over to sort the Illyrians out. Teuta immediately offered to give in, but the Romans didn't trust her and went to several Greek cities on the Adriatic coast and offered them protection in return for practical support. It was a brilliant gesture – Rome got a foothold across the Adriatic but without looking like a conqueror.

One of Teuta's supporters, Demetrius from the island of Pharos, went over to the Romans and was promptly made a Roman *amicus* ('friend'). As a result, other great Greek cities like Athens and Corinth also welcomed Roman diplomatic missions. But Demetrius blew it. Sensing the Second Punic War was brewing, he decided to return to piracy and attack the very Illyrian cities that were now loyal to Rome. Another Roman fleet was sent over in 219 BC, and Demetrius fled to Philip V of Macedon. He tried to get Philip to attack the Romans, but Philip held back.

Now back to the story.

The First Macedonian War (214–205 BC)

Just before the Second Punic War broke out in 218 BC, Rome had been trying to end the problem of the Illyrian pirates in the Adriatic. One of the players in the drama was Philip V, King of Macedon (refer to the preceding section). Philip was an opportunist. After the catastrophe at Cannae and with the impression that the Second Punic War was going against the Romans, Philip decided to make friends with Hannibal, at the time the new kid on the block in Italy (remember, this happened before Hannibal's final defeat). This was obviously a situation that Rome had to deal with, and so began the First Macedonian War.

Because the Second Punic War was using up almost all Rome's resources, the First Macedonian War didn't amount to much. Rome made an alliance with Philip's enemy, the Aetolian League led by its ally, the great Greek city of Pergamon on the west coast of Asia Minor (modern Turkey), then ruled by Attalos I (241–197 BC). The Aetolian League was a confederation of cities in central Greece formed to oppose the Macedonians. A bit of fighting took place, but in 205 BC, the Romans made peace with Philip, who had now wised up to the fact that Rome was likely to win the Second Punic War.

The Second Macedonian War (200–197 BC)

Philip, ever the opportunist, came up with another plan, one that he hoped would avoid attention from Rome. With support from the Seleucid Empire in Syria, his idea was to start attacking the Egyptians, then ruled by the boy-Pharaoh Ptolemy V, and to help himself to Egyptian possessions. The Seleucid Empire was formed in what is now Syria, Iran, and Iraq, by Seleucus, one of Alexander the Great's generals, out of Alexander's empire on his death in 323 BC. It had fallen into decline, but Seleucus's descendant Antiochus III revived its fortunes.

Thanks to the fact that Philip's forces attacked whoever they pleased in the Aegean, the Greeks got annoyed with him. Determined to protect its interests, the wealthy island of Rhodes made an alliance with Pergamon. In 201 BC, Pergamon and Rhodes turned to Rome for help after Philip's navy beat their combined forces.

Rome was exhausted and reluctant to go to war again. But when the news got out that Philip was in alliance with the Seleucids, led by the ambitious Antiochus III 'the Great' (242–187 BC), they decided they had no choice. Antiochus III had helped himself to Syria and Palestine. The Romans decided to make the war look as if it was as a campaign to protect the freedom of the Greek cities.

The Greek effect

The Romans had been fascinated by all things Greek for a long time. The Etruscans (read about them in Chapter 10) had picked up a lot from the Greeks. King Tarquinius Priscus once sent his sons to the oracle in Delphi for advice. As Rome's tentacles spread across the Mediterranean in the second century BC, the Romans became more and more impressed by the sophisticated Greek culture. Greek statues were brought to Rome and widely copied. Greek gods were matched with Roman gods. Greek literature was read and appreciated. The Roman playwright Terence (*c.* 190–159 BC) was translated and adapted into Latin works by the Greek playwright Menander and others for a Roman audience. The Greeks went on to influence Roman culture for centuries (see Hadrian in Chapter 17, for example).

The Second Macedonian War started when the Romans arrived in Illyria in 200 BC under the command of Titus Quinctius Flamininus. Frankly, the war got off to a slow start and stayed that way. The Romans tried to wear Philip down. Philip couldn't let that happen, so he forced a pitched battle by a ridge at Cynoscephalae in 197 BC. Racing down the hillside, Philip nearly demolished the Roman army, but Flamininus counter-attacked with his wing before the second wave of Macedonians had time to get into position. Philip was totally defeated.

The Greek cities were delirious with joy at their deliverance from Philip. At the Isthmian Games in Corinth in 196 BC, the Roman commander Flamininus proclaimed all Greece to be free. The Greeks were particularly impressed because Flamininus gave his speech in Greek. The Greeks decided that the Romans were thoroughly good types and their saviours and patrons, while the Romans indulged themselves in their love of Greek art and culture. But Greece remained a problem, and more to the point so did Antiochus III. What happened to Greece comes next (see Chapter 13 for the story about Antiochus III).

The Third Macedonian War (172–167 BC)

Philip V of Macedon died in 179 BC. The throne went to his anti-Roman son Perseus who had had his pro-Roman younger brother Demetrius executed. The Romans declared war in 172 BC on the pretext that Perseus had attacked some Balkan chieftains who were Roman allies. Perseus failed to take advantage of the general Greek back-pedalling about their love for Rome, but he still managed to defeat the Romans in 171 BC. It was the same old story – the

Romans were all the more determined to beat him. It took three more years of campaigns, but at Pydna in Macedonia in 168 BC, Perseus was crushed by the Roman army commanded by Lucius Aemilius Paullus. Perseus might have won if the Achaean League had formed an alliance with him. They certainly thought about it – until the Romans seized some key Achaean hostages to keep them on good behaviour.

After Perseus was defeated, the Romans decided they'd had enough of the Greeks and their internal disputes. Around 1,000 supporters of Macedonia in Greece were shipped to Italy for trial – 700 died in prison. In 167 BC, the region of Epirus was ravaged, and 150,000 people were sold into slavery. Macedonia was broken up into four republics.

Even so, the Romans didn't have any plans to conquer and govern the Greeks. The idea was to leave the Greeks free, but punish them so they'd never ally themselves with another enemy of Rome. The Romans even cut taxes to make themselves look like thoroughly reasonable people.

It's not really surprising that Greece wasn't Rome's greatest concern at this time. Between 151–146 BC, the Third Punic War was raging. More on that in Chapter 13.

The spoils of Greece (Achaea)

Despite Rome's plan to just punish, but not conquer, the Greeks, the last straw came with Andriscus, a pretender to the Macedonian throne claiming to be a son of Perseus, who managed to reunite Macedonia. The Romans abandoned the idea of leaving the Greeks free.

The sack of Corinth

According to the Roman geographer Strabo, Corinth was sacked partly by the Roman general Lucius Mummius because of the Corinthians' disgusting habits, such as pouring filth on top of any Romans passing by. But the main reason was to punish the city for its resistance and to wipe out a major commercial rival. The men were all murdered, and women and children enslaved. According to the Greek historian Polybius, Mummius was placed under huge pressure to be so cruel and didn't have the strength to stand up to it. He helped himself to Corinthian works of art, which were shipped back to Rome, including a painting of Dionysus which ended up in the Temple of Ceres. Polybius, who was there, watched with disgust as soldiers played dice on paintings they had chucked on the ground. A century later Julius Caesar founded a colony on the site of Corinth. The Roman colonists dug up the ancient Corinthian cemeteries and made a tidy living out of selling the terracotta reliefs and bronze vessels they found.

By 148 BC, a Roman army under Quintus Caecilius Metellus drove Andriscus off (sometimes called the Fourth Macedonian War). The Achaean League appointed Critolaos of Megalopolis their general. Refusing to negotiate with the Romans, he overran central Greece with his army. Metellus dealt with him, but Achaeans making a last stand near Corinth was destroyed by the Roman Consul Lucius Mummius.

Corinth was razed to the ground. The Achaean League was broken up. The Roman governor of Macedonia watched out for trouble, and Greece was forced to pay tribute to Rome. It was a turning point in Greek history that mirrored what had happened in Italy between 493–272 BC when the Romans systematically took control of Italian cities (refer to Chapter 11). Now the Greek city states lost their freedom; centuries of conflict, war, and destruction followed, with periods of brilliance in politics and art.

The Secret of Success: The Comeback

The Roman army didn't have a great deal of flair, but it was successful because it had a ready supply of manpower from the allies, it was the best organised, and it worked like a machine. Every soldier knew what his job was and where he was supposed to be, whether that was in camp or on the battlefield.

The setting up of colonies to guard ports, mountain passes, or major road junctions meant there was a Roman presence in crucial locations, acting as a military reserve. That colonies were laid out as if they were military camps, with institutions modelled on those in Rome, was part of the process.

Towns in allied territory continued to function much as they always had, but now under Roman supervision. All across Italy, communities found that being in Rome's orbit could be a big plus. In return for contributions to the Roman army, they received a share in the spoils of victory. The allies also benefited from stability, but without being oppressed. The Sabines, for example, had fought the Romans on four separate occasions, but instead of finding themselves sold into slavery and their settlements confiscated, by 268 BC they had been promoted to Roman citizens with full voting rights.

Chapter 13

While We're at It – Let's Conquer Everywhere Else, Too

*R*ome, having got Greece, Macedonia, and the Seleucids thoroughly under control, was by 146 BC a major power in the eastern Mediterranean (refer to Chapter 12 for details on these events). Rome's dominance was to have serious consequences for Asia Minor (modern Turkey) and Egypt. But history's never straightforward. Even though Greece, Macedonia, and the Seleucids were sewn up, Rome hadn't conquered the world – yet.

Rome still had problems, particularly in Italy, and also to the west in Spain, and in North Africa, Carthage's home. Despite being well and truly thrashed in both the First and Second Punic Wars (refer to Chapter 12), Carthage wasn't finished.

What happened between 200 and the 130s BC in the western Mediterranean and North Africa – the focus of this chapter – is the story of how Rome's power spread across the whole of the Mediterranean.

Conquering the Mediterranean was, by any standards, a simply flabbergasting achievement. No other ancient society (or any modern society for that matter) ever managed anything remotely like it. Even at the height of their power, the Egyptians had little influence beyond the Levant and Asia Minor. The Greeks, despite extensive colonisation around the Mediterranean, never had an organised political system to rival Rome's. The Greeks could hardly rule themselves, let alone anyone else. It was only thanks to the Roman fascination with Greek culture that Greek art, literature, and knowledge of Greece's experiments with democracy and philosophy were handed down at all.

How the West Was Won

Cisalpine Gaul (northern Italy) was something of a sideshow for the Romans whose main energies in the first half of the second century BC were concentrated on Macedonia and Greece. But northern Italy was still a vitally important area to the Romans. It was rich and fertile and part of the important overland route along the coast to southern France and Spain.

First stop: Northern Italy

At the end of the Second Punic War in 202 BC, Rome's first problem was to sort out and punish Rome's allies that had defected to Hannibal. Rome was in constant dread of Hannibal, fearing he planned to destroy Rome during his march through Italy (refer to Chapter 12).

Rome did what it had to do, meting out the punishment, which the defectors accepted. The turncoat city of Capua, for example, lost its right to self-government. And like other cities that had rebelled, Capua also lost much of its land as new Roman colonies were set up on Capuan territory.

Cisalpine Gaul was a different matter. No-one told the Cisalpine Gauls that the Second Punic War was over, so they carried on fighting for another ten years in an effort to fend off Roman reprisals for the help they'd given Hannibal. It took until 191 for the Gaulish Boii tribe to be knocked out. The man who did so was Publius Cornelius Scipio Nasica (a cousin of Scipio Africanus, who defeated the Carthaginians in the decisive Battle of Zama; see Chapter 12). Rome imposed heavy fines and took half the Boii's land as a punishment. What was left of the Boii drifted north-east and ended up in what is now Bohemia.

Northern Italy was resettled. Rome set up new colonies, like the one at Parma in 183 BC, and the land was broken up into individual parcels. New roads were built across the region, and within 50 years the whole area looked little different from the rest of Romanised Italy.

Relaxing by the Riviera

As usual, the Romans found that winning one bit of new territory, like northern Italy, meant that they had no choice but to take the next bit along as well. That's exactly what happened with the Italian Riviera, known as Liguria. Liguria was an undeveloped area with primitive inhabitants, but it was essential to Rome that Liguria should be under Roman control. Sailors in the ancient world liked to hug the coasts for safety and to make sure they didn't get lost. The Romans needed Liguria to guarantee the journey from Liguria to Spain was safe from enemies.

The Romans much preferred to fight great set-piece battles, but wearing down the tribes in this mountainous region meant they had to fight incessant small-scale skirmishes. After 186 BC, one Roman army after another was sent into Liguria. By 180, the tribes were exhausted by Rome's relentless ability to keep up the fight, and large numbers of tribal inhabitants gave up and moved away. Even so, it took Rome another 70 years before the coast road as far as Genua (Genoa) was completed and safe.

On the other side of Italy, the area we know as the Venetian Riviera, named after the Veneti tribe that lived there, was stable and generally friendly. The only problems came from Alpine tribes, so the Romans set up a colony at Aquileia (modern Aquila) – which became the major commercial centre of the region and the port-of-entry from Italy into Illyria, on the Adriatic.

The Reign in Spain, 197–179 BC

At first, Rome didn't have any great ambitions in Spain. But in the end, the Romans decided it was easier to take the place over to make sure that bolshie locals towed the line. Scipio Africanus had fought in Spain during the Second Punic War to stop the Carthaginians from establishing a power base in Spain that could be used to attack Italy. Hannibal had already tried to do this, and the Romans wanted to prevent him trying again (refer to Chapter 12).

Also, the Romans had been in Spain long enough to spot that the Iberian peninsula was heaving with mineral resources: tin, iron, gold, and silver. Strabo, the ancient historian and geographer, who wrote a description of the Roman world about 200 hundred years later, said Spain had the best and richest supply of metals of anywhere he knew.

Conquering Spain's tribes

In 197 BC, Rome created two new provinces: *Hispania Citerior* (Nearer Spain) and *Hispania Ulterior* (Further Spain). The locals in the new provinces didn't take too kindly to the idea of the Romans replacing the Carthaginians. Also, the nasty side of Roman administration came into play after Scipio Africanus left. The next few decades in Spain were brutal, oppressive, and unpleasant.

The Celtiberians

Celtiberians were tribes of Celtic origin living in defended hilltop centres in the Iberian peninsula (Spain and Portugal). Celtiberian was a name the Romans gave to a whole lot of different Celtic tribes living in the region, such as the Carpetani and Oretani. Like most Celts, the Celtiberians avoided fighting pitched battles, preferring to operate in small bands, using their knowledge of the local terrain to harass the Roman forces.

Constant rebellions by different tribes, especially the Celtiberians (people who lived in Hispania Citerior), followed. It took two Roman armies in 179 BC to corner the Celtiberians and Lusitanians (people from Hispania Ulterior, nowadays Portugal) into giving up the fight and accepting Roman rule. (Of course, it may have helped that the Roman commander Tiberius Sempronius Gracchus, who claimed to have captured 300 Celtiberian settlements, earned the Celtiberians' respect by his fair-mindedness.) Even so, Celtiberian guerrillas were trouble for decades to come.

Return to war

The peace Gracchus installed in Spain left the Romans in control of almost the whole Iberian peninsula (apart from the Atlantic coast), and lasted until 154 BC. The peace fell apart because, after Gracchus left, a number of Roman governors who followed abused their powers. Every time the Spanish tribes complained to the Senate, nothing was done. The Celtiberians and Lusitanians returned to war, and the situation worsened when some Roman commanders made unprovoked attacks.

The unrest in Spain became even more significant because, by 151 BC, the Third Punic War had broken out (see the section 'The Third Punic War (151–146 BC)' later in this chapter), placing greater pressure on Roman military resources. But ironically, it was the general who destroyed Carthage in the Third Punic War who brought his experience to Spain and brought the conflict to an end.

The Lusitanians were led by Viriathus, a herdsman, who through sheer force of personality became the Lusitanians' leader. From 146–141 BC, Viriathus beat the Romans every year. His success brought the Celtiberians back into the fight in 143 BC (they'd originally come to peace terms with the Romans in 153 after a year of fighting), though by 142 BC the Romans had driven the Celtiberians back to their hilltop settlements.

The Roman solution to the Lusitanians was sneaky. In 140 BC, the Roman leader, Servilius Caepio, bribed traitors in the Lusitanian camp to murder Viriathus. Without him, Lusitanian resistance collapsed in 139 BC.

All that remained were a few cities that refused to give up. Numantia, sitting between two rivers in deep ravines, was practically impregnable and managed to hold out for nine years. Despite Roman trickery and weight of forces, the siege of Numantia went nowhere until 133 BC.

The destruction of Numantia

Numantia's end came in 133 BC. The destroyer of Carthage in 146 BC, Publius Cornelius Scipio Aemilianus, the adopted grandson of Scipio Africanus (see Chapters 12 and 23 for more on Scipio Africanus, the hero of the Second Punic War), arrived at Numantia with a force of 60,000 made up of Roman soldiers, Spanish, and other allies. Aemilianus built seven forts around the town (some of which still survive), starved out the 4,000 Numantians who were sold into slavery, and destroyed the town.

Roman names are easily confused because they're often so similar, especially in the same family. Publius Cornelius Scipio Africanus got his title from his victories in the Second Punic War. His adopted grandson, Publius Cornelius Scipio Aemilianus, was also given the title Africanus for his efforts in the Third Punic War, and was confusingly called Africanus the Younger. But this man, Aemilianus the grandson, was also awarded the title Numantinus for the victory at Numantia. For Scipio Aemilianus's mysterious death, see Chapter 14.

Why the Spanish wars were different

The Roman wars in Spain were an ugly affair. They dragged on, and the Roman custom of appointing a new commanding officer each year didn't help. The Romans had a reputation, on the whole, for being magnanimous in victory and keeping their word. Not so in Spain. The Romans broke treaty after treaty, and the Senate did nothing to stop it. The sheer number of men conscripted for military service caused discontent at home in Italy and had a serious impact on Roman domestic politics.

The Third Punic War (151–146 BC)

While the war in Spain dragged on, Rome had another war on her hands: the Third, and final, Punic War. Rome had been remarkably generous in her peace terms with Carthage (refer to Chapter 12) at the end of the Second Punic War, given that Rome could have finished off Carthage as a trading power. In addition, Rome left Hannibal in power – he probably couldn't believe his luck.

Hannibal patches up Carthage

The Carthaginians soon got themselves on their feet again. In North Africa, Hannibal introduced more efficient farming and administrative reforms which meant that Carthage was able to start paying off its fines to Rome. Carthage even offered free gifts of corn to Roman armies fighting in Greece and Macedonia. Carthage had become so servile that Hannibal's political enemies decided to go to Rome and tell the Senate that Hannibal was doing deals with the ambitious king of Syria, Antiochus III (see Chapters 12 and 25 for more on Antiochus). A Roman deputation turned up to investigate, but Hannibal escaped and went to Antiochus III's court (see the later section 'Mopping Up the East' for information on Rome's problems with Antiochus).

Rome was clearly satisfied with the way things were in Carthage. But the aged King Masinissa of Numidia, Carthage's neighbour, had other ideas.

The ambitions of Masinissa: Provoke Carthaginians

King Masinissa did well in the peace at the end of the Second Punic War: The Romans made him King of Numidia. Over the next 50 years, Masinissa built up an army and improved the Numidians' standard of living. But then, like most rulers, power went to his head, and he thought his kingdom wasn't big enough. Masinissa had his eyes on North Africa where there were numerous Carthaginian settlements.

Thanks to Rome's peace terms at the end of the Second Punic War in 202 BC (refer to Chapter 12), the Carthaginians weren't allowed to defend themselves without Roman permission. Masinissa started helping himself to Carthaginian settlements and fended off Roman objections by falling over backwards to look pro-Roman by sending food and troops to the Roman armies in the East.

Naturally, the Carthaginians were provoked and in 150 BC attacked Masinissa, which was exactly what he wanted to happen. Masinissa knew the Romans had an obsessive fear of the Carthaginians and that Hannibal was Rome's ultimate bogeyman. The slightest suggestion of trouble from the Carthaginians meant that the Romans would crush the Carthaginians mercilessly.

Lucius Hostilius Mancinus's one-man show

Lucius Hostilius Mancinus was the first soldier over Carthage's walls in the campaign of 146 BC. When Lucius got back to Rome, he infuriated Scipio Aemilianus by holding live shows in the Forum telling a public audience all about the siege and his exploits. Lucius even put up a plan of the assault and displays of scenery. Lucius's one-man show was so popular that Lucius ended up as Consul at the next election.

Rome's response: Wipe out Carthage!

Marcus Porcius Cato, an 84-year-old veteran of the Second Punic War and the wars in Spain, and leader of anti-Carthaginian fervour in Rome, denounced the Carthaginians as proven treaty-breakers. Cato famously declared *delenda est Carthago,* which means 'Carthage ought to be wiped out' (for more on Cato, see Chapters 4 and 23). Cato's opponents disagreed, thinking Carthage ought to be left as it was because it presented no real threat to Rome and fear of Carthage would hold the Roman people together. But Cato won the day, though he died almost as soon as the war started (as did King Masinissa, who had started the whole thing in the first place).

A Roman army arrived at Carthage in 149 BC. The Carthaginians promptly surrendered and handed over hostages and their military equipment. But the Romans demanded more and more. To destroy the Carthaginians once and for all, the Romans demanded that the Carthaginians abandon their city and move inland, which meant that Carthage as a trading power would cease to exist.

The Carthaginians were enraged by Rome's demands. Deciding they had nothing to lose, the Carthaginians prepared for war. Unfortunately for Carthage, most of their neighbours had already sided with Rome. The Carthaginian fortifications helped to keep the Romans back, and they sent out bands of soldiers to slow up the Roman supply lines. They held out until 147–146 BC when a new campaign began. The Roman commander Publius Cornelius Scipio Aemilianus arrived and utterly wiped out the city.

The final indignity: Salt on the wounds

There was no grand battle in Scipio Aemilianus's campaign of 147—146 BC. Aemilianus simply wore the Carthaginians down, smashing his way through Carthage's outer defences. Then, inch by inch, his troops fought hand-to-hand to reach the inner citadel. Only 50,000 Carthaginian citizens were left, which came to a tiny number, given the trouble Rome thought Carthage was. The citizens were captured and sold into slavery. The city library was broken up and its books given to neighbouring African rulers. According to legend, the Romans sowed salt on the land round Carthage to sterilise it and make it into a wasteland. Whether this legend is true or not makes no difference: Carthage was finished and in ruins. The ruins which can still be seen today lie not far from the city of Tunis. Some time later, a Roman colony was founded nearby: the final insult.

Mopping Up the East

Asia Minor (modern Turkey) was only as far away from Rome as Spain. However, the difference was that Asia Minor had a long history and established cities and kingdoms. Rome first got involved in Asia Minor during the Macedonian Wars when the Seleucid king Antiochus III 'the Great' (242–187 BC) made an alliance with Philip V of Macedon (check out Chapter 12).

The ambitions of Antiochus III

Antiochus III had been seen off by the Romans in the Second Macedonian War (200–197 BC; see Chapter 12). But he remained powerful in Asia and for the moment concentrated his ambitions in the East instead. Antiochus had married his daughter to Ptolemy V Epiphanes, Pharaoh of Egypt, as part of a treaty that secured Antiochus's conquest of Syria and Palestine, and he had also added the south coast of Asia Minor to his land.

The wealthy Greek communities of the island of Rhodes and the city of Pergamon, which headed the Aetolian League in Asia Minor, were starting to get twitchy. In the aftermath of the Second Macedonian War, the Romans had guaranteed the liberty of Greek mainland cities. Now in 196 BC, Pergamon asked the Roman Senate to guarantee the liberty of cities in Asia Minor. It was an extraordinary request and shows how powerful Rome had become. It was also an amazing gesture of confidence in Rome, now seen as a benign and honourable power.

Rome protested to Antiochus III, but this wily operator brandished a new treaty he had signed with Egypt to show he was acting with Egypt's approval. So it was impossible for Rome to pretend it was acting to defend Egypt's interests. Flamininus, the Roman commander in charge of the Roman forces in Greece, fell for the story. Others, like Scipio Africanus, weren't so sure, especially as Antiochus had now been joined by Hannibal who'd fled from Carthage in 195 BC (Hannibal later committed suicide in 183 BC).

Rome carried on negotiations with Antiochus for the next few years without getting anywhere. In the meantime, Roman forces were withdrawn from Greece. By 191 BC, however, the Romans had to return to Greece.

Cramping Antiochus III's style

The Aetolian League felt cheated by the outcome of the Second Macedonian War; they'd helped out but had been prevented by the Romans from acquiring part of Greece as a reward. So the Aetolian League invited Antiochus III to invade Greece. He did, but was met by a Roman army under the command of Scipio Africanus the Elder, who soundly saw Antiochus off at Thermopylae and Magnesia with almost the total loss of the Seleucid forces. The peace of 188 BC ended Seleucid ambitions in Europe. Antiochus had to hand over most of his fleet, pay a vast fine to Rome (the biggest Rome ever imposed on an enemy), withdraw from much of his territory, and was left only with a right to defend himself. The Seleucids remained a force to be reckoned with in Asia, but the reality was that they were so damaged Rome was bound to be able to move into the power vacuum before long.

Antiochus was crushed and humiliated by the peace imposed by Rome. He had to say goodbye to his navy and pay a record-breaking fine of 15,000 talents. Antiochus had to pull out of western Asia Minor and was denied the right to hold any territory in Europe or the Aegean or have any allies there.

A *talent* was a unit of weight of gold or silver. It's hard to get an exact equivalent but suggested figures range from 25 kilograms to 42 kilograms (about 57–93 pounds) of gold for each talent. These days, gold has been hitting prices of more than £270 an ounce, which comes close to £280,000 a talent at the lowest estimate. Which means Antiochus faced the modern equivalent of about £4.2 billion in fines.

Scipio throws a sickie

Scipio Africanus threw a sickie on the day of the battle that defeated Antiochus III. The overall Commander of the Roman force was his brother, the Consul Lucius Cornelius Scipio. Probably Scipio Africanus wanted to make sure that his brother got all the credit, but on the other hand, the real reason may have been that it suited Scipio Africanus not to be there, because he had cut a deal with Antiochus who was holding Africanus's son as hostage.

The Romans then pulled out of Asia Minor. Pergamon did the best out of the peace in territorial terms, but what really happened is that the whole area was broken up into small units. By destroying Antiochus's power in the west, the Romans wrecked his prestige, and he lost some of his eastern provinces as well.

After this, the Romans only intervened occasionally in Asia Minor's affairs, despite having done a lot to destabilise the region. When Rhodes tried to act as a peacemaker in the Third Macedonian War, Rome destroyed the island's trading interests and power, and Rhodes's traditional role of policing the seas as well.

Winning the lottery: Gaining Pergamon

In 133 BC, Rome found it was the owner of Pergamon and its territory – without a drop of blood being spilled. King Attalus III of Pergamon (reigned 138–133 BC) had no heirs, and in his will he left his kingdom to the Romans on the basis that they were the only people likely to make good use of it. Because Pergamon and its other cities were amongst the wealthiest communities in the Greek-speaking East, it wasn't difficult for Rome to accept.

Pergamon became part of the Roman province of Asia, and Rome now had a gateway to the East. This gateway turned out to be

- ✔ A source of fabulous wealth

- ✔ Where some of Rome's greatest enemies would emerge

- ✔ The site for Constantinople, the new Rome, some 440 years in the future

- ✔ Where in AD 1453 the Roman Empire would fall and ultimately die

But that was yet to come. To date, Rome had faced some of her greatest trials so far, but other challenges were on the horizon. Unlike most of Rome's previous problems, these trials were to come from within Rome herself.

Part IV
When Romans Ruled the World

The 5th Wave   By Rich Tennant

STUMBLING BLOCK IN ROME'S CONQUEST OF NORTHERN EUROPE.

Hold on—I don't think I've got a bit of change!

Welcome to NORTHERN EUROPE

EXACT CHANGE ONLY

In this part . . .

By the late second century BC, Rome was the most successful state in the ancient world. She had more power and prestige than anyone else. Yet, in the next hundred years, the Roman Republic tore itself to pieces. All the wealth and power Rome had went to the heads of several very ambitious men. Civil war nearly destroyed the greatest phenomenon of the ancient world.

It could have been terminal but for the genius of one man: Augustus Caesar. Augustus reinvented the Republic by turning it into a hereditary monarchy. His genius was to pretend that he had restored the Republic. How he did that, and as a result made the Roman Empire more powerful than ever before, is what you'll read about in this part. At its climax Roman power spread from the hills of Scotland right the way across Europe and the Mediterranean to the remote southern deserts of Egypt.

Chapter 14

Reform and Civil War

In This Chapter

▶ The bitterness of Rome's class conflicts

▶ The reformers and the new men

▶ How military dictators seized power

▶ Why the First Triumvirate came into being

▶ How the Republic dissolved into civil war

*W*henever a country grows rich and powerful, it's usually the case that the rich get richer and all too often the poor get poorer. As Rome's power and wealth grew during the second century BC, all sorts of domestic political issues started to come to the front. Because the Romans hadn't planned to end up with a growing Empire, no-one had really given any time to wondering whether the now increasingly ancient institutions of the Republic were really up to coping with the new order.

Crisis in Rome

There was a sea change in Roman politics in the second century BC. The Roman Republican system was originally built around magistracies, like the consulship (see Chapter 3). The idea was that the system would roll on endlessly, year after year, with no one man becoming pre-eminent. But corruption and self-interest led to demands for reform, led by the Gracchi brothers (read about them in the section 'Enter the Gracchi', later in this chapter). Their campaigns, and the hostility from their enemies, showed how bitterly personal Roman politics was becoming. Meanwhile, the emergence of powerful generals, like Marius, who used their armies to increase their political power at Rome showed a different side to personality-based politics and led to the civil wars of the first century BC. These wars between generals with their rival armies brought the end of the Republic.

The Conflict of the Orders, the class war between patricians and plebeians, was beginning to look like a big waste of time (Chapter 10 explains how the Conflict of the Orders started). The aristocracy, which eventually included the most successful plebeian families, had ended up controlling the whole political system and held all the high offices, leaving all the other plebeians with no real power at all. This caused terrible tensions, as the plebeians and their representatives, like the Gracchi brothers, demanded reform from an aristocracy determined to do anything to stop them.

Power to the people! – Not

Unrest arose over who was going to benefit from Rome's new wealth and power. As Rome's territories increased, new tribes had been added with new voters. Since 241 BC, the Roman voting population had been divided into 35 tribes, the final total (for more on tribes, see Chapter 2). Citizens still had to do their voting through the *Comitia Centuriata,* the assembly of male citizens eligible for military service, but it just became impossible for many of the new Roman citizens to get to Rome to vote. They simply lived too far away. Only those citizens in and around Rome were able to use their vote.

Buying votes

In addition, Roman politics were getting too complicated for most Romans. It was the politically ambitious who were able to use the system to gain power. Roman society was based round rich, powerful individuals known as *patrons,* who surrounded themselves with hangers-on, their own freed slaves ('freedmen'), business associates, and so on, called their *clients.* Patrons looked after their clients in return for loyalty. This made it easy for the nobility to persuade their clients to vote for them, and buying votes became routine. Nobles simply paid clients cash for votes or, more subtly, put on free public entertainments. Case in point: A whole series of new public games were invented during the Second Punic War (see Chapter 8 for the gaming calendar).

The Roman mob was steadily getting bigger because of the influx of farm workers and smallholders to Rome. Rome's wars put these men out of work and also captured thousands of slaves who did the work instead, situations explained in more detail in the later sections 'A soldier's tale' and 'Slaves to circumstance'). Keeping this growing mob happy became more and more important to the aristocrats because of the risk of riots and disorder in Rome if the mob became hostile.

Aristocrats on top

The upshot was that all the power ordinary people had won in the Conflict of the Orders was being gradually worn down by the aristocracy. The power of the Comitia Centuriata was also weakened. Although most senators came from plebeian families, they had become known as *nobiles* ('nobles'). In theory, any plebeian could enter the Senate and hold office, but in practice, the new nobiles shut the door on aspiring plebeian senators.

Rome was now ruled by old and new aristocrats. No-one else could get a look in. By the year 134 BC, 25 families had dominated the consulship over the last 75 years. Although no individual could hold permanent political power, it was starting to look as if the family was becoming more powerful than the individual. Aristocratic families tried to hold on to their interests by forging political ties through marriage, and did anything they could to maximise their support and political strength. At the same time, they looked for any sign that a political enemy had broken the law and then set about having those enemies prosecuted.

The rise of the equestrians

The structure of Roman society was changing. Wealth was replacing birth. In the eighteenth and nineteenth centuries, countries like the USA and Britain saw the rise of families that had grown wealthy from trade, rather than from inheriting vast landed estates like the aristocratic families. These newly rich families had a dramatic effect on society, and that's pretty much what was happening in Rome.

The main beneficiaries were the equestrians *(equites),* originally Roman citizens wealthy enough to field a horse in battle. By the late Republic, this was long in the past, and the equestrians had evolved into a sort of second-grade aristocracy below the senators. There were now really two types: the 'financier equestrians' in Rome who had grown rich from trade and business, and the equestrians who belonged to local municipal aristocracies in Italian cities with Roman citizen status (refer to Chapter 2 for where equestrians fitted into Roman society and Chapter 3 for the sorts of jobs they could do).

The trouble with allies

Other tensions were simmering. Rome's allies wanted more of the rights that Roman citizens enjoyed, such as voting and the chance to take part in the colonisation of conquered territory. After all, the allies had put a lot into winning Rome's wars for her, providing around half the troops Rome had used to fight the war in Spain and the Third Punic War. Amazingly, in 177 BC, the allies were even told they were only entitled to war booty at half the rate a Roman citizen enjoyed. Insulting treatment by Romans made the allies even crosser. In 173 BC, the city of Cales banned its own townsfolk from using the baths when a Roman magistrate was staying there.

A soldier's tale

Fewer and fewer people, especially Romans, wanted to do Rome's fighting. Even the senators protested and led the way by organising draft-dodging for their sons who ended up with office jobs on a general's staff instead of fighting. Military leadership tended to be poor. Even though hardened professionals like Scipio Africanus and his adoptive grandson Scipio Aemilianus had triumphed in the Second and Third Punic Wars respectively, the Romans continued to rely on the system of sending out a new consul each year as general. This was what had contributed to the disasters of Trasimene and Cannae in the Second Punic War because there was no system of choosing men on ability or experience.

Traditionally, Rome had relied on part-time soldiers. Raised from the Roman citizenry based on a minimum property qualification, counted in the census, these men did not come from a background of solid military training and discipline. They were raised on an as-need basis, and at this time, no man could be made to serve for more than 16 years. Normally what happened is that the army was disbanded at the end of a campaign, so there was no means of creating an experienced army and keeping it together. It wasn't until the days of the late Republic and the Empire that the Romans developed a professional army (explained in Chapter 5).

This system of part-time soldiers worked well in the past, but it wasn't good for long-term campaigning abroad because as many as 100,000 men could be involved each year. Most of Rome's soldiers worked on farms. Taking them away from their land and families for years on end could mean ruin, not just for a man and his household, but also serious consequences for Roman society and the Roman economy, so it's no surprise that some men deserted.

In an effort to increase the number of available soldiers, the minimum property qualification had to be drastically lowered. But in practice, this seems to have had little effect on improving things. Nothing at all was done to build up a highly-trained, experienced, and fully-prepared army. Instead, Rome continued to call up inexperienced new troops when needed and to rely on her allies to bolster the numbers and also on her massive resources to keep pounding away until her enemies were worn down. But as Rome's power and influence grew, it became obvious this couldn't go on. It wasn't till Gaius Marius (discussed in the section 'Marius the New Man – and More Unrest') came on the scene that a professional Roman army was organised, providing the foundation of the army of the Empire, but that brought its own dangers, as you'll see.

Slaves to circumstance

Slaves were the lowest of the low in Roman society, and Rome's wars had generated thousands more of them. These slaves worked on aristocratic estates and in the city.

On the plus side, using slaves on farms helped make good the shortage of peasants who were away fighting. On the minus side, this meant that peasants came home from the wars to find they often couldn't get work on the land. This was especially true for those peasants who fell into debt while away. In addition, land speculation, which made for larger and more efficient estates, meant more slaves were needed, forcing even more free men off the land.

In Roman society, there's a difference between a 'free man' and a 'freedman'. *Free man* means someone like you and me. A *freedman*, on the other hand, is someone who was formerly a slave.

Slaves became essential to the Roman economy, but as their numbers grew, the fear of the Romans at the prospect of slave rebellions grew as well. At the same time, free men forced off the land to make way for these huge estates became more and more discontented.

Enter the Gracchi

The *Gracchi* (which is the plural of Gracchus) brothers, Tiberius and Gaius, came into the world with the perfect pedigree. Their mother Cornelia was the daughter of Scipio Africanus, hero of the Second Punic War (refer to Chapter 12). Their father, Titus Sempronius Gracchus, had been one of the more successful commanders in Spain (refer to Chapter 13). Tiberius Gracchus had fought with distinction in the Third Punic War (detailed in Chapter 13) and climbed the social ladder by marrying Claudia, daughter of Appius Claudius Pulcher, who had been Senator in 143 BC. Strange to say, Tiberius and Gaius Gracchus set out to reform the very system that had made themselves and their families powerful.

Tiberius and Gaius Gracchus tried to pass laws that would increase the Roman citizen base in Italy and make land distribution fairer, but both found themselves fighting the self-interest of the Senate and the aristocracy, who used underhand methods to undermine them. Even though the Gracchi brothers' reforms failed, they had made a name for themselves, and their violent deaths turned them into popular martyrs.

Tiberius Sempronius Gracchus

No-one knows what turned Tiberius Gracchus, a man born to privilege and wealth, into a social reformer. But while in Spain, he'd seen that Roman soldiers weren't as tough as they used to be and also noticed how free peasant farmers and farm-workers were being replaced by slaves. Tiberius had also been disturbed by how a massive slave revolt had exploded in Sicily in 135 BC, provoked by extremely harsh treatment and started by slaves working on a farm. Before long, more than 70,000 slaves had risen, murdering their masters and leading to minor copycat slave rebellions in Italy, too. It took a Roman army till 132 BC to crush the Sicilian slave revolt.

Tiberius Gracchus probably concluded that the Italian farming stock, which provided the backbone of the army, needed support with improved rights and privileges so that Rome would have a better and bigger source of soldiers for its wars, and not have to depend for agriculture on slavery, with all its dangers of rebellion. He also realised that a system where the aristocracy controlled so much of the wealth was bound to lead to civil unrest if something wasn't done (perhaps he'd looked into the future and seen the French Revolution!).

Proposing land reform

In 133 BC, Tiberius Gracchus was elected Tribune of the Plebs (see Chapter 3 for this important post). As tribune, he tried to bring in a law to distribute public land acquired since the Second Punic War more fairly to encourage the farming of land by free men rather than slaves (this wasn't an entirely new idea; his father-in-law Appius Claudius Pulcher had already suggested this). Tiberius Gracchus proposed that big landowners should be compensated and the land divided up into smaller parcels.

Because this was a slap in the face to all those senators who'd been profiteering from land over the past few decades, it's no great surprise to learn that the Senate refused to fund the commission to organise the reforms. But thanks to Attalus III of Pergamon in 133 BC and leaving his kingdom of Asia to the Romans (refer to Chapter 13), Tiberius brought in a bill to appropriate those funds instead and the commission set to work.

An ancient law of Rome held that no Roman could have more than 500 acres of land. No-one had taken any notice of the law for generations, but Tiberius Gracchus wanted the law restored in order that more people would benefit. Senators with vast estates were horrified.

A veto war, a new land law, and growing concern

The nobles, unhappy with Tiberius Gracchus's proposed change, were out to get him. They had the other Tribune, Marcus Octavius, on their side, and he vetoed Tiberius Gracchus's bill. A veto war broke out. Tiberius Gracchus vetoed all the other legislation going through at the time. Both Tiberius Gracchus and Marcus Octavius were determined not to back down.

Tiberius Gracchus finally told Marcus Octavius to abandon his veto or be thrown out of office by the plebs. Marcus Octavius refused, so he was removed by a vote of the plebs. The new land law went through, but there were deep concerns that Tiberius Gracchus had broken the law by having Octavius thrown out.

In 132 BC, Tiberius Gracchus stood for Tribune again, to protect himself and his new laws. He hoped this would make his position safe because the job of tribune was treated as inviolable. This strategy was both tactless and border-line illegal (a law of 180 BC banned holding the same magistracy two years running, though it wasn't clear to anyone if this included the tribuneship) – it was certainly bad practice, and Tiberius Gracchus lost a lot of support. A brawl broke out during the electoral meetings. A bunch of senators got out of control and, in their fury, clubbed Tiberius Gracchus and 300 of his senators to death. So much for the rule of law in Rome. The Senate went on to use the law to prosecute the rest of Tiberius Gracchus's supporters, though in reality it was more of a witch hunt.

Continuing Tiberius Gracchus's reforms: Scipio Aemilianus and Marcus Fulvius Flaccus

As a senator, Publius Cornelius Scipio Aemilianus denounced Tiberius Gracchus for his dubious actions. But Scipio Aemilianus, the great commander in the Third Punic War who'd destroyed Carthage and Numantia in Spain (refer to Chapter 13), knew how much Rome owed to its Latin and Italian soldiers. Scipio Aemilianus decided to promote the soldiers' interests, which irritated the Roman mob. Mysteriously, Scipio Aemilianus was then found dead. It was probably a natural death, but the situation had become so heated that there was talk of foul play. And the prime suspect was Scipio Aemilianus's wife Sempronia, sister of Tiberius Gracchus.

Marcus Fulvius Flaccus, Consul for 134 BC, took up Scipio Aemilianus's proposal to give the allies who wished, Roman citizenship. This was totally unacceptable to the senators who only wanted voters in Rome whom they could buy and control. The proposed extension of citizenship was a missed opportunity and started a time bomb ticking that would go off in 90 BC.

Gaius Gracchus

Gaius Gracchus, who in 123 BC became Tribune of the Plebs, followed up his brother's reforms and became one of the most important political figures in Rome's history. He was a brilliant speaker. Unlike his brother Tiberius, Gaius Gracchus was hot-blooded, but he knew what he was doing, kept cool, and avoided acting on impulse. If Gaius Gracchus got worked up, a slave calmed him down by playing the flute.

Reforms on his watch

As Tribune of the Plebs, Gaius Gracchus brought in social and economic reforms, including:

- ✔ **Land reforms:** Gaius Gracchus promoted his brother Tiberius's land reforms and arranged for new roads to be built in order that produce could be transported and sold more easily.

- ✔ **New colonies:** Gaius Gracchus founded new colonies to stimulate industry in Italy.

- ✔ **Agricultural reform:** Gaius Gracchus reorganised Rome's corn supply to prevent fluctuations in availability by arranging for storage, setting the amount for each person, and regulating prices.

- ✔ **Legal reform:** Gaius Gracchus decreed that Roman citizens could not be executed before the Roman people without a trial.

Gaius Gracchus also challenged abuses of the law, such as senators on juries who had acquitted fellow senators charged with extortion while serving as provincial governors. Gaius Gracchus's new law passed control of such juries to the equestrians, which everyone interpreted as an insult to the Senate. Senators would no longer be able to control and exploit provincial governorships. Gaius Gracchus also promoted the interests of the equestrians by making the tax collectors among them responsible for collecting revenue from the newly acquired province of Asia. By offering the equestrians so much power, Gaius Gracchus also bought their support.

Downfall of Gaius Gracchus

In 122 BC, Gaius Gracchus was re-elected tribune but with none of the trouble his brother Tiberius experienced. Wisely, Gaius Gracchus hadn't actually stood for re-election, but the people voted him in anyway. Gaius Gracchus proposed that the first overseas Roman colony be founded near the site of old Carthage. He also reintroduced the idea that the Latin allies be made full Roman citizens and the rest given Latin status. But a rival tribune called Marcus Livius Drusus, with secret Senate backing, vetoed Gaius Gracchus's ideas and offered an even more attractive package of reforms. They included 12 new settlements in Italy, open even to the poorest, and also total exemption for the Latins from execution or flogging by Roman military commanders.

Livius Drusus's laws were passed, though nothing was ever done about any of them; their sole purpose had been to undermine Gaius Gracchus, whose popularity was on the wane anyway, partly because rumours were circulating that his new colony near Carthage was encroaching on the 'cursed' site of the old city destroyed at the end of the Third Punic War in 146 BC. In 121 BC, Gaius Gracchus tried to get in as tribune for a third term, but failed.

The Senate told one of the new tribunes, Marcus Minucius Rufus, to propose annulling the law intended to create the new colony in Africa. One of the reasons was that the Senate had an abiding fear that one day a colony of Rome would end up being more powerful than Rome. After all, the original Carthage started life as a colony of the city of Tyre in Phoenicia (roughly where Lebanon is now) and had ended up totally overshadowing its mother city.

Gaius Gracchus's opponents in the Senate had a leader in the form of Lucius Opimius, a man who hated everything Gaius Gracchus stood for, and they made sure he was elected Consul. Lucius Opimius and his associates immediately started revoking Gaius Gracchus's laws. So Gaius Gracchus got his friends together to try and stop Opimius blocking his new colony by turning up at the Capitol to protest in force, but a fight broke out between the rival bands of supporters and one of Gaius Gracchus's men killed one of Opimius's servants. That gave Opimius the chance to declare Gaius Gracchus an enemy of the state, offering a reward for his capture and persuading the Senate to pass a resolution called *Senatus Consultum Ultimum* ('The most extreme Senatorial decree').

The Senatus Consultum Ultimum decreed that, when a situation was desperate, the Senate had to support magistrates bringing an action against an enemy of the state. That meant consuls could do away with someone like Gaius Gracchus and simply argue they were defending the state, and, of course, the consuls automatically had the support of the Senate.

121 BC: A vintage year

Funnily enough, 121 BC was also remembered for its excellent wines as well as the end of Gaius Gracchus. The summer of 121 BC was especially hot and sunny, producing a celebrated harvest of grapes. Two centuries later men were still drinking wine made that year and singing its praises.

In the riots that followed, hundreds of Gaius Gracchus's supporters were killed. Gaius Gracchus himself ordered his slave Philocrates to kill him, which he did, though another story has both men being caught and killed by rioters. Thousands more of Gaius Gracchus's supporters were later executed.

The aftermath of the Gracchi

With Gaius Gracchus out of the way, the Senate could do more or less as it wanted. The Senate was able to call on its new Senatus Consultum Ultimum resolution whenever it needed. Wisely, the Senate allowed most of the Gracchi brothers' reforms to go ahead, realising that any opposition would incur the fury of the people.

What the Gracchi brothers left to the world was the fact that the days when the people could reform Rome through their tribunes were over. Politicians now divided into two groups. The two groups weren't political parties as we would understand them; they were more simply ways of thinking:

- ✔ *Optimates* ('the Best Men'): These were political leaders who pursued their ambitions through the Senate and claimed moral and social superiority based on birth.
- ✔ *Populares* ('the People's Men'): These were political leaders who tried to work through the people and tribunes and claimed to defend the liberty of the people from the actions of the Optimates.

The identities of the Optimates and the Populares were easily blurred. For example, a noble starting out on his political career could serve as tribune of the plebs and use Populares' techniques like promising land and voting reforms. In the long run, this made it possible for the nobles, including emperors, to keep control.

Marius the New Man – and More Unrest

Gaius Marius (157–86 BC) had fought at Numantia in Spain (refer to Chapter 13 for more on Numantia). With the support of the Metelli family, one of the top senatorial families in Rome, Gaius Marius came to Rome to try his hand in politics as a *novus homo* ('new man'). A novus homo was a person who was able to get power, not by their wealth or birth, but through ability. As a 'new man', Gaius Marius was to become the most important military leader at the end of the second century BC.

Marius rose to the top purely because of his own talents. Marius came from a town called Arpinum, south-east of Rome, as did another brilliant new man, the orator Cicero, born in 106 BC. Both men eventually became consuls and made a permanent mark on Rome's history. Although they both came from affluent backgrounds, they couldn't rely on the network of support members of old aristocratic families and had to try much harder to get on. Such ambitious and committed self-made men were the shape of things to come. (Head to the section 'The Gang of Three: The First Triumvirate', later in this chapter, for details on Cicero's objections to the triumvirate system.)

Fighting the Jugurthine War

Masinissa's Numidia came back to haunt Rome. It was Masinissa's skilful manipulation of Rome's hysterical fear of Carthage that had led to the Third Punic War (see Chapter 13). By 118 BC, Masinissa was long dead and was so his son Micipsa, who had left Numidia to his two biological sons and an adoptive third son called Jugurtha. Jugurtha killed one of the two other brothers and defied all Roman attempts to impose a settlement between himself and the surviving brother.

So in 111 BC, Rome started the Jugurthine War. It didn't go well, which was bad news for the nobles, especially in the eyes of the Roman mob – because some senators had also been accused of corruption and accepting bribes. In 109 BC, Quintus Caecilius Metellus, a member of the vastly powerful Caecilii Metelli family whose members held many consulships and military commands, took command in the Jugurthine War. He improved discipline, but the Roman mob wasn't impressed by the slow progress of the fighting.

Gaius Marius, who was in Africa with Quintus Caecilius Metellus, seized his chance. He raced back to Rome, claiming that Metellus was dragging out the Jugurthine War for the sake of his own glory.

Marius, taking advantage of frustration in Rome at the way the Jugurthine War had not been brought to an end, severely criticised Caecilius Metellus. By presenting himself as an appropriate alternative, Marius managed to get himself elected as Consul in 107 BC, thus qualifying him to be made Commander in Africa, instead of Caecilius Metellus.

To improve the army, Marius brought in volunteers, rather than unwilling conscripts. He trained the new troops and led a highly successful series of campaigns against Jugurtha, bringing Jugurtha to Rome in 104 BC for execution. Marius became extremely popular in Rome – not surprisingly – and his military success was to have important consequences for Rome's politics.

Marius's mules

Marius helped start the process of creating the first professional standing army in Rome's history. In 107 BC, he started hiring, training, and equipping volunteers from amongst Romans who were too poor to have the normal property qualifications for military service. It's possible this had happened before, but Marius turned it into a major break with the past. Crucially, his troops were loyal to Marius, their leader, rather than to Rome. Soldiers were now disciplined, mobile, and self-sufficient. Marius improved the organisation of the army by introducing centurions (see Chapter 5). Having professional soldiers meant keeping them busy when there was no fighting, rather than sending them home. Marius used soldiers to build roads and bridges. The soldiers became known as 'Marius's mules'. The professional army was to be the backbone of the future Roman Empire.

The 'Northmen' advance

As soon as Marius returned to Rome, he was promptly appointed to train up and lead another army to fend off a tribal invasion from the north. The Cimbri and Teutones tribes, known collectively as the 'Northmen', terrified the average Roman. As a result of this fear, Marius was illegally made Consul five times between 104–100 BC (there was supposed to be a ten-year gap between being consul twice), because it was generally felt that having him in charge was more important than worrying about the law. Marius ended up being the first man to be consul seven times. In 102 and 101 BC, he destroyed the Northmen threat and made himself even more popular.

Suppressing a slave revolt in Sicily

Marius then suppressed a slave revolt in Sicily. Many of the slaves there had been free men, captured by pirates and sold into Roman slavery. In 104 BC, the Senate ordered that the kidnapped men be freed, but slave owners were determined not to lose their expensively purchased labour. The owners, led by the governor of Sicily, prevented the Senate's order being enforced, so in 103 BC, the kidnapped men seized a chance to escape and start a rebellion, encouraging other slaves to join them. It wasn't until one of Marius's armies arrived in 101 BC that the revolt was crushed.

Marius's downfall

Despite his many successes, Marius totally failed to use his position as Consul to reform the Roman state. More concerned with the welfare of his soldiers, he left all the moves for land reform to a tribune named Lucius Appuleius Saturninus. The two men fixed things so that Caecilius Metellus was the only senator to oppose the reforms and forced him into exile.

Saturninus had been placed in charge of Rome's grain supply in 105 BC. This was a good job for anyone with ambition because doing well meant more votes. But Saturninus was pushed out when the grain price went up thanks to a shortage caused by a slave rebellion in Sicily; instead the job was given to someone with more experience. Saturninus took this as a personal insult and was out to get the nobility from then on. He had himself elected as tribune in 103 BC and used the position to crank up demands for reform.

To begin with, Saturninus was the perfect friend for Marius. Saturninus attracted popular support by reintroducing low-price grain handouts and arranged for land grants for Marius's veteran soldiers. Saturninus used thugs from the Roman mob to attack anyone who criticised him and made sure of his own re-election as tribune by having a rival murdered.

Unfortunately for Marius, Saturninus's plans for Marius's veterans, and the Latin and Italian allies who had also fought for Marius, turned the Roman mob against Saturninus. There was an all-out riot in the Forum of Rome between Saturninus's supporters and the Roman mob. Saturninus won, but he organised the murder of another political rival called Memmius.

Marius decided enough was enough. The Senate demanded Marius use his powers as Consul to protect the state against Saturninus. Saturninus was trapped on the Capitoline Hill, but a crowd burst in and killed him. Marius was in a no-win situation. He had lost support in the Saturninus Populares camp, but because also Marius wouldn't let Caecilius Metellus come back from exile, Marius lost any standing with the Optimates.

Marius and the eagle

Marius came up with the idea to get rid of the different standards the legions carried into battle. The emblems represented a variety of real and mythical beasts like wild boars, wolves, and the Minotaur. But Marius wanted the eagle to be the great symbol of Rome's power. He had his way, and from 104 BC each legion carried a standard with a silver eagle into battle. The idea of eagles-only didn't last – the legions later went back to their own symbols as well as that of the eagle.

The Senate overturned all of Saturninus's legislation that would also have provided for Marius's veterans. The Senate's action created a divide between the soldiers and the Senate. From now on, soldiers looked to their generals and not to the Roman state for their future security.

Metellus was allowed back from exile anyway, and Marius had to leave for Asia. Marius was a military genius and a great commander, but he was no politician. But he was far from finished, even though he'd managed to annoy just about everyone.

Fighting Your Friends: The Social War (90–88 BC)

The word for an ally in Latin is *socius* (allies: *socii*); the name given to the conflict that now broke out: the Social War. The conflict threatened Rome's very existence – and was the worst crisis that Rome had had to deal with since Hannibal's exploits more than a century before.

Wrong-footing the allies

When the Senate overturned Saturninus's law reforms (refer to the preceding section, 'Marius's downfall'), Rome's Italian allies were bitterly disappointed. The allies had made a great contribution in recent wars, and they deeply resented being excluded from becoming full Roman citizens. Italians who'd gathered in Rome to support Saturninus now looked like serious trouble. Italian resentment was growing, and before long it was bound to explode.

Marcus Livius Drusus, Tribune of the Plebs in 91 BC, started the reform ball rolling again. He had the backing of the Senate, who hoped he would clamp down on the political power of the equestrians. The plan included the following:

- ✔ Drusus would restore control of the courts to the Senate and, in return, 300 top equestrians would be made senators.
- ✔ In his biggest move, Drusus's was to give the Italian allies full Roman voting rights. He did this because he realised giving the allies Roman citizenship was inevitable, and Drusus wanted to make sure it was done on the Senate's terms.

The Senate, equestrians, and the general Roman mob joined forces in total opposition to Drusus's reform. Even Drusus was alarmed when the cities of the allies started organising 'committees of action', and even more so by a plan to assassinate the Consul Lucius Marcius Philippus, one of Drusus's chief opponents. Drusus warned Philippus, but his good faith gesture did him (Drusus) no good. Philippus had all Drusus's previous reforms thrown out and had Drusus murdered.

The allies involved in the Social War that followed were mainly from the mountainous areas and were only a small proportion of Rome's allies – but they were good fighters. These allies organised a confederation. Considering that the allies had been trained and disciplined in warfare the Roman way, they were a deadly prospect.

Extending the franchise and ending the war

The Social War went badly for the Romans to begin with, as they'd been caught off their guard. Despite fielding a massive army, by the end of 90 BC, the Romans decided they had to stop the rebellion spreading. Therefore, they gave the full franchise – that is, Roman citizenship – to loyal allies and to those allies who hadn't joined in fighting. This move had the desired effect. (One of the Roman commanders, Lucius Cornelius Sulla, also did a great deal to bring the war to an end in 88 BC by fighting with uncompromising ruthless-ness. You can read about Sulla in the following section 'Think the unthink-able: A Roman captures Rome – Sulla'.) In the end, the war was said to have cost Italians more than 300,000 young men.

The upshot of the Social War is that Rome survived, but it was ironic that it had taken the conflict to bring about the franchise extension that had been such a source of unpleasantness and violence in Rome for decades. If what Gaius Gracchus and Drusus had asked for originally had been granted, war could have been avoided.

The outcome of the Social War was that by giving the allies the franchise, Rome in the long run became stronger. But the dogs of war had been let loose. The very same Roman armies created to fight and bring peace would soon tear the Republic apart.

Think the Unthinkable: A Roman Captures Rome – Sulla (88 BC)

Lucius Cornelius Sulla (138–78 BC) had a nickname: *Felix* ('Lucky'), and with good reason. But he also went down in history as one of Rome's greatest vil-lains (see Chapter 24). Because he had fought so well in the Social War, Sulla was in the perfect position to benefit from Marius's lack of political skills.

Taking Rome and settling Mithridates

Mithridates VI, King of Pontus, without difficulty, had occupied a large part of Asia Minor and Greece, the locals having decided that Mithridates's lordship was preferable to Rome's greed and bullying. Sulla was put in command of the army to fight Mithridates, but Marius wanted the job. The Tribune Sulpicius had the command transferred to Marius, with the idea that he, Sulpicius, could use Marius's support for his reforms. Sulla gave in, but finding that he still had the loyalty of the troops, Sulla decided to gamble everything and marched on Rome.

In 88 BC, Sulla marched on Rome and seized the city – an unbelievably dramatic and illegal act for which he was forever remembered as a criminal. Even his own officers deserted in disgust. Sulla had Sulpicius killed, and Marius then fled Rome and hid out with his veterans. Sulla forced through new laws, using his army's muscle to put down opposition. The die was cast for the future: Ambitious men and their armies would control Roman politics for the decades to come.

Sulla left Rome, ignoring a summons to stand trial, and fought Mithridates. In 87 BC, the Consul Lucius Cornelius Cinna tried to start reversing Sulla's legislation. He was expelled from Rome by his colleague, the Consul Gnaeus Octavius, who practically set himself up as sole ruler. So Cinna collected an army of legionaries and Italian allies, and Marius, who came back to Italy to join in. They marched on Rome – bad news for Sulla who was obviously desperate to get back. Sulla forced Mithridates to come to terms with Rome, ignoring the fact that Mithridates had murdered thousands of Romans while conquering Asia. Mithridates became a Roman ally in return for giving up all his conquests in Asia and Greece.

Marius and Cinna fight back

Marius and Cinna marched on Rome where they carried on a reign of terror and murdered many of the aristocrats, including Sulla's supporters.

During this campaign in 86 BC, Marius died (of natural causes, believe it or not – exhausted, he had a breakdown, started drinking heavily, and got pleurisy). Cinna was left the ruler of Rome. Keen to restore order and end the violence, Cinna promptly gave Roman citizenship to the new Italian citizens in Rome's 35 tribes and cancelled their debts. This made Cinna very popular, and he was re-elected to the consulship in 86 BC without opposition. Despite the reign of terror that lead up to his rule, Cinna managed to establish peace and stability for a few years, but Sulla was still a danger. Cinna prepared for war against Sulla, but Cinna was murdered by some of his own men in 84 BC.

I'll be back: Sulla comes home

Sulla had little trouble rounding up support from the aristocracy, thanks to Cinna and Marius's campaign against them. Amongst the aristocrats who joined Sulla were two future big names:

- Marcus Licinius Crassus
- Gnaeus Pompeius (known to history as Pompey)

Sulla needed just one year of fighting to deal with the opposition to his return. Only a force of 70,000 Samnites (for Samnites, see Chapter 11) ended up standing in his way. Close to Rome, in 82 BC, Sulla's army wiped out the Samnites and butchered and tortured the survivors. Pompey wiped out any support amongst forces in Sicily and Africa who supported Marius, and earned himself the title Magnus ('the Great'), which was supposed to be one of Sulla's jokes but the name stuck. By 80 BC, all resistance to Sulla ended.

Dictator of Rome

Sulla was elected Dictator of Rome in 81 BC. He organised the murder of his opponents by declaring them outlaws, putting a price on their heads, and displaying a list of their names. Funnily enough, the idea of the list was to save unnecessary worry for anyone not on it. Imagine what it did to those who were listed – all 500 of them!

Sulla's main targets were the new breed of financier equestrians, whose wealth came from business and trade, because they'd supported Marius. Sulla seized these equestrians' money and gave it to his veterans or his friends. Sulla freed the condemned equestrians' slaves and hired them as his bodyguards. He also seized land from cities that had supported Marius and gave it to his own soldiers. This last was a smart move on Sulla's part: Sulla needed to provide for his soldiers in order to stop them turning to crime and being a threat to Sulla's rule.

Despite his brutality, Sulla knew Rome needed the return of the rule of law and did the following:

- Increased the numbers of the Senate by promoting members of the equestrians in the Italian municipal aristocracy (not the same as the financier equestrians in Rome, whom he hated) to replace the men lost in the fighting. The Senate now numbered 600 and crucially the new members meant much better representation for Italy.

✔ Restored the Senate's right to veto legislation passed by the *Concilium Plebis Tributum* (the Council of Plebs, see Chapter 3), wiping out most of the tribunes' power at a stroke. That meant that men like Marius could no longer use tribunes to pass laws they had failed to get the Senate to introduce.

✔ Laid down that the career structure of magistracies held by senators would be strictly fixed by age to prevent overambitious young men reaching high office too early, but their numbers were increased to take into account Rome's increasing number of provinces (magistrates like quaestors and praetors, see Chapter 3, would serve a year at Rome and then be sent out to a province).

✔ Gave the Senate the power to select magistrates for posts in provincial government and, at the same time, prohibited them from fighting wars outside the borders of their provinces to stop them trying to seize power and destabilising Rome.

✔ Increased the number of Roman provinces to ten (in Spain, northern Italy, Africa, Sardinia and Corsica, and Sicily). Naturally, this increased Rome's wealth and call on resources.

✔ Left Italy's civil and political privileges as they were and promised not to revoke any earlier grants of Roman citizenship to Italian cities, except in one or two cases. In practice, many Italian cities started voluntarily remodelling their constitutions on Rome's anyway. It just showed how influential the Roman system was.

Retiring alive and dying peacefully

Sulla was dictator for three years, which was an incredible violation of the age-old principle of the Roman Republic: that no-one could hold permanent political power. In 79 BC, Sulla resigned, retired to the country and, living up to his name of 'lucky', died peacefully the following year, which was a remarkable achievement for him and the age he lived in.

Sulla's man Lucullus

Licinius Lucullus (*c.* 100–57 BC) was related to both Sulla and the powerful Metelli family. Lucullus had marched on Rome with Sulla and also fought with him in Asia against Mithridates VI, King of Pontus. In 74 BC, Lucullus got his own military command in the East because Mithridates had broken the 88 BC settlement with Sulla and started fighting again. Lucullus's army refused to fight, accusing Lucullus of dragging out the war to get rich. He was recalled and Pompey sent out in his place. Lucullus more or less retired to private life. Apart from obstructing Pompey's settlement of Asia in 62 BC (see Gnaeus Pompeius); Lucullus became notorious for his luxury lifestyle, extravagant gardens in Rome, and famously lavish banquets.

Despite his achievements, Sulla left Rome unsettled because:

- ✔ Although Sulla promoted Italian equestrians to the Senate, he only did that as a one-off. He failed to introduce a regular system of bringing in Italians, which would have invigorated the Senate and given it a broader appreciation of Rome's place in Italy and the world.

- ✔ He missed the chance to bring in long-lasting reforms to the Republic, for example, creating permanent representation of Italian cities in the Senate or making it possible to vote in places all round Italy for Rome's magistrates.

- ✔ He left many enemies such as Sertorius, who was leading a revolt in Spain (discussed in the later section 'Gnaeus Pompeius (Pompey)').

- ✔ In the East, Mithridates VI had overturned his settlement with Sulla and gone back to war, which meant a new Roman army had to be sent out to force a new peace. But it took till 62 BC to achieve this.

- ✔ Sulla had dramatically shown how a single general could rise to power at the head of an army. They owed their livelihoods and their retirement grants to him and him alone, and were liable to follow other military leaders once he was gone. This was a terrible sign for the future, and it echoed down the decades to come. Any man with an eye on power could see how Sulla had done it and made sure he did the same.

Well, They Started Out As Mates: The Age of the Generals

Instead of the Roman Republic being allowed to recuperate after Sulla's rule, it was plunged into more warfare. The traditional aristocracy carried on dominating all the senior positions in the Senate and the various magistracies, but spent most of its energies on its own internal quarrels and holding on to its privileges, rather than trying to carry on any reforms. What followed was the *Age of the Generals*, which brought the Republic to its final dizzying end.

The three generals who defined the shape of Roman history down to the 40s BC were Gnaeus Pompeius, Marcus Licinius Crassus, and Gaius Julius Caesar. They all led armies, jockeyed for power, worked together and against each other depending on the circumstances. And they all had violent deaths.

The time from Sulla down to Octavian (roughly the first 70 years of the first century BC) is sometimes called the *Imperatorial Age* from the Latin word *imperator,* meaning a general.

Gnaeus Pompeius (Pompey) (106–48 BC)

Pompey was the son of a general called Pompeius Strabo. He fought with great success and bravery under his father, and he was immensely popular for his looks and manner, which did a lot to overcome the fact that he was born an equestrian. He used three legions of his father's veterans to fight for Sulla against Marius.

Pompey earned his title Magnus ('the Great') during the campaign to clear Marius's supporters out of Africa (see the earlier section 'I'll be back: Sulla comes home'). But Pompey's rise to military and political power had also been achieved in other campaigns:

✔ **The revolt in Spain:** In Spain, the Marian Sertorius led a highly success-ful revolt that involved making a pact with Mithridates VI, King of Pontus; Sertorius followed this by stirring rebellions in southern Gaul; and he even planned an overland invasion of Italy, as Hannibal had done in 218 BC. In 77 BC, the Senate sent Pompey to Spain to finish Sertorius off. Sertorius had been waging a guerrilla war with about 2,600 men, and what was left of a Roman army that had fled Italy, led by Perpenna. Between them, Sertorius and Perpenna held off four Roman armies totalling about 140,000.

The war in Spain came to a rapid end in 73 BC when Sertorius was mur-dered by Perpenna. Pompey's settlement of Spain was generous and fair-minded. He even destroyed Sertorius's archives to prevent a *pogrom* (an organised persecution) of any of his associates in Rome. Because of this, Pompey's personal standing and popularity increased.

✔ **The slave war:** In about 73 BC a massive slave revolt broke out in Capua and spread across Italy, lasting until 71 BC. The revolt was led by a run-away gladiator called Spartacus. Marcus Licinius Crassus had defeated the slaves, but Pompey raced back from Spain with his army to help hunt down survivors and claim all the credit. That stole Crassus's thun-der, much to Crassus's fury, and had given Pompey an excuse to bring his army into Italy.

Spartacus and the slave revolt are immortalised in the famous movie made in 1960, starring Kirk Douglas as the hero. See Chapter 2 for more on the revolt, and Chapter 25 for more about Spartacus himself.

✔ **Making an alliance with Crassus:** Because of the bad blood between them during the slave war, Marcus Licinius Crassus and Pompey could have gone for each other's throats, but they were smart enough to realise they would be much more powerful working together. In 70 BC, Crassus and Pompey were made joint consuls and promptly gave back to the tribunes all the powers they had before Sulla was in power. It was a clever move. Crassus and Pompey depended on their armies for their power, but they knew the Senate hated this and would try to force them to give up their armies. Now the tribunes were restored to power, Crassus and Pompey could appeal to the tribunes for the necessary approval to keep their armies.

✔ **Pompey and the pirates:** In 67 BC, Pompey was given supreme command to get rid of the Cilician pirates in the eastern Mediterranean (Cilicia is where southern Turkey is now). Pompey did the job in three months, capturing 20,000 men and 90 ships, as well as huge quantities of treasure. Pompey's victory made him very popular because it at once cut the price of grain, and grain ships no longer risked piracy.

The Cilician pirates also feature in the movie *Spartacus* (1960). The pirates help the rebellious slaves by providing transport for the slaves out of Italy. There isn't a movie about Pompey and the pirates, but the movie *Ben Hur* (1957), set in the early days of Christianity, starring Charlton Heston as our hero, features a great sea battle between Roman warships manned by shackled slaves, pirate galleys, and shows how the ships tried to ram each other.

✔ **Defeating Mithridates and conquering other lands:** In 66 BC, Pompey was ordered to sort out Mithridates VI, King of Pontus. Pompey defeated Mithridates and followed that up by conquering Armenia, Syria, and Judaea. Pompey's settlement in 62 BC was brilliant: He founded colonies, gave the pirates land so they didn't need to be pirates, and set up a loyal client king in Judaea.

In 62 BC, Pompey came home and disbanded his army, to everyone's relief (and surprise). But in return, Pompey wanted land for his veterans and the Senate's approval of his settlement in the East. Pompey was frustrated by the Senate. In order to get what he wanted, Pompey joined forces with two other ambitious politicians – Marcus Licinius Crassus and Julius Caesar – in an alliance known to history as the First Triumvirate.

Pompey's victories

The victorious Pompey was a legend in his own lifetime and ever afterwards. Pompey had risen to the top through his own talents; he was merely an equestrian when his career started. Pliny the Elder (see Chapter 23) thought Pompey was quite equal to Alexander the Great, but Pliny then went over the top by suggesting Pompey was nearly as successful as the immortal Hercules. After the war in Africa, Pompey was the first equestrian to ride in a triumphal chariot. The chariot was towed by elephants, a sight never seen before in Rome. To commemorate the defeat of the pirates and his Eastern conquests Pompey paraded a costly portrait of himself made in pearls. He was later blamed for making precious stones and pearls fashionable. At the same time Pompey introduced fluorspar (calcium fluoride), translucent ornamental vessels, to Rome, as well as handing out vast sums of money to the state, his commanders, and every one of his soldiers.

Marcus Licinius Crassus (c. 115 to 53 BC)

Marcus Licinius Crassus's father had defended Rome unsuccessfully against Marius in 87 BC, and Crassus fled to Spain, later reaching Africa before returning to Italy where he joined Sulla in 83 BC. His reward was to make money out of Sulla's proscriptions against his enemies, even adding an innocent man to the list just to profit from confiscating this man's estate. Sulla never trusted him again after that, but Crassus could work a crowd and was popular with the Roman people.

After serving as praetor (see Chapter 3 for this magistracy), Crassus was made general of the army sent to defeat Spartacus and the slave revolt of 73–71 BC, in preference to sending out inexperienced consuls. He was victorious, but the way Pompey turned up at the last minute to take all the credit enraged him. Crassus's career was a constant struggle against Pompey, though they served together in the First Triumvirate (discussed in the later section 'The Gang of Three: The First Triumvirate') because he was too powerful to be left out.

The most famous Roman of them all: Julius Caesar

Gaius Julius Caesar (100–44 BC) – (see also Chapter 23), is the most famous Roman who has ever lived. Caesar's family claimed descent from Aeneas's son Anchises, known also as Iulus. Aeneas's mother was the goddess Venus; you can see what sort of pedigree Caesar was able to boast about. Caesar backed Marius's military leaderships and Pompey's restoration of the tribunes.

How Crassus got rich

Crassus was phenomenally wealthy, and it didn't all come from Sulla's proscriptions. One of the ways he got rich quick was by training up slaves to be builders and architects. When Crassus got news of a house on fire, he'd rush round and offer the owner a knock-down price.

The terrified owner usually sold up, as even a bad price was better than nothing. Crassus then had the fire put out and redeveloped the site for rent. The end result was that after a few years, Crassus owned a huge part of Rome.

Caesar was highly ambitious and extremely intelligent. He was also a brilliant leader and knew how to make himself popular. In 65 BC, Caesar became an aedile (the assistant to a tribune, refer to Chapter 3) and spent a huge amount of money (probably Crassus's money) on public works and entertainments, such as wild-beast fights and stage plays. Caesar also reinstated the trophies commemorating Marius's victories in the Jugurthine War and against the Northmen.

Caesar wasn't averse to underhand tactics. In 63 BC, he bribed his way into becoming *Pontifex Maximus* (chief priest). In 62 BC, an attempt was made to implicate Caesar in a conspiracy against the state (the Catiline Conspiracy; see the sidebar 'Marcus Tullius Cicero and the Catiline Conspiracy' for details), but Cicero proved this was impossible. The accusations against Caesar did him no harm, and Caesar was made governor of Further Spain (nowadays Portugal) in 61 BC.

The Gang of Three: The First Triumvirate (60 BC)

Triumvirate comes from two Latin words: *tres* ('three') and *vir* ('man'), and means 'rule by three men'. By the time of the Second Triumvirate, the triumvirate had become a legal Roman institution. But the First Triumvirate had no legal backing; it was a private deal between three immensely powerful men – Pompey, Crassus, and Caesar – who believed they would be even more powerful if they joined together. However, not everyone was so keen on the idea of the triumvirate, and the most conspicuous was Cicero.

Cicero (106–43 BC), like his famous forbear Marius, was a *novus homo* ('new man'). Unlike Marius, Cicero was a man of letters and brilliant orator (refer to Chapter 1 for details of what Cicero wrote). By the 60s BC, Cicero had a brilliant reputation following his success in the trial of Gaius Verres, accused of extortion in his time as governor of Sicily (Chapter 24). Cicero championed Pompey and also exposed the Catiline Conspiracy in 62 BC. Determined to remain politically independent, Cicero refused help from Caesar and fled Rome, returning several years later. Cicero's greatest wish was that all the various political groups would work together in what he called the Concord of the Orders. Cicero thought the best way forward was for the senators and equestrians to work together. In the end, Cicero had no choice but to accept the union of the First Triumvirate.

Cicero and the Catiline Conspiracy

Lucius Sergius Catilinus was one of Sulla's side-kicks during Sulla's dictatorship. Catilinus stood for Consul in 63 BC, but was defeated by Cicero. The next year Catilinus stood on a ticket to defend anyone who was poor and discontented. Catilinus lost, and Crassus dumped him. Catilinus got together the disaffected and organised a conspiracy to take over the state, hiding out with some landless veterans. Cicero got hold of evidence implicating the conspirators, who were rounded up and executed. Catilinus fled from Rome and was defeated in battle by Cicero's co-consul, Gaius Antonius. Cicero had the remaining conspirators arrested and executed without trial, an arbitrary act that ruined Cicero's reputation. For more about Catilinus, see Chapter 24.

By 60 BC, Pompey, Caesar, and Crassus had each been frustrated in their ambitions, mainly by the Optimates. As usual in Roman politics, aristocratic internal feuds came into play:

- **Pompey:** The powerful Optimates Metelli family blocked Pompey's request for land for his veterans. Pompey then had to look for support elsewhere.

  The Senate's rejection of Pompey's request shows just how personal Roman power politics had become. The Metellis were getting back at Pompey for having divorced his wife Mucia Tertia, a relative of the Metelli.

- **Crassus:** Despite Crassus achieving great fame in crushing the slave revolt in 71 BC, Pompey's victories in the East and late arrival to mop up the slaves had totally overshadowed him. Crassus's ambition involved using his money, connections, and financing any up-and-coming young man. This meant he 'owned' lots of politicians, earning him enemies amongst the Optimates. Crassus also came up against the conspirator Catilinus (refer to the sidebar 'Cicero and the Catiline Conspiracy' for that story).

- **Caesar:** Caesar was governor of Further Spain in 61–60 BC, where he defeated various tribes and settled disputes between creditors and debtors. Flushed with success, he set off for Rome in hope of a triumph and being elected as consul. Anyone hoping for a triumph had to wait outside Rome, but by law, a candidate for the consulship had to be in Rome. So Caesar asked to be considered for the consulship in absentia. The Senate turned him down, annoyed by this attempt to bend the law, and said he could only stand for the consulship if he came to Rome in person. So Caesar then came back to Rome.

Caesar returned to Rome and formed the First Triumvirate with Crassus and Pompey. In 59 BC, Caesar was elected consul. In practice, Caesar was also now the leader of the First Triumvirate.

Caesar, Crassus, and Pompey bombarded the Senate with their demands and, after some resistance, got what they wanted. Thanks to Caesar, Pompey got both the land for his veterans and ratification of his settlement at the end of the war with Mithridates VI. Pompey married Caesar's daughter Julia in 59 BC to bind their alliance. Caesar got the job of Proconsular Governor in Gaul together with an army, though the truth was, Caesar had awarded himself this powerful command. Crassus was sidelined for the moment and had to wait till 55 BC before he had a chance to gain himself a military reputation to rival Caesar and Pompey.

Building his power base: Caesar and the Gallic Wars

Caesar's governorship of Cisalpine Gaul gave him the best of both worlds. He was close enough to Rome to be able to remain at the centre of political developments, and he had a major provincial command with an army, which gave Caesar the prospect of conquest.

During a nine-year campaign known to history as the Gallic Wars, Caesar conquered Gaul. The war brought the huge area of Gaul into the Roman Empire, giving Rome an Atlantic and North Sea coastline. Caesar also led two expeditions to Britain (55 and 54 BC). With these exploits, Caesar gained a phenomenal level of personal prestige and box-office popularity. Reaching Britain at all was the stuff of legend, because Britain was popularly believed to be at the ends of the earth.

We know a great deal about Caesar's campaign in Gaul because he wrote a detailed account, which survives in full. Inevitably biased, because it was written as propaganda, it is still an extraordinary account of a generally highly successful campaign. Discipline, logistics, squabbling amongst the enemy, and the brutal suppression of rebellions against Roman rule, all play their part. There is no doubt, though, that the campaign was utterly ruthless, bloody, and caused colossal suffering to the Gauls – just so Caesar could make himself into a Roman hero. The final engagement against the Gaulish chieftain Vercingetorix came with the legendary siege of Alesia (modern Alise).

Some like it hot

One day, in 62 BC, publius Clodius Pulcher tried to seduce Caesar's wife. Caesar was out because his wife Pompeia was taking part in a women-only celebration of Ceres, also known as the Good Goddess *(Bona Dea)*. Clodius turned up disguised as a female lute player, but when a maid asked him who he was, his voice gave him away. Clodius hid, but was found and taken to court. Clodius declared he had been out of Rome on the day in question, but his former friend Cicero said that wasn't true. Other evidence emerged that Clodius had committed incest with his sisters. Clodius's accusers were bribed and Clodius got off scot-free. The outcome of the case was that Caesar divorced Pompeia, but Caesar refused to give evidence against Clodius. Caesar famously said he had divorced Pompeia not because of the allegation of adultery but because 'Caesar's wife should not only be free from guilt but free from any suspicion of guilt'.

Meanwhile back in Rome . . .

While Caesar was in Gaul and Britain, polishing up his curriculum vitae, tensions were mounting in Rome, where the tribune publius Clodius Pulcher had been left in control. Clodius Pulcher's actions promoted the vicious personal rivalries that characterised Roman politics at this time and showed how things were becoming more and more out of control. More importantly, Clodius Pulcher's behaviour gave Pompey an excuse to increase his power in Rome at Caesar's expense. Clodius Pulcher had

- ✔ Shamelessly courted the Roman mob with free handouts and kept gangs of thugs on Caesar's payroll.

- ✔ Used the doubtful legality of the executions after the Catiline Conspiracy to chase Cicero out of Rome, pursuing a personal vendetta (refer to the sidebar 'Cicero and the Catiline Conspiracy').

- ✔ Deposed the king of Cyprus in order to help himself to the treasury to pay for the free handouts.

- ✔ Locked Pompey up in his own house. Pompey responded in kind and organised his own gang of thugs and then passed a law which Clodius Pulcher failed to block, allowing Cicero back.

- ✔ Tried to seduce Caesar's wife. Clodius Pulcher was discovered, stood trial, and, through bribery and other underhand tricks, got off. (For the intimate details, read the sidebar 'Some like it hot'.)

Renewing the Triumvirate

By 56 BC, the First Triumvirate agreement between Pompey, Crassus, and Caesar was looking distinctly shaky. Pompey was asserting himself against Clodius Pulcher whose behaviour was out of control, and Crassus took the chance to bring Caesar, still on campaign in Gaul, up to speed with what was going on. A meeting was arranged at Luca (Lucca) in northern Italy to sort out all their differences and guarantee mutual support. Caesar's command in Gaul was extended, while Crassus took Syria and Pompey took Spain, all positions of enormous power.

Death of Crassus and the crumbling Triumvirate

Crassus was given a prestigious military command in the East to fight the Parthian Empire (roughly equivalent to modern Iran and Iraq). He went out in 55 BC and started off well. But in 53 BC, Crassus was defeated at Carrhae (modern Harran on Turkey's south-east border with Syria) and was killed trying to escape. The final humiliation came when the Parthians captured Crassus's legionary standards, not recovered until 20 BC when the Emperor Augustus negotiated their return.

The death of Crassus left Caesar and Pompey in open opposition by upsetting the balance of power. Unfortunately, Caesar's daughter Julia (Pompey's wife) had died in 54 BC, removing the only personal link between the two men.

Because of the problems in Rome, the Senate made various moves to recall Caesar from Gaul. In the end, an agreement was reached in which Caesar would get time to finish the war in Gaul, but he would give up control of Rome to Pompey. The problem was that Rome was dissolving into chaos. Gang warfare between supporters of Caesar and Pompey led to street riots, ending up in the burning of the Senate house in 52 BC and the death of Clodius. The Senate's solution was to give Pompey all the powers of a dictator in order to restore order.

A key turning point came in 52 BC because Pompey had just been awarded the power of *imperium* (see Chapter 3 for the power it conferred) for another five years. Everything hung on whether Pompey would support demands for Caesar's recall from Gaul, which would mean Caesar giving up his army and thereby all his power. Since Julia had died in 54 BC, Pompey was free to marry again and instead of marrying another woman in Caesar's family, he chose one from the Metelli family, cementing his new loyalty to the Optimates. Influenced by the Optimates, he supported demands that Caesar be recalled, and in 50 BC accepted command of the Roman armies in Italy. The balance of power was destroyed, and the Roman world dissolved into civil war, which is the story of the next chapter.

Chapter 15

Daggers Drawn – The Fall of the Republic

··

In This Chapter

▶ The rivalry of Caesar and Pompey

▶ How Caesar became master of Rome

▶ What happened on the Ides of March

▶ Why Octavian and Mark Antony fell out

▶ How an Egyptian queen nearly destroyed the Roman world

··

The Roman Republic – based on the ideal of rule by the people – had been falling apart for years, but finally ground to an end in 43 BC. Within 15 years the Roman Empire, ruled by an emperor, came into being. Or did it? At the time, many pretended that the Roman Empire was the old Republic reinvented. What couldn't be ignored though, was that one man, the 'general', held a lot more power than anyone else.

At first, believe it or not, no such thing as a Roman emperor officially existed. A Roman emperor actually called himself *imperator,* which means 'general'. Only later did the title 'general', commander of the Roman army, come to mean what we mean by the word 'emperor' – that is, a supreme ruler like a monarch.

During the Republic, different men of high rank did various jobs: consul, quaestor, praetor, tribune, censor, and so on (see Chapter 3 for descriptions of these positions). The same set-up carried on into the Roman Empire – but with a difference, the 'general' now held more and more of the jobs.

This chapter follows explains how the Republic collapsed and how one man, Octavian (known as Augustus), refashioned the rule of the Republic in such a way that he held absolute power.

Civil War

The seeds of the Civil War were sown with the creation of the First Triumvirate. Three men – Crassus, Pompey, and Caesar – backed by their own armies, individually forced the Senate to do what they wanted (refer to Chapter 14). Their personal struggle for power became the most important force in the Roman world.

Crassus, the third member of the Triumvirate, was dead by 53 BC, and Caesar and Pompey were left in opposition to one another. Caesar and Pompey weren't enemies (yet), but they *were* rivals. By the late 50s BC, both men had *imperium:* the authority to command an army. The crucial issue of the day was whether Caesar or Pompey, or both, could be made to give up their commands. No-one, not Caesar or Pompey or their supporters, was prepared to back down.

Deadly deals

The crunch came in 50 BC when the consul Gaius Marcellus demanded Caesar's recall from Gaul. A bankrupt tribune called Scribonius Curio, whose support Caesar had bought at vast expense, vetoed Caesar's recall. Marcellus begged Pompey to save the Republic by using his army to bring pressure on Caesar to give up his command. Caesar offered a compromise: that both he and Pompey would give up their commands. The Senate rejected Caesar's offer because they thought Pompey needed his army to bring Caesar to heel. The Senate appointed new governors to the Gallic provinces. The Tribune Mark Antony tried to veto the new appointments but was threatened with his life and had to flee.

Even Cicero, who opposed the Triumvirate and was Caesar's enemy (refer to Chapter 14), tried to negotiate a deal, in which Caesar would go to Illyricum and Pompey to Spain. But the deal fell apart when the Senate granted Pompey the *Senatus Consultum Ultimum,* which gave Pompey the power to declare Caesar an enemy of the state and then get rid of him.

Crossing the Rubicon (50 BC)

The Rubicon is a river (now the Rigone) on the border between the Gallic provinces and Umbria in northern Italy. Caesar had been presented by the Senate with the option of giving himself up as an enemy of the state or of being taken by his enemies in Gaul. Caesar spent hours thinking about it and decided that he had nothing to lose. If he gave himself up to the Senate, he would have to stand trial in Rome and be condemned by a regime that had become corrupt.

Caesar did the unthinkable: In 49 BC, he took his troops from Gaul across the Rubicon and invaded Italy, an act that would be seen as a declaration of war against the Republic. This was the occasion of Caesar's famous phrase: *Iacta alea est,* 'The die is cast'.

Nowadays, the phrase 'crossing the Rubicon' is used to mean there's no going back, whatever the situation.

Cutting off Pompey at the head (48 BC)

If Caesar had had his own way, he would have preferred to negotiate power sharing with Pompey. Pompey, who tended to be indecisive, gave in to his advisors and turned down Caesar's offer of a compromise. Pompey made a bad decision amounting to a declaration of war, but Pompey's army wasn't anywhere ready. Caesar, however, was more than ready for war and hurtled down through Italy in barely two months. Pompey fell back with his soldiers, got away to the port of Brundisium (Brindisi), and shipped his army across the Adriatic to the safety of Greece.

Caesar takes Rome

Caesar had time on his side. Having planned his attack, he then seized Rome. Most of the senators had fled out of blind terror, but thanks to Caesar's rigid discipline over his troops, no looting, destruction, or murdering of opponents took place. Caesar kept his reputation for fair play intact. Caesar's other goodwill gestures included cancelling debts, bringing Italians into the Senate, and allowing back to Rome men who had been exiled by Sulla and Pompey. Caesar even recruited Pompey's soldiers who had been left behind in Rome.

African setback

Caesar's first setback came in Africa. A rebellion by the governor Attius Varus, a supporter of Pompey, was met by an army sent out by Caesar under the command of the ex-tribune Scribonius Curio. Curio had no serious military experience, and even worse, a large part of the army he'd been given was made up of Pompey's former soldiers. Curio was totally defeated. Caesar himself went to Pompey's province of Spain to fight Pompey's two deputies and defeated them in little over a month.

Pompey's plan

Meanwhile Pompey was busying himself building up a colossal army in Greece. He took Roman soldiers from frontier garrisons and ended up with a force that vastly outnumbered Caesar's. Pompey's plan was to reinvade Italy, but like most military schemes, it didn't work out. Caesar took his army over the Adriatic to Greece in 48 BC. The campaign started out badly for Caesar when he had to abandon the siege of Pompey's Adriatic base at Dyrrachium.

The Battle of Pharsalus 48 BC

Pompey could have invaded Italy without any trouble but decided instead that his real target was Caesar and chased him into Greece. Urged on by the Optimates (refer to Chapter 14) to end the conflict as fast as possible, Pompey drew up battle lines at Pharsalus in the heart of northern Greece. Caesar had 22,000 men, but Pompey had nearly 40,000.

Pharsalus was a disaster for Pompey. Caesar's infantry stood firm against Pompey's cavalry and stopped them in their tracks. Next, Caesar threw in his reserves and overwhelmed Pompey's army. Pompey fled to Egypt, and Caesar captured most of his army, having told his troops to 'spare your fellow citizens'. True to his honourable reputation, Caesar burned Pompey's papers without reading them.

The death of Pompey

Pompey's end was ignominious. He might have preferred the honourable option of suicide. He was murdered in Egypt by Pothinus and Achillas, two members of the Egyptian court of the pro-Caesar boy-King Ptolemy XIII. Caesar turned up in Egypt in hot pursuit of Pompey and was proudly shown Pompey's severed head. Ptolemy rather hoped that Caesar would support him in the dispute with his sister Cleopatra VII. He was wrong.

Caesar gets a girlfriend

Caesar was disgusted at Pompey's humiliating end and had Pothinus executed. Caesar placed Cleopatra VII on the Egyptian throne by giving the crown to her other brother Ptolemy XIV, whom she married (brother-sister marriages were normal for Egyptian rulers). Cleopatra was known to be intelligent, politically astute, and manipulative. But Caesar's action involved him in an Egyptian civil war. Fortunately for Caesar, Ptolemy was killed in an attempt to attack the tiny Roman force Caesar had brought with him. For good measure Cleopatra became Caesar's mistress and had a son by him.

Wiping out the remaining opposition

On the way to returning to Rome in 47 BC, Caesar had to settle trouble in Asia Minor. Pharnaces II, son of Mithridates and now King of Pontus, had given help to Pompey. Caesar crushed all opposition from Pharnaces in a high-speed five-day war. Caesar summed up his victory over Pharnaces in the immortal words: *Veni, vidi, vici*, 'I came, I saw, I conquered'.

In 46 BC Caesar defeated an army loyal to Pompey in Africa, the campaign ending in the bloody Battle of Thapsus. After the battle, one of Caesar's most die-hard enemies, Marcus Porcius Cato, who had been in charge of the garrison at Utica in Africa, committed suicide.

Marcus Porcius Cato

Marcus Porcius Cato (95–46 BC) was a direct descendant of Cato, the renowned veteran of the Second Punic War and champion of traditional Roman virtues, who a century before had insisted that Carthage must be destroyed (refer to Chapter 4 for information on Cato's works and Chapter 12 for details on the Second Punic War). Like his famous ancestor, Marcus Porcius Cato was a dedicated Stoic and was committed to personal integrity and intolerance of weaknesses in others. He was also a wholehearted supporter of the Optimates and their thinking (explained in Chapter 14) and therefore totally opposed Caesar.

Caesar: Leader of the Roman World

Caesar's victory in the civil war at the Battle of Pharsalus in 48 BC and the death of Pompey left him in sole charge of the Roman world. The Senate created Caesar Dictator for ten years. The responsibility for repairing the damage, restoring the Republic, settling veterans, and recreating law and order was all down to him. Caesar was determined to avoid the bloody reprisals that Sulla had carried out during his dictatorship (refer to Chapter 14). Caesar's impact on the Roman state was colossal and his reforms much more far-reaching than those of the previous century.

Caesar's new order

Caesar's reconstruction of the Republic was a model of restraint and foresight. He brought in practical solutions to restore stability in the Roman world, such as extending the Romanisation of the provinces by bringing provincials into the heart of the Roman system. Caesar's reforms included:

- ✔ Forgiving Pompey's supporters, even Caesar's arch-enemy Cicero, if they agreed to come over to Caesar.

- ✔ More than halving the number of Romans who depended on the free corn dole in order to cut the numbers of idle troublemakers. Those who were disqualified were transported to colonies overseas.

- ✔ Settling Caesar's veterans in overseas colonies.

- ✔ Setting up new colonies, such as Arles in France and Seville in Spain, and giving them Roman or Latin status.

- ✔ Awarding Roman citizenship to worthy provincial individuals, and cities and soldiers Caesar had recruited overseas.

- Admitting Italians, and even some Gauls, to the Senate, thus broadening the Senate's understanding of issues outside Rome.

- Improving road links to the port at Ostia.

- Giving Latin status to Transpadane Gaul.

- Cutting taxes and reforming collection in some provinces.

Caesar raised vast sums of money by taking land off supporters of Pompey who hadn't surrendered quickly enough, fining provincial cities that had supported Pompey, and selling privileges to eastern cities and kingdoms. The income allowed Caesar to provide handouts for his soldiers, put in place a programme of public building, and fund free public entertainments.

Hey, we didn't want a king! (44 BC)

Caesar was widely admired – not surprising really – for his reforms. Caesar had done more than anyone else to bring stability to the Roman world. The Senate believed Caesar was still going to operate within the Republican system.

But Caesar had other ideas, and with the army behind him, he could do as he pleased. He took over the job of Consul several times and the powers of a tribune. Caesar's actions went down badly with traditionalists, who thought he was trampling on the Republican system. Caesar's biggest mistake was to remind Romans of the city's ancient past. He packed the Senate with his own men and, because of this, did more or less whatever he wanted, saying his word was law.

The Julian calendar

One of Caesar's most enduring reforms was the calendar, which was named after him. The Julian calendar is still the basis of the one used today. The Roman year lasted 355 days with an odd month inserted after February to make it fit the sun's year. However, thanks to various extra days put in by priests, the whole thing became hopelessly unworkable. Caesar's solution was to make the year 365 days long and add an extra day every fourth year. His new calendar, which included a month named after him (July), lasted for centuries, until it was found that the calendar didn't quite match the earth's orbit round the sun. By 1582, the Julian calendar was ten days out. The new calendar devised by Pope Gregory XIII modified Caesar's leap year allowances to correct the error but wasn't introduced in Britain until 1752. It's the one we use now.

Caesar's talents and weaknesses

Caesar had an exceptional reputation for energy, vigour, and multitasking. He could read and write, or listen and dictate, at the same time. It was said that Caesar was able to dictate four letters at once if they were important, and seven if they weren't. He had reputedly fought 50 battles, a record, but was considered the most merciful of men – though it's unlikely the Gauls would have agreed with that. Apart from vanity and a weakness for women, Caesar also suffered from epilepsy. He had a fit during the Battle of Thapsus in 46 BC. Several Roman historians refer to his condition, which probably got worse in later life.

But Caesar let his achievements go to his head. He allowed a statue of himself to be carried with those of gods at the beginning of games and another statue of himself to be placed with those of the kings, and he issued coins with his portrait on them. Even his reform of the calendar only made some men resent his power more. In 44 BC, Caesar was made *Dictator Perpetuus* (Dictator for Life), and to make sure everyone knew this, he accepted the offer of a gilt throne in the Senate house, a triumphal robe, and laurel crown. When he was once hailed as King he said, 'I am Caesar and not King', but the mud stuck.

The fatal blow (44 BC)

Most of the Roman population only wanted stability and leadership; they probably didn't care how Caesar went about it. Caesar's reforms were practical solutions to years of chaos. But many senators were angry and didn't want change – they wanted the Republic restored to the original way of working. Cicero called Caesar a tyrant, and the idea spread rapidly. Caesar was now so convinced of his invincibility that he felt he had no need of a bodyguard. He was planning a war against Parthia, and his supporters even put it about that there was a prophecy that only a Roman king could defeat Parthia.

Caesar's enemies knew he was leaving on 18 March 44 BC and would be out of their reach – they had to strike while the iron was hot. A motley collection of patriots plotted to kill Caesar in March 44 BC. Some, like Cassius and Brutus, were supporters of Pompey pardoned by Caesar. Others had personal grievances, but there were men who were still faithful to Caesar. Cassius wanted Mark Antony killed as well, but Brutus refused.

Omens of Caesar's death

The Romans loved the idea of bad and good omens and especially liked to watch out for clues that bad things were coming. Caesar is said to have sacrificed an animal that turned out to have no heart, but much more ominously a soothsayer warned that some great danger would come to him not later than the Ides of March. The night before the Ides of March, Caesar had a dream he was in heaven, and on the morning of 15 March, he hesitated to go out. But he did and was even handed a note warning him of an impending disaster. Caesar didn't read the note and was brutally assassinated. Just after Caesar's death, Caesar's great-nephew, the emperor Augustus, saw a comet during the games he was holding to honour Venus. Augustus later built a temple in the comet's honour.

Marcus Junius Brutus was descended from Lucius Junius Brutus, leader of the conspiracy to throw Tarquinius Superbus off the Roman throne (refer to Chapter 10) and credited with founding the original Roman Republic. This probably explains why the young Brutus was dedicated to the ideals of the Roman Republic. For example, although Brutus hated Pompey for killing his father, Brutus went over to Pompey, believing that Pompey was a greater Republican patriot than Caesar, and he fought for Pompey at Pharsalus. Brutus had other reasons to hate Caesar: Amongst Caesar's many female conquests was Brutus's mother Servilia Caepionis (half-sister of Caesar's sworn enemy Marcus Porcius Cato; for him, see the earlier sidebar by the same name) and his sister Junia Tertia, supplied by her mother for Caesar's pleasure. Others included Crassus's wife Tertulla and Pompey's wife Mucia.

In Rome, on the Ides of March 44 BC (15 March), Caesar arrived at a Senate meeting at a hall just next door to the great stone theatre built by Pompey – a classic twist of fate. The conspirators pounced on Caesar and stabbed him 23 times.

A hideous mistake and the rise of Mark Antony

Caesar's murderers thought that they had liberated the people from a tyrant and would be welcomed as the saviours of the Republic. The murderers made the mistake of assuming that the clock could be turned back and the Republic could once again operate in the way it was set up back in 509 BC. They thought wrong. Brutus planned to give a speech justifying Caesar's assassination, but the senators had all cleared off. Instead of cheering crowds, the conspirators found the Forum deserted. The conspirators marched through the streets brandishing their weapons and, protected by a band of gladiators, hid out on the Capitol.

Caesar's colleague in the consulship, Mark Antony, took charge, much to Cicero's regret (Cicero thought Antony should have been killed, too). Cicero hated the way Caesar had been behaving and was utterly delighted at the news of the assassination, but thought it was a wasted opportunity because Antony took over instead.

Antony and Caesar went back a long way: Antony had been on Caesar's staff during the war in Gaul, defended Caesar's interests when Antony became tribune in 49 BC, and commanded part of Caesar's army at Pharsalus.

To please those who had supported Caesar, Antony persuaded the Senate to pass any outstanding legislation of Caesar's and to approve an amnesty for the conspirators, suggested by Cicero. Antony also asked the Senate to vote for a public funeral for Caesar.

Caesar's funeral turned into a public frenzy. The crowd went crazy at the sight of Caesar's body and ransacked the Forum for anything that could be set alight. The crowd then lynched someone they thought was a conspirator (an act of mistaken identity), and some of the crowd raced to where Brutus and Cassius lived and tried to kill them. Brutus and Cassius fled Rome.

Et tu Brute?

The story goes that Caesar said *Et tu Brute?* ('And you, Brutus?') when faced with his murderers. The original source of the story is in Suetonius's *Life of Julius Caesar.* Caesar spoke in Greek, using the words *Kai su teknon,* which means 'You also, my child?' William Shakespeare changed the phrase to *Et tu Brute* for his play *Julius Caesar* (Act III, Scene I).

But whether you hear the words in Latin or Greek, the meaning is the same: Brutus was Caesar's old friend, but now one of his assassins. So what exactly was the relationship between Caesar and Brutus? When Pompey's troops, including Brutus, were defeated at Pharsalus,

Caesar ordered his troops not to kill Brutus because of Caesar's fondness for Brutus's mother Servilia, with whom he had had an affair. Caesar was uneasy about where Brutus's loyalties lay, but he made him a friend and supported his career, making Brutus Praetor in 44 BC.

And what of Brutus's character? Was he the idealistic Republican of literature? Well, yes, but he was also ruthless. Case in point: Brutus got himself a special exemption from a cap on interest rates and then lent money at a ruinous 48 per cent to the people of Salamis. Brutus enforced repayments by murdering city councillors.

Picking Caesar's heir: Mark Antony or Octavian?

Mark Antony managed to stabilise a potentially disastrous situation after Caesar's murder. He deliberately allowed the conspirators to escape, found land for Caesar's veterans to keep them away from Rome, and arranged for the abolition of the dictatorship. Antony made Brutus and Cassius Governors of provinces. Brutus and Cassius took exception to this treatment, but Antony threatened them and they fled to the East. However, Brutus and Cassius were awarded *maius imperium* (an enhanced form of the military command, *imperium*) by the Senate, giving them power over provincial governors. Brutus and Cassius helped themselves to all the resources Caesar had put in place for his campaign in Parthia, imposed ruthless taxation, and set about building themselves an army.

Not everything was going Antony's way. In Rome, the Senate objected to the way Antony was spending money and selling privileges and immunities using forged documents, which he claimed were Caesar's. And Caesar's great-nephew, Gaius Octavius – and not Antony – was named as Caesar's heir.

Octavian's relationship to Julius Caesar is complicated but important. Julius Caesar's sister Julia married Marcus Atius Balbus, a relative of Pompey's. Julia and Marcus's daughter Atia married Gaius Octavius, who died in 58 BC. Atia and Octavius had a son born in 63 BC, who was Caesar's great-nephew: Gaius Octavius with the addition of the name Thurinus to commemorate Thurii where his family had come from. Gaius Octavius Thurinus became known as Octavianus, and we call him Octavian.

Caesar named Octavian as his heir in his will and Octavian was adopted as Caesar's son. (Caesar had a son of his own by Cleopatra, called Caesarion. When Caesar died, Caesarion, who Octavian was to deal with later, was still alive in Egypt with Cleopatra.) The 18-year-old Octavian was in Epirus (north-west Greece) on military training when he heard he was Caesar's heir, and promptly came to Rome to claim his inheritance.

The history of the last 70-odd years of the Republic has been all about the careers of a few key men: Marius, Sulla, Crassus, Pompey, and Caesar. They'd totally dominated Roman politics and war. They had all challenged the fundamental principle of the Roman Republic: That no-one was supposed to have permanent political power. Caesar had overturned that principle, and the Republic had teetered on the brink of being ruled by a monarch and a tyrant. Caesar's mightiness was the cause of his downfall. The Republic was to last for just a few more years till 43 BC and the course of world history changed.

Octavian and the End of the Republic (44–43 BC)

Octavian arrived in Rome and changed his name to Gaius Julius Caesar Octavianus, knowing this was the best way to win over Caesar's troops. Octavian was annoyed to discover that Mark Antony had been merrily spending Caesar's private fortune, as well as any public funds he had been able to get his hands on. Octavian now had to raise the money that Caesar had left as a bequest to his troops. Octavian and Antony were instantly locked in a deadly feud.

The tense situation was made worse when Cicero interfered by issuing the First and Second Philippics, (a *Philippic* was a bitter critique, and comes from the Greek orator Demosthenes's criticisms of Philip II of Macedon in the fourth century BC). Cicero slated Antony for being an opportunist who had all Caesar's criminal ambitions, but none of Caesar's skills and restraint. Cicero praised Antony for getting rid of the dictatorship, but cursed Antony for turning government into 'monstrous marketing', and for protecting himself with a band of thugs against honest men.

Meanwhile, Antony had himself made governor in Gaul and planned to move troops from Macedonia into Gaul. Antony accused Octavian of plotting to assassinate him, which led Octavian to call on Caesar's old troops to come and join him.

Back in Rome, in 43 BC, Cicero continued to stir things up by unveiling his plans to undo Antony's legislation, just when Antony was planning to attack Brutus at Mutina in northern Italy. Antony offered not to go to war if his laws were left alone, but Antony's offer was rejected, and the Senate declared him a public enemy.

By now Octavian was approaching with his army, so Antony pulled back and joined forces with the governors of Gaul and Spain.

Octavian fell out with the Senate, who wanted him to become an ally of Brutus. The last thing Octavian was ever going to do was work with the murderers of Caesar. The Senate punished Octavian by holding back money for the troops. Octavian's answer was to march into Rome, have himself elected Consul, and cancel the amnesty for Caesar's killers.

Brutus and Cassius had their own armies so civil war was inevitable. Ever practical, Octavian could see that feuding with Antony wasn't going to help. Octavian saw that the time had come to strike a deal with Antony.

The second Gang of Three: The Second Triumvirate (43 BC)

Octavian met Antony, together with Marcus Aemilius Lepidus, the Governor of Spain. Lepidus had gone over to Antony's side, but had also negotiated to come back to Octavian. The three men made a five-year legal pact known to history as the Second Triumvirate, so unlike the First Triumvirate this one was official. The power of the Second Triumvirate made the Senate no more than a rubber stamp. Octavian, Antony, and Lepidus could appoint magistrates, and more importantly, they had the absolute freedom to go to war whenever they wanted. The law creating the Second Triumvirate was passed on 27 November 43 BC and marked the end of the Roman Republic, though no-one realised it at the time.

Blood, guts, and gods

The Second Triumvirate was bathed in blood from the start. Octavian, Antony, and Lepidus drew up a list of 300 senators and 2,000 equestrians who had been supporters of Caesar's assassination and, apart from a few lucky ones, massacred them. The Triumvirate's action wasn't just about fear of their opponents. Octavian, Antony, and Lepidus had 43 legions between them, and by confiscating the estates of the massacred senators and equestrians they could pay the troops. The money wasn't enough though, and the Triumvirate had to impose heavy taxes as well.

Cicero's Second Philippic to Antony was Cicero writing his own death warrant. Octavian spent two days trying to persuade Antony to let Cicero live, but Antony refused to listen. Cicero toyed with the idea of escaping to Greece, but decided to accept his fate. Cicero was caught in his villa and murdered. His head and hands were carried to Rome and Antony displayed them in the Forum, declaring the punishment of Caesar's supporters had now ended.

Octavian upstaged Antony and Lepidus by proclaiming his close relationship to the great god, Caesar. In 42 BC Julius Caesar had been created a god and a temple was built in his honour. As Caesar's adopted son, Octavian was able to bask in Caesar's fame – without any danger of being accused of thinking he, Octavian, was a god.

The Battle of Philippi

Octavian, Antony, and Lepidus split the Roman Empire between them. Octavian had Sicily, Sardinia, and Africa; Lepidus had Spain and part of Gaul; and Antony the rest of Gaul. All three shared Italy, and Octavian, Antony, and

Lepidus joined together with the common purpose of recovering the East from Brutus and Cassius.

In 42 BC Antony and Octavian left Lepidus in charge of Italy and set out for Greece, determined to wipe out Brutus and Cassius. At the Battle of Philippi, Antony took command because Octavian wasn't much of a general. In the first engagement Antony overcame Cassius's troops and Cassius committed suicide. In the second engagement, three weeks later, Brutus also took his own life after being defeated by Antony.

Octavian had never enjoyed good health. After the Battle of Philippi Octavian was said to have spent three days sick in a marsh with dropsy.

The bust up starts

The Second Triumvirate was made up of three ambitious men so they were bound to fall out. Antony was the main player in the Triumvirate because he had done all the fighting at Philippi. Antony and Octavian packed Lepidus (whom they had previously left in charge of Italy) off to Africa, accused him of disloyalty, and helped themselves to his provinces. Octavian was left to take care of Italy while Antony headed east to build himself an empire. Octavian planned to settle his own veterans on lands he had confiscated in Italy. But Octavian's plans were frustrated by Antony's family, who promised the people whose lands Octavian had taken that Antony would soon be back to restore the Republic.

Antony returned to Italy in 40 BC. Refused entry by Octavian's forces, he blockaded the port of Brundisium in retaliation. War almost broke out, but realising this wouldn't help anyone, the three triumvirs decided to join forces once again. Octavian suppressed revolts in Gaul and even settled some of his soldiers there. In 38 BC Antony helped Octavian defeat Pompey's son Sextus, who was leading a rebellion in Sicily. The Second Triumvirate was renewed for another five years, and then Octavian showed his true colours and had Lepidus driven out from the Triumvirate. Octavian followed this up by fighting his way into the East down through Illyricum.

As you can imagine, with Octavian and Antony left fighting for power the situation just got worse and worse.

Antony and Cleopatra

Antony's big problem was recovering Rome's eastern possessions. The Parthians had invaded Syria and most of Asia Minor. Although they were driven back, Antony also wanted to carry out the invasion of Parthia that Caesar had been planning just before his murder.

Antony met Cleopatra, queen of Egypt, while preparing to invade Parthia (refer to the section 'Caesar gets a girlfriend', earlier in the chapter). Antony demanded Cleopatra's presence to explain why she had supported Cassius. Cleopatra arrived on a magnificent boat, dressed as Venus, and Antony was completely bowled over. Cleopatra had charm, intelligence, could speak numerous languages, and, of course, had plenty of sex appeal.

To complicate matters Antony had married Octavia, Octavian's sister, in 40 BC, as a way of settling the differences between Octavian and himself. The idea for the marriage came from Octavia herself. But Antony left Octavia and their children behind when he went back to the East. Antony met up with Cleopatra in Syria in 37 BC – Antony couldn't resist Cleopatra; they fell deeply in love and had children together.

Antony went on to recover most of Rome's eastern territories, but when Antony invaded Parthia in 36 BC he was trapped and had to beat a hasty retreat, losing 22,000 soldiers, although he was left with most of his army. With his forces depleted and his money disappearing, Antony became totally dependent on Cleopatra's resources. In 35 BC, Antony divorced Octavia, which meant that he had cut himself off from Octavian as well.

Throwing down the gauntlet

In 34 BC, Antony held a triumph in Alexandria where he declared Caesarion, Cleopatra's son by Caesar, to be the true heir of Julius Caesar. Sometime around 33 BC Antony had agreed to marry Cleopatra. Antony's action was a blatant insult to Octavia, whom he did not divorce until the next year. Antony set about expanding Cleopatra's kingdom by unilaterally dividing up Roman and other territory in the East amongst Cleopatra's children, which threatened the strength of the Roman Empire.

In 32 BC, Antony and Cleopatra issued a coin with Antony's portrait on one side and Cleopatra's on the other. Cleopatra's legend read 'Queen of Kings, and of her sons who are Kings', a clear statement of Antony and Cleopatra's ambitions, and a direct challenge to Octavian.

The Battle of Actium (31 BC)

The Second Triumvirate broke up in 33 BC. Octavian instantly abandoned his title and powers, and drove out the consuls and 300 senators who had planned to condemn him. The consuls and senators left to join Antony, but a rumour blew up that Antony was planning to make Cleopatra queen of Rome, and rule the Roman Empire from Egypt.

Antony's silver

Mark Antony issued vast numbers of silver coins in order to pay his troops. Each coin had a picture of a war galley on one side, and a legionary standard with a legion's number on the other (coins were issued for each of Antony's legions). To make Antony's silver go further, the coins were debased with more copper than usual. The value of the coins was reduced, making the coins less useful for melting down or saving. Because the coins weren't all that valuable, Antony's coins were in circulation for hundreds of years after his death, and turned up all round the Roman Empire. Today, Antony's coins are common and relatively cheap in the coin-collecting market.

Octavian's next step was to publish Antony's will (there was no proof that it was genuine), which reaffirmed Cleopatra's son Caesarion as Caesar's true heir. Roman cities across the West promptly swore allegiance to Octavian, who took this as approval that he could go to war against Antony. In 31 BC Octavian was made Consul, and he got the Senate to declare war against Antony and Cleopatra, who were now in Greece.

Antony and Cleopatra defeated

Antony and Cleopatra were at Actium on the north-west coast of Greece with their fleet. Octavian's admiral and friend, Marcus Vipsanius Agrippa, used the fleet to cut off Antony's supplies. Octavian's army wore Antony's soldiers down. On 2 September 31 BC Antony tried to slip away with a force of 200 ships. Cleopatra escaped with 60 ships, and Antony followed her but with only a few more vessels. The rest of Antony's fleet, and the remains of Antony's army, quickly surrendered to Octavian.

Antony and Cleopatra made their way back to Egypt. But they knew the game was up and committed suicide.

The aftermath

Octavian spared Antony's children by Cleopatra but had his own cousin Caesarion killed. Egypt now became a Roman province after being an independent state in the ancient world for 3,000 years, but a special one because it was Octavian's personal property and was passed down to the emperors who succeeded him. As Octavian was now undisputed master of the Roman Empire, no-one was in a position to argue the toss.

Chapter 16

Augustus and the Caesars – Plots, Perverts, and Paranoia

*A*fter the Battle of Actium in 31 BC (refer to Chapter 15), the government of the Republic was in tatters. Men like Marius, Sulla, and Caesar had destroyed the prestige and power of the Senate and Rome's nobility. Rome had grown too powerful, had too many possessions, and needed powerful leadership, yet the rulers of the previous century had pursued their own ambitions and, far from creating stability, had undermined the stability of the Roman world. One thing was certain, no-one wanted to go back to a monarchy.

One of the most famous books written by a Roman historian is the *Twelve Caesars* by Gaius Suetonius Tranquillus. Starting with the life of Julius Caesar, it continues with biographies of the first 11 emperors up to AD 96. The first five emperors (Augustus, Tiberius, Caligula, Claudius, and Nero) were members of the Julio-Claudian dynasty, which means they were all linked by family connections to Julius Caesar and Tiberius's father, Tiberius Claudius Nero. The next three (Galba, Otho, and Vitellius) were short-lived emperors of the civil war of AD 68–69, and were followed by the three emperors of the Flavian dynasty: Vespasian and his sons, Titus, and Domitian. The rule of the 11 emperors covers one of the most dramatic and decisive periods in Roman history.

Augustus (aka Octavian) and His Powers

Octavian arrived in Rome from Egypt in 29 BC absolutely unchallenged. His enemies were all dead. He controlled the whole Roman army. He had seized Egypt's riches. What's more, so much time had passed that no-one could remember the Republic working properly. Octavian could have become a power-crazed megalomaniac tyrant, but he didn't – and that's one of the most remarkable things about his rule.

Restoring the Republic

Octavian had a dilemma. If he gave up command of the army or shared it with anyone else, then he risked a return to more civil war. If he held onto his control, then he was flying in the face of the Republican tradition of outlawing permanent political power in the hands of one man. And he knew what had happened to Caesar.

Octavian had to find a solution. He returned to Rome, was elected Consul, and set to work. He also:

- ✔ Restored the institutions of the Republic, but under his direction, giving him complete control of the army and foreign policy

- ✔ Discharged some of his troops, gave them land, and cancelled anything illegal he'd done in the preceding years of war

- ✔ Placed day-to-day government of non-military affairs under the control of senators and the equestrians

- ✔ Got rid of unsuitable senators and came up with a list of qualifications for entry to the Senate: military service, personal qualities, and financial standing

During these first few years, Octavian ruled in a strictly unofficial way, biding his time and working out the best things to do. He got away with it because of his personal prestige and because everyone was exhausted by the chaos. He also had two extremely important friends who helped him:

- ✔ **Maecenas:** Gaius Maecenas (died 8 BC) was an equestrian and had been at the Battle of Philippi with Octavian. In 40 BC, Maecenas negotiated the settlement with Antony at Brundisium. Maecenas was often left in control of Rome during the 30s BC. His relationship with Octavian cooled in later years, because Maecenas's wife became Octavian's mistress; however, he still left his old friend Octavian all his property in his will. Maecenas was a great patron of poets and writers, and it's thanks to him that the influential propaganda poetry of Virgil and Horace praised Octavian's rule.

✔ **Agrippa:** Marcus Vipsanius Agrippa (64–13 BC) came to Rome with Octavian when Octavian claimed his inheritance after Caesar's death. Agrippa was a brilliant soldier and naval tactician, responsible for most of Octavian's military successes. Not only did Agrippa manage Italy together with Maecenas, but Agrippa was also given control of the East and later solved problems in Gaul as well. He spent lavishly on public building projects in Rome. Agrippa married Octavian's daughter Julia. Down that line, the Emperors Caligula (AD 37–41) and Nero (AD 54–68) were descended from both Agrippa and Octavian. The most remarkable thing about Agrippa is that, despite being so able, he always put Octavian's career first.

Octavian's wife Livia (58 BC–AD 29) was another important person in Octavian's life. His first wife, Scribonia, was Julia's mother, but Octavian divorced Scribonia in 39 BC, claiming he couldn't get on with her. In 38 BC, Octavian married Livia, wife of a Pompeian supporter called Tiberius Claudius Nero, in order to cement political ties with potential opponents. Octavian even got Livia to divorce her own husband to marry him. Octavian adopted Livia's son Tiberius as his heir, but Octavian and Livia had no children of their own.

The Emperor who wasn't an Emperor

In 27 BC, Octavian gave up all his powers and all his provinces to the Senate and to the people of Rome. The Senate and the people of Rome promptly (and tactfully) gave most of the power and territory back to Octavian. Octavian now held his powers as a gift from the Senate and the Roman people. It was a brilliant move: Octavian's tactic had made him the legally elected Emperor and, more importantly, the legal holder of supreme power.

Octavian was re-elected Consul annually until 23 BC. He was given control of the provinces of Spain, Gaul, and Syria with the power of *imperium* (refer to Chapter 3 for the significance of this title) and was allowed to assign the imperium to his representatives (known as *legati* – from which we get our word 'delegate') in those provinces. Octavian also held Egypt as his own property. Governors of other Roman provinces (*proconsuls;* see Chapter 3) were appointed by the Senate. The Senate became a law court.

Becoming Augustus

In 27 BC, Octavian's name was changed to Augustus (meaning 'venerable'). It was a symbolic gesture that proclaimed his status. During his reign, Octavian had acquired several titles, showing his power and position. The titles include *princeps, imperator,* and *pater patriae* (from 2 BC), reinforced by personal qualities such as *dignitas* and *auctoritas*. (The titles apply to all emperors to a greater or lesser degree; you can find them explained in more detail in Chapter 3.)

To let things settle down, Augustus left Rome for nearly three years to attend to Gaul, and campaign in Spain. Soon after returning to Rome in 23 BC, Augustus fell seriously ill, and the year went from bad to worse. Augustus's nephew and intended heir Marcellus died, leaving his wife Julia (Augustus's daughter) a widow. Augustus briefly made Agrippa his successor in place of Marcellus. Agrippa divorced his second wife and married Augustus's daughter Julia to ensure the line of succession from Augustus. But Agrippa's early death in 13 BC, and the deaths of Agrippa's sons by Julia, ruined Augustus's plans (see the section 'A son, a son! My kingdom for a son!', later in this chapter).

Defender of the people – Populares methods for an Optimate

Augustus made some clever moves. He gave up the consulship after 23 BC for the time being (he held it twice more, in 5 BC and 2 BC). In return, the Senate each year made Augustus Tribune of the Plebs for the rest of his life. He was now firmly established as the representative of the people, with the power to summon the Senate, propose legislation, and veto any laws that he thought not in the people's interest. Augustus also had the right to nominate candidates to magistracies, and the imperium over his provinces was renewed. Being a noble, Augustus belonged to the *Optimates,* but by acting as the defender of the people he had adopted *Populares* ways of operating (refer to Chapter 14 for the distinction between Optimates and Populares). Augustus's position made him popular with the people, though in reality the plebs had even less power than they had ever had.

Augustus's political genius

With patience, tact, and diplomacy, Augustus had made himself an elected official of the state, subject to the law, with powers given to him by the Senate and the people. What is remarkable is that the principles of the Roman Republic had been upheld, while at the same time, Augustus, with the approval of the Senate and the people, held all the offices of state in his own hands.

Imagine if the President of the United States was also the Chief Justice of the Supreme Court and the leading member of the majority party in both the Senate and the House of Representatives – with everyone accepting that the Constitution of the United States was still functioning legally. You get the picture. Augustus's rule worked because he didn't abuse his exceptional powers. Unfortunately, not all of Augustus's successors were as trustworthy.

Augustus: The radical conservative

Augustus was a true conservative. He made changes, but at the same time Augustus wanted the people to believe he was keeping to the old ways.

Augustus used his powers to encourage all sorts of traditional values, such as encouraging men to wear togas. He passed laws against adultery and bribery, and men and women who failed to marry were barred from receiving inheritances, even though this was unpopular. Augustus's conservatism even went as far as being reluctant to give citizenship to non-Latins, and he placed a limit on the freeing of slaves.

Augustus enhanced the Roman religion by increasing the number of priests and reviving old rites. Augustus also:

- Built and restored temples

- Revived the night-time Saecular Games, for young people

- Made himself *Pontifex Maximus* ('Chief Priest') in 12 BC

- Revived in 11 BC the office of *flamen dialis,* 'priest of Jupiter' (from Diespiter 'Day father', another name for Jupiter)

Augustus set about reviving Roman religious customs, not because he especially wanted to restore Roman religious faith, but because it was a way of strengthening Rome's image and political status. With help from his friend Maecenas, Augustus encouraged writers to set down the myths and legends of Rome's origins. Virgil's *Aeneid* not only tells the story of Aeneas's adventures, but also presents Rome's destiny, reinforcing Aeneas's descent from Venus, a lineage claimed by Julius Caesar and Augustus himself (refer to Chapter 1 for more on Virgil).

How the Aeneid survived

When the poet Virgil died, he left instructions that the *Aeneid,* his great poem about the foundation of Rome, which foretold the coming of Augustus, be burned. Augustus, knowing the propaganda value of the *Aeneid,* ignored Virgil's will. Thereafter, generations of Roman schoolchildren memorised passages from the *Aeneid* as part of their reading and writing instruction, and quotations from Virgil's epic poem entered everyday speech, much as William Shakespeare's work has influenced modern English. Manuscripts of the *Aeneid* survived and were copied by early Christian monks in the fourth and fifth centuries AD. Preserved in monasteries, these copies formed the basis of some of the first printed editions in the fifteenth century. Today, the *Aeneid* is widely available in its original Latin and numerous other languages around the world.

Coinage

Augustus knew the importance of coinage as a way of publicising his regime. Until Caesar's time, coinage had mostly only portrayed gods. Augustus issued hundreds of different types of coins, many with his likeness and featuring various appropriate virtues and subjects. There was the comet type – featuring Augustus's head on one side and the comet that appeared after Caesar's assassination in 44 BC on the other. Another coin issued was the 'For preserving the citizens' type – with the legend *Ob Cives Servatos*. Augustus's coins circulated throughout the Roman Empire and beyond. It was the first major advertising campaign in history.

Finding it brick and leaving it marble

Augustus understood perfectly the importance of a public image. Although he had been a good-looking young man, he wasn't especially tall. He was said to be spotty, had various birthmarks, a limp, and suffered from bladder stones and a variety of serious illnesses. Rome had suffered, too, and needed a thorough restyling.

The ever youthful Augustus

Statues of Augustus portray him as a handsome, imposing, and vigorous warrior. Like all the greatest heroes, Augustus never aged. By the end of his reign, in his late 70s, no statue or coin had ever shown him as an old man. It was a trick that rulers often used. Queen Victoria (1837–1901) issued coins for the first 50 years of her reign, with the same youthful portrait, until advancing age and photography made it impossible for her to get away with it. Augustus was luckier. Most people in the Roman Empire had never seen him, so he was eternally youthful in their imaginations.

Rebuilding Rome

Like Augustus, Rome needed updating. Augustus spent a huge amount of money on improving the city. He increased the number of officials looking after public buildings and services. This meant hiring large numbers of equestrians to take charge of the many jobs in finance and administration, as well as using freedmen and slaves to do the routine administrative and clerical work. Augustus created what could be called a civil service. Rome was the Washington DC or Whitehall of its day.

Augustus's proudest boast was that he had found Rome a city built of brick and left it made of marble. It was a bit of an exaggeration, but Augustus was responsible, with Agrippa, for constructing a number of magnificent public buildings that can still be seen today. Augustus and Agrippa also introduced a sort of combination fire brigade and police force *(Vigiles)*, and put on more public entertainments than ever before. You can find details of what Augustus and Agrippa achieved in Chapter 6.

Sorting out the borders

Rome's wealth and prestige depended on the existence of the Empire, which provided the money and resources for turning Rome into a fabled city of marble and the proof of Rome's superiority as a military, political, religious, and moral power. So keeping it in order was a vital part of Augustus's work.

Taxing business

Augustus had to pay out large sums of money to his veterans but had huge reserves from legacies and money he'd confiscated in the provinces, especially Egypt. Taxation was another source of income, but here Augustus had to tread carefully. Antony, Brutus, and Cassius had overdone taxation to fund their wars, and look where they ended up.

Administrative reform was essential. Because of this, Augustus ordered a census (the same census written about in the New Testament at the time of the birth of Christ in Judaea). Augustus introduced a land tax *(tributum soli)* and a poll or property tax *(tributum capitis);* however, Italy and Roman citizens were exempt from the land tax and probably the poll tax. Taxes were also imposed on goods at borders, based on a percentage of the value of goods. Augustus set up a fund for retired soldiers, giving soldiers a lump sum, and he paid for it by imposing sales taxes and death duties. In his own imperial provinces, Augustus appointed equestrians as *procurators* (financial managers) to look after his personal property (as his province of Egypt was governed by an equestrian; see Chapter 3 for the role of procurators).

Colonies

In Italy, Augustus set up 28 Roman colonies alone, like Turin, and provided each one with public buildings, rights, and constitutions, really making them into mini-Romes. Cities like these could now provide new recruits to Rome's senators and equestrians. Roads were rebuilt and repaired to maintain communications with Rome. A police force was created to deal with bandits who infested the countryside. The net result was that Rome and Italy became really two halves of the same being.

The frontiers

Augustus was determined to make the Empire's frontiers strong and secure. He had no plans to conquer more territory, because Rome already had the wealthy (and conquerable) places under her control. Not only that, he also knew that if he gave a man an army and told him to conquer somewhere, then that man had all the resources he needed to challenge Augustus.

Egypt's southern borders were made safe in 22 BC after war with the Ethiopians. Fighting in Arabia gave the Romans commercial access to the Red Sea and the Indian Ocean, and Augustus was rewarded for his involvement in the area by visits from Indian ambassadors. In Asia Minor, eastern mountain robbers were beaten off and colonies established.

Augustus and his immediate successors made use of *client kings* – tame rulers in strategically important locations around the Empire whose territories made a convenient buffer zone between potential enemies of Roman territory. Client kings could rely on Roman military support in return for their loyalty; in the East, for example, client kings helped Rome by protecting the frontier with Parthia. Yet client kings weren't always reliable and could change sides without warning.

North-western Europe

North-western Europe was a different problem. In 19 BC in Spain, Agrippa finally defeated the mountainous tribes, founded colonies, and set up a permanent garrison in Spain. Gaul remained peaceful, but unlike Greece and Asia, Gaul needed to be equipped with all the trappings of a Roman province, which meant creating administrative districts, building roads, and constructing public buildings. Gaul had become so settled that Augustus established a mint at Lugdunum (Lyons) in 15 BC, which became the main source of silver and gold coins for the next half century.

Britain still lay beyond the borders of the Roman world, but Augustus interfered in tribal politics to make sure pro-Roman rulers were in charge by subsidising them. Two British rulers even dashed to Rome for help from him in their dynastic feuds.

Augustus had much more trouble with Germany and the Rhine. German tribes constantly harried the Rhine frontier. Augustus authorised an invasion beyond the Rhine to push the frontier back farther. A series of wars began against the German tribes in 12 BC, led by Augustus's stepson, Drusus the Elder. Drusus died in 9 BC and his brother Tiberius continued the wars. By AD 5, Germany was largely under Roman control, but there was a long way to go before the area could be called a Roman province.

The disaster of AD 9

It's beginning to read as if Augustus was a one-stop brilliant success story. He wasn't. Frontier control went spectacularly wrong in the year AD 9. Augustus sent out a Governor called Publius Quinctilius Varus to Germany. Varus was tactless and high-handed. He tried to impose taxation and Roman jurisdiction. Varus's actions led to a revolt by a chieftain called Arminius, who had actually been fighting in the Roman army and even been made an equestrian.

Arminius fell back into the forests, and like a fool, Varus followed him right into the trap. Deep in the Teutoburg Forest, Arminius pounced on Varus and wiped out three legions (the XVII, XVIII, and XIX) in one fell swoop. Augustus was devastated but had to make instant preparations against riots in Rome and allies defecting.

On hearing the news from Germany, Augustus was plunged into despair; *Quinctili Vare, legiones redde,* 'Quinctilius Varus, give me back my legions!' he wailed.

In AD 14, an army of revenge was sent out under Tiberius, led by his nephew Germanicus, who found the forest littered with the remains of Varus's army; the soldiers had been massacred, and some were tortured to death. Germanicus pacified the region, as well as recovering the standards of the lost legions. But that was the end of any attempt to push the frontier beyond the Rhine.

A son, a son! My kingdom for a son!

Augustus was plagued by the problem of choosing an heir. Augustus's only child, by his first wife Scribonia, was Julia. Julia's first husband Marcellus had died in 23 BC, leaving no children. Augustus was left with three grandsons by Julia's second husband, Agrippa: Gaius, Lucius, and Agrippa Postumus – but they were all too young to be named as Augustus's heir.

Tiberius, Augustus's stepson by Livia, was the only male choice left. Augustus adopted Tiberius and forced Tiberius to divorce his wife Vipsania and marry Julia. Tiberius was furious because he loved his wife and cleared off to Rhodes for seven years; Tiberius had absolutely no desire to succeed Augustus.

Gaius and Lucius died in AD 2 and AD 4, and Agrippa Postumus was banished by Augustus for his bad behaviour. Augustus also banished Julia and her daughter, also called Julia, because of their immoral way of life. That left Tiberius as Augustus's only possible heir.

The deeds of a lifetime: The Res Gestae

As well as his will, instructions for his funeral, and a statement on the condition of the Empire, Augustus left a summary of his lifetime achievements, called the *Res Gestae*.

In the *Res Gestae,* Augustus proudly listed all the things he had done. These included:

- ✔ The wars he had fought to 'restore liberty to the Republic'

- ✔ His reform of the Senate

- ✔ The honours and triumphs given to him

- ✔ The gifts he had made to the people

- ✔ The temples and other buildings he had constructed

- ✔ The funding of public entertainments

- ✔ His settlement of the provinces

Augustus was bragging, but he was also telling the truth. No other document like the *Res Gestae* exists, which is as it should be, because no other Roman emperor like Augustus ever lived.

In AD 4, Tiberius adopted his nephew Germanicus, and the next year Germanicus married Augustus's granddaughter Agrippina, the sister of Gaius, Lucius, and Agrippa Postumus, and the banished Julia the Younger. Tiberius did inherit the Roman Empire, but the rest of the plan didn't quite work out (see 'Tiberius – part good, part bad, part pervert').

Augustus's death

Augustus died peacefully at the age of 75 on 19 August AD 14. Not many of Augustus's successors enjoyed such a long life or were lucky enough to have a peaceful death.

Augustus is phenomenally important in Roman history because, almost single-handedly, he created a political system that lasted. Augustus was widely worshipped after his death, both publicly and privately. His successors tried to live up to him. From now on, the reigning emperor would be known as the *Imperator Augustus;* later on, an emperor's successor would be known as the *Caesar.* The most difficult thing Augustus tried to do was to establish a secure line of succession – but that was beyond even his control!

Augustus's Dynasty: Tiberius, Caligula, Claudius, and Nero (AD 14–68)

Augustus was followed by four Emperors who all belonged to the Julio-Claudian dynasty: Tiberius, Caligula, Claudius, and Nero. The last three, like Augustus, were all descended from Julius Caesar's sister Julia (that's the Julio- bit), while Tiberius was brought in by adoption when Augustus married his mother Livia. Tiberius, Caligula, Claudius, and Nero were also descended from Tiberius's father Tiberius Claudius Nero (the last three via Tiberius's brother Drusus, making the Claudian bit).

Whatever their pedigree, if you believe the Roman historians Tacitus and Suetonius, the four emperors were nothing but megalomaniacs and perverts. Up to a point, Tacitus and Suetonius were right, although they weren't altogether fair. Tiberius and Claudius had their excesses but were actually quite good rulers. Even Caligula and Nero had their better moments. But the bad things the four emperors did angered people, and many wanted to see the old style Republic restored – not just Augustus's version of it.

Tiberius – part good, part bad, part pervert (AD 14–37)

Tiberius never wanted to be Emperor. He resented having to divorce his wife Vipsania in 12 BC and marry Augustus's ghastly daughter Julia (later exiled for immoral behaviour). Tiberius spent a large part of Augustus's reign knowing perfectly well that Augustus would have preferred the succession to pass to Augustus's own grandsons, Gaius and Lucius, who had died young.

Augustus had groomed Tiberius for the succession by allowing him to share some of his own jobs. While he was alive, Augustus made Tiberius a tribune and also gave him the imperium. Tiberius won for himself a great military reputation, thanks to recovering, in 19 BC, the standards lost by Crassus to the Parthians back in 53 BC (refer to Chapter 14) and for his leadership of the campaign in Germany after the disaster of AD 9 (refer to the section 'The disaster of AD 9'). Because of this, no-one opposed Tiberius's succession.

Tiberius abroad

Tiberius, who was 56 when he became Emperor, had always had a great sense of duty. He was determined to continue Augustus's reconstruction of the Roman Empire and followed Augustus's plan to keep the Roman Empire within its existing boundaries. That meant holding back his popular nephew (and heir) Germanicus (d. AD 19) from trying to conquer more of Germany, although Tiberius gloried in Germanicus's magnificent triumph in AD 17.

Tiberius was smart. He named Commagene and Cappadocia in the East as new provinces when the client kings died, and continued Augustus's policy of Romanisation of the provinces by constructing new public buildings and roads. When a massive earthquake with an epicentre close to Sardis wrecked many of the cities of Asia, Tiberius sent relief and issued coins commemorating his generosity.

Piso and Germanicus

Tiberius made Cnaeus Calpurnius Piso Governor of Syria to keep an eye on Germanicus. Piso had a reputation for ferocity and insubordination. Before he died, Germanicus claimed he had been poisoned by Piso. Germanicus was extremely popular, and his death was greeted with despair by the Roman people. Before long, stories started to circulate that Tiberius and Piso had conspired to murder Germanicus, because Tiberius didn't like anyone else being too popular, and because Germanicus had been planning to restore the Republic. Tiberius had enemies within his own family, namely Germanicus's wife Agrippina. The stories were a gift to her, because she planned that her own sons, and not Germanicus, should succeed Tiberius. Piso later committed suicide.

Home rule

Tiberius was really quite modest in his public image. He refused to call himself Imperator, was consul only three times during his reign, and increased the Senate's powers. Tiberius saved cash by not putting on public entertainments. Imperial mines were taken over by imperial equestrian procurators (Roman financial agents) rather than being run by private individuals, and he made soldiers stay on after they should have retired. The changes weren't popular, but they did save money. The economies meant that Tiberius was able to cut taxes. When Tiberius died, he left a large surplus, even though he had provided relief for natural disasters and let people off their debts.

Flies in the ointment

Although Tiberius made some sound political moves, he lacked tact and was highly suspicious. That made his relationship with the Senate difficult. Worse, Tiberius became far too dependent on Lucius Aelius Sejanus, the Prefect commanding the Praetorian Guard in Rome (refer to Chapter 5 for the role of the Praetorian Guard). Sejanus was a man on the make who fancied himself as the next emperor. Tiberius became a recluse, preferring his villa on Capri to Rome, which meant he took his eye off the ball.

The rise and fall of Sejanus

In AD 19, Germanicus died in Syria where he had been campaigning. Augustus's scheme for Germanicus to become emperor after Tiberius had been foiled. Next in line was Tiberius's own son, Drusus the Younger. In AD 23, Drusus died, murdered by Sejanus. Tiberius, trusting Sejanus entirely, was totally unaware of his treachery. Sejanus encouraged Tiberius to stay on Capri so that he could fill the army and administration with his own men. In AD 31, Tiberius's sister-in-law, Antonia, informed Tiberius about Sejanus's disloyalty and his murder of Drusus.

Tiberius brought down Sejanus with a masterpiece of subterfuge and revenge. Tiberius appointed a soldier called Macro, then Prefect of Rome's fire brigade (*Vigiles*) to be the praetorian prefect, and got the Praetorian Guard over to his side with an offer of cash. Tiberius then sent a long letter from Capri to be read in the Senate. Sejanus listened eagerly, thinking he was to be made a Tribune. The letter started well for Sejanus, praising his virtues and achievements, but ending with Tiberius denouncing Sejanus as a traitor. Within hours, Sejanus, his family, and supporters, were all viciously killed by a mob.

Family paranoia

Tiberius's suspicious nature wrecked family relations. After Drusus's death, Tiberius had accepted his nephew Germanicus's eldest sons, Nero and Drusus, by his wife Agrippina (Augustus's granddaughter), as his heirs. Tiberius later became convinced that Nero and Drusus were conspiring with Sejanus. Tiberius had Agrippina banished and her sons killed.

Paranoia was one of Tiberius's weaknesses and made him the prey of political opportunists. Tiberius believed what he was told and used *delatores* (informers) to build up evidence against anyone said to have spoken or acted against him. The delatores stood to get 25 per cent of the property of anyone they informed against who was successfully convicted of treason (*maiestas*). Naturally, there was a huge incentive to inform on anyone, and the richer the better.

Tiberius expires

Tiberius died on 16 March AD 37 on his way back to Capri after an abortive attempt to visit Rome. Stories were put about that Tiberius had been murdered. It was said that his great-nephew Caligula had poisoned him and that the praetorian prefect Macro (whom Tiberius had used to put down Sejanus) had suffocated Tiberius to show his loyalty to Caligula.

Caligula was made emperor, despite Tiberius's plans that his own grandson, Tiberius Gemellus, would succeed him.

Making your horse a consul is a bad idea: Caligula (AD 37–41)

Caligula, who succeeded Tiberius, was Germanicus and Agrippina's third son. His father's immense popularity helped him a great deal. But Caligula was a very different man.

Caligula's real name was Gaius. As a child he was immensely popular with his father Germanicus's troops on the Rhine frontier, and his father gave him a pair of military sandals to wear. The name *Caligula* means 'little army boot'. The name Caligula stuck, and it's what he's still known as today.

Tiberius stories

Thanks mainly to the historian Suetonius have so many stories about Tiberius's paranoia and debauchery been preserved. Tiberius's victims, half-dead from torture, were supposedly flung off a cliff on Capri where a naval unit waited below to beat them to death if, by chance, they'd survived. Tiberius had young people called *spintriae* perform perverted sexual acts for him. But it was Tacitus who painted a devastating portrait of Tiberius as a crazed recluse.

The truth is that both historians had a hidden agenda. Suetonius and Tacitus were Senators and had seen the Senate's power dwindle as the emperors ruled. Tacitus used Tiberius's hang ups as a way of getting at an emperor much closer to his own time: Domitian (AD 81–96). (More on Domitian at the end of this chapter.) Tiberius did become a recluse and was paranoid, but is now known to have been a competent ruler.

Caligula was hailed on his way to Rome as if he was a superstar. As Germanicus's son, Caligula was welcomed with open arms as emperor in Rome, especially because people hoped the money-saving and paranoia of Tiberius's reign would be cleared out. They were, but were replaced with something far worse: murderous megalomania. Unlike Augustus or Tiberius, Caligula had absolutely no suitable qualifications to be an emperor. He had no experience of the Republic's institutions, no military reputation, no idea of tact and diplomacy, and no idea how to get along with the Senate.

Despite Caligula's lack of experience, he started off well and made himself popular, by

- ✔ Reducing taxes
- ✔ Bringing back men exiled by Tiberius
- ✔ Throwing out any outstanding legal cases
- ✔ Banishing sexual perverts
- ✔ Allowing freedom of speech
- ✔ Reviving elections
- ✔ Paying out Tiberius's legacies
- ✔ Finishing public building works
- ✔ Governing conscientiously

Caligula put on endless expensive public entertainments and paid the Praetorian Guard generously. Caligula then fell ill. When he recovered, he was a changed man. Caligula turned into a tyrant and a lunatic. His expenditure became more reckless and, despite imposing a wide range of new taxes, he managed to squander Tiberius's huge cash reserves within a year. Caligula rapidly descended into madness and did the following:

- **Declared himself a god:** Caligula posed as an absolute monarch, declaring one day 'Let there be one Lord, one King!' After their deaths, Julius Caesar and Augustus had been elevated to the status of gods (Tiberius, not surprisingly, wasn't given that status). In reality, being named as a god was a political gesture, and for Caesar and Augustus, it was a way of acknowledging their great achievements as emperors. Caligula, however, decided he already *was* a god. He planned to replace statues of other gods with a bust of himself, set up a priestly cult to 'Caligula', and spent the day 'talking' to Jupiter.

- **Purged the Senate:** Caligula slated the Senate for supporting Sejanus (refer to 'The rise and fall of Sejanus', earlier in the chapter). Men were executed without trial, including Macro, and Caligula brought back the use of the *delatores* (informers; refer to 'Tiberius – part good, part bad, part pervert').

- **Acted the hypocrite:** He cursed the equestrians for being obsessed with the theatre and the arena – which, frankly, was a cheek because he was a fanatical supporter of the Green faction at the chariot-racing circus himself. He had the neighbourhood silenced so that his favourite horse, Incitatus, would not be disturbed before a race. Apparently, he even toyed with the idea of making Incitatus a consul, though it's unknown if this actually happened.

- **Was fanatically cruel:** Caligula's cruelties never stopped. He flung men of rank into the mines or the circus, and had a playwright burnt alive because the writer had dared to put an indelicate joke into one of his own plays. One of Caligula's most famous remarks was 'I wish the Roman people had a single neck' – meaning that Caligula would be able to execute the Roman population in one go.

- **Made a complete fiasco of foreign policy:** Caligula had a client king called Ptolemy (grandson of Antony and Cleopatra) of Mauretania in North Africa murdered for turning up in Rome wearing a purple cloak (that smacked of imperial rivalry). Caligula provoked Mauretania and Judaea to the point of rebellion. On the way to visit a rural shrine, Caligula got it into his head to invade Germany and, while there, gave the chief centurions the sack.

Adminius, a British warrior prince, fled to Caligula for help. Caligula then announced proudly that he had conquered Britain. Next, Caligula sent his troops to the shores of the North Sea and told the men to collect sea shells as spoils of war.

✔ **Plotted against his family:** Caligula declared his mother Agrippina was the offspring of an incestuous relationship between Augustus and Augustus's daughter Julia. Caligula had his grandmother Antonia poisoned and his cousin Tiberius Gemellus (Tiberius's grandson) murdered.

✔ **Indulged in incest:** Caligula had incestuous relationships with his sisters Drusilla, Julia, and Agrippina (the younger). He even issued a coin portraying himself on one side and his sisters on the other. Caligula carried on with Drusilla, Julia, and Agrippina despite the fact that he was married to Caesonia and had a daughter by her.

There was no way Caligula was going to die peacefully in his own bed. He'd signed his own death warrant, several dozen times! A plot implicating two of his sisters was uncovered, but another was organised involving senators, imperial freedmen, and the Praetorian Guard. On his way to a public performance on 24 January AD 41, Caligula was set upon and hacked to death, despite being protected by his German bodyguards who killed some of the conspirators.

One of the most controversial movies made about the Roman Empire is the 1979 film *Caligula,* starring Malcolm McDowell in the title role and Peter O'Toole as Tiberius. Written by Gore Vidal, the movie features scenes of extreme violence and sexual perversions, but nevertheless reflects what the historian Suetonius recorded about Caligula's reign.

The dribbling old halfwit done good: Claudius (AD 41–54)

Caligula, of course, had made no plans for the succession. Neither had his murderers, whose only concern was to get rid of a dangerous madman. (They also killed Caesonia and Caligula's daughter.)

The Senate spotted its chance and decided it was the time to throw away Augustus's principate and restore the 'good old days' of the Roman Republic. They'd forgotten, however, that for the last 150 years, the Senate had had to do whatever the generals and the army had told them to do. And that's what happened now.

In the plots against his family, Caligula left his uncle Claudius, Tiberius's nephew, unharmed. Claudius had a reputation as the family idiot because he dribbled, stammered, and had a limp. Caligula thought he was a joke, but Claudius was highly intelligent. Augustus knew that Claudius was clever and made sure that Claudius had an education. But Claudius was never allowed to gain experience as a soldier or administrator, because his physical handicaps would have been bad for Augustus's image.

Claudius was found by the Praetorian Guard hiding behind a curtain when Caligula was murdered. The Guard wrong-footed the Senate by declaring the 50-year-old Claudius their new Emperor and champion. Claudius, being a historian, was smart enough to realise that the only power that mattered was military power. If Claudius had said no to being emperor, he would probably have been killed. Claudius accepted the job and promised the Praetorian Guard a handsome sum of money in return for their support.

The making of a man: Conquering Britain

Rome's secret of success was adapting to new circumstances while clinging on to tradition, and Claudius knew this. He also knew that his personal reputation was a handicap: Claudius had to prove himself as a leader and as a conqueror. He started off by settling the war in Mauretania, made Mauretania into two new provinces, and created a client kingdom to stabilise Judaea. Claudius also added Lycia and Thrace to the Empire.

Claudius's greatest opportunity came in AD 43 when a British tribal chieftain called Verica fled to him for help. Britain, like most parts of the world ruled by tribes, suffered from endless petty dynastic and territorial disputes. The disputes weren't of much importance to Rome, but Britain was important, because of its valuable mineral resources.

Claudius mounted a major military expedition to Britain, led by the general Aulus Plautius. Caligula had left some of the preparations to invade Britain in place from his abortive effort a few years earlier. Claudius was able to take advantage of Caligula's arrangements. Julius Caesar had failed to hold on to Britain, and now Claudius was given the chance to outdo the greatest Roman of them all.

To begin with, the invasion of Britain went remarkably well. Plautius advanced inland and then sent to Rome for the Emperor. Claudius marched at the head of his army to the great tribal capital of Camulodunum (Colchester), returning to Rome after 16 days. Claudius put on a triumph, erecting arches and issuing coins to commemorate his mighty achievement. The war in Britain continued on and off for more than a century, but Claudius had achieved his goal. He was now a fully-fledged Roman emperor who had proved himself as a victorious commander. To celebrate, he named his son Britannicus.

Running the Roman Empire

In AD 48, Claudius encouraged the senators to admit leading Gauls to the Senate, a liberal gesture on Claudius's part, which gave provincials more power. Part of Claudius's original speech announcing this survives on a bronze plaque in Lyons. Claudius was also keen that the Senate felt free to express its own views, rather than just agreeing with imperial decisions.

The Druids

The Druids were a priestly caste in Gaul and Britain. The word *druid* comes from the Greek for an oak tree: δρυς, pronounced *drys*. Groves of oak trees with mistletoe were sacred to the Druids. The Druids controlled tribal religion, law, and politics, enforced with human sacrifices, which disgusted the Romans. The Druids hugely resented the Romans for denting their power. In Britain, Druids continued to lead resistance to the Roman invasion until AD 60 (see the later sidebar 'The Boudican War').

Claudius built a large new harbour for the port at Ostia to improve the grain supply to Rome, and he reformed the grain supply's administration (see Chapter 7 for information on the importance of the grain supply). He also built a new aqueduct and handed out gifts to the people.

Claudius revived Roman religious customs, discouraged emperor worship, and generally tolerated foreign cults, but only if they didn't directly challenge Roman power. Jews were allowed to worship freely, but Claudius ordered that the Druids in Gaul be wiped out.

Claudius's shortcomings

Apart from his physical handicaps, Claudius had an unpredictable temper. Sometimes he was careful and considerate, at other times thoughtless and impatient, which led to hasty judgements in the Senate. Claudius relied on his wives and freedmen for advice, which made the senators and equestrians distrustful and resentful.

Claudius's Chief Secretary Narcissus, Chief Assistant Pallas, and Examiner of Petitions Callistus were all freedmen and the most senior men in Claudius's government. Narcissus, Pallas, and Callistus wielded unprecedented influence, sold offices and privileges, and made themselves wealthy over and above the gifts they received from Claudius.

Senators and equestrians themselves hadn't been above such practices in the past. The use of freedmen and slaves was simply more efficient, and Claudius's dependence on a personal bureaucracy was probably better for the Empire.

Claudius's wives

Claudius had four wives (not at the same time), but it was numbers three and four who annoyed the Senate, more even than Claudius's freedmen. His third and fourth wives, Valeria Messalina and Caligula's sister Agrippina (Claudius's niece), both played on Claudius's fears of conspiracies. Suetonius said that thanks to Messalina and Agrippina's denunciations, 35 senators and 300 equestrians were executed.

- ✔ Messalina, mother of Claudius's son Britannicus, was a bigamist and a nymphomaniac. Claudius had Messalina executed in AD 48 when he discovered she had secretly married another man, Gaius Silius. Disgusted and disappointed, he was determined not to marry again, but there's no fool like an old fool, and he fell for his niece Agrippina (Caligula's sister).

- ✔ Agrippina ensnared Claudius easily. Claudius had the law changed to make it legal to marry his niece. Agrippina wanted her son Lucius by Cnaeus Domitius Ahenobarbus to become Emperor (he did: as Nero). Agrippina persuaded Claudius to adopt Lucius, which placed him second in line to the throne after Britannicus. Lucius's name was changed to Nero Claudius Caesar Drusus Germanicus.

The end of Claudius

Nero, still too young to succeed as emperor, fell increasingly under Agrippina's control. In AD 54, when Nero was nearly 17 (five years older than Britannicus), by a lucky chance, Claudius died. The story at the time was that Claudius had been murdered, but this was not proved. The smart money was on Agrippina, who was said to have served him up a plate of poisoned mushrooms.

Claudius's death was kept quiet until Agrippina could arrange for Nero's smooth succession. The reign of Nero, probably the most notorious in Roman history, was about to begin.

Robert Graves wrote a couple of novels, *I, Claudius* and *Claudius the God,* which trace how Claudius became Emperor and tell the story of the reigns of Augustus, Tiberius, and Caligula. *I, Claudius* is a great yarn and was brilliantly televised in a 1976 BBC series with Derek Jacobi, superb as the stammering Claudius. John Hurt as Caligula was a tour de force of hysterical menace.

Where mother went wrong: Nero (AD 54–68)

Nero was a melodramatic, ridiculous, and posturing egomaniac who had unlimited faith in his own creative, artistic, and sporting skills. In Suetonius's words, Nero was obsessed with a 'craze for popularity'. Still only in his mid-teens, Nero had been handed the whole Roman world and its resources with which to indulge himself. At that point in his life, he was still, by most standards, pretty normal. He had spent his childhood honing his interest in horses, sport, art, music, and painting.

The Boudican War

The Boudican War in Britain was no sideshow. The war nearly cost Rome a province; if Rome had lost, the Empire's prestige would have been permanently destroyed.

The client king of the Iceni in Britain, Prasutagus, died around AD 59. Prasutagus left half his kingdom to Nero in the hope the tribe would be left in peace, but Roman administrators moved in to ransack Iceni territory. Boudica, Prasutagus's wife, was famously flogged and her daughters raped. The Iceni, taking advantage of the governor's absence (he had taken a large chunk of the Roman army on a campaign to wipe out the Druids on the island of Anglesey, off the Welsh coast), rose in rebellion and were soon joined by some of their neighbours.

Although the Iceni had serious grievances, there's no doubt that many of the rebels were more interested in loot and plunder. Three Roman cities (Colchester, London, and St Albans) were burned to the ground and their inhabitants massacred. The Roman army in Britain suffered defeats until the governor, Gaius Suetonius Paullinus, forced the rebels into a pitched battle and destroyed them. In the aftermath, the Roman army moved more troops into Iceni territory and punished the rebellious tribes.

The Iceni rebellion was a devastating blow to Rome, and news of it was kept as quiet as possible to stop other provinces rebelling. No victory coins were issued. Nero had already thought about abandoning the war in Britain because of the cost, but decided it would have been an insult to Claudius and his victories in Britain. The Iceni rebellion made it impossible for Rome to withdraw from Britain. For more about Boudica, see Chapter 25.

Nero's reign in a nutshell

During the early years of Nero's reign, the Roman Empire carried on much as it had under Claudius. The efficient new bureaucracy continued to work. In the East, the general Cnaeus Domitius Corbulo conquered Armenia and installed a client king. In Britain, the war of conquest was steadily proceeding north and west with the ultimate target being the destruction of the Druid stronghold on Anglesey, off the north-west coast of Wales. But as Nero's reign wore on, his lack of ability led to instability in Rome and the provinces.

As the Roman poet Juvenal once said, 'no-one ever reached the depths of depravity all at once'. It took Nero a few years, but he got there alright. Towards the end of his reign, things got really out of control. The advisors who had held Nero in check – his praetorian prefect Burrus and his tutor Lucius Annaeus Seneca – were no longer around. (Burrus had died in AD 62 and Seneca retired.) Nero fell into a life of depravity and wild extravagance and abandoned any attempt to govern the Empire.

Nero's reign had many memorable moments. Here are some of the highlights (or lowlights):

- **Clearing the way:** In AD 55, Agrippina poisoned Claudius's son Britannicus, to wipe out the chance of a rival faction.

- **Nero killed his mother Agrippina:** He was driven to distraction by her constant interference. Nero wasn't the only one who hated Agrippina; Seneca and Burrus both resented her power and influence. Much as he loved his mother, Nero threw Agrippina out of the palace. Nero couldn't take any more when Agrippina interfered over his mistress, Poppaea. He decided to have Agrippina killed. (Seneca put it about that Agrippina was plotting to kill Nero, to stop Nero from getting any bad publicity.) But Nero didn't find the task of getting rid of Agrippina easy:

  - Nero tried poisoning Agrippina, but he was foiled because Agrippina had all the necessary antidotes.

  - Nero planned to have ceiling panels dropped on Agrippina while she slept, but his wicked scheme got about before he could arrange the 'accident'.

  - Anicetus suggested that Nero build a collapsible boat for Agrippina so that she would drown. When Agrippina came to see Nero, she went home in the boat, but when the boat fell apart Agrippina saved her life by swimming home.

  - Nero gave up and sent Anicetus and some other thugs round to beat Agrippina to death, which they did.

- **Rebellions in the provinces:** AD 60 and AD 61 were terrible years for Rome. In Britain, a rebellion led by Boudica, ruler of the Iceni tribe, devastated the new Roman province and was put down with great difficulty (see the sidebar, 'The Boudican War' for details). In Armenia, in AD 62, a Roman army was defeated and forced to surrender. Armenia was only brought to heel by sending in the general Corbulo with a new and much bigger army.

  Nero sent out an expedition of Praetorian Guards under a tribune to Africa in AD 61, because he was planning an attack on Ethiopia. It took the soldiers around 1,000 miles beyond the Roman frontier in Egypt – probably the furthest the Roman army ever reached – but because all they found was desert, the idea of an invasion was abandoned. Given what had happened in Britain, perhaps it was just as well.

- **Nero killed his wife Octavia and seduced Poppaea:** Nero divorced and murdered his wife Octavia and then married his mistress Poppaea (who died in AD 65). Poppaea was the wife of Nero's friend, Marcus Salvius Otho, who had helped Nero kill Agrippina. Not surprisingly, Nero and Otho fell out, and Nero sent Otho to govern Lusitania in Spain. Otho took his revenge by becoming emperor after Nero's death, (explained in the section 'A man of many enemies: Otho', later in this chapter).

✔ **Great Fire of Rome:** In AD 64, a catastrophic fire destroyed a large part of Rome, and, as the famous story goes, 'Nero played the fiddle while Rome burned'. The disaster was a heaven-sent opportunity for Nero to regain public support and esteem by funding the rebuilding of Rome and helping out the homeless. Nero did give some help in organising repair work, but he was more interested in helping himself to a huge chunk of the land (120 acres) to build himself a palace, known as the *Domus Aurea* ('Golden House'). People seethed with resentment, believing that Nero started the Great Fire in order to fund his new palace. Nero, with the help of the new praetorian prefect Othonius Tigellinus, responded by putting about a rumour that it was the Christians who were responsible for the fire, and Nero organised a hasty round of persecutions to prove the story.

Quo Vadis (1951) is all about a general called Marcus Vinicius, who returning home to Rome, falls in love with a Christian girl called Lygia. Vinicius gets Nero to give Lygia to him, but when Nero starts persecuting Christians after the fire in Rome, Vinicius has to rescue Lygia and her family. Peter Ustinov as Nero is particularly memorable.

✔ **Nero tried people for treason on the smallest pretence:** In AD 66, a philosopher called Publius Paetus Thrasea was tried and executed for treason for mildly criticising Nero. Others, like Nero's old tutor Seneca, who had been implicated in a plot against Nero, were told to commit suicide. As time went on, Nero suspected anyone and everyone. He executed his General Corbulo, as well as other military commanders. The executions were a bad move on Nero's part. Nero had killed off men of real power and influence. Now powerful men had to choose between execution or rebellion; they chose rebellion.

✔ **Nero took a holiday in Greece at the wrong time:** Nero, ignoring all the signs of a conspiracy against him, took a vast entourage to Greece, after declaring the whole province to be free. From AD 67 to 68, Nero had a great time in Greece taking part in games he was always allowed to win, and giving musical performances to captive audiences who were literally locked in the theatre. While Nero was enjoying himself, a famine broke out in Rome because grain ships bringing corn to Rome were being diverted to take the grain to Greece instead.

Nero's coins

Not much coinage was struck by Claudius after AD 41, and the shortage continued into Nero's reign. But in AD 64, Nero ordered a massive new issue of coins to be struck, employing the finest engravers available. The new coins, especially the large brass sestertii (34 millimetres wide), carried dramatically realistic portraits of Nero.

He was shown in his late bloated and preening years, complete with designer hairstyle and stubble, bull-neck, and double-chin. In the Renaissance, scholars wondered at the coins, which so brilliantly reflect the personality of Nero described by Suetonius and Tacitus.

TECHNICAL STUFF

Domus Aurea

Nero's *Domus Aurea* ('Golden House') sprawled across a large part of central Rome. Nero employed two architects, Severus and Celerus, to design his new residence, and building was in progress from soon after Rome's Great Fire in AD 64, until Nero's death in AD 68. The Domus Aurea had an artificial lake, parks, and forests, as well as an array of buildings that included covered passages connecting the complex to the palaces of Augustus and Tiberius. Although some of the Domus Aurea was destroyed after Nero's death, a fair-sized part was later buried to provide the site for baths built by Trajan (AD 98–117) and has survived. It can still be seen today, complete with wall-plaster and ceilings.

By the late 60s Nero's reign was falling apart. To pay for foreign wars, Nero had to lower the bullion content of silver coinage. Then Nero had to send Titus Flavius Vespasianus to Judea with a huge army to suppress a rebellion. Unwittingly, by giving Vespasian the command of an army, Nero had given Vespasian the power to bring Nero down and the means of becoming Emperor himself.

The rebellions start

Out on the Rhine frontier, the Roman army had a reputation for being mutinous: The troops were sick of waiting for their pay or retirement papers. Nero let their pay get even more behind, and as they had no personal loyalty to him, it would only take a spark to start a mutiny. In AD 68, the governor of Gallia Lugdunensis, Gaius Julius Vindex, led a rebellion against Nero. Vindex was the descendent of Gallic tribal chieftains, and although he had been 'Romanised', the legions on the Rhine saw Vindex as a Gallic rebel and destroyed the rebellion.

After Vindex had been put down, the victorious soldiers were keen to march on Rome and make their own commander, Lucius Verginius Rufus, emperor. Rufus said no to the soldiers, but news of the plan reached Rome, and the Praetorian Guard's new commander Nymphidius Sabinus told the Guard that the governor of Hispania Tarraconensis in Spain, Servius Sulpicius Galba, was prepared to give the Praetorian Guard a large cash reward to make *him* emperor. The Guard promptly sided with Galba.

Nero panicked. He tried to get an escape fleet organised, but no-one would help him. Next, he considered surrendering to Galba; then he thought about making a speech in the Forum begging for forgiveness and asking for the governorship of Egypt instead of being emperor. But Nero realised he would be lynched before he got as far as the Forum. Nero was left with just a few trusty servants; one of them, called Epaphroditus, in the summer of AD 68, helped Nero commit suicide.

As Nero died, ever missing the point about what an emperor needed to be, he declared: *Qualis artifex pereo,* 'What an artist I die!'

The Year of the Four Emperors (AD 68–69)

There were, quite literally, no Julio-Claudians left to succeed Nero. The mechanism of choosing a successor by family connection to the Julio-Claudians was broken. The historian Tacitus said this was when the terrible secret of the Roman Empire was exposed: An emperor could be made in a place other than Rome. It looked like Rome was going to turn back the clock to the days of the Republican generals in the first century BC. What followed is sometimes called the Year of the Four Emperors.

Too old and too tight: Galba (AD 68–69)

Galba was chosen by the Senate to replace Nero. Galba came from an old Republican family, was 71 years old, and suffered from gout. He seemed to have all the right qualifications but started out completely on the wrong foot:

- ✔ He made himself look like a tyrant by executing Nero's supporters.

- ✔ His strict economies annoyed the mob, especially the army, which had been hoping for a large payment in return for their loyalty.

- ✔ He removed Lucius Verginius Rufinus from his command on the Rhine, infuriating the troops, and sent in two new commanders (Flaccus and Vitellius – more of them shortly) who were unable to control the troops.

- ✔ He upset the former Governor of Lusitiania, Marcus Salvius Otho, who had supported him, by making a young and untried man called Lucius Piso Licinianus the new commander on the Rhine.

The army on the Rhine swore allegiance to Vitellius, but Otho, whose hopes of being adopted by Galba as his successor had been dashed by Piso's promotion, seized his chance to become emperor.

A man of many enemies: Otho (AD 69)

Otho had himself declared emperor on 15 January AD 69 simply by offering the Praetorian Guard a large sum of money. Galba and Piso were promptly murdered.

Greedy Vitellius

Vitellius was said to have spent time with Tiberius's *spintriae* (young people who performed sexual perversions; refer to the earlier sidebar 'Tiberius stories') on Capri. Vitellius had been popular with Caligula because he liked chariot driving and with Claudius because he liked playing dice. But Vitellius is remembered most for his greed.

Vitellius used to invite himself to people's houses for dinner, forcing his hosts to spend a fortune on food, nearly ruining them. Vitellius even helped himself to food intended for religious sacrifice, and he designed a gigantic dish called the 'Shield of Minerva the Protectress' that included food from every part of the Empire.

Otho, like Galba, had a bad start. Having been one of Nero's closest friends, Otho wasn't trusted, and with the powerful Rhine armies supporting Vitellius, civil war looked unavoidable. Vitellius's forces divided into two and set out across the Alps for Italy. Vitellius's troops met Otho's army at Cremona, and thanks to the help of Batavian auxiliaries, Otho's army was defeated. Otho's troops surrendered to Vitellius, and Otho, after a reign of just three months, committed suicide. The Senate immediately declared Vitellius emperor.

The gluttonous emperor: Vitellius (AD 69)

Not a lot is known about Vitellius's family background. Vitellius's uncle, Quintus, had been involved in Sejanus's conspiracy against Tiberius (refer to the earlier section 'The rise and fall of Sejanus'). Vitellius's father Lucius had been close to Caligula, even worshipping him as a god. Lucius had also taken care of the Empire while Claudius was campaigning in Britain in AD 43.

Vitellius had been a competent provincial governor, but he had no experience on the battlefield and had relied entirely on his troops in the campaign against Otho at Cremona. After defeating Otho, Vitellius dismissed most of the Praetorian Guard as a punishment for killing Galba. Leading a triumphant march to Rome, Vitellius stopped at the battlefield at Betriacum near Cremona and, drinking plenty of wine to overcome the stench of corpses, made the tactless comment that only the smell of a dead fellow citizen was sweeter than the smell of a dead enemy.

Vitellius appointed unsuitable advisors, including an insolent thief of a freedman called Asiaticus. He also had men tortured and executed on the slightest pretext. Vitellius was on the way out soon after he got in.

The Revolt of Civilis

Gaius Julius Civilis was a Batavian tribal chieftain who had served in the Roman army and earned Roman citizenship. Antonius Primus asked Civilis to create a diversion and prevent Vitellius's troops slowing down the pro-Vespasian forces in Italy. Civilis decided to pretend to be pro-Vespasian, in order to fight a war of liberation. Various border tribes joined Civilis and, amazingly, Roman troops at Neuss. Civilis's army managed to defeat a legion, and Civilis even started striking Roman-type coinage to pay his troops. But when Vespasian sent a Roman army to put down the revolt, Civilis gave up, and no-one knows what happened to him.

The rise of Vespasian

Out East, Vespasian, with his son Titus, had been fighting a major war against the Jews in Judaea. Unlike Nero, Galba, Otho, and Vitellius, Vespasian was a trained and successful soldier and was smart enough to wait for the right moment to make a bid to be emperor.

When Vitellius had been emperor for eight months, Vespasian's army in the East declared Vespasian as emperor, making him the fourth emperor in the 'Year of the Four Emperors'. Vespasian also had the support of legions in the Danube area. Vespasian's army, commanded by Antonius Primus, set out for Italy and defeated Vitellius's forces at Cremona, almost at the same place where Vitellius's forces had defeated Otho earlier in the year. Cremona was sacked and governors across the western provinces went over to Vespasian.

Vitellius made a deal with Vespasian's brother Sabinus, who was in command of what was left of the Praetorian Guard, that he would abdicate. Vitellius's troops, however, refused to let him give up. Vitellius drove Sabinus and his supporters into the Capitol, lynching them and burning down the Temple of Jupiter. When the Danube troops who supported Vespasian reached Rome, Vitellius tried to escape in disguise, but was soon caught, tortured, and flung into the river Tiber.

Starting Well and Finishing Badly – the Flavians (AD 69–96)

The Year of the Four Emperors had changed everything for the Roman Empire. Not only was it clear that an emperor could be made outside Rome, but it was also clear that being emperor was open to people who were not from ancient aristocratic families. Vespasian (full name Titus Flavius Vespasianus) and his sons Titus and Domitian would rule as the Flavian dynasty.

From Augustus to Nero, the name 'Caesar' was a family name – the holder was a member of the Julio-Claudian dynasty. From the reign of Galba onwards 'Caesar' became a mark of rank: the title given to the named heir, or heirs, of the emperor, who were later given the title of Augustus on becoming emperor. Vespasian's sons Titus and Domitian were named as Caesars. When Titus became emperor in AD 79, he became Augustus, and Domitian remained a Caesar until AD 81, when he, too, became Augustus.

Mr Down-to-earth: Vespasian AD 69–79)

Vespasian (full name Titus Flavius Vespasianus), and his sons Titus and Domitian, ruled as the Flavian dynasty. Vespasian's family were equestrians from the Sabine town of Reate (modern Rieti), but Vespasian and his brother gained promotion to senatorial status. His father was a tax collector and banker, with a reputation for honesty. Vespasian won fame as a brilliant soldier during the invasion of Britain in AD 43 and later in Africa, and then in Judaea under Nero. Nero banished Vespasian for walking out of (or falling asleep during) one of Nero's recitals. But luckily for Vespasian, Nero recalled him because of his military abilities, and he was sent to Judaea with Titus and a large army to put down the Jewish revolt.

Vespasian was a practical man. He had no great vision like Augustus, but he was tireless, straightforward, and blissfully free of delusions of grandeur. Thanks to Vespasian, the office of emperor survived the war of AD 68–69 instead of being abandoned.

When in Rome

In AD 70, Vespasian made an important change to government by reviving the censorship. A censor's chief job was to organise a census of the population, but more importantly, a censor could nominate men to the Senate. Vespasian was able to bring men into the Senate with the right abilities and experience to serve the Empire – in fact, men like himself. Vespasian got rid of unsuitable senators, and if the right man wasn't able to fulfil the property qualification (refer to Chapter 2), Vespasian made up the shortfall in cash. Vespasian's new men included not only Italians but also men from farther afield. Vespasian took the important step of broadening the make-up of the Senate by filling it with men from backgrounds other than the Roman aristocracy.

Vespasian no longer relied on freedmen to do the clerical work as Claudius and Nero had done. He retained a few freedmen, but their duties were given to equestrians. Because of Nero's excessive spending, Vespasian had to raise taxes and invent new ones, and take back estates former emperors had given to their friends. Vespasian, though, wasn't above dubious practices; to raise cash, he sold offices and, for a price, acquitted men being prosecuted.

Vespasian had the loyalty of the army and escaped having to make extra payments to the soldiers for their support. He managed to offset opposition to his rule by organising a programme of public building, including the building of the Colosseum, Rome's famous amphitheatre, and also allowing anyone to build on sites in Rome left vacant by fire or ruin.

In the provinces

Administration of the provinces became easier when Vespasian brought in the post of *legatus iuridicus* (the judicial legate). Judicial legates were posted to certain provinces where they could take care of legal cases while the governor-proper had other things to worry about, such as in Britain, for example, where the governor was still busy conquering the west and north of the country. The settled part of Britain was recovering from the devastation of the Boudican revolt. Public buildings were being constructed, and the Britons were encouraged to adopt the Roman way of life.

Elsewhere, Vespasian brought in new provinces by taking away their liberty; for example, revoking Nero's grant of freedom to Greece meant that Greece was obliged to pay taxes to Rome.

Vespasian's heirs

Vespasian believed in omens. He was committed to establishing a Flavian dynasty and believed he had been given all the right signs. Vespasian told the Senate that only his sons Titus and Domitian would succeed him as Emperor. When Vespasian died on 23 June AD 79, the succession was clear-cut, something that had not happened since Augustus died in AD 14, 65 years earlier.

Vespasian was the first emperor to use Imperator as a title, rather than as part of his name. Legends on Vespasian's coins start 'Imperator . . .'. The fiction that Augustus had 'restored' the Republic was giving way to the hard fact that the real power now belonged to the emperor.

The much-loved Titus (AD 79–81)

Titus, Vespasian's son, was a popular young man; he had been a childhood playmate of Claudius's son Britannicus. Titus was good at almost everything, from warfare to music, and he had an exceptional memory. He had fought with his father in the Jewish revolt and then came to Rome, where he served a fellow official of his father's who was consul and tribune. But Titus wasn't perfect and could be arrogant. He had a reputation for murdering anyone he suspected of conspiracy and had a taste for all-night revels. Titus was infatuated with a Judaean Queen called Berenice and brought her back to Rome; he might have married her if it had not been for Vespasian's death.

As Titus was so clearly his father's designated heir, the succession went smoothly. Titus got rid of disreputable friends, gave up misbehaving for good, and sent Berenice, the Judean Queen, home. Titus quickly developed a reputation for fair dealing, confirmed any favours done by previous emperors rather than overturning them as previous emperors usually did, and avoided helping himself to people's estates. Titus had the *delatores* (informers) publicly humiliated and sent out of Rome. He also continued Vespasian's building projects and completed the Colosseum, which he opened with a spectacular cycle of public games and entertainments.

Dealing with disasters

Barely two months into the job of emperor, Titus faced the most famous disaster in the history of the Roman Empire. On 24 August AD 79, Mount Vesuvius erupted and devastated the Bay of Naples. Villas owned by wealthy Romans were destroyed by lava and pumice, and thousands of people were killed by poisonous fumes. Two major towns, Pompeii and Herculaneum, were wiped out. The following year a serious fire and also a plague hit Rome. Titus gave huge amounts of cash and practical aid to both disasters and tried, without success, to have a cure found for the plague.

A sudden death

Titus had made himself very popular by his generous response to the disasters, and his unexpected death caused widespread mourning. On a journey into Sabine territory, in the late summer of AD 81, Titus caught a fever and died on 13 September, leaving a daughter called Julia Titi.

Judaea and Masada

Judaea was a nightmare province, seething with resentment at Roman control. Titus was left to finish off the war that had broken out in AD 66 under Nero. This war involved fighting for every last yard until the temple and citadel in Jerusalem were destroyed. Judean rebels held out against Rome until AD 73, in the Judean hilltop fortress of Masada. An army of 7,000 legionaries beseiged the fortress for six months, until the people inside set the fortress on fire and then committed suicide. To this day, the siege works used by the Roman army are still visible at Masada, including a huge ramp that was built up one side to gain access. The conquered Judeans became Roman slaves and Jews around the Empire were taxed to pay for the new Temple of Jupiter in Rome.

Flavian propaganda

Titus, or one of his officials, had a brainwave. A whole series of coin types issued by previous emperors was revived and issued in large numbers. It wasn't a new idea, but no-one had done it on this scale before. The old coins were copied but had a legend added to them saying 'the emperor Titus restored this coin'. The new coin was a clever way of showing how the Flavian dynasty represented continuity. Augustus, Tiberius, Claudius, and Galba were included (Galba being there to show you didn't have to be a Julio-Claudian to be emperor: pretty important for the Flavians), as well as imperial family members and associates like Germanicus (Tiberius's nephew) and Agrippa (nominated by Augustus as his heir). But Caligula, Nero, Otho, and Vitellius weren't represented – they had been classed as imperial outcasts; no-one in their right mind was going to celebrate their reigns.

Paranoid fly-killer: Domitian (AD 81–96)

Domitian, Vespasian's other son, was everything Titus was not. Domitian had spent much of Titus's reign plotting his brother's downfall. Once, when Titus fell ill, Domitian ordered Titus to be left for dead. Titus left no sons, and as Domitian had been named by Vespasian as his heir, there was no opposition to Domitian becoming emperor.

Vespasian and Titus had kept Domitian under control by letting Domitian serve as consul, but Vespasian and Titus didn't allow Domitian the command of an army in case Domitian attracted a following. With Vespasian and Titus gone, Domitian had a free rein. Domitian showed all the signs of a cruel and despotic ruler. He boasted that he was the one who had placed Vespasian and Titus on the throne. He had people executed or banished on the slightest pretext; Sallustius Lucullus, the governor of Britain, for example, designed a new type of spear, but Lucullus stupidly named it after himself rather than after Domitian. As a punishment, Domitian had Lucullus executed. When Domitian became emperor, it was said that he spent his spare time stabbing flies.

Domitian as ruler

Domitian, for all his defects, was a surprisingly competent emperor. He maintained a popular programme of public entertainments and gifts, insisted on proper Roman dress amongst spectators, and encouraged the cult of his favourite goddess, Minerva. He had public buildings repaired and built new ones, but committed a public-relations crime by putting his own name on the restored buildings instead of the names of the emperors who had originally built them.

In the Piazza Navona in Rome, you can still see the outline of Domitian's stadium, which replaced a wooden one from earlier times. Parts of the brick and stone substructures of the circus (which held 20,000 people) are still visible, but the stadium was destroyed in the Middle Ages, and the bricks and stones used as foundations for houses and a church. Large parts of Domitian's palace on the Palatine Hill are still standing.

Meanwhile, on the frontiers

Domitian had money problems because of excessive public spending, and his solution was to cut back on the army and military expeditions. In AD 87, he abandoned a long-standing campaign to conquer northern Britain, including Scotland. The reality was that securing Britain's far north wasn't going to make Rome any safer, but holding the German frontier would. The Rhine-Danube frontier had never been secure in the areas where the two rivers rise, because both rivers turn southwards to their sources, leaving a large gap between them. This created a sharp 'V' in the Roman frontier, which the Chatti tribe took advantage of. Domitian's answer was to push the frontier northwards and create a network of fortifications, which made the frontier in Germany secure for generations.

After strengthening the borders in Germany, Domitian's troops were ready to go to war against the Dacians. The Dacians' chieftain Decebalus was determined to make himself an empire out of Roman territory. Domitian wasn't able to deal with Decebalus because he was distracted by a Roman general who had picked the same time to rebel. Domitian set a precedent by paying Decebalus a large subsidy to keep the peace. (See Chapter 17 for the more about the Dacians.)

Damnatio Memoriae

Domitian was convinced that he was surrounded by enemies. Despite his achievements, he was widely loathed. Domitian acted like a despot and was far too keen on the trappings of the job. He liked it when poets called him 'Master and God'. Domitian had an ongoing affair with his niece, Julia Titi, and a taste for prostitutes, which might explain why his wife Domitia (daughter of the general Corbulo, discussed in the earlier section 'Where mother went wrong: Nero') seems to have been one of the main players in his assassination. He dreamed that Minerva (his favourite goddess) had told him she could no longer protect him. On 18 September AD 96, Domitian was murdered.

Domitian's death caused mixed reactions. Most people didn't care. The soldiers, however, were furious; Domitian had increased soldiers' pay by a third, and now it was likely that they would lose the increase. The Senate was delighted to get the news of Domitian's death, so delighted, in fact, that they ordered statues of Domitian be torn down and Domitian's name chiselled off every inscription in the Empire that named him. This was a Roman punishment known as *damnatio memoriae,* 'the damnation of (his) memory' – simply a way of wiping someone from the record.

At the museum in the Roman town of St Albans, you can see an inscription with Domitian's name deleted. The text has been restored from the few surviving fragments; Vespasian's name can be seen along with that of Agricola, the Governor of Britain. The bit where Domitian's name was hacked out is plain to see.

Chapter 17

The Five Good Emperors

In This Chapter

▶ How a stopgap emperor saved the Empire from another civil war (AD 96–98)

▶ Trajan makes the Roman Empire as big as it ever got (98–117)

▶ Why Hadrian stopped conquest and fixed the frontiers (117–138)

▶ How Antoninus Pius managed to be so nice (138–161)

▶ Marcus Aurelius's admiral reign – and unfortunate choice of successor (161–180)

After Nero died in 68, the civil war and three disastrous emperors (Galba, Otho, and Vitellius), one after another, took Augustus's world to the brink. Fortunately, Vespasian came next. His common sense, patience, and hard work saved the day. Vespasian's son Titus continued to provide competent leadership and stability. When Titus died, his brother Domitian took over. Domitian might have been a bad emperor in some ways, but like his brother Titus and his father, he was really a competent ruler. Not only that, but by the end of the first century AD, no-one could really imagine the Roman world without an emperor, most of all the provincial senators who now packed the benches in the Roman Senate.

After Domitian's death the Senate had a choice: restore the Republic or pick another emperor. The Senate went for emperor, and what followed was a series of rulers called the Five Good Emperors. It was the climax of Rome's power, when the Empire was at its richest and most settled.

Edward Gibbon, the famous historian, in *Decline and Fall of the Roman Empire,* published in 1776, talked about the time of the Five Good Emperors as 'the most happy and prosperous' in all human history. Maybe Gibbon was right, but what is certain is that when Marcus Aurelius, the last of the five emperors, died in AD 180, the Roman Empire was on the long road into decline.

We've now passed the time of the last, greatest Roman historians, Tacitus and Suetonius. As the second century opened, they were busy writing down their work, much of which has survived. But no-one wrote anything quite so detailed after that – at least, nothing that has survived. So instead, we have to fall back on what's left of Dio Cassius's history, occasional other histories, biographies of emperors written hundreds of years later, inscriptions, and scattered other bits and pieces. If that sounds a lot, it isn't – at best the sources are patchy; at worst they're non-existent or chronically unreliable.

Nerva: A Good Stopgap (AD 96–98)

In AD 96, the senators got together to find a new emperor instead of fantasising about restoring the Republic. They came up with a veteran Senator called Marcus Cocceius Nerva. He was the first of what are now known as the Five Good Emperors, whose rule covered the climax of Rome's power, when the Empire was at its richest and most settled.

As a young man Nerva had been a close friend of Nero's, but he was trusted by Vespasian and Domitian to serve as consul. Nerva might have been in on the plot to assassinate Domitian. No-one knows, but as he was made emperor the same day, he must have known about it. He also must have been politically astute – perfect to calm the crisis down.

Nerva was 64 years old when he became emperor, and he was just a good stopgap. He didn't have foolish ambitions, nor did he have children, but he did have the necessary political and administrative experience for the job.

As luck would have it, Nerva and the next three emperors would be childless (or outlive their sons), giving them all the luxury to choose the right successor, rather than passing on the Empire to an unsuitable son.

Smart moves and good deeds

After the nastiness of Domitian's reign and its violent end (refer to Chapter 16), Nerva had to restore public confidence in the position of emperor. He wanted to show that an enlightened emperor could do good things for the people of Rome and Italy and make their lives better. His policies addressed the following:

- ✔ **Public funds:** Nerva saved on public spending by cutting back on the gladiatorial games and religious sacrifices. He sold off imperial treasure and appointed a commission to find different ways of saving money. Because of the economies, he was able to cut taxes. He also abolished the way local communities had to pay for the imperial post (the communication system introduced by Augustus; see Chapter 6 for details).

- **Public policy:** Nerva probably introduced the *alimenta,* a scheme to finance the education and welfare of poor Italian children, which was developed further by Trajan, Nerva's successor (see Chapter 2 for how it worked). Nerva also spent a huge sum of money on buying land to give in allotments to poor Romans. And, best of all, Nerva restored free speech.

Pliny the Younger, writing a letter to a friend, captured the mood of the times: 'Liberty was restored,' he said. Tacitus, delighted by the new free-doms, said, 'It's the rare fortune of these times that a man can think what he wants and say what he thinks.'

- **Public works:** Nerva appointed Sextus Julius Frontinus to sort out Rome's water supply system (described in Chapter 7).

Foiling plots and picking a successor

Nerva wasn't completely up to the job. A tactful coin issue bearing the legend *Concordia Exercituum* ('The harmony of the army') and showing a pair of clasped hands couldn't conceal the fact that he had no military credentials to impress the soldiers, and his old age meant he wasn't likely to be around for too long. So there was a danger the soldiers would hunt around for a successor of their own choosing. Told of a plot against his life hatched by a senator called Calpurnius Crassus, Nerva invited the conspirators to a public event and even offered them swords. Stunned by his coolness, Calpurnius Crassus abandoned the plan.

Nerva solved the problem of the army and the succession a year into his reign by adopting Marcus Ulpius Trajanus, then aged 41, as his heir in October 97, who was then commanding the army in Upper Germany and had just won a victory. It was a brilliant move. With Trajan's protection, Nerva could rule safely for the last four months of his life. He died on 25 January 98.

Trajan: Right Man for the Job (AD 98–117)

Nerva's selection of Trajan as his successor was a delight to the Senate and the army, but it was a good deal more radical than it first appears. If the year 68 (the Year of the Four Emperors; refer to Chapter 16) revealed that an emperor could be made in a place other than Rome, then the year 98 revealed that the emperor didn't have to be Roman or even Italian. In fact, Trajan's remote family origins were in Umbria in Italy, but his ancestors had settled at Italica in Spain, and his mother was Spanish. Unthinkable as little as a generation earlier, Trajan's succession was a major innovation.

Italica

Scipio Africanus, the great hero of the Second Punic War back in the days of the Roman Republic (refer to Chapter 12), founded Italica in Spain as a Roman colony. Scipio couldn't possibly have imagined that he had created the future home of two of the greatest of all the Roman emperors: Trajan and Hadrian (see the section 'Hadrian, Artist and Aesthete', later in this chapter), and much later the emperor Theodosius I (AD 379–395), who would hold the Empire together in its darkest days (see Chapter 21).

Trajan in Rome

Trajan didn't rush to Rome. He made sure everyone knew he was in charge and started with the army. He made certain the Rhine and Danube frontiers were safe and secure first, reduced the bounty to soldiers before having any troublesome praetorians forced into retirement or executed, and confirmed all the Senate's privileges.

Once in Rome, Trajan took care to guarantee the corn dole to the Roman mob. The alimenta, which might have been started by Nerva, was certainly operating now and improved the lot of poor Italian families. Taxes were reduced and another vast programme of public building initiated, including baths on the site of Nero's Domus Aurea, a new aqueduct, and a forum. Large parts of the Forum of Trajan can still be seen in Rome today, including its multi-level terraced shopping precinct.

War with Dacia and Parthia

Trajan paid for the tax reductions and costly building programme from the booty earned by going to war with Dacia and Parthia. Dacia and Parthia were the Roman Empire's furthest boundaries (see Figure 17-1).

Fighting the Dacians

Trajan resented the large subsidies being paid to Decebalus, the Dacian leader, to keep peace with Rome (refer to Chapter 16). In AD 101, Trajan crossed the Danube to finish off Decebalus, who was building up Dacian power.

By AD 104, Trajan had defeated Decebalus and installed garrisons in Dacia. A magnificent bridge across the Danube designed by the architect Apollodorus gave Trajan access into the Romans' newly won territory, but in AD 105, Decebalus restarted the war with Rome. Trajan marched back into Dacia and destroyed Decebalus's army (Decebalus committed suicide in shame). Trajan turned Dacia into a Roman province and took over Dacia's rich mineral mines.

Trajan's letters

Trajan was a hands-on ruler, and there's no better evidence for this than the unique series of letters exchanged by him and Pliny the Younger, governor of Bithynia and Pontus. They show that Trajan was constantly personally consulted on almost every aspect of provincial government, whether that meant enfranchising a soldier's daughter, arranging for new architects to oversee inept local building projects, or dealing with Christians who were refusing to go through the motions of paying homage to the imperial cult (for more on the tension between Christianity and the Roman state, see Chapter 9).

To make navigation on the Danube safe, Trajan's military engineers in AD 101 dug out a canal to bypass the lethal rapids of the Iron Gate gorge. The construction of the canal is just one of the Roman's phenomenal engineering achievements. No-one else was able to rival the skill of the Romans until the Industrial Revolution in the eighteenth century.

Figure 17-1: The Roman Empire in AD 116, at its greatest extent.

Parthian problems

Parthia in the East was a constant irritation to Rome. The Parthian king Osroes threw out the client king in Armenia, and Trajan set off for Parthia in AD 113 to defeat Osroes. Within a year, Trajan had recaptured Armenia and made it into part of the province of Cappadocia. By AD 115, Trajan had captured the Parthian capital at Ctesiphon; the next year, he crushed a revolt.

Trajan's legacy

As Trajan was travelling home from his victory over the Parthians, he had a stroke and died on 8 August AD 117.

Trajan never abused his power and treated his position as a privilege and a responsibility. Although Trajan spent much of his reign away from Rome, his authority was so respected that the machinery of government throughout the Roman Empire went on working efficiently without his presence in Rome.

Trajan created the archetype Roman emperor: powerful, paternal, able, and effective. The Senate awarded Trajan the title *Optimus Principorum,* 'the best of princes'. However, Trajan's territorial ambitions left the East far from settled, and the Empire was becoming overstretched. The Roman Empire had now reached its territorial limit.

IN THEIR WORDS

'Veni, vidi, vici...'

The Vindolanda archive

Vindolanda, the British fort in Northumberland, was used during Trajan's reign, and amazingly some of Vindolanda's archives survived. The story of Vindolanda is written down on wooden writing tablets, and no other place in the Roman world has records to match the Vindolanda archive. The archive survived because the waterlogged conditions in the remote north British fort preserved the wooden tablets. Dozens of wooden tablets from Vindolanda have been dug up and studied. The Vindolanda archive gives a unique picture of Roman frontier life around the years AD 95–105. The tablets record the arrangements to celebrate a commanding officer's wife's birthday, food supplies, a list of the troops and the reasons for absence,

from sickness to being posted away, and even a complaint about poor roads. One of the units based at Vindolanda was the Ninth Cohort of Batavians, who pop up almost 400 years later as the last-ever-heard-of-unit of the Roman army in the West (see Chapter 5). You can see the Vindolanda archive in the British Museum in London.

Here's a quote from one of the tablets:

'Octavius to his brother Candidus . . . send me some cash as soon as possible . . . I would have already been to collect the [hides] except that I did not care to injure the animals while the roads are bad.' (For more on Roman roads, see Chapter 6.)

Trajan's column, one of Rome's most famous monuments, celebrates Trajan's greatness. Trajan's cremated remains were buried in its base. The column is decorated with a continuous spiralling relief from top to bottom, and illustrates Trajan's campaign against the Dacians, including Trajan's journey, warships, sacrifices, forts, battles, and prisoners. The column is one of the most valuable sources of information on the Roman army. It's hard to see detail on it today, because the surrounding Roman library with its viewing galleries has long gone, but you can go to the Victoria and Albert Museum in London and see full-size plaster casts of the column taken long ago before modern traffic pollution damaged the original. In the sixteenth century, the statue of Trajan on top of the column was replaced by one of St Peter.

Hadrian, Artist and Aesthete (AD 117–138)

Publius Aelius Hadrianus is one of the most famous Roman emperors of all. He was a highly intelligent man who took a great interest in military discipline and organisation, architecture, and Greek culture. He travelled throughout the Roman world, visiting as many provinces as possible, and made the crucial decision to end the conquest of new provinces. His reign represents a turning point in Roman history.

A dodgy succession

Like Trajan, Hadrian was Spanish and came from Italica. Hadrian's father died when he was young, and he was taken on by the childless Trajan and his wife Plotina. Hadrian took up a high-profile career, making his mark in senatorial magistracies and military posts. By AD 114, he was governor of Syria and was left in charge of the East when Trajan set out for home. But Trajan made a bad move: He never publicly named Hadrian as his successor.

Hadrian's succession was anything but smooth. The day after Trajan's death, Trajan's wife and her lover (a former compatriot of Trajan's) made an announcement that Hadrian had been adopted by Trajan on his deathbed. At the time plenty of people, including Roman historians, thought the whole thing had been made up; nevertheless, the Senate agreed to accept Hadrian as Emperor.

Hadrian was Plotina's favourite, despite other more senior men pushing to be Trajan's successor. Unfortunately, Trajan hadn't specified his intentions for the succession, and there were several other possible candidates, all of whom were more experienced. The last thing the Empire needed was a disputed succession – look what happened in 68–69 (refer to Chapter 16). Hadrian moved quickly to secure the Senate's approval. But his reign started badly because the Senate had four alleged conspirators executed on his say-so, though Hadrian blamed this on the praetorian prefect. Fortunately, civil war was avoided because Hadrian had moved so fast. Hadrian had to promise the Senate never to have anyone executed again without the Senate's approval.

Hadrian in Rome

Hadrian's rule was remarkably successful, but he faced an instant problem: tying up Trajan's affairs. Hadrian had to suppress another revolt on the Danube frontier before reaching Rome to establish himself as emperor. Arriving in Rome, Hadrian put on public entertainments, provided handouts to the mob, and gave a general pardon to debtors, celebrating his generosity by throwing all the relevant paperwork onto a bonfire in the Forum.

Hadrian, like Trajan, spent little time in Rome (his travels are detailed in the next section), but his administration was well set up and worked effectively without him. He generally carried on the work of his predecessors, for example Trajan's alimenta, and kept extortion in the provinces to a minimum. He also encouraged the use of equestrians, rather than freedmen, as administrators.

Enough's enough: Touring the provinces

Hadrian called a halt to further expansion of the Roman Empire. Augustus, more than a century before, had held the view that the Empire should stay within its borders. Conquests by Claudius, Vespasian, Domitian, and especially Trajan, had broken that rule and left the Empire struggling to maintain its frontiers.

Hadrian decided enough was enough: The Empire would expand no longer. He set out on a famous tour of the provinces, the only emperor ever to do so, reviewing the army and the frontiers. Under Trajan, there'd been a series of governors being prosecuted for extorting their provinces, so it was clearly time for some hands-on attention from the emperor. The travel was part supervisory, part sightseeing, and part military. The journey was commemorated on a remarkable, unparalleled series of coins that show Hadrian being greeted by each province he visited.

Restoring military discipline on the frontiers

Hadrian was an absolute stickler for military discipline and swept away any nice, relaxed frontier living amongst garrison troops, especially in Germany and Britain during AD 120–122 where he tightened things up and had the frontiers redesigned, building his famous Wall across Britain (see Chapter 5 for more on that). He was particularly annoyed to discover the soldiers had nice dining rooms and ornamental gardens. He had no time for fancy imperial dress himself and went about in the most basic clothing he could get his hands on.

Giving back provinces and hostages

By 123 Hadrian had headed to the East. Provinces which he decided were a step too far, like Armenia and Mesopotamia, he simply gave up. The Parthian king's daughter, taken hostage by Trajan, was returned.

When in Greece . . .

Hadrian reached Greece in 125 and visited again in 128. He loved Greece and all things artistic, as well as mathematics and architecture. It affected his dress and appearance – he grew a beard as Greeks did (though apparently this was to cover blotches on his face), a fashion followed by his successors and many men of rank throughout the Empire. He was also responsible for great building projects like the Temple of Olympian Zeus and a library in Athens.

The Bar Cochba Revolt

During AD 132–135, Hadrian had to deal with a major revolt in Judaea led by Bar Cochba. Trouble started under Trajan when Roman troops were diverted to the war in Parthia. The trouble was suppressed, and generally Hadrian was enlightened and tolerant towards the Jews. But he came up with the foolish idea of forcing the Jews in Palestine to be assimilated – in 131 BC, for example, he declared circumcision to be illegal. That provoked Jewish nationalist hopes which threatened to destabilise the Roman East. (For more on Bar Cochba himself and the revolt, see Chapter 25.) After Hadrian put down the revolt, the Jews lost their land and became nationless. The historian Dio said 'Judaea was made desolate'.

Building more than walls: Hadrian the architect

Hadrian seems to have been behind the reconstruction of the Pantheon in Rome. Built originally by Agrippa in Augustus's reign, the Pantheon was rebuilt as a magnificent domed structure with a vast pedimented façade supported by Egyptian granite columns. Agrippa's original dedication inscription of 25 BC was modestly reproduced with no mention of Hadrian. Incredibly, the building survives virtually 100 per cent intact in Rome today, having been used as a church in the Middle Ages. Hadrian also built the Temple of Venus and Rome, and a new imperial mausoleum in Rome, which survives today as the Castel San Angelo (it was turned into a castle in the Middle Ages). To the east of Rome at Tivoli, Hadrian built his vast sprawling villa covering 160 acres (65 hectares), known today as the Villa Adriani. An almost endless complex of buildings, each of which was individually designed by Hadrian to reflect his interests or the places he had visited around the Empire, it was where he spent most of the last part of his life. Today the Villa is in ruins, but large parts of it can still be seen and enjoyed.

Hadrian and Antinoüs

Hadrian, on his grand tour of the provinces, reached Egypt in AD 130. Egypt was where Hadrian's favourite, a youth called Antinoüs, had drowned in an accident. Hadrian may well have had a homosexual relationship with Antinoüs, but what is known is that Hadrian was absolutely devastated by the loss of Antinoüs and was said to have 'wept for him like a woman'. Hadrian founded a city called Antinoöpolis in Antinoüs's memory.

Hadrian was married to Trajan's great niece, Sabina. No-one knows what Sabina thought of Antinoüs. Popular gossip had it that Hadrian's marriage to Sabina was unhappy, but there's no evidence, and Hadrian granted Sabina all the usual honours, as well as striking coins with Sabina's portrait on them.

Growing ill in mind and body

As Hadrian grew older, his health began to fail. All Hadrian's travelling caught up with him. He seems to have lost his reason because there are various stories about him ordering the death of various people, including a would-be successor called Servianus (though this is impossible nonsense as Servianus was over 90 years old) and even possibly his wife Sabina. The signs had been there already though. He'd been keen for years on using imperial spies *(frumentarii)* to keep him fully informed about the private business of people in court, his friends, or, in fact, anyone.

Hadrian also suffered from oedema (a build-up of water in the body) and felt so ill that he asked a slave to stab him to death. Antoninus, the senator Hadrian appointed as his successor (see the next section, 'Choosing a successor'), stopped the slave, but Hadrian hadn't much longer to live anyway.

Choosing a successor

Hadrian, racked with illness, had to choose a successor. Like Trajan before him, Hadrian had no children. Hadrian's first choice was Lucius Ceionius Commodus (renamed Lucius Aelius Verus Caesar), whom Hadrian adopted in AD 136. Aelius was made a consul and given a governorship. Unfortunately, Aelius was a sick man and died on 1 January AD 138, after taking too much medicine.

Within a few weeks of Aelius's death, Hadrian adopted as his successor a senator and distinguished governor of Asia, with the exaggerated name of Titus Aurelius Fulvus Boionius Arrius Antoninus. In AD 138, shortly after Antoninus's nomination, Hadrian died.

The frumentarii

No self-respecting totalitarian state could do without its spies. Originally, frumentarii (imperial spies) were soldiers in charge of the corn stores, but the frumentarii ended up being used as couriers on imperial business. Emperors, by Hadrian's time, were using the frumentarii to spy on anyone and everyone. They were a gift to bad emperors, like Commodus (see Chapter 18), but the frumentarii became so unpopular that Diocletian (see Chapter 20) had to get rid of them.

Antoninus Pius: Nice and Vice-free (AD 138–161)

Antoninus succeeded as Antoninus Pius, a name he acquired either because of the honours he heaped on Hadrian after his death or because he took great care of his aged father-in-law. He certainly had to persuade the Senate to make Hadrian a god, which they were reluctant to do after all the carryings-on at the end of Hadrian's reign.

Antoninus in Rome

The most remarkable thing about Antoninus Pius is that he really was apparently without any vices whatsoever. He was the last word in decency and honesty and scrupulously respected the Senate. Even a senator who confessed he had killed his own father was marooned on an island instead of being executed. When there was a shortage of wine, oil, and wheat, Antoninus bought in extra stocks at his own expense and gave them out for free. He refused to travel abroad on the grounds that putting up an emperor and all his entourage cost the provinces far too much. He placed a maximum cost on gladiatorial games to save cash, which helped him finance new public buildings and the repair of old ones.

Antoninus adored his wife Faustina and set up an order of homeless girls called the Faustinianae in her honour. When Faustina died in AD 141, Antoninus issued a magnificent series of coins commemorating her life. How much nicer can you get?

Largely as a result of this, practically nothing of any great note happened during Antoninus Pius's reign, especially in Rome, apart from a disastrous collapse of a stadium (probably the Circus Maximus) causing the deaths of more than 1,000 spectators. There were no proscriptions, no executions, no sexual scandals, no vice. Nor were there any significant innovations in imperial government, though he did establish some important legal principles concerning inheritances, adoptions, and the treatment of slaves.

Whenever he could, Antoninus Pius avoided war. His favourite saying was that he would 'rather save a single citizen than a thousand enemies', a quote he apparently found amongst the sayings of Scipio Africanus.

On the borders

Out in the provinces life wasn't quite as settled. In Britain, a northern war led to the temporary abandonment of Hadrian's Wall and a trial new frontier made of turf called the Antonine Wall farther north. But after little more than a generation, this was given up and the garrisons returned to Hadrian's Wall. Various other risings in Numidia, Mauretania, and Egypt all had to be suppressed, and Dacia had to be divided into three provinces to settle it. None of the rebellions were very serious, but together they gave a hint that had any or all of them blown up into something really dramatic, the Empire would have been hard put to cope. That was really the key to stability under Antoninus Pius: He had the good luck to rule over a world largely at peace.

Smelling the Storm Brewing: Marcus Aurelius (AD 161–180)

Marcus Aurelius was the son of Antoninus Pius's brother-in-law and came from a family of Spanish origin. He'd been educated under Hadrian's supervision and married Antoninus Pius's daughter Faustina the Younger in 145.

Mr Sensitivity

Marcus Aurelius was, by nature, a man of peace. He wasn't paranoid like some of his predecessors, such as Domitian, who saw conspiracies everywhere. Aurelius always tried to think well of everyone. He avoided executing or imprisoning Avidius Cassius's co-conspirators (see the section 'Marcus the warrior' for details on this episode). Although Aurelius's wife Faustina had been implicated in the same plot, she died soon afterwards, and Aurelius burned all Faustina's papers to avoid reading about the plot, because it could force him to hate the conspirators. Even at the games, Aurelius couldn't bear the idea of gladiators getting hurt and made them fight with blunt weapons.

Appointing a partner

Marcus Aurelius took over smoothly, but unlike his predecessors, he promptly organised the who-comes-next problem. He appointed Lucius Verus, son of Aelius (the designated heir of Hadrian who had died in 138 before he could succeed), his co-Augustus immediately. This was a radical step, placing the Empire under the control of two emperors of equal rank for the first time.

Lucius Verus's position was enhanced when he was married to Aurelius's daughter in 164. Great scheme, but like all the best ideas, it was susceptible to things going wrong. Verus was an effective military commander but had none of his colleague's qualities. He was thought by some to be like another Nero but without the cruelty.

Marcus the warrior

Marcus Aurelius would definitely have rather spent his life poring over books and meditating rather than running an Empire. So it's ironic that much of his reign was spent in war. Aurelius sent Lucius Verus to deal with the Parthians who had invaded Armenia and Syria, and by AD 166 the Parthians were defeated. A great triumph took place in Rome, but the war had terrible consequences. The soldiers brought a plague back with them to Rome, and large numbers of people died, causing a famine.

Tribes in Britain and the Chatti in Germany took advantage of Roman troops being away to fight the Parthians and rebelled, causing trouble for Aurelius. It was now clear that Rome could not deal with multiple frontier problems; the Empire simply did not have the manpower to cover distances that would challenge even a modern mechanised army today.

Although the German and British rebellions were put down, a major invasion by German tribes in AD 166 threatened Italy. The invaders were brought to terms by AD 168, but then Aurelius faced more trouble from the Sarmatians along the Danube. Worse, Marcus Aurelius had to deal with the troubles on his own because Lucius Verus died in AD 169 after suffering an apoplexy.

Next came a revolt in 175 by Avidius Cassius, commander in the East, who thought Aurelius was dead. Aurelius had to set out for Syria before news came that Avidius had been murdered. Another German invasion, by the Quadi and Marcomanni, followed and Aurelius headed out on campaign once more in 178.

Who comes next? Picking a successor

Marcus Aurelius didn't get round to appointing a replacement successor until AD 177. Aurelius appointed his son Commodus as his co-Augustus. Commodus was fighting with Marcus Aurelius at Vindobona (Vienna), and with the war almost won, Aurelius passed away (although he took a week to do it) on 17 March AD 180, facing death like a true Stoic.

Unfortunately, Commodus didn't have any of his father's qualities, or any of those of the four emperors before Aurelius. With the death of Marcus Aurelius, the good days were over. The historian Dio Cassius said 'our history now descends from a kingdom of gold to one of iron and rust'. Dio Cassius should know – he watched the Roman Empire begin to decay with his own eyes.

Marcus Aurelius features in two epic movies: *Fall of the Roman Empire* (1964), starring Alec Guinness as the emperor (the film was a flop), and *Gladiator* (2000), starring Richard Harris as Aurelius and Russell Crowe as Maximus the Gladiator (a monster international hit). *Fall of the Roman Empire* wins the prize for historical accuracy, but *Gladiator,* which is only half true and half nonsense (Maximus didn't exist), is rather less boring.

The End of the Good Old Days

Antoninus Pius and Marcus Aurelius were good and honourable men with exceptional qualities, and their reigns were the high summer of the Roman Empire. Antoninus and Aurelius had ruled over an Empire that stretched from northern Britain to Egypt. But all things must pass.

By the time Marcus Aurelius died, Rome had been ruled by emperors for nearly 200 years. The system had survived the die-hards who wanted to go back to the old days of the Republic, the reigns of Caligula and Nero, and the civil war of AD 68–69. Along the way there had been imaginative reforms, which now meant emperors of Gaulish and Spanish origin could rule the Roman world, while the Senate was filled with men from all over much of the Empire.

The Roman Empire was far from perfect but it was truly remarkable that, despite the frontier problems, a colossal land area was kept very largely at peace for two centuries. You have only to think of all the wars that have crippled Europe and the rest of the world over the past 1,500 years to appreciate that this was no mean feat. Of course, it couldn't last, and it didn't.

Part V
Throwing the Empire Away

The 5th Wave   By Rich Tennant

FALL OF THE ROMAN UMPIRE

Holy Caesar...

@RICHTENNANT

In this part . . .

A century of brutal thugs ruled the Roman world after Marcus Aurelius, and very few of them died in their beds. The Roman Empire even started splitting up into rival Empires as one general after another decided to try and become emperor himself. Meanwhile, war broke out constantly on the borders. As long as this went on, the very existence of the Roman world was at stake.

Along came Diocletian at the end of the third century. Diocletian's system was completely different – in an effort to keep the Roman world functioning, he tied Roman citizens to their homes and jobs. The medieval feudal system had been born. The rich grew very rich, and the poor grew poorer. But the Roman Empire was still under attack on all its borders and from within. Diocletian's new order started falling apart over the next hundred years as his successors squabbled over power and territory. It's no great wonder that the barbarians found their way in and sacked Rome. The Western Roman Empire fell to pieces. Perhaps the strangest thing of all, though, is that the Eastern Roman Empire had another thousand years to run.

Chapter 18

More Civil War, Auctioning the Empire, and Paranoid Lunatics

- -

In This Chapter

▶ The mad, bad, crazy world of Commodus

▶ How the Roman Empire got auctioned off

▶ Why the Roman world collapsed into civil war

▶ How Septimius Severus established a new dynasty

- -

A Roman emperor could do pretty much what he wanted because he had
the money and there were plenty of people hungry for power who'd let
him. Which wasn't a bad thing, if the emperor was good at his job and didn't
let it all go to his head. Nerva, Trajan, Hadrian, Antoninus Pius, and Marcus
Aurelius, who ruled between AD 96 and 180 (see Chapter 17 for details), did
this. They put the Empire first and didn't use the power at their disposal to
pursue their own selfish ambitions. Apart from a few ructions, their reigns
were the high summer of the Roman age. The Empire had never been richer,
more powerful, or more stable.

The same can't be said of the emperors who followed. The men discussed in
this chapter put their personal ambition first. The result was intermittent
civil war as one man after another used the Empire's resources for his own
ends. The good times were over.

I Think I'm Hercules: Commodus (AD 180–192)

Marcus Aurelius (whose reign is discussed in Chapter 17) lost quite a few
sons, including one half of a pair of twins. The other twin, Lucius Aurelius
Commodus, lived and was 17 when his father died in 180.

Marcus Aurelius hadn't planned on having Commodus succeed him. But
Lucius Verus, the man he had picked to succeed him, died in 169. Marcus

Aurelius, being a Stoic (refer to Chapter 1), seems to have accepted that things were the way they were.

Like Caligula in AD 37 (refer to Chapter 16), Commodus was too young and inexperienced to be emperor. Other emperors, Hadrian and Antoninus Pius, for example, had been trained up to the job. They'd commanded army units and had served as magistrates in Rome and as provincial governors abroad. Commodus hadn't done any of those things.

Depending on which Roman historian you read, Commodus was either a simple coward who fell in with a bad lot, or he was cruel, foul-mouthed, and debauched. Either way, he certainly ended up debauched, and Rome suffered for it. Incidentally, the Latin word *commodus* means 'pleasant' or 'obliging'. Rarely was a man more inappropriately named.

Commodus and the affairs of state

Because Commodus was too busy spending his time chariot racing and carousing with his friends, he used the praetorian prefect Perennis to run not just the army but also all the other affairs of state. Perennis (an equestrian like all prefects) started making equestrians into legionary commanders, largely because Commodus hated and distrusted anyone of senatorial rank. Following Perennis's death – he was executed for treason; see the section 'Plots against Commodus and his demise' – Commodus gave a freedman called Cleander control of the Praetorians and pretty much everything else.

Cleander was an operator. Realising his master wasn't in the least bit interested in affairs of state, he turned his job into a business trafficking in jobs. He sold senatorships, governorships, and military commands, charging his customers as much as he could. He even sold 25 consulships alone in a single year – one of the lucky buyers was a man from North Africa called Septimius Severus (see the section 'Septimus Severus' later in this chapter for more on his political career). Commodus let Cleander get away with it because Cleander gave Commodus some of the cash. When a riot broke out during a famine, the crowd blamed Cleander. All this terrified Commodus, who ordered Cleander executed.

After the fall of Cleander in 189, the last three years of Commodus's reign descended into mayhem. Men he'd once regarded as favourites were murdered for their money or, in one case, simply because Commodus was jealous of his sporting skills.

Things were so bad that when plague broke out in Rome, killing as many as 2,000 in a single day, no-one took any notice. They were far more frightened of Commodus, who in a fit of egomania had decided Rome should be renamed Commodiana.

Commodus the gladiator

Commodus was obsessed with fighting in the arena, killing animals, and riding chariots. He decided he was the reincarnation of Hercules, so he dressed up like the mythical hero with a lion skin headdress and waving a club. That is, when he wasn't parading around dressed as the god Mercury. Unlike Nero, who wasn't particularly good at sport or performing, Commodus was actually quite accomplished, and one day killed 100 bears himself. He fought as a gladiator and paid himself a fortune out of the gladiatorial fund. Senators were forced to attend and watch what everyone regarded as a thoroughly humiliating spectacle. On one occasion, Commodus decapitated an ostrich and waved its head at the senators as a reminder of what he'd like to do to them.

The movie *Gladiator* (2000) begins in the reign of Marcus Aurelius. But the story carries right on into the reign of Commodus, who is one of the chief characters. Despite the way the script plays fast and loose with historical fact, the portrayal of Commodus by Joaquin Phoenix as a half-bonkers, bloodthirsty stadium and circus fanatic is really pretty good.

Plots against Commodus and his demise

Throughout his years as emperor, Commodus had to deal with a series of conspiracies against his life. The first was orchestrated by his sister. After that, Commodus was very wary of plotters and used secret police (known as *frumentarii*) to root them out. The following sections share the highlights.

Plot 1: The loving sister

When Marcus Aurelius died, Commodus was on campaign. Upon hearing the news of his succession, he abandoned the war against the German tribes, negotiated a treaty on favourable terms, and headed back to Rome with his best friend Saoterus, parading him in a triumphal chariot and kissing him. One historian said Saoterus was Commodus's 'partner in depravity'.

Commodus's sister Lucilla started a plot as a result. It was uncovered and Lucilla was forced into exile, but the commanders of the Praetorian Guard killed Saoterus anyway.

Plot 2: Rumour has it . . .

Although Perennis (refer to the earlier section 'Commodus and the affairs of state') was good at his job, the soldiers were annoyed at how he'd pushed his rival out of the way for the post of Prefect. They mutinied. A band of soldiers came all the way from Britain to Rome and told Commodus in person that Perennis was plotting to kill him.

Commodus believed the soldiers and promptly allowed the troops to kill Perennis and his family in the year 185.

Plot 3: The end of Commodus

It was unlikely Commodus would die in his bed, and he didn't. In 192, the praetorian prefect Aemilius Laetus and Commodus's chamberlain Eclectus decided to kill Commodus when news got out that the emperor was planning to execute both consuls and replace them with gladiators. While everyone was distracted by the mid-winter festival, the Saturnalia (see Chapter 8), they had Commodus fed poison by his mistress Marcia who was in on the plot. Commodus was already so drunk, he vomited the poison up, so they had an athlete strangle Commodus on the last day of December in 192.

Pertinax: The 87-Day Wonder

When Commodus died, he left no successor. Laetus and Eclectus, who had arranged Commodus's death (see the preceding section), went to see Publius Helvius Pertinax, the 66-year-old consul and prefect of Rome, who the Roman historian Dio said was an 'excellent and upright man'. The son of a freedman, Pertinax grew up to become an equestrian, before Marcus Aurelius made him a senator. He was rich and had governed various provinces including Africa and Britain. He was a stickler for discipline and tough enough to suppress a mutiny in the army in Britain where he was nearly killed, and he also put down several rebellions in Africa.

Reintroducing discipline

Before Pertinax accepted Laetus and Eclectus's offer, he sent a friend to see Commodus's body, just to make sure the story was true. He then went in secret to the Praetorian Guard and offered them a fat bonus to accept him as emperor. Pertinax said he was going to put everything right again and sort out discipline. To that end, he did the following:

- He had all the statues of Commodus knocked down and declared the dead emperor a public enemy.
- He reordered government and had himself declared 'Chief of the Senate'.
- He gave posthumous pardons to people unjustly put to death.
- He sold off Commodus's possessions to raise money so that he could pay the soldiers and the mob.

Ticking off the soldiers

After the debauchery of Commodus's reign, you'd think that everyone would be relieved to have someone competent in charge, but Pertinax's intentions worried the soldiers and the imperial freedmen, who could see all the privileges awarded them by Commodus disappearing in a puff of smoke.

Soldiers were no longer allowed to behave as they please, which had included (incredibly) hitting passers-by as they went about Rome and waving axes. Pertinax put a stop to the axe-carrying and told them to stop insulting the public. But that just made the soldiers nostalgic for the 'good old days' of booze-fuelled chaos under Commodus.

Biting the dust

To rid themselves of Pertinax, the Praetorians and Laetus started a plot to put a consul called Falco on the throne. Pertinax found out about it and pardoned Falco. To cover his back, Laetus then turned on the soldiers. Terrified that they were going to be killed, 200 of them went round to the palace and murdered Pertinax along with Eclectus.

Pertinax had managed a reign of 87 days, five less than the previous record for the shortest reign of a Roman emperor held by Otho in 69 (refer to Chapter 16).

Didius Julianus and Civil War

When Pertinax died, Didius Julianus, a former colleague of Pertinax's in the consulship who'd been exiled by Commodus, raced to the Praetorians' camp and offered them serious cash to make him emperor. He had a rival, the new city prefect Sulpicianus (Pertinax's father-in-law), and the two men competed to outbid one another in the auction of the Roman Empire. If that sounds incredible now, it was considered no less incredible at the time. It went on until Didius Julianus suddenly increased his bid by a huge amount and won the auction (see Chapter 24 for details of Didius's personality).

The people of Rome were not amused and called Didius 'Empire robber'. A mob raced to a circus and held out there, demanding that soldiers in the East under the governor Pescennius Niger in Syria come and save them from Didius. They resented Didius because they'd hoped that Pertinax would do away with all Commodus's abuses. Didius didn't care. He was having the time of his life, handing out favours, going to the theatre, and having banquets. It was bound to end in tears, and it did.

Immortalised in bronze

The Senate voted Didius a statue made of gold, but he refused because he'd noticed that gold and silver statues were always destroyed and asked for a bronze one instead so that he would be remembered forever. But as the historian Dio pointed out, the only worthwhile way to be remembered was as a man of virtue. The bronze statue was knocked down when Didius was killed. So much for immortality then.

When the soldiers in Syria, under the command of the governor Pescennius Niger, heard the appeal from Rome to come and get rid of Didius Julianus, they promptly declared Pescennius Niger emperor. Niger wasn't the only one who had such aspirations. Two other men threw their hats into the ring: Clodius Albinus, a North African who was governor in Britain (even Commodus had once considered him an heir) and Lucius Septimius Severus, another North African in Pannonia who was declared emperor by his troops.

The scene was set for an almighty civil war. Severus was the cleverest. He knew that once Didius Julianus was dead, the three of them would have to fight it out, and it was unlikely anyone would be a clear winner. And as Severus had every intention of being the winner, he came up with a cunning plan.

Severus pretended to be friends with Clodius Albinus and said that Albinus could be his declared heir. Albinus fell for the trick hook, line, and sinker, believing this meant he had a share in imperial power without having to fight for it, and waited in Britain. Severus marched on Rome where Didius Julianus tried to turn the city into a fortress. The problem was that the Praetorians were so used to easy living, none of them knew how to build fortifications properly, and some of them were going over to Severus. In the end, Didius was done for by Severus's promise that if they handed over the men who'd killed Pertinax he would protect them. The Senate assembled, approved the soldiers' action, sentenced Didius to death, and declared Severus emperor.

Didius Julianus was executed after a reign of 66 days, which was another new record for the shortest reign in the history of the Roman Empire. He cried as he was killed, 'What evil have I done? Whom have I killed?'

Septimius Severus (AD 193–211)

Lucius Septimius Severus was born in 145 at Leptis Magna, a major city of North Africa on the coast of what is now Libya. He came from a wealthy family of Punic and Italian descent, was a scholar, and his favourite childhood game was playing at being a judge. He came to Rome to finish his education and, with family backing, became a senator under Marcus Aurelius (see Chapter 17 for his reign). He bought one of the consulships sold by Cleander under Commodus (refer to the section 'Commodus and the affairs of state', earlier in this chapter). Highly superstitious, Severus was always on the look out for omens and was convinced that he was destined to be emperor because, amongst other signs:

- He once dreamed that he'd been suckled by a she-wolf like Romulus (refer to Chapter 10 for more about this mythic figure).
- When he married his second wife Julia Domna (a Syrian) in Rome in AD 173, the reigning emperor Marcus Aurelius's wife Faustina had prepared their nuptial chamber.
- An astrologer had once predicted that Julia Domna would marry a king (and, in fact, that's why Severus chose her as his wife).
- A snake once coiled itself round Severus's head but did him no harm.
- While governor in Gaul, he'd dreamed the whole Roman world had saluted him.

Securing the throne

After the death of Didius Julianus, Septimius Severus had a long way to go before securing the throne. Leaving Clodius Albinus in Britain optimistically assuming he was a permanent fixture in the new regime, Severus could safely head out East to clear Pescennius Niger off the map. Niger hadn't been wasting his time and had sewn up the whole region. But Severus defeated Niger's forces three times and caught up with him while he tried to escape towards the river Euphrates. Niger was promptly executed in 194 along with anyone even suspected of being a supporter. Severus fined cities that had supported his rival and punished them by taking away municipal status.

Pertinax's funeral

Septimius Severus put on a massive show for Pertinax's funeral before setting out to defeat Niger. An effigy of the dead man was made and treated as if it was a real man asleep, even with a slave to wave flies off. A procession of soldiers, senators, and equestrians and their families was followed by an altar decorated with ivory and jewels from India. Finally the 'body' was placed in a three-storey tower and set ablaze.

Next on Severus's list was Clodius Albinus, who'd realised he'd been stitched up and had strengthened his army. Albinus's soldiers declared him emperor and together they crossed from Britain to Gaul and set out for Rome. Severus met them near the city of Lugdunum (Lyons) in 197. The battle, supposedly involving 150,000 soldiers on each side, was a close-run thing, and Severus was very nearly killed, but he won the day. Because the last thing Severus wanted was a rival dynasty, he ruthlessly ordered Albinus executed and had his head displayed on a pike. Then he ordered the killing of Albinus's wife and children and all his supporters. Albinus's body was left to rot before it was thrown into a river.

Dividing and ruling

Severus was undisputed master of the Roman world by 197. Britain and Syria were each subdivided into two provinces so that never again would an upstart of a governor be able to call on either province's garrison to try and seize power. (Actually Severus was wrong about this, as Chapter 20 explains.)

Building a dynasty

Severus purged the Senate of any supporters of Niger and Albinus and set about establishing a dynasty, claiming to be the son of Marcus Aurelius. It was obvious nonsense, but lots of emperors over the turbulent decades to come did the same thing to appear legitimate. His eldest son was named Bassianus at birth but was now renamed Marcus Aurelius Antoninus as part of Severus's spurious lineage, pretending to be descended from the famously good emperors of the second century AD. But the boy was always known as Caracalla because he wore a hooded Gaulish cloak called a *caracalla.*

Severus was particularly dependent on his praetorian prefect, Fulvius Plautianus. Plautianus ruthlessly stole whatever he could, tortured people for information, and had so much influence he even got away with being rude to Julia Domna. In 202, Plautianus's daughter Plautilla was married to Caracalla, even though Caracalla loathed them both. When Severus's brother denounced Plautianus in 205, the game was up and Plautianus was killed (reminiscent of what happened to Sejanus under Tiberius, see Chapter 16).

Severus and religion

Thanks in part to his exotic Syrian wife, Julia Domna, his own origins, and his campaigns, Severus was very interested in eastern cults. While Severus was visiting Egypt, he worshipped Serapis (a hybrid Egyptian god made up from Osiris and Apis), and it was probably while Severus was in Britain that a legionary commander of his in York dedicated a temple to Serapis.

The Arch of Severus

The arch of Septimius Severus in the Forum in Rome is one of the most complete monuments still standing in the city. At 23.2 metres (76 feet) wide and 21 metres (68 feet) high, it's one of the biggest. It has one large central arch and a smaller one on each side and is covered with carvings commemorating Severus's campaign against the Parthians.

Dealing with the frontiers

Severus was lucky. The borders on the Danube and Rhine were peaceful, and he could afford to go and deal with the Parthian threat in the East. He dealt the Parthians a fatal blow from which they never recovered and reconquered territory given up under Hadrian. He made the city of Palmyra into a colony, and it rapidly grew into one of the greatest cities of the Roman Empire as it lay on the great trade route to the Far East.

Palmyra's growing power meant in the decades to come that the city became a huge threat to Rome's power in the East (see Chapter 19).

Dealing with the Roman Senate

Severus only came back to Rome in 202. He had no interest in pretending to co-operate with the Senate, the last bastion of the Republic. He started giving administrative jobs to the equestrians and even made them commanders of new legions, as well as putting them in charge of some provinces (a process which had begun under Commodus). He brought in many provincials from the East, which is hardly surprising given where he and his wife came from, and he must have extended Roman citizenship to do this.

Severus was keen on putting up public buildings, and he also increased military pay. Some of the cash he raised by confiscating estates from Niger's and Albinus's supporters. The rest he raised by increasing taxes and by reducing the silver content of the coinage so that he could mint more coins with less silver. That caused inflation (refer to Chapter 7) and would have a disastrous impact on Roman currency.

Beefing up his sons in Britain

By 208, Severus was off again, this time to Britain. Britain's northern frontier was a constant irritation, and he'd already had to order the repair and reconstruction of Hadrian's Wall. But the real reason was to toughen up his two sons, Caracalla and Geta, whom he was determined would succeed him. These two needed all the prestige of a great war of conquest and preferably one that didn't mean any risk for Rome.

The war was a farce. The Roman army headed into Scotland, plagued by guerrilla tribesmen who kept agreeing to peace and then breaking their word. The Romans found it impossible to fight the enemy properly, because small bands of tribesmen just lurked in swamps and disappeared into the forests and mists after attacking the Roman column. The Roman army, weighed down by equipment, got dragged farther and deeper into northern Britain.

Severus's death

After three years of fighting in Britain, Severus died, worn out with old age and gout, in the northern British city of York in 211. Needless to say, he'd seen omens of his own death – he dreamed he was being carried up to heaven and was terrified when an Ethiopian soldier said, 'You've been a conqueror, now be a god!'

Severus's reign was a sign of the future:

- ✔ He was born a long way from Rome.
- ✔ He was made an emperor in the provinces.
- ✔ He died an emperor in the provinces.
- ✔ He spent most of his reign away from Rome.
- ✔ He brought more provincials into the Roman elite than ever before.

Not Living Up to Dad's Expectations – Caracalla (AD 211–217)

Septimius Severus had the succession all nicely worked out when he died. Caracalla had been lined up as co-emperor since 198 and was joined in 208 by his brother Geta. For the first time in Roman history, there were three emperors *(Augusti)* of equal rank. It was a great plan except that the brothers hated each other, and hating each other was of far more concern to them than anything else.

As a boy Caracalla was sensitive, intelligent, and compassionate; he even restored rights to the cities of Antioch and Byzantium which his father had punished for supporting Niger back in 193. But as he grew up, he turned into an arrogant and ambitious thug who loathed his brother and fancied himself as Alexander the Great.

Getting rid of Geta and a host of others

Severus's death in 211 couldn't have come soon enough for Caracalla, who amazingly had already tried to kill his father during the campaign in Britain. Now Caracalla took care to have any of his father's closest advisers murdered, as well as Severus's doctors for not speeding up his death. Caracalla and Geta abandoned the war in Britain and headed home.

Caracalla had his own wife Plautilla murdered, too. She was daughter of his father's favourite, the praetorian prefect Fulvius Plautianus (see the earlier section 'Building a dynasty'). Caracalla had had her exiled to Sicily years before. He then told the praetorians that Geta had plotted against him and had him killed. To do this, he had to get their mother Julia Domna to summon them to her room, so that Geta would be without his bodyguards. Two soldiers rushed in on Caracalla's orders and killed Geta in his mother's arms. Caracalla forced Julia to treat the murder as a deliverance. He had to calm the soldiers down with money and then proceeded to murder any other relatives or members of Marcus Aurelius's family that looked like potential rivals. He didn't stop there and had any supporters of Geta killed, too.

Caracalla's problem was that he refused to take advice from anyone, and resented anyone who knew something he didn't. He was determined to have total power and to prevent anyone else from having power of any sort.

Universal citizenship (AD 212)

In the year 212, Caracalla made the most dramatic change to Roman society for centuries. He declared that all free men within the Empire's borders were to be Roman citizens. The edict is called the *Constitutio Antoniniana* ('the Antoninian Decree'). It finished off a process that had been going on for years, but it was a remarkable gesture, even though Caracalla's real reason for issuing the edict was to raise money.

Caracalla used to demand money with menace from anyone and everyone. He also loaded the population with more taxes – he doubled the tax on freeing slaves, for example. Caracalla desperately needed cash for the soldiers' pay rises and hand-outs to his friends and favourites. So he cancelled exemption from tax on legacies for Roman citizens. By making everyone into Roman citizens, they all became liable for the tax (refer to Chapter 3 for more on the rights and responsibilities of Roman citizens). No wonder he declared 'no-one in the world should have money except me, and I want to give it all to the soldiers!' The army changed, too – because citizenship was a qualification for being a legionary and a reward for an auxiliary soldier, the army started to evolve into a different kind of force.

Caracalla's indulgences

Caracalla had an insatiable blood lust. He loved seeing killing in the arena and even took part in the games himself. He forced senators to provide huge numbers of animals at their expense; he also made them build houses all over the place so that he could stay there if he fancied (but almost never did). He also drove around in chariots dressed in the colours of the Blue faction (see Chapter 8 for circus factions) and had a champion charioteer, called Euprepes, killed just for being a member of a rival faction.

On a journey to Gaul, Caracalla suddenly had a governor killed, and thanks to inscriptions found in Britain with a scrubbed-out name, it seems he might have ordered the execution of a governor there, too. He had four of the Vestal Virgins killed on the grounds that they were no longer virgins, even though he had defiled one of them himself (for information on Vestal Virgins, see Chapter 10).

Caracalla swaggered around with weapons he thought had once been used by Alexander the Great, decided he was a reincarnation of Alexander, and even organised a 16,000-strong force of Macedonians on the lines of Alexander's *phalanx* (a close order of Macedonian infantry). Despite that, he decimated the population of Alexandria and then built a kind of Berlin Wall to divide the survivors because he'd heard that the Alexandrians had treated him as a joke.

The end of Caracalla

Caracalla's opportunity for war came first with fighting off more threats along the Danube; then he set his sights on trying to conquer more territory in the East. He asked the Parthian king Artabanos for the hand in marriage of his daughter, which was instantly rejected, so Caracalla began a war to attack the Parthians. He met his end on that campaign in 217 at the hands of Macrinus the praetorian prefect, who murdered him – events you can read about in the next chapter.

Chapter 19

The Age of the Thug – The Third Century's Soldier Emperors

In This Chapter

▶ Why a Sun-God worshipper became an emperor

▶ How one soldier after another ruled the Roman Empire

▶ Why the Empire started splitting apart

▶ How Aurelian and Probus repaired the Roman world

*B*efore the Severans of 193–235, the emperors had ruled with the Senate, generally treading carefully and going to a lot of trouble to try and maintain a semblance of the old Republican system. Many of them had a genuine sense of duty and a belief that they had a responsibility to the state and that the state came first.

Septimius Severus (refer to Chapter 18) changed all that. He was supremely in charge. The Roman Empire became a tool he used to advance himself and his family. Severus had enough personal prestige to hold the Empire together, but the soldiers knew they held all the trump cards. Macrinus, Elagabalus, and Severus Alexander were made emperor because of the soldiers; the Senate had no choice. In any case, the Senate was unrecognisable from the one Augustus had known. There were far more senators, very few were from Italy, and most spent little or no time in Rome. These days the emperor made the laws and the Senate just rubber-stamped them.

The decisive power in the Roman world was the army. It always had been, but now it was absolutely out in the open, and the soldiers knew it. The army made and broke emperors. Because the Roman army was never a single organisation but a collection of dozens of units scattered across the Empire, there was plenty of potential for rival claims on the throne. During the next 50 years, the Roman Empire tore itself apart.

The First Thug on the Throne: Marcus Opelius Macrinus

Marcus Opelius Macrinus came from Caesarea in Mauretania in North Africa. Not much is known about him because he came from such a modest background. Even so, he'd worked his way up from nowhere to equestrian status. Despite his obscure origins, he was a lawyer with a reputation for having a healthy respect for the law. This probably explains why he was given the prestigious job of procurator in charge of Caracalla's private property (to read about Caracalla, go to Chapter 18). Macrinus was then promoted to prefect of the Praetorian Guard, a job he did so well he was more or less left to get on with it by himself.

How to take the throne

An African soothsayer announced that Macrinus and his son Diadumenian were destined to be emperors. This prophecy put Macrinus in a fright because it was inevitable Caracalla would have him killed if the story got out. So he promptly organised a conspiracy and had Caracalla murdered on campaign.

Macrinus had been clever enough to put it about that a conspiracy of soldiers had killed Caracalla, so that his own hands seemed clean. To cover his tracks even more, he made Caracalla into a god, though it's hard to think of a less deserving candidate.

Despite murdering Caracalla, Macrinus took Severus as part of his own name, added Antoninus to his son Diadumenian's name, and made him heir apparent.

Macrinus had achieved a first. Because he was an equestrian, he'd never served in the Senate, which means he'd never served in any of the posts all the other emperors had held at least some of. It was a major precedent. Many of the emperors who followed came from what would have seemed impossibly obscure origins a few years before.

How to lose popularity

Despite whatever talents he may have had, Macrinus didn't secure his position as emperor very well. Already unpopular because of his modest origins, he made several mistakes and misjudgements:

✔ **He lost Roman territory.** After killing Caracalla, Macrinus carried on the campaign against the Parthians, but after losing two battles, knocked up a compromise peace and had to hand over Armenia. It was a bad move because it made him look like a loser and meant he lost any prestige he might have earned himself through murdering Caracalla.

✔ **He failed to get rid of any other potential Severan candidates for the throne.** Macrinus had forgotten that Septimius Severus's widow, Julia Domna – who had committed suicide after Caracalla's death – had a sister (see the next section, 'How to lose the throne').

✔ **He made several unsuitable appointments.** Macrinus promoted Adventus, a former imperial spy. Macrinus made Adventus into a senator, a consul, and even prefect of Rome, despite the fact that Adventus was old and blind, had no relevant experience, and was so uneducated he knew nothing about how the Roman administration worked. The idea seems to have been to divert attention from Macrinus's obscure origins, but along with several other unsuitable appointments and acting high and mighty, all it did was provoke resentment.

✔ **His behaviour alienated the soldiers.** Macrinus had a curious taste for taking part in mime shows; he also liked walking about wearing brooches and a belt decorated with gold and jewels. As far as the soldiers were concerned, this was all too decadent and much too much like a barbarian's taste for them. The fact that Macrinus lived in luxury while they were having a tough life in forts annoyed them, too. They added all these to their list of resentments and felt that killing him was totally justified.

How to lose the throne

Macrinus was eventually deposed by Julia Domna (Caracalla's mother) and her daughter Julia Soaemias, who installed Julia Soaemias's son Elagabalus as emperor. Although Macrinus sent some troops to get rid of Elagabalus, the troops promptly changed sides. At the battle that followed, even more soldiers went over to Elagabalus, and Macrinus was doomed. He and his son escaped but were soon caught and executed.

Elagabalus (AD 218–222)

Caracalla's mother, Julia Domna, had a sister called Julia Maesa (who died in 225). Julia Maesa was massively ambitious. She was also boiling with rage that Macrinus had thrown her out of the palace when Caracalla was killed.

Julia Maesa did not let the fact that she was only related by marriage to Septimius Severus impede her (see Figure 19-1 to see the Severan family tree). She decided that her grandsons, Elagabalus and Severus Alexander, were the ideal candidates to replace Macrinus. There was also a handy rumour going about that Caracalla was the real father of Elagabalus (he looked like Caracalla, too), which Maesa encouraged because Caracalla's popularity with the troops would help her cause.

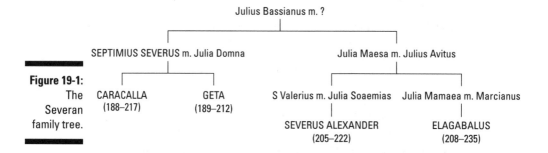

Figure 19-1: The Severan family tree.

Maesa used hard cash to buy the soldiers at Emesa in Syria, and they declared Elagabalus emperor in 218. Elagabalus took the name Marcus Aurelius Antoninus so that he could pretend to be part of the direct descent from the original Marcus Aurelius.

Thanks to all the spurious descents from Marcus Aurelius and Antoninus Pius being claimed, Caracalla's and Elagabalus's coins bear similar names to those of their so-called illustrious forbearers. Thanks to realistic portraits, the coins can be distinguished, but with imperial inscriptions sometimes it really isn't possible to tell the difference between those of Caracalla and Elagabalus.

The 14-year-old Elagabalus might have been Emperor, but the people who were really in charge were his grandmother Julia Maesa and his mother Julia Soaemias (Julia Soaemias was allowed to watch the Senate and even run her own women's senate). What they'd established was a new eastern Severan dynasty at Rome. Initially, Rome welcomed Elagabalus because he was good-looking and seemed a better bet than Macrinus, but from day one he took no notice of worrying about government. The Roman people were horrified at what followed.

Elagabalus's god

Elagabalus's real name was Varius Avitus Bassianus. He was a fanatical worshipper of the sun-god Heliogabalus (or Elah-Gabal) of Emesa, and that's how he got his nickname.

The Sun-God Heliogabalus was worshipped at Emesa in Syria where there was a black conical stone, which was generally believed to have fallen from the sky and landed on the spot. It might, in fact, have been a meteorite. Once he became emperor, Elagabalus had the stone taken to Rome.

Elagabalus had only one serious agenda: imposing the worship of the Sun-God and preventing any other cults apart from that of the Great Mother *(Magna Mater)*, another Eastern religion. To that end, he built a temple to the Sun-God.

Elagabalus's government

Rumours started circulating about Elagabalus's homosexuality, the way he posed as 'Venus' for the purposes of copulation, and his interest in well-endowed men to whom he gave all sorts of high-profile jobs. He made a barber, for example, the prefect of the grain supply and a mule-driver the collector of the inheritance tax. Elagabalus sold off any positions or privileges he could, purely to raise cash. His freedmen were made commanders of legions or governors of provinces. His favourite, whom he 'married', was an athlete called Zoticus who threw his weight about in the palace.

The difference between Elagabalus and, say, someone like Antoninus Pius (138–161), discussed in Chapter 17, is so colossal it's sometimes hard to believe it's the same Empire. Even more incredibly, Elagabalus actually took the official name 'Antoninus Pius' himself, and called himself that on his coins.

Elagabalus's women

Elagabalus's first wife in a marriage arranged by his grandmother Julia Maesa was Julia Paula, who was disgusted by him. Because she came from an old Roman aristocratic society, that's no surprise. He divorced her in 220, and she retired into private life. (In the mayhem that followed, Julia Paula was one of the few lucky ones. She lived.)

His second wife was his lover and Vestal Virgin called Aquileia Severa. Their marriage caused such outrage, even though Elagabalus claimed to the Senate any children they might have were bound to be divine, he had to divorce her, too.

Wife number three was Annia Faustina, a descendant of Marcus Aurelius. This marriage was clearly an attempt to reinforce his crumbling regime. (During this marriage, Elagabalus went back to Aquileia, whom he seems to have really liked, though this just made him more unpopular than ever.)

Elagabalus's tastes

Elagabalus devoted his life to pleasure. These are some (and only some – there are plenty more) of the things he liked:

✔ His pool had to be perfumed with saffron.

✔ He had couches made of silver and cushions stuffed with rabbit fur and partridge feathers.

✔ He had lions and leopards for pets.

✔ Presents at his banquets included eunuchs and four-horse chariots.

✔ He drove various chariots pulled by elephants, stags, tigers, dogs, and lions.

✔ He wore clothes made of pure silk – the first in Rome to do so – and never wore the same shoes twice.

✔ He sometimes invited eight men with the same disability to dinner, such as eight deaf men, eight one-eyed men, or eight bald men.

The end of Elagabalus

Elagabalus went too far when he decided to do in his cousin Alexianus (who succeeded as Severus Alexander, see the next section). Alexanius, adopted as Elagabalus's heir in 221, was a decent young man who was loved by the soldiers. Elagabalus seems to have had a sudden whim to order Alexanius's execution. The troops raced round, rescued Alexanius, his mother, and grandmother, and told Elagabalus that if he wanted to stay emperor he'd have to give up his favourites and all his degenerate activities.

Elagabalus pretended to make peace, but he was still hell-bent on killing Alexanius. On 6 March 222, the praetorians had had enough – Elagabalus and his mother Julia Soaemias were killed and their bodies dragged around Rome before being thrown in the Tiber. No emperor ever before, however degenerate, had been humiliated that way.

Severus Alexander (AD 222–235)

Despite the horrors of his cousin Elagabalus's reign and the distinctly unpleasant family he seemed to come from, Alexianus was a thoroughly decent boy. In fact, if he'd been born a century earlier into an altogether better time, he might have been one of the Five Good Emperors of the second century (refer to Chapter 17). But he wasn't. He was only 13 when he was made emperor, changing his name from Alexianus to Alexander and becoming Marcus Aurelius Severus Alexander.

A little stability in a sea of chaos

Back in the first century, Nero (54–68) had got sick of being dominated by his mother Agrippina and killed her (refer to Chapter 16). But Alexander didn't do that – he put up and shut up. He was under the power of his grandmother Julia Maesa until she died in 226 and then his mother Julia Mamaea who even declared herself to be Augusta, as if she was empress in her own right.

Julia Mamaea was no idiot. Realising that her and Alexander's lives would be at risk if another bout of military anarchy followed, she decided that a show of respect to the Senate would pay dividends. So 16 senators were appointed to the imperial council, and it was made possible for a senator to be Praetorian prefect. One of the greatest lawyers in Roman history, Domitius Ulpianus, was made Praetorian prefect, but in reality he ran the government of the Roman Empire under Mamaea's supervision.

If that sounds bad, it wasn't – at least, not all of it. The equestrian administrators under Ulpianus did a good job generally, and the Roman Empire was temporarily restored to stability and sanity. For a good ten years the frontiers were peaceful, hand-outs to the mob were maintained at a sensible level, cash was found to subsidise teachers, the special money *(alimentia)* for poor families was increased, and the imperial court went on an economy drive to pay for all this.

But not all is well

Despite the benefits of a more stable government, things were far from sorted. The praetorian prefect Ulpianus was murdered by his own Praetorian troops by 228. They also wanted to kill the historian Dio Cassius, consul in 229, on the grounds that he was too severe for them. Dio was saved when Alexander discharged him.

The Sassanids

By AD 224, the Parthians had ruled Persia since 247 BC. In about AD 10, a Parthian king called Artabanos II threw off Greek cultural influence and restored old Persian traditions and religion. Ardashir, also known as Artaxerxes, was descended from a man called Sassan. He overthrew the last Parthian king, Artabanos IV, in AD 224, establishing the Sassanid dynasty and restoring the ancient Zoroastrianism religion. Zoroastrianism was one of the first ancient religions to teach monotheism, the idea of a resurrection after death, and eternal life for the reunited body and soul. It still exists today in the Middle East.

And then there were the frontiers. The Parthian Empire collapsed in 230, and into the power vacuum came a Persian dynasty called the Sassanids under a king called Ardashir, who was determined to recover all the land the Persians had once ruled – which meant much of the Roman Empire in the East. Alexander did defeat Ardashir, but it cost him dearly in men, which damaged his prestige. Meanwhile, the Alamanni tribe in Germany decided to take advantage of the Eastern war. Alexander headed for the German frontier in 234, but his troops mutinied and he had to bribe the Alamanni to hold off.

The end of Alexander and Julia

The frontier trouble was the chance Maximinus Thrax ('Maximinus the Thracian') needed. He'd served in Alexander's Eastern war and was now one of the commanders in the German war. To the soldiers who were disappointed by Alexander's lack of military skill, Maximinus looked a much better bet. Alexander and Julia Mamaea were murdered in their camp near Mainz in Germany.

Blink and you'll miss them: A slew of emperors who followed Alexander

If it wasn't for the coins of the soldier emperors we'd know a lot less about them. Coins provide names, portraits, and records of some of these rulers' deeds and in a few cases are the only evidence we have at all. (But see Chapter 7 for the effect of all the instability on the coinage's quality.) Portraits of emperors on coins from the years AD 235–284 tell the story. Almost to a man they show brutal, unshaven thugs because these were the men who appealed to the soldiers. Usually men who had risen from the ranks, they cared little or nothing for the Senate or traditional Roman virtues, though, of course, they pretended they did. Hardly a single one died in his bed. While they battled it out, Rome's enemies on the borders started to move in for the kill.

- ✔ **Maximinus 'Thrax' I (235–238):** He set the pace. A huge man, he fought the Germans successfully, but he was ruthless and cruel and hated the Roman aristocracy. The Senate tried to get rid of him by supporting a coup in 238 led by the governor of Africa, Gordianus.

- ✔ **Gordianus I and Gordianus II (238):** The former Governor of Africa ruled briefly with his son, but Maximinus's friends killed them.

- ✔ **Balbinus and Pupienus (238):** The Senate made these two senators into joint emperors in 238. The Praetorians killed them, but not before Maximinus's own men had mutinied and killed him, too.

✔ **Gordianus III (238–244):** Gordianus I's grandson was made emperor. He was killed on campaign against the Persians by the praetorian prefect, a soldier called Philip I the Arab who became the next emperor.

✔ **Philip I the Arab (244–249):** Philip defeated the Persians and celebrated the thousandth year of Rome with a vast festival of games. Philip sent the governor of Lower Moesia, Trajan Decius, to suppress a rebellion amongst the Danube legions. But the rebels made Trajan Decius emperor, and he defeated and killed Philip in a battle near Verona.

✔ **Trajan Decius (249–251):** Decius lasted two years, during which he famously started a ruthless persecution of Christians. Trajan Decius was killed fighting the Goths.

✔ **Trebonianus Gallus (251–253):** He replaced Decius and ruled jointly with Decius's son Hostilian. Gallus made a humiliating peace with the Goths, but it was becoming difficult for any emperor to manage the various border threats. He also faced a devastating plague that swept across the Roman world and killed Hostilian. Gallus was killed in 253 by his own soldiers who preferred the idea of being ruled by a governor called Aemilian, who had succeeded in defeating the Goths.

✔ **Aemilian (253):** Aemilian only lasted about three months: He was murdered by Valerian, who had been gathering an army to help Gallus. Read more about Valerian in the next section.

Valerian 1 (AD 253–260) and Gallienus (253–268)

Valerian was a decent man, but he faced all the consequences of years of anarchy which had allowed frontier defences to fall to pieces. He ruled jointly with his son Gallienus, realising it was the only way to try and manage the frontier troubles and run the Empire. By 256, Valerian had set out to fight the Persian Sassanid king Shapur.

While his father Valerian was fighting in the East, Gallienus was supposed to be in charge of the western provinces of the Roman Empire; in reality, he was trying to rule an Empire rent by revolts, plagues, and famine. By 262, following hot on the heels of a catastrophic earthquake that wrecked cities in Asia and shook Rome, a plague reached Rome that, at its height, was said to be killing up to 5,000 people in a single day across the Empire. In the East Gallienus faced the rising power of the Palmyrenes, and in the West something unprecedented happened: Part of the Roman Empire broke away to create the Gallic Empire.

Valerian dies and a rebellion starts

Four years into the war against the Persians in 260, Valerian's army was crippled by plague. During peace negotiations, Valerian was captured by Shapur and died in prison. It was a spectacular and unprecedented humiliation for a Roman emperor.

An officer called Macrianus in Valerian's army promptly took his chance and proclaimed his two sons, Macrianus the Younger and Quietus, emperors in 260. The two Macriani headed west with an army to get rid of Valerian's son Gallienus.

Events in the Palymrenes

Palmyra, an oasis on the great trade route into Mesopotamia and farther east, was one of the largest and richest cities in the Eastern Roman Empire. The people had nomadic origins, a tradition they put to good use when Mark Antony tried to capture Palmyra in 41 BC just to plunder its riches. Hearing he was coming, the people carted their goods across the Euphrates, and Antony's men found the city empty. Later, Palmyra was given privileges by various Roman emperors, including being allowed to tax all traffic passing through, which made it even wealthier. Palmyra was made into a Roman colony by Septimius Severus (193–211; refer to Chapter 18). Publius Septimius Odaenathus was a member of the most important Palmyran family and declared himself King of Palmyra after Valerian I was killed in 260.

Actually, Odaenathus had done Gallienus a favour because this was the only way the East could possibly be held against the Sassanids and get rid of the usurper Quietus. Gallienus made Odaenathus 'Duke of the East' and commander of all Roman forces in the region. Odaenathus attacked and killed Quietus at Emesa in 261.

Under Odaenathus, Palmyra became the major force in the Roman East. Odaenathus recaptured Mesopotamia for the Roman Empire and was even given the title *imperator*. But Palmyra's power was growing unchecked. Odaenathus was assassinated in 267 as part of a local dynastic plot. His son Vabalathus inherited the throne, but had to share power with his beautiful, highly intelligent, and ambitious mother Zenobia. But time was running out for the Palmyrenes.

The Gallic Empire breaks away

Valerian had made Marcus Cassianus Latinius Postumus commander of the Rhine garrisons. In 259, Postumus was declared emperor at Cologne by his troops. Unlike a lot of other pretenders, he wasn't stupid enough to think he could have the whole Empire to himself.

Postumus had control of Gaul, Spain, and Britain, and he ran it like a proper Roman Empire. Today it's known as the Gallic Empire. It was truly astonishing because he adopted all the trappings of a Roman emperor and set up his own Senate with consuls and all the usual magistracies. He was a generally popular and sensible ruler who tried to reform the coinage and posed with all the proper Roman virtues. The only difference was that his empire wasn't centred on Rome, but Trier.

Gallienus's death and the next emperor, Claudius II

Gallienus was educated, interested in Greek culture, and tolerant of Christians. He preferred men of ability, which was why he used experienced soldiers who had reached equestrian status to command his legions and relied increasingly on a crack body of mobile troops to reach trouble spots.

Gallienus beat off an invasion of Greece by a Germanic tribe called the Heruli. He had left a general called Acilius Aureolus in charge of the war against Postumus, but Aureolus took his chance and headed towards Rome. Gallienus caught him up and besieged him at Milan, where Gallienus was murdered in 268 by some of his own officers, who included the future emperors Claudius II and Aurelian. Gallienus's death was a waste.

Claudius II Gothicus (268–270) was one of the conspirators involved in Gallienus's death. He earned his title after winning a massive victory over the Goths in the Battle of Naissus. His reign was short-lived, however, because he caught the plague and died in 270, a rare instance of an emperor *not* being murdered during the third century.

Aurelian (AD 270–275)

Succeeding Claudius II was a highly effective general called Aurelian. Aurelian was a rare instance of a Roman emperor in the third century who could control the army, put down rebels, hold the frontiers, and tackle domestic problems. As the sections 'Annihilating Palmyra' and 'The end of the Gallic Empire' explain, he settled the Palmyra dispute and reclaimed the Gallic Empire for Rome. During a great triumph held in Rome to celebrate his victories, he had both Tetricus of the Gallic Empire and Zenobia of Palmyra walk in the procession, but he pensioned both off and allowed them to live out their days in peace.

The ruins of Palmyra

Palmyra, which sits on top of an underground spring, means *city of palms*. Today, it's Syria's number one tourist attraction. Visitors today can see the Street of Columns, a triumphal arch, the remains of several temples, and other buildings scattered over an area of more than 6 square kilometres (2 square miles). The on-site museum has mosaics and paintings that testify to the huge wealth enjoyed by the Palmyrenes before Aurelian destroyed the city.

Annihilating Palmyra

In Palmyra, when Vabalathus was declared emperor in 271, it was the last straw for Aurelian. Aurelian headed east and defeated the Palmyrenes at Antioch and Emesa. Next he crossed the desert and besieged Palmyra. During the siege, Zenobia was captured while trying to escape and hire Persian reinforcements. She was deposed, and a Roman garrison established. Aurelian headed to the Danube to deal with the frontier only to hear that a revolt in Palmyra had killed the whole garrison. Aurelian raced back to Palmyra and wiped the city out, totally destroying it. Palmyra wasn't rediscovered until travellers from Europe made it there in the 1700s.

The end of the Gallic Empire

Everything started going wrong for the Gallic Empire in 268 when a revolt against Postumus was put down. Postumus refused the soldiers permission to sack Mainz as punishment. So they killed Postumus. A succession of very short-lived emperors followed, ending with Tetricus I (270–273) and his son Tetricus II. Aurelian, just back from wiping out the Palmyrenes, invaded Gaul in 273. The two Tetrici promptly (and wisely) surrendered, and that was the end of the Gallic Empire.

Aurelian at home

Aurelian tried to reform the coinage and end the skyrocketing inflation with modest success, but he used the money he had taken from Palmyra to pay for handouts of bread, meat, oil, and salt in Rome. He repaired the Tiber's banks and started making food and shipping guilds into semi-official organisations to improve commerce and production.

The Aurelian walls of Rome

Although he was a brilliant general, Aurelian knew only too well how real the threat was to Rome from rebels and barbarians. He ordered the building of a massive new circuit of brick and concrete walls to protect the city. Nineteen kilometres long (12 miles), they were finished under Probus (276–282) and had watchtowers and massive gates all the way round. The walls were constantly improved over the next 200 years and eventually had 383 towers, 14 gates, and 116 latrines for the guards. Large stretches survive more or less intact and are one of the most impressive sights in Rome today.

Aurelian co-operated with the Senate and involved it in his reforms though he was always ready for trouble – his nickname was *Manu ad ferrum* which translates as 'Hand on iron', meaning he was always ready to draw his sword if necessary.

The death of Aurelian

In 275, Aurelian was in Thrace, heading off to deal with the Persians once more. Along the way, he was murdered by Praetorian officers who'd been told (falsely) by an imperial secretary that they were on the list of men to be executed. Thoroughly ashamed of their actions, the soldiers asked the Senate to pick the next emperor, the first time anything like that had happened probably since Nerva's accession in 96.

The Sun-God

Interest in monotheism (belief in one god) was becoming more and more common in the Roman world. Aurelian was especially keen on the god called the 'Unconquered Sun-God' *(Sol Invictus)* and had been impressed by Sun-God worship in places like Palmyra. He built a temple to Sol in Rome and created a college of priests to man it. He posed as a priest of Sol on his coins, which was a big step towards a world in which the emperor presented himself as a divinely appointed representative of a god on Earth. Sol's feast-day was 25 December, later adapted to be the winter festival of the Christians. But Aurelian had no intention of getting rid of the old gods – he just wanted Sol to be the most important.

The Senate picked an elderly senator called Tacitus after a delay of six months. Tacitus successfully defeated the Goths in Asia Minor but died from old age after a reign of only about seven months in the summer of 276. His half-brother Florianus, the praetorian prefect, declared himself to be emperor. Unfortunately for him, he wasn't the only candidate. Probus, Aurelian's former general in the East, was also declared emperor. Florianus's troops decided Probus was the better bet and killed Florianus.

Probus (AD 276–282)

Probus was young enough, wise enough, and capable enough to have restored the Roman world. He made his way to Rome, was approved by the Senate, and promptly set out on a war to defeat German tribes. He was successful and also put down rebellions in Britain, Gaul, and Germany; he even hired some of his prisoners-of-war as soldiers to strengthen his own forces.

Probus kept his soldiers busy with public building projects and even planting vineyards when they weren't fighting. Word seems to have got out that Probus thought conditions were improving so much that soon the army, or large parts of it anyway, could be discharged. That didn't go down well amongst an army already resentful at being made to work on building sites, and as a result, Probus was murdered by troops in the provinces of Raetia and Noricum. A waste of a potentially good emperor.

The End of the Principate

Things became chaotic again following Probus's murder. The troops who murdered Probus proclaimed the praetorian prefect Carus emperor in 282. Carus (282–283) promptly appointed his sons Numerian and Carinus his heirs and set off with Numerian to finish off the Sassanid Persians. Carus defeated the Persians but had an amazing stroke of bad luck in his camp: He was struck by lightning and killed. At least that was the story put about. Another possibility is that he was killed by Numerian's father-in-law, the praetorian prefect Aper, who fancied seeing his descendants on the throne more quickly. Either way, Numerian (282–284), who preferred writing poetry to fighting, set off back to Rome but was mysteriously murdered in his litter in 284, probably also by Aper. That left Carinus (282–285) in charge.

In the spring of 285, Diocles, head of the imperial bodyguard, was chosen by the army in the East to avenge the death of Numerian. Diocles headed west and met Carinus's army near the Danube. Carinus, who was extremely unpopular, was killed by one of his own men, and his troops went over to Diocles.

Carinus's death marked the end of the principate, the system established by Augustus 300 years earlier and which had evolved over the years. It's pretty obvious it was in a very dodgy state, so it's just as well that Diocles was something of a visionary. He realised that the Roman world had changed beyond recognition. It needed a new system, it needed it fast, and he decided he was the man to bring that about.

Chapter 20

East Is East and West Is West: Diocletian and Constantine

*B*y the end of the third century, the days when the emperor could do much of his ruling from Rome, or concentrate on one war at a time, were long gone. Roman emperors, good or bad, were spending virtually all their time on campaign. Instead of just relying on well-established garrisons around the Roman world, highly mobile units had also to be created so that soldiers could race from one trouble spot to another. When the emperors weren't fighting one another, they were moving from one frontier to another, shoring up the defences, fighting back barbarians, and negotiating peace deals. The coasts of Britain and Gaul, for example, were plagued by pirates from Northern Europe, so a series of coastal fortified compounds were installed to help protect commerce, towns, villas, and farms. New fortifications were being built on new frontiers as well.

Meanwhile, society across the Roman Empire was changing. The endless parade of rebel emperors disrupted provincial government. As vast quantities of resources were being poured into the army and defences, provincials found themselves being taxed to pay for all the various rebellions as well as the legitimate army. Some lost their land and livings and formed marauding bands of landless outlaws.

This chapter tells the story of how one soldier emperor named Diocletian tried to transform the Roman world in an attempt to repair the damage before it was too late, and how another Roman emperor named Constantine issued an edict that changed Rome forever.

On the Case: Diocletian (AD 284–305)

Diocles, born around 240 to a poor family in Dalmatia, had spent a lifetime witnessing the chaos of the soldier emperors. Like so many of the emperors of the third century, he rose through the ranks of the army entirely on merit. That was how he ended up on the imperial bodyguard under the emperor Numerian (282–284) and why he was chosen to avenge Numerian's death (refer to Chapter 19 for the details on this episode).

When he became emperor in 284 (following the murder of Carinus, who ruled from 282 to 285, and the defection of Carinus's men to his side; refer to Chapter 19), Diocles changed his name to Gaius Aurelius Valerius Diocletianus. It helped echo former emperors' names.

Diocletian moved fast and decisively after getting rid of Carinus. In 285, he made his comrade Maximian his Caesar and, therefore, his heir. The next year, he made Maximian into a joint Augustus and sent him to Gaul to sort out the Bagaudae, a mob of landless peasants who were ravaging the countryside. Maximian soon defeated Bagaudae, with the help of another soldier called Carausius, who went on to become one of the most successful rebel Emperors of the time (more on him in the section 'The rebellion in Britain: Carausius', later in this chapter).

Four emperors are better than one: The Tetrarchy

Diocletian knew that the Empire was too big, too unstable, and too insecure for one emperor to run alone. Although the Roman Empire had had joint emperors before, Diocletian did something different: He split the Empire in half. Maximian would rule the Latin West, and Diocletian would rule the Greek East.

In 293, Diocletian came up with the idea of the *Tetrarchy,* in which four men would rule the Roman Empire. He appointed two junior emperors, known as Caesars: Constantius Chlorus in the West and Galerius in the East. Constantius would assist Maximian, and Galerius would assist Diocletian. Then, at an appropriate point in the future, Maximian and Diocletian would abdicate, and Constantius and Galerius would succeed them as the Augusti and appoint their own Caesars.

Tetrarchy comes from two Greek words: *tetra-* ('four') and *archos* ('chief' or 'commander'). So Tetrarchy means 'four chiefs'.

Each tetrarch had his headquarters. Diocletian ruled from Nicomedia in Asia Minor (Turkey), Galerius from Sirmium in modern Serbia, Maximian from Milan in Italy, and Constantius from Trier in Gaul. So much for Rome. Now the original city wasn't even an emperor's base. It was too far from the trouble areas.

The idea was to create a self-perpetuating system in which the succession was assured and the best men were selected for the job. On paper it looked like a brilliant system, and in the beginning, it went well. Constantius was able to deal with the rebellion of Carausius and Allectus in Britain (described in the section 'The rebellion in Britain: Carausius'), Diocletian was able to successfully deal with rebellions in Egypt, and Galerius sorted out the troublesome Persians.

Repairing the broken Empire

During the 20 years of his reign Diocletian energetically restored cities, roads, and infrastructure. Maximian, for his part, ran a major building programme in Rome. (It's a mark of just how much there was to do and the nature of the times that Diocletian didn't even visit Rome for the first time until 303, by which time he'd reigned for nearly 20 years.) But the greatest impact came from a series of major reforms.

The army

Diocletian started the process of turning the enlarged army into two halves: the mainly cavalry mobile field force called the *comitatenses* and the frontier garrisons called the *limitanei*. This system which became fully established under Constantine I (307–337). You can read more about the organisation of the army in Chapter 5.

Provinces

Provinces were divided up, roughly doubling the total, so that no individual governor would be powerful enough to start a rebellion. Britain, for example, had started life as one province, was divided into two by Septimius Severus (see Chapter 18), and was now made into four. Even Italy was broken up this way. Regional groups of provinces were arranged into *diœceses* (districts; singular *diœcesis*), 13 in total, each of which was overseen by a *vicarius* (vicar). The vicars were under the control of four Praetorian prefects, one for each of the four emperors. Provinces were no longer governed by a senatorial *legatus* (see Chapter 3); instead the position was variously called *praes* ('protector') and *rector* ('leader').

The *diœcesis, vicarius,* and *rector* of Diocletian's new system probably look familiar. That's because the Christian church modelled some of its own government on Diocletian's system. So today bishops run dioceses, and the Anglican church's local priests are called vicars. A rector is a priest or layperson in charge of an institution like a college.

Tax reform, Roman style

The tax assessment system that Diocletian set up may seem complicated, but it isn't. This is how it worked:

1. Land was now counted across the Empire by a fixed unit called the *iugerum* (plural: *iugera*).

2. Each iugerum was measured for how much it could produce according to a fixed unit of production called the *iugum* (plural: *iuga*).

3. Iugera that produced more or higher-value crops had to pay more tax. So 5 iugera of vineyard was assessed at 1 iugum, but it took 40 iugera of poor mountain land to be assessed at 1 iugum. Likewise 40 iugera of vineyard would be assessed for 8 iuga.

Money matters

Running Diocletian's new system cost a fortune. Taxes were levied not just in cash but also in kind, meaning people found themselves obliged to hand over money as well as produce and goods that the Empire needed. So if you made woollen goods, then you paid over some of your woollen goods to the government for tax. Paying in kind helped get round inflation. To halt the roller-coaster inflation of the third century, Diocletian fixed the prices in an Edict of Maximum Prices in 301. The same year he also fixed maximum salaries.

To make taxes less painful, in 296 Diocletian changed the system of assessment so that people only paid what was fair. The idea was to get rid of an almost infinite number of different local systems. Under Diocletian's system, better land was liable for more tax, poor land for less. The number of people was counted as well, so that a poll tax could be levied. This way each farm or villa ended up with a taxable value that took into account the people who lived and worked there and how much the estate could produce. Every year, the government announced how much it needed and divided that up amongst all the *iuga* which had been counted. (If you're interested in the details of this system, head to the sidebar 'Tax reform, Roman style'.)

But Diocletian's monetary and tax reforms didn't work properly in practice:

- Diocletian didn't have enough gold and silver to make coinage stable. Inflation continued upwards, and many goods just disappeared from the market. Eventually the Edict on Maximum Prices had to be withdrawn.

- Corrupt tax assessors over-measured estates' liabilities and pocketed the difference.

- ✔ Tax collectors could over-collect and pocket the difference (though if they under-collected, they had to pay the shortfall).
- ✔ The system of assessments effectively forced people to stay where they were permanently.

The Dominate: A new order

The result of Diocletian's new world was the beginning of the totalitarian state: interfering in every aspect of people's lives, and restricting freedom and movement. The new order is called the Dominate because the emperor was now called *Dominus* ('lord'), styled *Jovius* ('Jupiter's Chosen One'), and was treated as if he was a god. Appropriately enough, he was shown in statues and on reliefs wearing a halo. It's also very striking how emperors were no longer portrayed as individuals. Each of the Tetrarchs looks like all the others – a deliberate way of making rulers into a generic type.

But unlike the madmen who came before him, such as Commodus (discussed in Chapter 18) or Elagabalus (discussed in Chapter 19), Diocletian was just creating a new imperial image rather than actually deluding himself into believing he really was a god.

Persecuting Christians

In 303, Diocletian and Maximian began a major persecution of Christians. Maximian's suppression of Christianity in North Africa was especially severe. Actually, it remains something of a mystery why this happened because the Christians had been left more or less alone ever since the last persecution under Valerian I, which came to an end in 260. Diocletian even had a Christian wife. But his sidekick Galerius was fanatically anti-Christian. Galerius must have convinced Diocletian that the Christians were subversive and dangerous, and that the new totalitarian state had no room for any religion that undermined total loyalty to the regime. The persecution involved destroying churches and confiscating any holy texts, but Diocletian ordered no bloodshed, perhaps out of deference to his wife and his personal tendency to toleration. Galerius had a deathbed change of heart in 311 (see the later section 'Issuing the Edict of Milan').

Diocletian's spies

Diocletian did away with the *frumentarii* spies (see Chapter 17), who were extremely unpopular, and replaced them with *agentes* (agents). They did much the same job, but because their main role was carrying despatches, they were probably able to operate rather more undercover.

Diocletian's palace

Diocletian built himself a huge fortified palace at Split on the Dalmatian coast of the Adriatic, now part of modern Croatia. Split was then called *Spalato,* which means 'little palace', though it was anything but small. After he abdicated in 305, Diocletian spent most of the rest of his life there. Modelled on a Roman fort, the palace had the imperial apartments in the southern half, while the north was given over to servants, slaves, and soldiers. Huge parts of the palace have survived.

The rebellion in Britain: Carausius

During Diocletian's reign an extraordinary rebellion broke out in Britain. In many ways it was the most unusual rebellion of the whole of Roman history. It was certainly the cheekiest. It was led by a man called Carausius whose breathtaking front, swaggering bravado, and creative political spin were without parallel.

The making of a pirate

Mausaeus Carausius grew up on the coast of where modern Belgium is now. He became a soldier in Maximian's army and was so successful at defeating the Bagaudae in Gaul, that he was given the job of clearing Saxon raiders who were sailing down the North Sea and attacking towns and villas in Gaul and Britain.

Carausius used a Roman fleet to attack the raiders. He was so effective at this and became so popular that Maximian became annoyed. A story circulated that Carausius was waiting for the raiders to help themselves to loot, then he attacked them and took what they'd stolen. Maximian declared Carausius a criminal and offered a bounty for his capture.

Maximian might have put the story out himself, perhaps because he was jealous. We don't know. But what is certain is that Carausius now had nothing to lose. In 286, he declared himself emperor in Britain and part of Gaul. He was clearly popular because there isn't a hint of opposition to his rule.

Carausius's cheek

Carausius was a propaganda genius. Not only did he declare himself emperor, but he also

✔ Renamed himself Marcus Aurelius Mausaeus Carausius, echoing Septimius Severus 80 years before (Chapter 18) in creating a pseudo-claim to be descended from the 'good emperors' of the second century.

- ✔ Issued the first good silver coinage for generations (so perhaps he had indeed helped himself to loot!) to ensure his soldiers' loyalty, which Diocletian hadn't been able to produce.

- ✔ Posed on all his coins as a real toughie but associated himself with all sorts of proper Roman virtues like *pax* ('peace') and *uberitas* ('fertility') and claimed to be renewing the Roman Empire.

- ✔ Put slogans from the poetry of Augustus's state poet Virgil, written 300 years before, on his coins (for Virgil, see Chapter 1). This was an absolutely unprecedented move because no-one, even Augustus himself, had ever done that before.

What Carausius was saying was that his regime was the new Roman Empire. He was 'restoring' all the qualities of Augustus's world but in Britain, not in Rome.

- ✔ Declared he was a member of the Tetrarchy, too – adding insult to injury – and struck coins showing him with Diocletian and Maximian and the legend *Carausius et Fratres Sui*, 'Carausius and His Brothers'.

As you can imagine, the Tetrarchs were spitting with anger and called Carausius 'the pirate' and other insulting names. They tried to send a fleet in 289 to destroy Carausius, but it was wrecked by a storm.

Done in by a coup: Allectus

Carausius lasted in power till 293, swaggering away in Britain to Diocletian and Maximian's fury. But Carausius was murdered in a coup in 293 by his finance minister Allectus. Allectus made himself emperor, but it couldn't last.

The Empire strikes back

In 296, a huge fleet was gathered in Boulogne on the north coast of Gaul. The praetorian prefect Asclepiodotus invaded southern Britain, fought a battle with Allectus, and killed him. Meanwhile, Constantius Chlorus took another part of the fleet and seized London. A magnificent medal was issued to celebrate the event with the legend 'restored to the eternal light', which was how the Tetrarchy modestly liked to see itself.

The rebellion was over. It wasn't the last, in Britain or anywhere else, by any means. But it was certainly the most remarkable.

Like all the best ideas: The Tetrarchy falls apart

The Tetrarchy was a good idea. Too good for the Roman Empire, as it turned out. What Diocletian hadn't taken into account was other people's ambitions.

Because Galerius and Constantius had married their respective seniors' daughters, there was the making of a dynasty. There were also other interested parties, each of whom had an eye on getting a slice of the action.

Following Diocletian's and Maximian's retirements on 1 May 305, Galerius and Constantius succeeded them just as they were supposed to. Galerius appointed his ambitious nephew Maximinus II Daia as his Caesar, and Constantius recruited a man called Severus II. In theory, the Tetrarchy was now in its next phase. But then things started to go wrong

Too many cooks

When Diocletian and Maximian retired, and the new Augusti Galerius and Constantius had appointed their own Caesars (Maximinus II Daia and Severus II, respectively), a few people were a bit disgruntled by the way things had shaken out, particularly

- ✔ **Maxentius:** Maximian's son
- ✔ **Constantine:** Constantius I's son by an earlier marriage (a lot more on him in the section, 'Constantine I, the Great', later in this chapter)
- ✔ **Licinius:** Diocletian's adopted son

If that sounds like a recipe for disaster, it was.

Succession woes

Maximian's son Maxentius took grave exception to being cut out, and so did Constantius's son Constantine.

In 306, Constantius died in York, Britain, while on campaign. His troops rejected the idea of Severus II succeeding him and promptly declared Constantius's son Constantine emperor instead. It was an act that changed the history of the world.

Galerius was furious, but was very wary of letting a civil war break out. So he offered a compromise: Severus II would become Augustus in the West, as planned, and Constantine would become Severus's Caesar and thus the heir. Unfortunately, things started to heat up. Maximian's son Maxentius, still resentful at being cut out of the deal (any deal in fact), decided to throw his hat into the ring, and then things really got wild. Here, in the general order in which they happened, are the events that kept people guessing about who was *really* in charge between 305 and 308:

1. Maxentius led a coup in Rome and recalled his father Maximian who became emperor again.

2. Galerius sent Severus II against the usurpers, but his own soldiers abandoned him, and Severus was imprisoned and killed.

3. Maximian married his daughter Fausta to Constantine and made him Augustus in the West.

4. Galerius tried to seize Rome but was forced to retreat.

5. Maximian fell out with his son Maxentius and was made to give up and go and live with Constantine.

6. A conference followed in 308, in which both Diocletian and Maximian turned up. At this conference

   • Maxentius was declared a public enemy, though he remained a serious problem.

   • Constantine was demoted to Caesar, though he refused to accept it.

   • Galerius's comrade Licinius was made Augustus in the West.

   • Maximian was told he had to stay abdicated.

So by 308, here's where things stood:

✔ In the East, the Augustus was Galerius, with Maximinus II Daia as his Caesar.

✔ In the West, the Augustus was Licinius, with Constantine as his Caesar.

✔ Meanwhile, regardless of who was in charge in theory, Maxentius was in control of Italy and North Africa.

The final death throes of the Tetrarchy

As you may have figured out by now, in Roman history, even the things that are settled are never really settled. So you can expect that things didn't go smoothly for the Tetrarchy once the dust had settled in 308.

In 310, Maximian fell out with Constantine and declared himself emperor again (for the third time). This time Maximian was forced to give up by his own men and was found dead soon afterwards, probably murdered by Constantine. The wars that followed over the next 15 years wiped out Diocletian's Tetrarchy for good and left one man in sole charge of the Roman Empire: Constantine I, the Great. His reign would do more than any other to transform the Dominate and the Roman Empire and make changes that echo right down to the present.

Constantine 1, the Great (AD 307–337)

In 311, Galerius died from an agonising illness. Maximinus II succeeded him as Augustus in the East.

Constantine made an alliance with Licinius, who was Augustus in the West, and then he marched into Italy to defeat and kill Maxentius at the Battle of the Milvian Bridge on 28 October 312. (Remember, Maxentius was neither Augustus nor Caesar for any of the regions, but he had control of Italy and North Africa.) The victory meant Constantine had total control of the western Roman Empire, which set him up directly against Maximinus II in the East. What's more, the Senate declared Constantine was the senior Augustus, so it was a moment of enormous significance.

The Battle of the Milvian Bridge, at Rome, was one of the most decisive moments in the history of Europe and all Western civilisation because Constantine was convinced his victory had been caused by the Christian God. According to legend, Constantine claimed to have had a vision of Christ before the battle. In this vision, he was told to place the Chi-Rho symbol on his soldiers' shields, and he heard the words *in hoc signo vinces,* 'in this sign you shall conquer'.

Taking control of the West

After his victory at Milvian Bridge, Constantine's first job was to get shot of Maximinus II Daia, who was Augustus of the East. Constantine's motivation was simple: He had no intention of sharing the Roman world with anyone, and he was also determined to defend the interests of Christians.

Maximinus had gone back to persecuting Christians and had even tried to create a rival pagan church organised like the Christian church. As the senior Augustus, Constantine ordered him to stop. Maximinus didn't. Instead Maximinus set off to try and defeat Licinius who, in return for recognising Constantine in the West, had been awarded the right to rule in the East. Unfortunately for Maximinus, Licinius defeated him in Thrace. Maximinus disguised himself as a slave to escape; he also started trying to undo his Christian persecutions by issuing an edict of toleration. But it was too late. Before his change of heart had any impact, he died in the summer of 313.

Maximinus's death left Constantine undisputed master of the West and Licinius undisputed master of the East.

The two met in Milan in 313. Licinius married Constantine's half-sister Constantia to cement the alliance. To help their claim to rule, Constantine said he was descended from Claudius II, and Licinius said he was descended from Philip I (refer to Chapter 19 for information on both men). They also issued the Edict of Milan.

Issuing the Edict of Milan, 313

On his sick bed in 311, Galerius had orchestrated an edict with his fellow Tetrarchs that ended the persecution of Christians. All the persecutions had done was harden the Christians' resolve and divide the Roman world. The edict asked that Christians pray to their God to help the Roman state.

It was one thing to announce that Christians were free to worship, as Galerius had done in 311. It was another thing altogether to start turning the Roman state into a Christian one. The toleration of Christians was renewed in the 313 Edict of Milan, but this was a far more significant moment.

What the Edict of Milan said was that all religions would be tolerated and that anything that had been confiscated by the state from the Christians would be returned unconditionally. What the Edict didn't say was that Christianity was now the only legal religion. But it started the process that eventually led to the outlawing of paganism.

East vs. West: Fighting Licinius

A power struggle gradually ensued between Constantine and Licinius, despite their personal (and admittedly political) connections. In a way, it's reminiscent of how the First and Second Triumvirates of the late Republic fell apart around 400 years before even though their members were tied together in political and personal alliances (refer to Chapters 14 and 15). It just seems that sharing the Roman world was something few rulers could bear the idea of.

This power struggle eventually broke out into open war. Constantine was convinced he had the Christian God on his side.

Trouble brewing

Religion has a bit of a track record of being used to divide people, and that's what happened now. Constantine was also a smart operator. He used Christianity as a means of establishing a new power base. He could appoint new men to government and high rank in the army, men who owed their new status to Constantine, while old pagan families got pushed out. Constantine gave the church and its members all sorts of privileges, like exemptions from taxes, favouritism for jobs, and so on.

Licinius got suspicious when Constantine made his own brother-in-law, Bassianus, his Caesar in charge of Italy and the Danube provinces. Licinius encouraged Bassianus to revolt in 314, but the plot was uncovered and led to open war between Licinius and Constantine in 316 though the tensions between them had never gone away.

By 316, Constantine and Licinius had negotiated a truce. Part of the deal was sorting out the succession. In 317, Constantine's two sons, Crispus and Constantine II, were named his Caesars, and Licinius's son, also called Licinius, was named his. That held off the fighting for a while, but Licinius senior was still not satisfied. He believed that Constantine was using Christianity to undermine him by filling the East with Christians who were loyal to Constantine and not him. In retaliation, Licinius began to clamp down on the Church in the East, and he threw Christians out of the top jobs.

Licinius also thought Constantine was preferring his own sons for all the consulships. Although in the days of the Dominate, being consul amounted to nothing more than taking part in public ceremonials, it was a great way to promote someone. Licinius believed that Constantine was giving his own sons preferential treatment to make sure they would succeed as emperors, at the expense of Licinius's son.

The end of Licinius

In 322, Constantine entered the East, supposedly to see off another Gothic invasion. Licinius took this as a direct infringement of his control of the East, and war broke out. But Licinius had a series of disasters: In July 324, he was defeated at the Battle of Hadrianopolis; shortly afterwards the 350 ships of his fleet were destroyed by 200 ships commanded by Constantine's eldest son Crispus at the Battle of the Hellespont; and then in September Constantine totally defeated Licinius at the Battle of Chrysopolis. Licinius fled but was soon captured. He was later executed after being accused of plotting a comeback; his son's execution followed.

The Empire goes Christian

With Licinius out of the way, Constantine was left in sole control of the Roman Empire. Convinced that Christianity was the best way to hold the Empire together, Constantine began in earnest to Christianise the Roman Empire, a process that had started with the edicts of 311 and 313 (see 'Issuing the Edict of Milan, 313').

Clamping down on paganism

Constantine I's mother was Helena, said to be from Britain. She might have been Constantius's first wife, or a mistress. She was later made into a saint because she travelled to Judaea in 326 to visit places associated with Christianity. She believed she had found the major locations in Christ's life, including where he was born and where he was crucified. A dig led to the discovery of what were thought to be the three crosses and helped create a trade in fragments of the 'true cross'. Some shrines were multi-faith and were visited by pagans of all types as well as Christians. Constantine's mother-in-law, Eutropia, was horrified at one such shrine at Hebron and had Constantine destroy all the pagan monuments and install a church: Early Christianity often 'hijacked' pagan monuments and traditions and refranchised them as Christian.

The new imperial court

Constantine called himself 'Equal of the Apostles' and presented himself as the Christian God's representative on Earth. He maintained Diocletian's Dominate. The totalitarian state became more and more a fact of life. The Senate was a total irrelevance, and the old distinction between senators and equestrians was abandoned. Constantine had a council, the *sacrum consistorium* ('sacred body of those standing together'), which stood in his presence. It was all about pomp and circumstances, honorific titles, with everything being labelled *sacrum* ('sacred'). There was a vast imperial court, which was made up of Constantine's

- household staff, including eunuchs.

- his bodyguard (*scholae palatinae*, literally 'the corporation of the palace').

- ushers (*silentarii*).

- secretaries (*notarii*, from *nota* for a 'letter' or 'memo').

- ministers for the following: dealing with imperial lands (*comes rei pirivatae*, 'count of private affairs'), the palace (*quaestor sacri palatii*, 'quaestor of the sacred palace'), jobs (*magister officiorum*, 'master of jobs'; *magister militum*, 'Master of the Soldiers' – the latter becoming especially important in the late fourth and fifth centuries), and finance (*comes sacrarum largitionum*, 'count of the sacred largesse'), and their respective staff.

Celebrating Christianity in architecture

New architectural forms were developed to celebrate Christianity, like Constantine's Church of the Holy Apostles in his new capital of Constantinople, built in the form of a cross. The old pagan government basilica design, a hall with a nave and aisles, was adapted as a church design and formed the basis of all the great medieval cathedrals. The new designs appeared in Rome, too, like the first Basilica of St Peter (now beneath the modern St Peter's).

Vast statues of the emperor were carved. Fragments of two in Rome survive (one bronze, one marble), as well as one in York in northern Britain, where Constantine had been declared emperor. Totally unlike the lifelike classical statues of old, the new imperial images show an impersonal face with eyes rolled heavenward.

Christians at each other's throats

The Christians ought to have been delighted at their new-found freedom to worship. They probably were, but instead of automatically holding the Empire together, as Constantine had hoped, Christians proved as liable to squabble as – well, any other bunch of human beings. For a start, some of the Christians were as intolerant of pagans as some pagans had once been of them. This intolerance encouraged a long-term, ongoing process of bringing in anti-pagan laws banning pagan worship and temple building.

The Arian theology – it's all in a letter

The Arian schism in the end hinged on the letter 'i'. The orthodox (Catholic) Church defined their belief in the prayer called the Creed with the Greek word *homoousios,* which described how God the Father and God the Son were coeternal and coequal – in other words, exactly the same. The Arians added an 'i' and got *homoiousios* from *homoios* ('similar'), which meant God the Father and God the Son were similar but not identical. The Creed, which comes from the Latin *credo,* 'I believe', is a statement of what Christians believe about God the Father, God the Son, and God the Holy Ghost. The Arian schism resulted in two rival versions: the Nicene (orthodox) Creed and the Arian Creed.

To many Romans, Christianity was just one more religion to add to the many available. Some dedicated Christians rejected all other religions. But many people were prepared to worship Christ alongside pagan gods. Even Constantine continued to issue coins with the Unconquered Sun-God and the Genius of the Roman People on them as well as other traditional Roman pagan symbols and personifications.

However you look at it, Christianity at this time was not one single, uniform religion. Christians fell out with one another in splits called *schisms:*

- ✔ **Catholic (Orthodox):** These Christians believed that Christ was God in his own right alongside God the Father and that while they were separate they were also one (the idea of Three Gods in One as the Trinity was still evolving). This was the teaching promoted by the leadership of the Christian church in Rome – so orthodox also means anything they said.

- ✔ **The Arians:** A North African priest called Arius declared in the early 300s that Christ was not God in his own right, but only as a creation of God the Father as an instrument to create the world. Arius soon had quite a following, including some bishops. As you can imagine, this outraged orthodox believers.

  Constantine called a council at Nicaea in 325 to settle the matter. The Arians were banished, but before long, Constantine started to think the Arians might be right and started reinstating them. The furore carried on for decades after Constantine's death in 337 while various councils tried to thrash out a form of words that would satisfy everyone and hold the Church together.

- ✔ **The Donatists:** Some members of the African church objected in 311 to the consecration of a bishop of Carthage called Caecilian by Felix of Aptunga, who had given up his holy scriptures during Diocletian's persecution. As far as they were concerned, anyone who'd shown weakness during persecution should be cut no slack. So they appointed a rival, himself succeeded by a man called Donatus, who gave his name to the schism. Donatus had quite a reputation, having put up with a series of torture bouts during the persecution. A commission of 313, a synod at Arles in 314, and Constantine in 316 found against the Donatists, whose supporters rioted at the bad news. Constantine tried to suppress them but gave up in 321. Amazingly, the Donatists were around for another 400–500 years before finally fizzling out altogether.

Moving house: The capital goes to a new location

The showcase of Constantine's new order was to be his new capital. He chose Byzantium, an ancient Greek city which controlled the Bosphorus strait between Europe and Asia. He selected this site for his capital for the following reasons:

- ✔ It had a harbour.
- ✔ It could be defended by a land army and a navy.
- ✔ It was much closer to the wealthy and productive eastern provinces like Egypt and Asia.
- ✔ It was closer to the most important frontiers (the East and the Rhine-Danube).

Rome remained the Empire's first city on paper, but Byzantium was the future. It was treated to all the necessary public buildings like a senate house, a horse- and chariot-racing stadium (known as the *Hippodrome*), forum, and libraries. Various ancient sites were plundered by Constantine so that his new capital could have instant pedigree (see the sidebar, 'Instant heritage'). In 330, the city had its official opening as *Nova Roma,* 'New Rome', but was soon renamed Constantinopolis (Constantinople; today it's called Istanbul).

Instant heritage

Constantinople was kitted out with all the trappings of a great city by filching them from other places. Constantine's Hippodrome in Constantinople was decorated with four bronze horses, cast more than 700 years earlier in Greece. Around 900 years later in 1204, those same horses were taken from Constantinople in the Fourth Crusade and were installed on St Mark's church in Venice where, apart from being briefly stolen by Napoleon, they remained until the 1980s, when they were removed to a museum (replicas stand in their place). Other decorations included the fifth century BC bronze Tripod of Plataea, which had been made to commemorate the Greek victory over the Persians in 479 BC. It was brought to the Hippodrome from the Temple of Apollo at Delphi in Greece. Unlike the four horses, the Tripod (or what's left of it) is still in the Hippodrome and is known as 'the Serpentine Column'.

Managing money

Unlike Diocletian, Constantine did manage some sort of stability of the coinage. He introduced a gold coin called the *solidus* which was smaller and lighter than the old *aureus,* but it was highly successful and became a staple coin for centuries to come.

To cope with the increased costs of a vastly enlarged army and his own colossal staff, Constantine added new taxes and confiscated temple treasures. Landowners, whose responsibilities for tax assessment and collection were vital, were prevented from getting into occupations that were exempt from such work, such as senators, civil servants, and the Christian clergy. That meant landowners were condemned to stay as they were, just like the millions of ordinary people in trades and professions. Bakers and butchers, for example, were obliged to stay in their jobs, and so were their sons. Tenant farmers were stuck, too, and could even be chained to the ground to stop them leaving. The idea was to keep the wheels of the economy turning and prevent bands of landless and jobless outlaws growing up, but it was done at a terrible price. It essentially was the end of personal freedom.

Paranoia and the succession

Constantine was determined to settle the future, but in 326, he got it into his head that his wife Fausta and his son Crispus (born to his first wife Minervina) had been plotting against him. He executed both and made his three other sons – Constantine II, Constantius II, and Constans – and two of his nephews, Delmatius and Hannibalianus, into five potential successors. Constantine seems to have been under the illusion, or perhaps delusion's a better word, that they would all rule happily together after his death. Some hope.

Constantine was finally baptised a Christian on his death bed, having fallen ill while planning a war against the Persians. (Death bed baptisms were quite common in those days because it meant you could die in the purest possible form. The idea was that there wouldn't be time to sin again between baptism and death and compromise any chance of getting into Heaven.)

There's no doubt that Constantine's reign had been a truly remarkable one. He had turned Diocletian's Dominate into a workable system. The frontiers were in better shape, and the Empire's prestige as a whole was restored in the eyes of the rest of the world, even if most people in the Roman world were tied to their homes and their jobs and could only imagine how much freedom there had once been as a Roman citizen.

Constantine's loving family – not!

Constantine planned that his three surviving sons, Constantine II, Constantius II, and Constans, and his two nephews Delmatius and Hannibalianus, would succeed him. All were made Caesars except Hannibalianus, who was made King with power over the provinces of Armenia, Pontus, and Cappadocia. Considering what a taboo the idea of Roman king was, Hannibalianus's position was remarkable. They did all succeed Constantine, but not in the way he'd hoped. Unfortunately, Constantine had ignored Diocletian's plans to have successors chosen by merit and had gone for the right to inherit through birth instead.

Fighting over everything

In 337, Constantine II was about 21 years old and had already fought a successful war against the Goths. Constantius II was about 20, and Constans about 17. Not much is known about the nephews Delmatius and Hannibalianus, and it doesn't matter much either because the first thing that happened is that they were both murdered, probably on the orders of Constantius II. He and his brothers became the three Augusti, and the Empire was divided up between them, recalling the Second Triumvirate (refer to Chapter 15):

- ✔ Constantine II got Gaul, Spain, and Britain.
- ✔ Constantius II got the Eastern provinces.
- ✔ Constans got Italy and Africa.

With the stakes so high, it's not surprising that the arrangements didn't last. Arguments soon broke out, and the ante was upped by religion. The Arian controversy (see 'Christians at each other's throats', earlier in this chapter) was still simmering. The orthodox (Catholic) Bishop of Alexandria, Athanasius, had been sent into exile when Constantine I started favouring the Arians. Athanasius found refuge in Trier, which became Constantine II's capital. Athanasius was given permission to go back to Alexandria in Constantius II's territory. Constantius II was furious because he favoured the Arians and Athanasius was forced to flee to Rome in 339.

The deaths of Constantine II and Constans

Meanwhile, the imperial brothers held a meeting in 338 to sort out their differences. Constans was awarded more land: the Danube provinces, Thrace, Macedonia, Achaea (Greece), and Constantinople.

Constantine II felt hard done by, especially as he considered himself the senior emperor, and started quarrelling with Constans. In 340, he led an army over the Alps to invade Italy but was ambushed near Aquileia and killed. Constans helped himself to his brother's territories. Within three years of his death, Constantine I's five successors had been reduced to two.

The birthday party coup

The coup to topple Constans took place in January 350 when Marcellinus, chief finance minister of Constans, held a sham birthday party for his son at Augustodunum (Autun) in Gaul. Along with Magnentius and others, he had hatched the plan when Constans was out hunting. Magnentius attended along with a number of other important men and, at an appropriate moment, disappeared as if to relieve himself. He returned dressed up in purple and was promptly acclaimed as the emperor. The army instantly declared for Magnentius, and Constans had to make a hasty escape. Not hasty enough as it turned out. One of Magnentius's supporters caught him and killed him.

Constans was a committed orthodox Catholic and had even been baptised in 337. He actively supported the Church in the West and sided with Athanasius at the Council of Serdica in 342. The Empire was beginning to split down the middle between the orthodox West and the Arian East. War nearly broke out in 346, but Constans and Constantius II overcame their differences.

Constans lasted until 350. Although he was a popular emperor for his support of the Church, he had a terrible personal reputation for depravity and promoting men in return for bribes, which disastrously cost him the support of the army. In 350, he was killed in a coup led by a soldier called Magnentius.

Constantius II (AD 337–361)

After the death of his brother Constans, Constantius II might now have had the pleasure of running the whole Roman Empire, but he also had the humiliation of the rebel Magnentius running a breakaway empire in Spain, Gaul, Britain, and even Africa (refer to the preceding section). Magnentius had also killed a nephew of Constantine I's called Nepotian who had tried to seize power in Rome when Constans was killed.

The Magnentian Revolt

Magnentius, a pagan, posed as an orthodox Christian on his coins and even had the Chi-Rho symbol prominently displayed on the reverse of one type. He was using the split in the Church to rustle up support in the Catholic West against the Arian East.

IN THEIR WORDS

'Veni, vidi, vici...'

Eyewitness

The historian Ammianus Marcellinus was in Rome in 357 when Constantius II visited. This is his eyewitness account of an emperor in the days of the Dominate:

> 'He did not stir while being hailed as Augustus by supportive acclamations while the hills resounded to the roar, and showed himself to be as calm and imperturbable as he had in the provinces. Although he was very short, he stooped to pass below high gates. He fixed the gaze of his eyes ahead and did not turn to left or right, as if his head was in a vice. He did not nod if a wheel jolted, and he wasn't once seen spitting, wiping or rubbing his face or nose, or moving his hands about – as if he was a dummy.'

War was inevitable. Constantius II made his cousin Gallus into his Caesar and put him in charge of the East so that he could go off and fight Magnentius. In 351, Magnentius and Constantius met at the bloody Battle of Mursa Major in Pannonia. It was an expensive stalemate. Constantius's cavalry defeated the Magnentian legions, but it cost Constantius 30,000 men and Magnentius 24,000. A series of engagements followed that gradually pushed Magnentius back into Gaul. In 353, Magnentius was defeated again and committed suicide.

Constantius came down on Magnentius's supporters with utter totalitarian ruthlessness. Anyone suspected of supporting the rebel was liable to be executed or at the very least be thrown into prison, his estates and wealth confiscated. The historian Ammianus Marcellinus thought Constantius was more paranoid about treachery than any other emperor of the past, even Domitian (Chapter 17) or Commodus (Chapter 18). Some of the plots were genuine ones, but where cases were doubtful, Constantius was quite happy to use torture to extract confessions.

The first Santa Sophia

In 360, Constantius II's great church *Santa Sophia* ('Holy Wisdom') was dedicated in Constantinople. Two hundred years later, it was rebuilt by the Byzantine emperor Justinian I (see Chapter 21). Although today it is a mosque, it stands as one of the most remarkable structures to have survived from the Roman world.

While at Mursa Major, Constantius had met the local Arian bishop, a man called Valens. Valens had a huge amount of influence on Constantius, who became even more dedicated to the Arian cause. Athanasius, the orthodox Catholic bishop of Alexandria, was forced into exile once again.

Gallus was summoned after reports that he was acting like a despot, but he was tried and executed before he even reached Constantius. He was soon replaced in 354 by his brother Julian who became Constantius's designated successor.

Constantius II in power

As a ruler, Constantius was relatively competent. He fancied himself as an intellectual but really hadn't any abilities, unlike in sport, military skills, and hunting, which he was extremely good at. He only promoted men in the army on merit, but avoided handing out the highest titles unless thoroughly deserved. Conversely, he was rather too quick to commemorate his own military exploits on triumphal arches, and because he was indecisive, he listened to his eunuchs, his wives, and other officials too readily. Taxes were already heavy, but he did nothing to stop tax collectors extorting people, which only made him unpopular.

Resolving the Arian versus Catholic crisis

In 359, Constantius organised a two-part council to resolve the Arian versus orthodox tussle so that Christianity could work as the state religion of the Roman Empire. The Arian bishop Valens suggested a compromise wording that glossed over the key bone of contention (whether Christ *was* God or was *like* God, see the earlier section 'Christians at each other's throats') and it looked for a bit if everyone would be happy. The orthodox diehards led by Athanasius and Basil, Bishop of Ancyra, rejected that totally. But before too long, the Arians were weakened by splitting into three groups, each of which with its own idea about the precise difference between Christ and God. Finally, a council at Constantinople in 381 ratified the decisions made at Nicaea in 325. Arianism became a legal offence and disappeared from the Empire, though it remained popular for another century amongst some German tribes.

Bringing Back Pagans: Julian II 'the Apostate' (AD 360–363)

For most of the last part of his reign, Constantius II dealt constantly with trouble on the borders. He fought on the Danube and then had to head east once more to fend off the Persians. Constantius sent his cousin Julian to clear out Germans who had crossed the Rhine and sacked Cologne.

Riots in Alexandria

Julian's restoration of paganism sometimes had unfortunate consequences. In Alexandria, the people hated their bishop Georgius, believing that he had denounced all sorts of people to Constantius. The last straw was when Georgius threatened to pull down a pagan temple dedicated to the pagan Genius of the City (see Chapter 9 for information on the Geniuses). A riot broke out, and Georgius was lynched. Other officials were murdered, and even the Christians put up with it because they hated Georgius, too. Julian was appalled but cooled the situation by doing no more than threatening severe punishments if anything else happened.

Julian's father was another Constantius, a half-brother of Constantine I, who was killed along with various other relatives as soon as Constantine died in 337. Julian was born in 332 and was educated by a eunuch called Mardonius, who taught Julian all about the old pagan gods and classical literature. It had a permanent effect on Julian. Julian had been made Caesar in 355 by his cousin Constantius II because he was one of the very few family members left.

Julian spent the next few years successfully campaigning on the Rhine frontier. He was popular with his troops and even lowered taxes in Gaul. Of course, this made Constantius II jealous. He ordered some of Julian's troops to come back, but they refused and promptly declared Julian to be the Augustus. Negotiations followed, but got nowhere. Constantius set out to deal with Julian, but died from a fever in 361 along the way.

Turning back the clock

Julian now had the Roman world to himself, and he immediately turned back the clock. Some of Constantius's men were executed, but the big change was that all anti-pagan laws were overthrown. He threw money at pagan cults and encouraged them to create the sort of organisation that had made the Christians so strong. He punished the Christians by taking away their privileges, especially the financial ones like tax breaks, and even stopped them from serving as teachers.

Julian wasn't alone in his interest in paganism. Quite a few people regarded schisms like the Arian row, the Donatist heresy, and Christian intolerance of paganism as cast-iron evidence that the Christian church was an unstable and dangerous innovation. Julian saw how his Christian cousins in the family of Constantine had committed all sorts of crimes and found it absurd that, however much a Christian sinned, all he had to do was apologise and be forgiven. Like many other traditionalists, Julian grew up believing that the old tolerance, old gods, and the old beliefs were the way to keep the Roman Empire together. He grew a beard, became interested in the Greeks, mysticism, and magic. But he was so keen on sacrificing animals that if he had lived longer it was said there would have been a shortage of cattle!

Julian in charge

When he wasn't knocking Christians, Julian was a decent emperor who tried to control inflation and reduce the vast heaving mass of imperial bureaucracy and hangers-on. He was particularly shocked when an extravagantly dressed court barber came to cut his hair. Julian discovered the barber received various food allowances and other perks of the job, and promptly threw all such attendants out of the palace. In the East, he paid for repairs to the city of Nicomedia, wrecked by an earthquake.

Julian's final great ambition was to defeat the Persians. He arrived in Antioch in 362 to start getting ready. In March 363, he set out with 65,000 men and soon reached the Persian capital of Ctesiphon. He decided to pull back and join the reserves. The Persians used the opportunity to harass Julian's army, and in one attack, he was wounded and died, probably from an infection.

As he died, Julian admitted Christianity had defeated him. *Vicisti Galilaee*, 'You have conquered, Oh Galilean [Christ]'.

History remembers Julian as the man who turned his back on Christianity, and so he is usually known as 'Julian the Apostate' (*apostasy* means to abandon Christianity). Some see him as a man who committed a crime by going back to paganism while others see him as a man of intellect and reason.

Julian the writer

Julian wrote more than any other Roman emperor. Some of his work survives, showing he was an accomplished writer in Greek. He wrote letters and speeches, as well as critiques of Christianity like his *Against the Galileans,* and a hymn to the Sun-God. He also composed a series of satirical biographies of former emperors. He installed a vast library in Constantinople, housing 120,000 books.

Chapter 21

The Barbarians Are Coming! The End of Rome

*T*his chapter is about the last act in the great drama that was the history of a city called Rome. When Julian II died in 363 (see Chapter 20), Rome was, if we accept the traditional date of its founding in 753 BC, 1,116 years old. The Roman world stretched from Egypt and the Middle East to the British Isles and the furthest tip of Spain. It had gone through colossal change, but it was still essentially 'Roman', and the city of Rome was its spiritual heart.

But for more than a century, few emperors had done much more than pass through Rome. They spent most of their time campaigning or basing themselves closer to the frontiers. They'd shown that emperors could be made and die in places other than Rome, because the only power that mattered was military loyalty to the man who led the soldiers, wherever he was.

Constantine I (307–337) had made the most symbolic, permanent change for centuries. He'd recognised that Constantinople was the key to holding on to the Roman Empire because Rome had become more of an idea, a state of mind, than a physical place. Constantine's contribution was enormous, but even he could do nothing about the mounting pressure on the frontiers from barbarians. Worse, his plan to divide the Empire between his sons led to more civil war and rebellions that only weakened the Roman world further. During the fourth century, the Western Roman Empire began to crumble under the barbarian onslaught, and in the end, Rome herself would fall.

A Rundown of Barbarians

The Romans called 'barbarians' anyone who wasn't like them – that is, civilised, living in cities, with a taste for art and architecture, literature, and polite living. These included the inhabitants of some of their own remoter provinces, like the Britons, but mostly they meant tribes beyond the Roman frontiers of the Rhine and Danube. Naturally, the Romans were biased. Some of the barbarians were highly accomplished and could create great things, but what matters here is what the Romans thought of them.

The Romans had a thoroughly ambivalent relationship with the barbarians. For centuries, they had been trying to civilise tribes along the frontiers and had hired tribal warriors to fight in the Roman army in the hope that they would be an effective force against other barbarians trying to invade. By the fourth century, many people in the Roman world – especially in the frontier provinces – had barbarians amongst their ancestors. But everyone in the Roman world was terrified by the thought of the tribes beyond who were on the march in search of new lands and who saw the Roman Empire as either a place they were determined to be part of or as a place to sack and pillage.

The important thing to remember is that, although we have names for some of these barbarians, they were in a constant state of flux, moving about from place to place, forming alliances one minute and starting wars the next, with no regular chain of command or line of succession. The information we have about them is sporadic and incomplete, not least because we rely on Roman sources, and they were often fairly confused about who they were dealing with. No wonder the Romans who ruled by a system looked at barbarians with horror: They had no idea what to do with them or how to handle them.

Following are some of the most important barbarians. Notice how they fought one another as well as the Romans, and at times even *joined* the Romans:

✔ **Goths:** The Goths were divided into two: the *Ostrogoths* ('Bright Goths') and the *Visigoths* ('Wise Goths'). The Ostrogoths lived where the Ukraine is today, and the Visigoths where Romania is, but they originally came from Scandinavia. By the mid-third century AD, the Goths were on the move towards the Roman Empire, pushed forward by the Alans, a tribe on the Asiatic steppes. In 251, the Gothic king Cniva killed the emperor Trajan Decius (refer to Chapter 19). Then they experimented with joining the Romans as confederates, but the Visigoths killed the emperor Valens in 378 (see the later section 'Valens in the East' for details of these events). In 410, the Visigoth chieftain Alaric sacked Rome, but after that, the Visigoths became confederates with what was left of the Western Roman Empire.

- **Vandals:** The Vandals were a German tribe who originated in Scandinavia and first turn up causing trouble under Marcus Aurelius (refer to Chapter 17) when they crossed the Danube. They fought their neighbours, the Visigoths, and the Romans as the mood took them. Apart from those who joined the Roman army (like Stilicho, discussed in the later section 'Sacking Rome'), they were really just a nuisance till 406 when, pushed forward by the Huns, they crossed the Rhine with the Alans and Suebi and laid waste parts of Gaul and Spain. The Vandals were ruled in Spain by their king Gunderic until his death in 428, after which they moved to North Africa.

- **Huns:** Outstanding horsemen, the Huns first turn up in south-east Europe in the late fourth century. They drove the Visigoths out, forcing them to invade the Roman Empire, and later pushed the Vandals into Italy and Gaul. The most significant leader was Attila (434–453), but after his death the Huns were largely a spent force.

- **Franks:** The Franks were a collection of German tribes on the Rhine who started attacking Gaul and Spain in the late third century. Julian II (refer to Chapter 20) pushed back a major invasion in 355, and until 425 the Franks served under the Romans as confederate troops, helping to prop up the frontiers. In about 425, one of the new leaders, Chlodio, started a new invasion. By the end of the fifth century, the Franks had largely taken over Gaul which now bears their name: France.

- **Alans:** The nomadic Alans lived in southern Russia, trapped behind the Caucasus. The Roman Empire frequently fought off their efforts to break out, but in the end it was pressure from the Huns that forced them out. The Alans finally reached Gaul in 406 and Spain in 409, where they met the Vandals, after which they simply merged with them and disappear from history.

- **Alamanni:** The Alamanni was a collection of Germanic tribes who crossed the Roman frontier in *c.* 260. They remained a constant problem thereafter, even though Julian managed a major defeat of them in 357 at Strasbourg. By the fifth century, they had settled in Alsace before being conquered by the Franks.

Going Downhill – Barbarians at the Door

After Julian II died in 363, the captain of his imperial guard, Jovian, was declared emperor. The first thing Jovian did was negotiate a humiliating peace to abandon all the Persian territory won since the time of Diocletian more than 60 years earlier. When Jovian later set out for Constantinople, he was suffocated in an extraordinary accident when a brazier was left burning in his bedroom. It was a bad time to lose an emperor. The barbarians were knocking at Rome's door, and the next 50 years were going to be decisive.

Breaking the Empire into East and West

Valentinian was in Julian and Jovian's army. Following Jovian's death, Valentinian was made emperor at Nicaea. For one month, he was sole ruler of the Roman world from West to East, and he was the last there ever was. After four weeks in the job, he made his brother Valens co-emperor. Valentinian took the West and Valens the East. The division was permanent. Now Rome's future depended on how the emperors dealt with the barbarians.

Valentinian 1 in the West (AD 364–375)

Valentinian based himself in Milan to be closer to the frontiers. He upgraded the soldiers' status, providing them with tools so that they could farm during quiet periods. That meant higher taxes, but he softened the blow by limiting tax breaks for the rich. Valentinian loathed the wealthy and privileged, especially anyone who thought himself above the law. So he was especially concerned with the lot of ordinary people and made every one of the regional Praetorian prefects appoint a Defender of the People to protect their interests. Valentinian was also determined that Christianity not oppress other religions. So in 371, he declared that all religions would be tolerated and no-one should be made to worship any god other than the one he wanted to.

It was just as well Valentinian was in Milan and improving the army. He was faced almost immediately with a dramatic series of barbarian invasions. First the Alamanni crossed the Rhine, only to be beaten off by the Roman armies. Then in 367, a 'barbarian conspiracy' burst across Britain and devastated it. Valentinian had to send Count Theodosius to rebuild Britain's defences and drive out the invaders. In 374, a swarm of Germans crossed the Danube. Valentinian fought back over the river, but when an embassy of Germans arrived to broker a deal the following year, they so infuriated Valentinian he burst a blood vessel and expired on the spot.

Valens in the East (AD 364–378)

Valens had his own problems. First he had to put down a rebellion by a soldier called Procopius who declared himself emperor. Next he crossed the Danube to head off a potential invasion by the Visigoths. Unlike Valentinian, Valens was a dedicated Arian and started a series of persecutions of orthodox Catholics.

Next the Visigoths and Ostrogoths invaded en masse, forced out of their own lands by the Huns of the North. They were allowed to settle in the Eastern Empire, but broke out into rebellion when they were oppressed and exploited. More German tribes crossed in behind them to add to the chaos.

The Aqueduct of Valens

The rebel Procopius had been supported by the city of Chalcedon. To punish Chalcedon, Valens destroyed their defences and used stones from the city's walls to build a mighty aqueduct in Constantinople. The aqueduct crossed a valley in the city between two hills, carrying water to a reservoir called the *Nymphaeum Majus* ('Great Fountain'). Eighty-six arches still stand in Istanbul today.

The Visigoths, having been pushed out of their territory by the Huns, became one of the most important threats to the Western Roman Empire. Once inside the Empire, they soon decided they wanted better land than the Balkans and headed for Italy.

Valens launched a hasty counter-attack and met the Visigoths at the Battle of Hadrianopolis in 378. Valens was catastrophically defeated and killed, and his body was never found.

At Last! Someone Who Knows What He's Doing: Theodosius I the Great (AD 379–395)

In 375, Valentinian's sons Gratian, then 15 years old, and Valentinian II, aged 4, succeeded their father in the West (the two were half-brothers). In 378, with Valens dead, too, Gratian had the wit to see he was completely unable to cope with the whole Empire because they were both too young. He chose Flavius Theodosius, the son of the Count Theodosius sent to Britain after the disaster in 367, and made him Augustus in the East. Flavius Theodosius had been born in Italica in Spain, the same place as two of the greatest of all Roman emperors, Trajan (98–117) and Hadrian (117–138), and in many ways he lived up to his predecessors' reputations. (To read about Trajan and Hadrian, two of the 'Five Good Emperors', go to Chapter 17.)

Theodosius might have been forgiven if he had turned down his new job. His father, Count Theodosius, had been executed in about 375 on a charge of treason, and he had retired to Spain. But he accepted Gratian's offer of a command on the Danube in 378 followed by promotion to being the Eastern Augustus in 379.

Hiring the Visigoths

Theodosius started out by fighting the Visigoths but found the job impossible. His solution was on the 'if you can't beat them, join them' principle, except that he had the Visigoths join the Romans rather than the other way round. The Visigoths were made into federal allies within the Roman Empire. The deal was that they were given land in Thrace and in return provided soldiers (*foederati*, 'federates') for the Roman army and farm workers for the Roman economy.

It was a clever idea, bringing desperately needed reinforcements for the army. But it established the idea of independent barbarian states within the Empire, and it cost a lot of money. Theodosius declared that anything and everything could be taxed. Just how much freedom had been lost is summed up by the fact that now a tenant who left his land could be prosecuted for 'stealing himself' away from his job. Even tax collectors could be whipped for failing to collect everything due.

Breaking it up again: Revolts

In the West, Gratian's government was really controlled by Ausonius who, as well as being a famous poet, was chief minister and also praetorian prefect over Gaul, Italy, and Africa. Gratian monitored the frontiers from his base at Trier.

In 383, disaster struck when a soldier in Britain called Magnus Maximus was declared emperor and promptly set out for the Continent to get rid of Gratian. Gratian was betrayed by his own troops, who went over to Magnus Maximus. One of them killed Gratian in 383. Maximus then added Gaul, Spain, and Africa to his new empire.

In 387, however, Magnus Maximus got too ambitious and invaded Italy. Valentinian II fled to Theodosius, who was really in charge of the Roman Empire. Theodosius marched west and destroyed Maximus at Poetovio in 388. Valentinian was made emperor of the West again, but in 392, he was throttled by his Frankish general Arbogastes.

Arbogastes wasn't stupid enough to make himself emperor; instead he found a puppet in the imperial court called Eugenius and declared him emperor, while Arbogastes controlled everything. Theodosius refused to accept a barbarian general ruling through a puppet and invaded Italy in 394, defeated Eugenius's army, and then executed Eugenius on 6 September 394. Arbogastes fled and committed suicide.

Death of Theodosius

Theodosius died four months later at Milan in January 395 from dropsy. His sons Arcadius (aged 18) and Honorius (aged 11) succeeded him. They'd already been made into Augusti. Arcadius (383–408) took the East and Honorius (393–423) the West. Being young, both were easily led by powerful men in their courts. Arcadius, controlled by a succession of Praetorian prefects, staggered on in the East until 408 when he was succeeded by his 7-year-old son Theodosius II. The real story (told in the next section), however, belongs to Honorius and his father-in-law, Stilicho.

Sacking Rome

Rome wasn't built in a day, so the saying (actually a twelfth-century French proverb) goes. It wasn't destroyed in a day, either. The end was humiliating and rather slow, but the key point is that, whereas Rome had once been the hub of the Roman world, now it was almost an irrelevance. Of course, it had tremendous symbolic importance, but in a practical sense it was a sideshow. One of the ironies is that it was the very barbarians the Romans had been trying to keep out who kept Rome going as long as it did.

Stilicho: Buying off the Visigoths

In 395 when Theodosius died, his son Honorius was only 11, so it's no great surprise that the real power lay with Honorius's Master of Soldiers and later father-in-law, a Vandal general called Flavius Stilicho.

Stilicho fought off a Visigoth invasion of Italy under Alaric in 402 at Pollentia (Pollenza), and then fought off an Ostrogoth invasion in 405 at Faesulae (Fiesole), but he was unable or unwilling to hold back the relentless Visigoths who now had their sights set on Italy. Stilicho kept letting them get away, because he had lurking ambitions to conquer the Eastern Roman Empire. His chief rival was Rufinus, one of Arcadius's officials.

In 406, a horde of Vandals and other tribes, including the Alamanni and Alans, crossed the Rhine and devastated Gaul. Stilicho did little or nothing to fight them off because he wanted to use his forces to attack the Eastern Empire. In the meantime, he agreed to hand over a fortune in gold to the Visigothic leader Alaric, one of the Visigoths that Theodosius I had allowed to settle in the Roman Empire, who was demanding to be bought off. That only gave rise to suspicions that Stilicho was using Alaric to help make his (Stilcho's) son emperor. His troops mutinied, and Stilicho was executed in 408.

During this period, the imperial court was in Ravenna in north-east Italy, protected by the swamps that surrounded the city. Ravenna's late Roman churches and other buildings are some of the most magnificent surviving monuments from antiquity. They owe their preservation largely to their remote location.

As if the battles with the Visigoths weren't enough, in 407, Britain produced yet another rebel, this time the so-called Constantine III whose sole appeal seems to have been his name, which reminded the troops of the great days of Constantine I. Spotting the chaos in Italy, Constantine III led another rebellious army into Gaul. By 409, he had seized Spain, too, but was overwhelmed by barbarians himself. He was defeated and killed by Honorius's army in 411, which was remarkable given what had been happening in Rome in the meantime (explained in the next section).

Alaric and the fall of Rome in 410

In 408, Stilicho was murdered in a palace coup when the story got around that he might be planning to make his own son emperor with Alaric's help. German troops in the Roman army, now terrified for themselves and their families, promptly joined Alaric and the Visigoths. With Stilicho dead, Alaric had no useful friends at the Roman court. He saw his chance and burst into Italy.

'And when Rome falls – the world' (Lord Byron)

The Visigoths surged down to Rome and started a series of three sieges of Rome:

- ✔ In 408, after Stilicho's execution, many families of federated barbarian troops were murdered. Those troops fled to Alaric, who set out to besiege Rome in September 408. Facing the prospect of starvation, the Senate ordered the payment of a huge ransom to persuade Alaric to withdraw. All Alaric wanted was official recognition by Honorius. When that didn't come Alaric besieged Rome again in 409.

- ✔ In 409, Alaric forced the Senate to come to terms. He put his own puppet emperor, Attalus, on the Roman throne. Attalus was hopeless, so Alaric deposed him and decided to open talks with Honorius in 410. Unfortunately, a rival Visigoth leader called Sarus used his influence to wreck the negotiations. Alaric decided that Honorius must have been responsible and set off to besiege Rome again as a punishment.

- ✔ In August 410, Alaric was let into Rome by traitors. For the first time since the Gauls sacked Rome in 390 BC (refer to Chapter 11), the city was captured by an enemy. Actually, the Visigoths did relatively little damage: They left churches alone and anyone taking refuge in them, for example. But they may well have burned down the Basilica Aemilia in the Forum, which was certainly destroyed about this time.

Galla Placidia's husbands

Galla Placidia married Alaric's successor, Ataulf, in 414. Honorius refused his consent, and his general Constantius drove Ataulf into Spain and had him murdered. Placidia was returned to the Romans by Ataulf's successor, Wallia. As a reward, he was allowed to set up a Visigothic state in Gaul.

In 417, Galla Placidia married the general Constantius. Their son Valentinian was born two years later. In 421, Constantius was made joint-emperor with Honorius but died later the same year. Things took an odd twist next when Honorius took a fancy to his half-sister Placidia. His public displays of 'affection' caused a public outcry and her fury, so she fled to Constantinople in 423, the same year as Honorius died.

The fall of Rome in 410 was a horrifically demoralising experience, not just for the Romans, but also for Roman citizens everywhere. It was, literally, like facing the end of the world.

Actually Alaric only stayed three days in Rome before heading off to southern Italy with Honorius's half-sister Galla Placidia. He died before he could start a planned invasion of Africa and was reputedly buried under a river (the river was diverted first so that the grave could be dug).

Abandoning Britain

The year 410 was generally a bad one. In addition to the fall of Rome, Britain was also abandoned. Honorius told the island province to take care of its own defences, though actually the frustrated Britons had already thrown out the Roman officials a year before. What few troops were left were withdrawn. The rebel Constantine III had taken most of what was left.

Staggering On

For the rest of the fifth century, barbarians from central and northern Europe steadily moved into the Roman Empire. The fact that independent barbarian states had been established within the Roman Empire anticipated the future.

During this time, the sitting Roman emperors were not always the ones who held the real power.

In the East, Theodosius II (402–450) was Augustus, but the real power was held by his sister Aelia Pulcheria (ruling as co-regent from 414). She stayed in power for the rest of her life and died in 453. A devout Christian, she took a vow of chastity to avoid being forced into marriage. Many of her decisions were affected by her Christianity; she had Theodosius send the Jews of Constantinople into exile, for example.

In the West, the struggle for power continued:

- **Johannes (423–425):** Honorius's secretary Johannes succeeded Honorius. The Eastern emperor, Theodosius II, sent an army to get rid of Johannes. A Roman general called Flavius Aetius had fetched an army of Huns to support Johannes, but they turned up too late. Galla Placidia had paid off his Huns and sent him to deal with the Visigoths and Franks in Gaul.

- **Valentinian III (425–455):** Galla Placidia's son Valentinian became Augustus of the West when they returned to Rome. Galla Placidia spent the next 12 years as regent in the West until she retired to building churches in Ravenna (she died in 450). The real power was then held by Aetius, the emperor's *Magister Militum* ('Master of the Soldiers'). There was no stopping the relentless disintegration of the Western Roman Empire. By 429, the Vandals under Gaiseric had crossed Gaul and Spain, and were conquering Africa, which they seized by 439. By 429, Aetius could do nothing about the Vandals in Africa. But he did manage to push back the Germans, suppress peasant revolts, and defeated the Burgundians.

Attila the Hun (ruled AD 434–453)

Everyone has heard of Attila the Hun. Here's the chance to find out what he did. Attila was brought up as a barbarian hostage at the court of the emperor Honorius. The idea was that he would grow up more sympathetic to the Romans, but it meant he also grew up knowing how the Roman world worked. In 432, Attila and his brother Bleda inherited control of the Huns from their uncle Ruga. They followed this up with an invasion of Persia, followed by assaults on the Roman Empire, crossing the Danube in 440 and sacking cities in Illyria. In 443, another invasion followed, climaxing in their siege of Constantinople which ended only because they hadn't any proper siege equipment to scale the walls. In 447, Attila attacked the Roman Empire again and defeated a Roman army in Moesia before fighting his way south to Thermopylae in Greece. Constantinople was saved because the damage of 443 had been repaired, but the Eastern Empire agreed to pay Attila off.

Meanwhile, the Huns had been supplying the Western Roman Empire with troops. In 450, the Eastern Empire stopped the cash payments to Attila. Valentinian III ordered his sister Honoria to marry a Roman whom she disliked, so Honoria sent her ring to Attila and begged for rescue. Attila took this as an offer of marriage and demanded half the Western Empire as his dowry. Valentinian III said no to Attila, so Attila the Hun invaded the West.

In 451, Flavius Aetius defeated Attila at the Battle of Maurica (also known as the Battle of Chalons), the only time Attila was ever defeated. Attila withdrew but invaded Italy again in 452. Aetius used his troops just to harass Attila who was busy sacking various cities and demanding Honoria's hand. Eventually a Roman embassy met up with Attila and persuaded him to give up. He pulled back and left. In 453, Attila died from a burst blood vessel. The Hun Empire collapsed as barbarian kingdoms often did because they were totally dependent on the prestige of particular leaders.

The murders of Aetius (AD 454) and Valentinian III (AD 455)

In 454, the general Flavius Aetius was murdered by Valentinian III for threatening the Emperor's court eunuch Heraclius and the powerful Petronius Maximus (twice prefect of Rome and twice praetorian prefect of Italy). This ended the life of one of the most important men in Roman history over the preceding 20 years. And this time it was actually the emperor who did the killing, stabbing Aetius. The story goes that, after the killing, someone told Valentinian 'with your left hand you have cut off your right hand', meaning that Valentinian had now ruined his chances of ruling properly.

Petronius Maximus assumed he would now become the top man at Valentinian's court, but the eunuch Heraclius told Valentinian this was a bad idea. In retaliation, Petronius hired two of Aetius's soldiers to avenge their master. In 455 they killed Heraclius and Valentinian.

Petronius Maximus was proclaimed emperor on 17 March 455 and married Valentinian III's reluctant widow, Licinia Eudoxia. But he lasted about 70 days because she sent a message to Gaiseric, the Vandal king in Africa. Gaiseric had his own designs on the imperial dynasty and had plans to marry his son Huneric to Valentinian and Eudoxia's daughter Eudocia.

When Petronius heard the Vandals were on their way from Africa to Rome, he panicked and fled. But before he could get out of Rome, a mob killed him. Gaiseric arrived and carted off both Eudoxia, Eudocia, and her sister Placidia the Younger to Carthage. They were later released, and Placidia the Younger still had a part to play in Rome's last act. (For another of Galla Placidia's legacies, see the sidebar on 'Buildings').

Valentinian III's death was a disaster for the West because it marked the end of a dynasty that could be traced back to Valentinian I and Valens, nearly a century earlier. For all its faults, the dynasty had managed some sort of central stability even though the power nearly always lay in the hands of men like Stilicho and Aetius, and the Western Empire had been steadily eroded by barbarian invasions.

Buildings

The fifth century might have been a time of increasing chaos, but some of the great surviving buildings of the Roman world date from this era. Santa Sabina in Rome, begun in 422, is an immaculate basilican church largely in its original state, with columns dividing a nave and aisles. Galla Placidia's elegant brick cross-shaped and barrel-vaulted tomb in Ravenna is one of the great sights of the city, and its interior preserves all its wall and ceiling mosaics.

The next few emperors and the rise of Ricimer

Following Valentinian III's death, a series of emperors claimed (or were persuaded to claim) the throne of the Western Roman Empire, which by that time didn't amount to much more than Italy. All had to deal with the *Magister Militum* Ricimer, a general of mixed Visigoth and Suebian descent who was the real power in the West between 455–472. Here's a quick rundown of the last Western Roman emperors:

- **Avitus (455–456):** The Visigothic king Theodoric II persuaded Avitus to take the throne. So crushed was the West that the new emperor resorted to stripping bronze from public buildings to pay the Goths in his army. It was too much for the Romans, who forced him to flee. He was later defeated and deposed by Ricimer, whom he had promoted.

- **Majorian (457–461):** Majorian, who had served under Aetius, followed Avitus. Majorian defeated the Vandals in Gaul, but thanks to treachery, his fleet, prepared in Spain to attack the Vandals in Africa, was destroyed before it left. Majorian was deposed and executed by the general Ricimer, who installed a puppet called Libius Severus.

- **Libius Severus aka Severus III (461–465):** The real power behind the throne was Ricimer. Practically nothing is known about Libius Severus as a result. It might have been Ricimer who killed him.

- **Anthemius (467–472):** Leo I (457–474), who was now the Eastern emperor, appointed Anthemius himself. Anthemius was Leo's son-in-law. He had been hoping to succeed Leo but accepted the Western throne. He reached it in 467 and was immediately proclaimed emperor; his daughter even married Ricimer. A joint West-East expedition to attack Gaiseric and the Vandals in Africa ended in disaster when Gaiseric routed the Roman fleet. Events in Gaul further complicated things: The

Visigothic kingdom had been taken over by Euric who murdered his brother Theodoric II and started planning to seize the whole of Gaul and separate it from the Roman Empire. Euric defeated a Roman army. Bad feelings between Ricimer and Anthemius followed, and Leo I sent a man called Olybrius to sort out the quarrel between the two. Ricimer, however, decided Anthemius was a lost cause and set Olybrius up as a rival emperor. Olybrius happened to be married to Valentinian III's daughter Placidia the Younger. Ricimer besieged Rome. Anthemius fled and disguised himself as a beggar but was found and executed. Ricimer died a few weeks later.

- **Olybrius (472):** Anicius Olybrius, a member of the senatorial Anicii family, died in 472 of natural causes only a few months after being made emperor. After Olybrius died, four months passed before anyone suitable to be made emperor could be found.

- **Glycerius, Count of the Domestics (473–474):** He was proclaimed emperor at Ravenna in 473 by the current Magister Militum, Gundobad (in post 472–473). Glycerius's sole achievement was to persuade invading Ostrogoths to invade Gaul instead of Italy.

- **Julius Nepos (474–475):** The Eastern emperor Leo I refused to recognise Glycerius and sent Julius Nepos, his wife's nephew, to be emperor instead. Gundobad abandoned Glycerius, who Nepos easily dethroned. Nepos took over in June 474. He lasted barely a year before the new Magister Militum, Orestes (475–476), led a rebellion.

The last emperor in the West: Romulus Augustus (AD 475–476)

Orestes, who led a rebellion against the emperor Julius Nepos, made his own 16-year-old son emperor. By some extraordinary coincidence, the boy's name, Romulus Augustus, recalled the founder of Rome and also its first emperor. Of course, Orestes was the real power, and he ruled what was left of the Western Empire though Romulus Augustus lasted for less than a year. In August 476, Orestes's barbarian troops rebelled, killed Orestes, and made their leader Odovacer king of Rome. Romulus Augustus was allowed to retire (he lived on till 511 at least).

It was 1,229 years since the traditional date of the founding of Rome and 985 years since the last king of Rome, Tarquinius Superbus, had been ejected.

Odovacer sent a senatorial deputation to Constantinople and declared the West no longer needed an emperor. Strictly speaking, Julius Nepos was, on paper, still the 'legitimate' emperor – if anyone could really be called that – but in Rome itself, the last one was Romulus Augustus.

The new Eastern emperor, Zeno (474–491), had no choice but to accept. He made Odovacer Magister Militum and incorporated the West into the East once more. Italy was now under the rule of Germanic kings, based at Ravenna, from 476.

Far from destroying Roman traditions, Odovacer (King of Italy 476–493) and Theodoric the Great of the Ostrogoths (King of Italy 493–526) went out of their way to preserve them. Odovacer continued the tradition of public entertainment in the Colosseum and even restored the ageing arena. Theodoric, despite fighting his way into power and murdering Odovacer, had been educated at Constantinople. He maintained Rome's institutions under a system of law and did a good job of looking civilised, while at the same time bringing in 200,000 Ostrogoths. But there's no getting away from the fact that the Roman Empire in the West was over, though Rome remained home to the pope.

What Became of Rome's Western Provinces

The history of Western Europe after the fifth century is an incredibly complicated one and the subject for another, enormous, book. But in essence what happened is that the provinces of the Roman West simply fragmented into a huge variety of kingdoms, chiefdoms, dukedoms, and fiefdoms, though that process was already well advanced by the time Rome fell in 410 and even more so by 476.

The crucial difference from the days of Roman rule is that these various states depended far more on the prestige of their individual rulers, rather than institutions of government, and they laid the foundations for what Europe is today: a collection of different countries with their own languages, traditions, and identities. Here's a rundown of what happened:

- ✔ **Italy:** In 536, the Byzantines retook Rome (see the section, 'In the East: The Byzantine Empire'), but in 568, Italy was conquered by the Germanic Lombard peoples. In 756, the Papal States, ruled by the pope from Rome, were created. By 800, Italy was part of Charlemagne's Holy Roman Empire. Italy remained part of the Holy Roman Empire, but power struggles developed with the Papal States and the independent Italian cities. By the fifteenth century, Italy was made up of the rival kingdoms of Milan, Florence, Venice, Naples, and the Papal States. It took until 1870 for Italy to become one nation again for the first time since 476.

- ✔ **Britain:** Britain had been cast off since 410. The Church remained in some control into the fifth century, but all the Roman towns, forts, villas, and infrastructure fell steadily into disrepair. It wasn't till after the Norman Conquest in the eleventh century that England became ruled as a single nation. Wales was added in the fourteenth century. In 1707, Scotland was joined to England and Wales to create Britain. Ironically, during the eighteenth and nineteenth centuries, Britain established a vast Empire that dwarfed the Roman Empire – remarkable for a place the Romans regarded as a barbaric nowhere on the edge of the world.

- ✔ **Gaul:** The Roman provinces of Gaul were overrun by Germanic tribes including the Franks. The Frankish king Clovis (481–511) founded a Christian Frankish kingdom with a capital at Paris, but it fell apart until Pepin the Short (751–768) reunified it and founded the Carolingian dynasty. His son Charlemagne created the Holy Roman Empire (refer to Chapter 1) in much of Western Europe.

- ✔ **Spain and Portugal:** In the fifth century, Visigoths and Vandals overran the Roman province of Hispania and created a Visigoth kingdom.

- ✔ **Germany:** Only small parts of Germany were ever in the Roman Empire. Charlemagne of the Franks took Germany into the Holy Roman Empire.

In the East: The Byzantine Empire

With the Western Empire no more, the East was left on its own. Historians call it the Byzantine Empire, from Constantinople's old name of Byzantium, though the name wasn't even coined until the sixteenth century AD, decades after it had ceased to exist. The Byzantines called themselves the Roman Empire because, as far as they were concerned, it was no more or less than a continuation of the old Empire. In fact, the East continued to behave as if Rome and the West were still a fully functioning part of the Roman world. The pope remained in Rome (in the West), and even Latin remained the everyday language of government in Constantinople despite the fact that most people in the East spoke and used Greek.

The truth is that the history of the Byzantine Empire is a whole massive story in its own right, but until someone writes *The Byzantine Empire For Dummies* the best I can offer is the briefest of brief summaries. It's a story with its ups and downs, but the relentless fact is that the Byzantine Empire spent most of its time getting smaller, weaker, and poorer. To the Byzantines' credit, it took another thousand years to come to an end.

Religious tensions

The Christian church had been good at producing reasons to split ever since Constantine I issued his Edict of Milan, which imposed religious toleration on the Roman Empire, back in 313 (refer to Chapter 20). Now was no different. Theodoric the Great, the Arian king of the West, was fairly inspired when it came to religious tolerance, but the Eastern church started to insist on everyone singing from the same hymn sheet, so to speak.

Theodora

Justinian's wife Theodora (*c.* 500–548) was a considerable individual and a major force behind Justinian's throne. She started life as an actress, performing nude on stage – a career regarded then as tantamount to prostitution. She became a Monophysite (she believed that Christ had a single Divine nature), gave up the stage, and went to Constantinople where she worked as a wool spinner. Justinian came across her and had his uncle Justin I change the law so that he could marry a former actress. After saving the day during the 532 riot, she encouraged Justinian's building programme in Constantinople and supported his legal and religious reforms, though she remained a Monophysite till her death from cancer in 548.

The problem came over Christ's 'nature': Did he have a single, Divine nature, or did he have a double nature, both Divine and Human (which was the Catholic Orthodox teaching)?

Monophysitism means the doctrine of 'one nature'. Monophysites believed that Christ had a single Divine nature. *Dyophysitism* means the doctrine of 'two natures'. Dyophysites believed Christ had a double nature: Divine and Human.

The Catholic Orthodox teaching (that Christ had a dual nature) held sway in Constantinople. They wanted everyone to follow suit so that the Western and Eastern churches could all operate together. The new Eastern emperor, Justin I (518–527), supported this policy. Theodoric in the West was upset by all this. Even so, Theodoric allowed Pope John I to visit Constantinople in 526, but was horrified to hear that John had been mobbed by enthusiastic crowds. When John returned to Rome, he was imprisoned and died, followed soon after by Theodoric. Theodoric's dynasty gradually crumbled over the years that followed, while Justinian I started a massive campaign to recover the West.

Justinian 1 (AD 527–565)

If he had lived 400 years earlier, Justinian (Justin I's nephew) would have been one of the great Roman emperors. As it was, he remains probably the most important Byzantine emperor and the one who did a huge amount to preserve much of what has survived from the Roman Empire.

Hopeful signs and good moves

One of the first things Justinian did was order the codification of Roman law (see Chapter 1). His *Digest* contains vast quantities of vital information about how the Roman world had run itself, while the various case histories preserve all sorts of examples of how Roman society had functioned in the days of the Republic and Principate.

Riot in Constantinople

Justinian wasn't a total success. The mob in Constantinople was divided into groups based on factions of circus supporters. They didn't like Justinian's ministers and rioted in 532, trying to set up another emperor and burning down large parts of the city. Justinian was only saved by his wife Theodora, who rallied the resistance, and by his generals Belisarius and Mundus, who attacked the crowd. Thousands were killed in the clampdown, but the destruction left room for great new building projects. This was when Constantius II's church of Santa Sophia was rebuilt into the form it survives in today.

With his general Belisarius (*c.* 505–565), Justinian started to recover the Roman Empire. In 530, Belisarius defeated the Persians, and in 532, the 'eternal peace' was signed. It didn't last, but the border was fortified. Between 533–534, Belisarius defeated the Vandals in Africa. By 535, he had taken Sicily, and by 536, he led a victorious entry into Rome. In 540, the Ostrogothic capital at Ravenna fell. Belisarius had to leave to fight the Persians again. He was back in Italy in 544 to fight the Ostrogoths, but by then Justinian had started to get suspicious of Belisarius's success. Another general, Narses, finally defeated the Ostrogoths and reorganised the government of Italy in 554. After that date, the Senate in Rome was never heard of again.

The Empire after Justinian

Justinian died in 565. He had ruled over more territory than any other emperor for 150 years. It's an irony that his reconquest of the West ended the rule of Germanic kings in Italy who'd been looking after Roman institutions. It wouldn't be until the reign of the Frankish king Charlemagne that anything remotely resembling a Roman Empire would return to the West.

As for the Eastern Empire, it lasted another 900 years. But Justinian had over-stretched its resources. Most of Italy was lost again by 570. Maurice Tiberius (582–602) managed to consolidate and hold on to the East, fighting back the Persians. But in the Balkans, he couldn't hold back the Slav and Avar peoples which severely dented the Byzantine Empire's prestige. More threats came from the Bulgars and the Muslims. In the eighth century, Leo III (717–741) and Constantine V (741–775) held back the Muslims. Constantine V also forced the Bulgars to a peace in 774. The coronation of Charlemagne as Holy Roman Emperor in the West in 800 by the pope was another blow to Byzantine prestige.

A Macedonian dynasty of emperors, started by Basil I (867–886), heralded in a time when the Byzantines recovered their position. Basil made great advances in the East towards the Euphrates and used conversion to integrate

The Muslims

On the death of the prophet Mohammed in 632, the Islamic religion was confined to part of Arabia. But within 25 years, Islam had spread across the Middle East and Egypt. By 750, Muslims controlled all of the former Roman provinces of North Africa, Sicily, and most of Spain. By the late eleventh century, the Muslims were in Asia Minor (Turkey) and controlled almost all of it by 1250. The Byzantine Empire spent this time fighting an increasingly futile rearguard action, and in the end, Byzantium itself would fall to the Muslim Ottomans in 1453.

Slavic peoples into the Empire. Nicephorus II (963–969) took Cyprus and Antioch, which had been out of Byzantine hands for three centuries. John I Tzimisces (969–976) defeated the Russian prince Svjatoslav and advanced into Palestine, garrisoning bases all the way. By 1025, the Byzantine Empire was made up of what is now: southern Italy, Croatia, Serbia, Bulgaria, Albania, Macedonia, Greece, Turkey, and Cyprus.

Thanks to his epileptic fits, Michael IV, the Paphlagonian (1034–1041), relied on his brother John the Eunuch to run the Empire. John was a ruthless tax collector and the Slavs rebelled. Michael defeated the rebels, but the effort killed him. Byzantine power, increasingly depending on buying in mercenaries, was declining steadily.

The Great Schism of 1054

Under Constantine IX (1042–1055), the East and West churches finally split. Pope Leo IX excommunicated the Byzantine Patriarch Michael Cerularius, who excommunicated the Roman delegates to Byzantium (a patriarch was the name given to the bishops of Rome, Alexandria, Antioch, Jerusalem, and Constantinople, the five chief sees of Christendom). The East and Western churches, now known as the Western Catholic Orthodox and the Eastern Orthodox churches respectively, came to a sort of accommodation in 1274 when Michael VIII (1261–1282) recognised the papacy in order to get support for a war against his enemy, Charles of Anjou. But the real differences remained. Both claimed to be the One Holy Catholic and Apostolic Church, and it wasn't until 1965 that the churches met and committed themselves to reconciliation, even though in the intervening centuries various members of the Eastern Orthodox Church had rejoined Rome and created the Eastern Catholic Church.

The toll of the Crusades

Under Constantine X (1059–1067), the Byzantine Empire suffered terrible setbacks but enjoyed a brief revival under Alexius I (1081–1118). The next problem came from the Crusaders. The Crusades were essentially armies that came from Western Europe to recapture the Holy Land from the control of non-Christians. That was the theory, but in practice a lot of the Crusaders were only really interested in fighting and looting. Here's a quick rundown of the four Crusades:

- ✔ **First Crusade of 1095–1099:** During this Crusade, the Crusaders recovered Jerusalem and it culminated in an alliance with the Holy Roman Empire of the Germans.

- ✔ **Second Crusade of 1144–1150:** The Western crusaders had their eyes on Byzantium itself. Although the Eastern Emperor Manuel I (1143–1180) was able to hold them at bay, in doing so, he allowed the Normans to plunder Greece. The Byzantines suffered a total defeat at the Battle of Myriocephalon against the Turks, supported by the German Empire under Frederick Barbarossa (1155–1190), who was now an enemy.

- ✔ **Third Crusade (1189–1192):** This Crusade is known primarily for one of the crusaders – Richard I of England (1189–1199) – and was intended to recapture the Holy Land from the Muslim warrior Saladin. It didn't, but an agreement was gained which allowed Christian pilgrims to visit Jerusalem.

- ✔ **Fourth Crusade (1201–1204):** This Crusade was a catastrophe for Constantinople. Funded by the Venetians, the original plan was to invade Egypt to recover holy places, but the Venetians were determined to cash in on their investment and ordered the crusaders to sack Constantinople. And that's exactly what they did. The Byzantines fled, and the crusaders established a Latin dynasty of emperors in Byzantium.

The fall of Byzantium

Even though the Byzantines recaptured Constantinople after the Fourth Crusade, the last 250 years of the Byzantine Empire was a sorry tale of trying to fend off various would-be invaders. The last gasp at restoring the Empire came in 1261 when Michael VIII (1261–1282) retook Constantinople. His biggest threat came from the Norman Charles of Anjou, King of Sicily, who was rounding up an alliance to attack the new Byzantium. Michael agreed to recognise the pope. This made the Byzantines furious (see the earlier section 'The Great Schism of 1054'), but it did mean Pope Gregory X persuaded Charles of Anjou not to attack. Charles was overthrown in 1282.

It really was the last gasp. By the mid-1300s, all the Byzantines could do was watch what was left of their Empire disappear.

The end of the ancient world

The last Byzantine emperor was Constantine XI (1448–1453). It was his bad luck to preside over the end. The Sultan Muhammed II started his assault on Constantinople on 7 April 1453. Constantine heroically held out for seven weeks, but the city fell to a new discovery the great Roman Generals of the remote past, like Scipio Africanus and Caesar, or Emperors like Augustus and Vespasian, could never have dreamed of: gunpowder. The ancient world had met the modern world. Cannon fire breached the walls and, appropriately enough, Constantine died with a sword in his hand. His Empire consisted of little more than the city of Byzantium itself.

The Roman Empire, in its last guise as the Byzantine Empire, had finally fallen, 2,206 years after the legendary founding of Rome itself.

Part VI
The Part of Tens

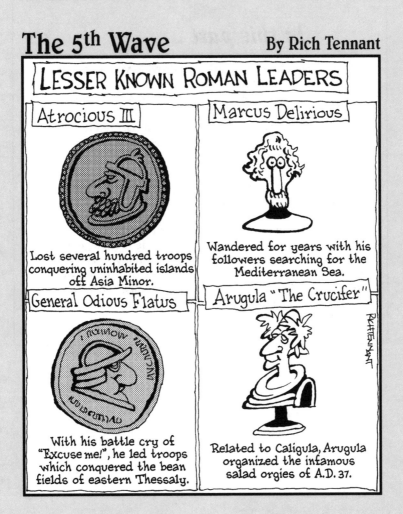

The 5th Wave — By Rich Tennant

LESSER KNOWN ROMAN LEADERS

Atrocious III
Lost several hundred troops conquering uninhabited islands off Asia Minor.

Marcus Delirious
Wandered for years with his followers searching for the Mediterranean Sea.

General Odious Flatus
With his battle cry of "Excuse me!", he led troops which conquered the bean fields of eastern Thessaly.

Arugula "The Crucifer"
Related to Caligula, Arugula organized the infamous salad orgies of A.D. 37.

In this part . . .

The idea behind this part is to provide you with meaty but digestibly-sized chunks of facts about the key events, people, and places that made Roman history happen the way it did. I'll freely admit it's a purely personal selection, and if someone else had written this book, he or she might have chosen a different list, but hopefully not that different!

What you'll find here is a list of ten crucial moments in Roman history when everything changed – for better or worse; ten Romans who were good or interesting people; ten award-winning villains; as well as ten anti-Romans whose opposition to Roman power made them legendary in their own time and afterwards. And finally, because I know you'll be itching to go out and see the Roman world for yourself, I've listed my top ten (actually, I've sneaked an extra one in, so make that eleven) places to start looking.

Chapter 22

Ten Turning Points in Roman History

In This Chapter

▶ Key events that changed the shape of the Roman world

▶ Wars, conquest, and social revolutions

*T*urning points are those moments in history when everything changes for a civilisation forever. The significance isn't always obvious at the time, but it is to historians, and that included Roman historians who could look back and see some of the decisive moments in Rome's past.

Kicking out the Kings (509 BC)

When the Romans turfed out Tarquinius Superbus in 509 BC, they established a principle that would last for centuries: no more kings. The Roman Republic that was created as a result defined the whole Roman system for the next five centuries, and even when Augustus became emperor, he had to make it look as though he'd done so within the Republican system. You can find the chucking out of the kings in Chapter 10, and how Augustus solved the problem of being a monarch without looking like one in Chapter 15.

Creating the Twelve Tables (450 BC)

When the plebs forced the patricians into accepting a written code of law that protected the plebs' interests, the Romans created something they'd all be immensely proud of in the long run: the idea of the rule of law, a principle most modern countries have inherited. For the Romans, it was also the opening skirmish in the Conflict of the Orders, which saw the plebs exert more and more political control through their tribunes. You'll find the Conflict of the Orders at the end of Chapter 10 and its next phase in Chapter 11.

Winning the Second Punic War (218–202 BC)

Rome's rivalry with Carthage was the greatest conflict of the age. The First Punic War (covered in Chapter 12) had nearly put pay to Carthage's ambitions and put Rome on the map. In the Second Punic War, the struggle became truly international with much higher stakes. The catastrophic defeats at Lake Trasimene (217 BC) and Cannae (216 BC) ought to have wiped Rome off the map. The fact that Rome held onto her allies, came back for more, and ended up defeating Carthage at Zama in 202 BC convinced Rome even more of her destiny and showed the world what she was capable of. The Second Punic War is discussed in Chapter 12.

The year 146 BC

This is a critical year for the Romans because it settled them as the supreme power in the Mediterranean. It marked the permanent destruction of Carthage as a rival, wiped out in a bitter and petty war of revenge that did Rome no great credit but showed what she could do if she wanted. The year also saw the end of Greece as an independent nation of any sort. With so much power, the Romans now did what so many successful states do: started falling apart as men squabbled over the riches. For more than a century, Rome was torn apart in a series of social struggles and the age of the imperators. Chapters 12 and 13 cover the climactic events that led to 146 BC, and Part III picks up what happened afterwards.

Augustus's settlements with the Senate in 27 and 19 BC

Augustus's proudest boast was that he had restored the Roman Republic. He gave up all his powers so that the Senate could give them back to him. It was the greatest political spin in Roman history and one of the greatest in all world history. Augustus clearly was a de facto emperor, but he created the brilliant fiction that he merely held positions within the Republican system and defined how Roman emperors ruled for centuries to come. The genius was that by doing this, Augustus made it possible for the Republic to survive at all. Turn to Chapter 16 to find out how he did it.

Breaking the link between the emperor and Rome (AD 68–69)

The historian Tacitus spotted the key significance of the Civil War of 68–69: Emperors did not have to be made at Rome. They could declare themselves anywhere so long as they had an army to back them. From then on, the Roman Empire was always going to fall prey to ambitious men who had the men and resources at their disposal. It's frankly amazing, then, that the next 120 years were so stable, but from the death of Commodus in 192, the revelation of 68–69 came back to define much of the rest of Roman history. The civil war of 68–69 is discussed in Chapter 16, and the chaos of 192 and later starts in Chapter 18.

Ending the tradition of conquest (AD 117–138)

Hadrian was one of Rome's most interesting emperors. An aesthete, architect, and inveterate traveller, he created some of the Roman Empire's most remarkable buildings, like the Pantheon in Rome. But he made a key decision that flew in the face of everything the Empire stood for and was based on: Realising that the Empire was too big to manage and defend itself, he pulled back and fortified the frontiers and said 'that's that'. From his reign on, the Roman Empire trod water and then went on the defensive, fighting sometimes desperately for its very existence. Hadrian comes in Chapter 17.

Dividing the Roman world (AD 284–305)

Diocletian was the last in a line of soldier emperors in the third century. But unlike so many of his predecessors, he knew the Roman Empire was going to have to change to face the challenges of the future. It had grown too big and had too many border problems for one man to rule. So Diocletian split the Empire in two: East and West. At the time, the devastating significance wasn't too obvious, but he'd created the division down which the Empire would split in the fifth century. The West would crumble, while the East would go on for another thousand years. Diocletian's radical step comes in Chapter 20.

The Edict of Milan (AD 313)

Rome's destiny had been 'preordained' by the pagan gods – a story which plays a central part in Virgil's *Aeneid* – yet the genius of Constantine I (AD 307–337) was to realise that Christianity might help to hold the Empire together. His Edict of Milan started the process that turned the Roman Empire into a Christian state by declaring that all religions would be tolerated – it was a way of letting the Christians in. The change brought its own problems, but it took Roman history into a completely new direction and defined not just the fourth century but the whole nature of power and the identity of the Eastern Roman Empire, which would last for another 1,100 years. See Chapter 20 for how he did it.

The fall of Rome (AD 410)

When Rome fell to Alaric the Goth in 410, the psychological impact was colossal. It's almost impossible for us to imagine just how devastating this event was. It wasn't just the practical implications of an assault on a city, but the mind-numbing sense that the whole foundation of the known world had turned out to be so vulnerable. The Roman world had been unnerved by decades of warfare, but once Rome fell, even though the end wouldn't come until 476, everyone no doubt knew that nothing would ever be the same again. Chapter 21 tells the story.

Chapter 23

Ten Interesting and Occasionally Good Romans

. . . .

In This Chapter

▶ Men who set the standards for being Romans

▶ Dictators, emperors, politicians, farmers, and ordinary soldiers

. . . .

*I*n every historical era, a few people really stand out from the rest for help-ing define the age they lived in. They don't always have to be the great movers and shakers, but they're usually somehow in the centre of events.

Cincinnatus (519–438 BC)

Lucius Quinctius Cincinnatus is one of the great traditional figures of the Roman Republic. Cincinnatus was a consul in 460 BC, but in 458 BC, while ploughing his fields, he was made dictator and placed in charge of the war against the Volsci and Aequi. Cincinnatus did the job in just 16 days, after which he laid down his command and went back to the plough. In 439 BC, he was made dictator again, despite being 80 years old, to put down a conspir-acy. He gave up the post again after 21 days and turned down any rewards. Cincinnatus sums up the Roman Republican ideal – a man of honour and leadership who wanted nothing more than the chance to plough his fields. The American city of Cincinnati in Ohio is named after him.

Scipio Africanus the Elder (236–185 BC)

Publius Cornelius Scipio Africanus was the great hero of the Second Punic War. In fact, the war had been the backdrop to the whole of his early life. Not only was he at Cannae in 216 BC, but in 211, he heard his father and uncle had been killed in the fighting in Spain. Catapulted to being head of his family at only 24, Scipio was given the unprecedented award of proconsular *imperium* at so young an age and was sent off to avenge his family. His triumphant defeat of the Carthaginians in Spain by 206 BC and then in Africa at Zama in 202 BC made him a great Roman hero. Ruined eventually by corruption charges brought by Cato (see the later section on Cato), Scipio ended up dying in exile. But Scipio went down in Roman lore as a heroic Roman of great honour and was revered for it. His family later included Scipio Aemilianus Africanus the Younger and the Gracchi brothers, whom you can read about in Chapter 14.

Marcus Sergius (late third century BC)

Marcus Sergius was said by some to have been the bravest Roman who ever lived. By the time of the Second Punic War, he'd already been wounded 23 times, including losing his right hand, and fought four battles using his left hand only. He ended up apparently unable to use his feet or his remaining hand, presumably temporarily. Hannibal captured him twice, but he escaped both times despite being banged up in chains for 20 months. Plans were made to disqualify him from the praetorship for being disabled, but Sergius was persistent and was elected anyway. He had an iron right hand made for himself and proceeded to raise the siege of Cremona in 200 BC during the war against the Cisalpine Gauls, and captured 12 enemy camps. Ironically for such a brave man and an inspiration to the Romans, his great-grandson was the arch-villain Sergius Catilinus (more about him in Chapter 24).

Marcus Porcius Cato (234–149 BC)

Cato (sometimes called 'Cato the Elder') was admired in Roman history as the ultimate stickler for traditional Roman virtues. He fought in the Second Punic War (covered in Chapter 12) while still only 17. Cato earned a reputation for ignoring any temptations to indulge himself. He stuck to water and simple meals. Cato hated luxury, decadence, and corruption of any sort and was even disgusted by Greek art, believing it would undermine the great Roman tradition of rural simplicity. You can read about his influential farmer's manual which celebrated the Roman myth of rural bliss and purity in Chapter 4. His moral strictness echoed down later generations, and Virgil even made him one of the judges of hell in the *Aeneid*. Cato sounds like a pretty dreadful person, and indeed it was Cato who called for Carthage's final destruction (described in Chapter 13). But there's no getting away from the fact that Cato summed up what some thought Rome stood for and the way Rome should have stayed.

Gaius Gracchus (d. 121 BC)

Gaius Gracchus (see Chapter 14) was a remarkable man who, like his brother Tiberius, knew that Rome couldn't possibly survive so long as the senatorial aristocracy tried to keep all Rome's wealth to themselves. Unlike Tiberius though, Gaius Gracchus was far more organised and had a much bigger programme of reform. Gaius Gracchus also understood that Rome's Italian allies needed to be rewarded with citizenship and Latin status. His legal measures to recover the liberty of the people earned him the loathing of the aristocracy, and like his brother, he paid with his life. But the Gracchi became martyrs in the cause of political reform, and the Senate had no choice but to accept a lot of what they'd done. Their violent deaths set the tone for Republican politics that lasted until nearly a century later when Augustus took power.

Julius Caesar (102–44 BC)

Caesar deserves his place in this list because he's the most famous Roman who ever lived. Let's get one thing straight: Caesar wasn't an emperor, though he's sometimes described as if he was. But he was a consummate politician who worked the mob like a genius and manipulated his rivals. He was also one of Rome's greatest generals and a brilliant leader of men. A relentless self-publicist, Caesar always had an eye on posterity and left behind his own account of some of these activities. In the end he went too far for the reactionaries who thought he was turning himself into a king. They might have killed him but all they did was cement Caesar's place in history and created a crisis which led to Caesar's nephew Augustus establishing a monarchy. Caesar himself has echoed down the ages, influencing every great military leader ever since.

Augustus (63 BC–AD 14)

Augustus is an obvious choice, but I'm making no apologies for including him here. He was no great general, but he was the winner at the end of all the ghastly civil wars of the first century BC, and instead of using his power to make himself fantastically rich and turn himself into a despot, he created the principate (the Empire disguised as a restored Republic with himself as 'first citizen' – see Chapter 16). What he also achieved was the image of the emperor himself, a kind of universal ageless identity that linked every part of the Roman world together under a single umbrella. Few of his successors were his equal in any way, and it was Rome's great and good fortune that he was the man he was. Augustus wasn't perfect by any means, but considering how some of his successors behaved, he was about as good as a Roman emperor could be.

Pliny the Elder (AD 23–79)

I love Pliny the Elder. He was fascinated by the world around him and, thank goodness, he wrote it all down for his own time and for ours. His *Natural History* is packed from end to end with what passed for Roman science, together with an endless parade of anecdotes, half-baked theories, historical facts, and yarns. It's completely absorbing, as well as amusing. Pliny's total fascination with what made the world tick makes him truly one of the first 'moderns' – if he'd lived centuries later he'd have been one of the geniuses of the Renaissance or a Victorian scientist, and he'd have got on like a house on fire with Thomas Jefferson. It's only appropriate he died when he went to view the eruption of Vesuvius at first hand in AD 79. What a truly fascinating man he must have been.

Carausius (reigned AD 286–293)

Including Carausius is blatant favouritism on my part. I'm intrigued by this man who emerged from total obscurity on the North Sea coast of Belgium to command the Roman fleet sent to clear out pirates. He ended up declaring himself emperor in Britain and part of Gaul, to the fury of Diocletian and Maximian. Simultaneously a rebel and a patriot, his revolt was just as much about frustration at the destruction caused to Rome's reputation by generations of civil war. Carausius resurrected ancient Roman traditions, myths, and literature, and declared his regime to be a brand new, restored Roman Empire. His front was breathtaking, but he's also a symbol of Rome's extraordinary impact on communities all round her Empire. He was the ultimate product of Augustus's branding and anticipated the medieval imitation Roman emperors because the Roman world had created the template for power.

Sextus Valerius Genialis (late first century AD)

Sextus Valerius Genialis was a nobody, but I'm including him because he sums up the Roman Empire. The only thing that survives of this man is his tombstone. It tells us he came from Frisia, just beyond the Rhine frontier. Genialis joined the Roman army and served for 20 years, dying at the age of 40 while on campaign in Britain in the late first century AD with a wing of cavalry from Thrace in northern Greece. His *tria nomina* (see Chapter 2 for Roman naming practices) shows that, unusually for an auxiliary, he hadn't had to wait until retirement to become a Roman citizen and was probably awarded it while in service. His name is totally generically Roman, blurring his own ethnic identity into a Roman one. Without the mention of Frisia, we'd otherwise have no idea at all where Genialis came from. Genialis is a symbol of untold millions of other men from places hundreds of miles from Rome, a city he probably never even saw, whose greatest ambition in life was to become a Roman. The fact that they wanted to and were allowed to is one of the reasons the Roman Empire became so powerful.

Chapter 24

Ten (Mostly) Bad Romans

. . . .

In This Chapter

▶ Men who didn't live up to Rome's great ideals

▶ Lunatics, thugs, and crooks

. . . .

*L*ike all the best history, Roman history is packed with villains. Villains make for great stories, and the Romans revelled in making sure none of their worst offenders went forgotten. I've picked ten here, but I can promise you I could have picked out ten times as many and still had room for more.

Tarquinius Superbus (535–509 BC)

In the annals of Roman history, Tarquinius Superbus (see Chapter 10) went down as one of the greatest villains of all time. Not only was he an Etruscan, but he'd only become king by arranging the murder of his father-in-law. He was called *Superbus* because of his pride and insolence (*superbus* means 'arrogant, overbearing'). He ignored the Senate and the public assemblies, so he ended up being hated by both. It was said that many of the citizens forced to work on his public sewer system tried to commit suicide, they were so exhausted. Tarquinius crucified the bodies of those suicides so that they could be eaten by animals. He emptied the treasury. When his son Sextus committed the Rape of Lucretia, it was the last straw for the Roman people. When Tarquinius was thrown out, it was the end of the rule of kings for good.

Coriolanus (527–490 BC)

Caius Marcius was the hero of the Battle of Lake Regillus in 496 BC in the war with the Latin League (refer to Chapter 11). He'd killed one of the enemy soldiers who was going to kill a wounded Roman. He took part in a later siege of the town of Corioli, which belonged to the Latin Volscian tribe. The Volscians came out to attack the Romans, but Marcius led a very small force and pushed them back into Corioli. For this he was given the name Coriolanus. But Coriolanus was a patrician and the plebs resented his attitude – he even tried to hold back a grain handout until the plebs agreed to give up their tribunes. He was forced to leave Rome and amazingly joined the Volscians and led their assault on Rome. This was regarded as the most scandalous and outrageous betrayal imaginable, guaranteeing his infamy. He only pulled back when his wife and mother came out of Rome to ask him to. One day William Shakespeare used the story for one of his most famous plays.

Sulla (138–78 BC)

Sulla (see Chapter 14) went down in history as the man who marched on, and captured, Rome. For that, he was damned to all eternity in Roman history. One of the men responsible for the fall of the Roman Republic, he rose to fame and power as the arch-rival of the general Gaius Marius (also in Chapter 14) and justified taking Rome because it was in the grip of mob rule led by Marius. Sulla was totally ruthless in his annihilation of his enemies, but it's a mark of the age that the relative order he imposed meant he was appointed dictator. Roman historians remembered his rule as a terrible time of proscriptions, arbitrary execution, banishment, and confiscations. No wonder the historian Appian (a Greek who wrote in the early second century AD) called his rule an 'absolute tyranny' of force and violence.

Sergius Catilinus (d. 63 BC)

Lucius Sergius Catilinus was one of Sulla's (see the preceding section) lieutenants, so perhaps it's not surprising he was such a bloodthirsty thug. In every sense a product of the age, Catilinus divorced his wife and married an heiress to underwrite his political ambitions. As a provincial governor, he extorted money and disqualified himself from becoming consul when placed under investigation. His conspiracy (see Chapter 14) was his solution to his money troubles and his thirst for power. He was damned by Cicero in famous speeches in which Cicero condemned Catilinus for being the kind of crook who needed to be driven out if the Roman Republic wasn't to be overrun with men like him.

Gaius Verres (c. 109–c. 43 BC)

Verres had an appalling reputation for milking dry the provinces he was sent to govern. Verres seized inheritances, passed laws to take money off farmers, took bribes to let guilty men off, and even – and this was considered the worst of all his crimes – tortured and executed Roman citizens as if they were slaves. He was absolutely the worst kind of Roman administrator imaginable, because men like him could wipe out Rome's claim she was acting for the good of the places she conquered. In 70 BC, the lawyer Cicero (refer to Chapter 14) was responsible for the prosecution of Verres on charges of extortion. Despite attempts by Verres and his associates to bribe their way to freedom, the evidence was overwhelming. So before the trial ended, Verres exiled himself and was then made an outlaw together with punitive fines. He was executed in about 43 BC by Mark Antony.

Caligula (reigned AD 37–41)

Caligula's villainy is one of the most priceless stories of the days of the Roman Empire. But let's face it, the odds were stacked against him. He was only the third emperor and had to follow in the footsteps of Augustus and all his achievements, and then the miserable Tiberius who at least had a track record as a war hero. Caligula had none of these things to offer the Roman people, and he was totally out of his depth. Add to that the fact that he seems to have become seriously ill, and it was a recipe for disaster. The rest of his reign was a cycle of manic self-delusion, perversion, crazed indulgence, and merciless brutality. The incredible thing is that the brand-new institution of the principate (the rule by an emperor, see Chapter 16) survived this devastating body-blow.

Nero (reigned AD 54–68)

Nero, the last of the Julio-Claudians, is more of a comical figure, but he was a gift to the historians Suetonius and Tacitus who positively revelled in telling the tale of this absurd posturing youth. Convinced of his own great artistic talents, Nero's adult life (once he had done away with his mother Agrippina) was a reckless cavalcade of self-indulgence, violence, narcissism, and eccentric extravagance that included building himself a vast sprawling palace in Rome and performing in Greece. No wonder the tales of his reign made him a byword for tyranny in later ages.

Commodus (reigned AD 180–192)

Commodus earns his place in this list because he was the emperor who brought to an end the Age of the Five Good Emperors. From 96–180 (see Chapter 17), the Roman Empire and most of the free people who lived in it enjoyed an amazing period of affluence and stability. It all went wrong because Commodus was Marcus Aurelius's son but wasn't up to ruling (all the other emperors had had no sons, so the best man for the job had been chosen instead). Commodus was a weak-minded fool who handed over power to corrupt officials and spent his time performing in the arena. It was a tragedy for Rome, because his violent death was inevitable and it heralded in a century of intermittent civil war and a succession of soldier emperors.

Didius Julianus (reigned AD 193)

Frankly, from Commodus's reign on, I'm spoilt for choice for bad Romans, but I've chosen one of his immediate successors. What marks Didius Julianus out is that, unlike all previous emperors, he was out for himself and his family and nothing else. He didn't even have an army of supporters. All he had was his ambitious wife Manlia Scantilla and daughter Didia Clara. In early 193, he offered 25,000 sesterces per soldier if they'd make him emperor, to the disgust of everyone. A call went out for revenge, and as a result, the Roman Empire exploded into civil war as the rival avengers fought it out for supreme control (refer to Chapter 18). Didius Julianus had taken the Empire to a new low – ironically he never paid the soldiers and was murdered after two months.

Caracalla (reigned AD 211–217)

When Septimius Severus made Caracalla and his brother Geta joint emperors and his heirs, the idea was to establish a new imperial dynasty. How wrong can a man be? Once Severus died in 211, Caracalla let rip. The brothers fell out, and Caracalla murdered Geta and his supporters, and his own wife. The rest of Caracalla's short and brutal reign was a reckless cycle of murder and intrigue as he pursued his obsessive belief that he was a reincarnation of Alexander the Great. No wonder he was murdered himself. His short, thuggish reign was the first of many similar ones that followed over the next century, and the sad truth is that he really helped the set the pace.

Elagabalus (reigned AD 218–222)

I doubt if Augustus would have bothered with establishing himself as emperor if he'd known who'd come along 200 years after his death. Elagabalus, born Varius Avitus Bassianus, was the victim of his mother's ambitions (Chapter 19). But he compounded that with his own obsessive sexual perversions, which included marrying a vestal virgin. That outraged the Romans who were equally horrified by his Sun-God cult which he celebrated by building a massive temple on the Palatine hill in Rome to their disgust. What matters, though, is that Elagabalus had absolutely no idea what being a Roman emperor meant apart from an opportunity to indulge himself with complete and utter indifference to the dignity of the position he held, the needs of imperial government, or even a sense of honour and respect. He outraged Rome and the Empire, making sure he died a violent death.

Chapter 25

Ten of Rome's Greatest Enemies

In This Chapter

▶ Men, women, and tribes who hated Rome and everything she stood for

▶ Wars, rebellions, double-crossing, and feminine wiles

*T*his motley collection of characters all in their own way resisted the Romans. In a way, the very fact that they did as they did was a recognition of Rome's power. If any one of them had succeeded, the history of the Roman Empire would have been very different. There's no doubt this is only a selection of Rome's greatest enemies. Like all major powers, Rome spent most of its existence facing opposition who viewed Rome with a mixture of awe, envy, and loathing.

Hannibal (247–182 BC)

The prize for Rome's ultimate bogeyman goes to Hannibal of Carthage. His father Hamilcar made him swear lifelong hatred of the Romans, and his campaigning in Spain guaranteed Rome would go to war. Hannibal's greatest years were during the Second Punic War (218–202 BC) when he led his army in an epic and legendary march across the Alps into Italy where he defeated the Romans at Trasimene and Cannae. He survived the war and remained in power in Carthage, but that only gave Rome the excuse to suspect what he was up to. He ended up fleeing to Antiochus III, but after Rome defeated Antiochus, too, Hannibal committed suicide. It was an ignominious end for a brilliant soldier whose fame and notoriety was so great that Carthage remained Rome's nightmare, leading ultimately to the vicious and gratuitous Third Punic War. To read more about Hannibal, go to Chapter 13.

Antiochus III (242–187 BC)

Antiochus III 'the Great' of Syria succeeded his father Seleucus II in 223 BC, whose reign had been a series of misfortunes, including defeat by Egypt and by the Parthians. Antiochus was determined to rebuild the Seleucid kingdom of Syria and, by 206 BC, had taken Armenia and also brought Parthia under his control. The problem for any expansionist monarch like Antiochus is that coming up against Rome was almost inevitable. So his plan to divide up Egypt's possessions with Philip V just put Rome on her guard, and when he invaded Thrace and then Greece, war ensured. It was probably Hannibal who urged Antiochus on to provoke Rome into war and also suggested that Antiochus invade Italy. Unfortunately for both of them, Antiochus was defeated at Thermopylae and Magnesia, as well as at sea, and the peace he was forced into in 188 BC destroyed the Seleucids' chances of being a force to be reckoned with in the Mediterranean. Antiochus was killed in 187 BC while trying to seize the temple treasure of the eastern kingdom of Susiana so that he could pay the annual fine to Rome. You'll find more about Antiochus's antics in Chapter 13.

Mithridates VI, King of Pontus (120–63 BC)

Rome's most relentless opponent in the East, Mithridates, was an admirer of Alexander the Great. When Mithridates V of Pontus (in Asia Minor) was murdered at Sinope, probably by his wife Laodice, Mithridates VI fled and had to hide out until he'd gathered the resources to come back. Mithridates captured Sinope, killed his brother, and slapped his mother into prison and took over the kingdom. He carried on his father's work of expanding the kingdom, but he came up against Rome when he tried his luck in Cappadocia and war broke out. Unfortunately for the Romans, ripping off provincials made Mithridates a popular alternative – when the Romans got it wrong, they often created their own enemies. Mithridates was defeated by Sulla in 85 and thrown out of Greece, but by 81 was fighting the Romans again. War broke out once more in 74 when Rome tried to take Bithynia and lasted till 63 BC when Mithridates's own oppressive treatment of his subjects generated a rebellion led by his own son Pharnaces. He was killed by a guard.

Spartacus (fl. 73–71 BC)

Spartacus was a Thracian slave who ended up in a gladiator school at Capua. He was educated and physically powerful. The revolt broke out thanks to the cruelty of the owner *(lanista)* of the school, Lentulus Batiatus, and Spartacus was elected one of the leaders. The slaves ran riot through Italy, defeating several Roman armies, one after another. But Spartacus found it impossible to persuade the slaves to flee Italy because they were more interested in pillage. He was finally cornered by Marcus Licinius Crassus in 71 BC and totally defeated, being killed then or amongst the survivors who were crucified. Pompey raced back from Spain to join in the hunt, which gave him the perfect excuse to keep his army together and also gain even more credit than he already had for protecting Rome.

The epic movie *Spartacus* (1960), starring Kirk Douglas as the rebel slave, Laurence Olivier as Crassus, and Peter Ustinov as Batiatus, is not only one of the greatest motion pictures set in the ancient world but also fairly authentic to the story and setting.

Cleopatra VII of Egypt (69–31 BC)

Unlike the other enemies of Rome in this list, Cleopatra played the Romans for fools rather than fighting them. She understood the Romans had colossal power and that the best thing was to harness it to her own interests. Celebrated for her looks and intelligence, Cleopatra made the most of them to beguile Julius Caesar and then Mark Antony. Caesar had become totally infatuated with the Egyptian queen even though she was only about 17 years old (he was 52). She bore him a son called Caesarion and later had children by Antony.

The affairs Cleopatra she had with both men is one of the great stories of the ancient world, and it's no surprise it was the subject of one of the most famously expensive epic movies of all time: *Cleopatra* (1963), starring Rex Harrison (Caesar), Richard Burton (Antony), and Elizabeth Taylor as guess-who. There's a lower-key and much funnier version called *Caesar and Cleopatra* (1945) starring Claude Rains as Caesar and Vivien Leigh as Cleopatra, based on the play by George Bernard Shaw. There's an even lower-key version called *Carry on Cleo* (1964) but the less said about that, the better.

Vercingetorix (fl. 52 BC, d. 46 BC)

Vercingetorix led the Gauls in a revolt against Julius Caesar in 52 BC. It was six years into the war against the Gauls, and Vercingetorix presented Caesar with an unprecedented challenge: the united tribes of Gaul. Vercingetorix destroyed farms and villages to stop the Roman army getting supplies. The

Gauls had hilltop strongholds with fortifications that were strong enough to resist Caesar's battering rams. His troops managed to burst into Avaricum (Bourges) and massacred almost 40,000 inhabitants, but Vercingetorix defeated Caesar at Gergovia which humiliated him and only helped spread the revolt. The climax came at the siege of Alesia (Alexia) where Caesar, vastly outnumbered, built massive siege works that separated the Alesians from a relief army. Alesia fell in the final battle, and Vercingetorix surrendered, being executed by Caesar in Rome in 46 BC. But he became a watchword for Gallic nationalism.

Christopher Lambert plays the hero in *Vercingetorix,* a French movie made in 2001, though the whole war is much more humorously commemorated in the *Asterix the Gaul* comic books and films created by Goscinny and Uderzo in 1959.

Caratacus (d. AD 43–51)

Caratacus led the resistance against the Roman invasion of Britain from the moment the Romans arrived in 43. Unlike most anti-Romans, he lasted a remarkably long time, considering the forces thrown against him. A prince of the Catuvellauni tribe, his domain was quickly overrun, so he escaped to the hills of Wales where he joined tribes together and held the Romans at bay in difficult upland country. He had the time of his life, giving the ancient world's superpower a monumental runaround (sounds familiar, doesn't it?). The Romans finally defeated him in a major battle, but Caratacus fled for sanctuary with a tribal queen called Cartimandua. Unfortunately for Caratacus, she handed him over to the Romans, and he was taken to Rome. Unlike Vercingetorix, however (see the preceding section), he was treated with respect by the emperor Claudius who pensioned him off. He spent his retirement in Rome, wondering why the Romans could possibly have been interested in conquering a remote and primitive place like Britain.

Boudica (d. AD 61)

In 60–61, Boudica led a destructive rebellion in Britain against Roman rule (see Chapter 16). Said to have been a powerful and impressive woman with a mane of red hair, she seems to have provided historians like Tacitus and Dio with a certain amount of suppressed erotic fascination at her dominatrix role in the uprising. Boudica and her family were the victims of oppressive Roman provincial administration. But what makes her really fascinating is how those historians portrayed Boudica as the exact opposite of Nero. It makes one wonder how true the picture is, but it tells us a huge amount about what Romans thought their rulers should be like. Nero was the effeminate man with none of the virtues a Roman leader should have, but Boudica was the masculine barbarian woman with all the virtues of leadership, bravery, and patriotism.

Boudica has been a frequent theme of television documentaries and dramatisations but oddly never a motion picture for cinema.

Simon Bar Cochba (fl. AD 132–135)

Bar Cochba's name means 'son of a star'. Because actual letters by him have been found, we now know his original name was Shim'on Ben Cosiba. He led the great Jewish revolt against the Romans in Palestine under Hadrian, the result of decades of resentment ever since the destruction of Jerusalem and the Temple in 70. Hadrian provoked the rebellion by banning circumcision and planning to build a new city on Jerusalem's site. Bar Cochba created an independent Jewish state and was even thought by some to be the Jewish Messiah. Hadrian sent a general called Julius Severus, who'd been toughened up by campaigning in Britain, and he successfully put the revolt down. Dio says the war cost the destruction of 50 fortresses and 985 villages, and the lives of 580,000 men. The figures are probably exaggerated, but it's clear it was a bloody war. When the revolt fell apart, some of the rebels hid out in Dead Sea Caves, but Bar Cochba was killed in a Roman attack on a place called Bethar. Jerusalem was replaced by a city called Aelia Capitolina.

The German tribes

As soon as Rome advanced north into Gaul and central Europe, she became exposed to the tribes of Germany. If you've seen *Gladiator* (2000), you'll remember the vicious opening battle between Marcus Aurelius's army in 180 and a horde of barbarian tribesmen. The Rhine marked the barrier, and throughout Rome's imperial history, holding that frontier was a constant nightmare on which Rome's very existence depended. The Germans started to become a real problem under Augustus, despite the efforts to integrate German tribal leaders. The catastrophe of AD 9 when three legions were lost (see Chapter 16) was psychologically devastating for Rome. One of the tribes involved was the Chatti, who later took part in the Revolt of Civilis (69–70) (also in Chapter 16). Domitian (81–96) had to fortify the gap between the Rhine and Danube to hold the Chatti back. It was largely successful, but by Marcus Aurelius's time (161–180), war had broken out on the frontier again (Chapter 17). Throughout the third and fourth centuries (Chapters 11, 12 and 13), the fighting continued on and off. The Germans played their own part in the last days of the Roman Empire in the West, even annoying Valentinian I so much in 374 that he literally died of rage (Chapter 21).

Chapter 26

Ten (or So) Great Roman Places to Visit

In This Chapter

▶ Places to see that still evoke Rome's extraordinary history

▶ Towns, amphitheatres, forts, frontiers, and plenty more

*T*here are remains of Rome's civilisation to be seen in just about every part of the world the Romans ruled. In this chapter, I list 10 (okay, I list 11; consider the last a bonus). You'll have heard of some of the places but might not be sure what there is to see. Other places you probably won't have heard of, but I've included them because they're truly marvellous and not to be missed at any price.

Rome and Ostia

Yes, I know this is an obvious one. Rome has remains of the forums, the imperial palaces, the Pantheon, original Roman bridges, and the Colosseum, of course, all of which have popped up throughout the book. But Rome has all sorts of other extraordinary remains a little off the beaten track. You can see the exceptional fifth-century late Roman church of Santa Sabina, for instance, and not far away is the amazing Monte Testaccio (the heap of Roman waste-oil *amphorae* from Spain; refer to Chapter 7). But nothing can be beat the ruins of the port of Rome at Ostia, now half an hour away by train on the coast at the mouth of the Tiber. With its streets, granaries, apartment blocks, and tombs, it evokes what everyday Rome once looked like for the ordinary Roman.

Pompeii and Herculaneum

Pompeii is the only place in the Roman Empire, apart from Ostia, where you can get a real sense of the Roman town as a functioning organism. The big sights here are the amphitheatre and the houses with their painted walls. But to get a real feel for the place, linger in the streets and look at the deeply-worn ruts in the flagstones – the evidence of real lives eked out here before the place was destroyed by Vesuvius in August 79. A few miles north are the even more outstanding, but less often visited, ruins of Herculaneum. Swamped by a pyroclastic mud flow, Herculaneum was much more deeply buried, with all sorts of organic remains preserved, right down to the carbonised bread in a street-side tavern. Here you can see Roman houses with upstairs rooms and a shop with a wooden rack for *amphorae* pottery containers.

Ravenna

Almost forgotten in north-east Italy, Ravenna was where the imperial court of the west holed itself up in the late fourth century. Thanks to its isolation, many of the magnificent late Roman churches and other buildings have survived almost totally intact. My personal favourite is the neat little Tomb of Galla Placidia with its extraordinary vaulted roofs covered with brilliantly coloured mosaics. Perhaps the most astonishing building of all is the mausoleum of Theodoric the Great, king of the Ostrogoths (ruled Italy AD 493–526) with its vault made of a single piece of Istrian stone, 35 feet (10 metres) wide and weighing about 300 tons. These buildings, although built later than most Roman buildings, preserve examples of technique that just don't survive as well elsewhere. Go to Chapter 21 for information about Galla Placidia and Theodoric the Great.

Ephesus

Sitting on the west coast of Turkey not far from a resort called Selçuk and an hour's drive south of the major port at Izmir is Ephesus, once one of the greatest cities of Asia Minor. Once a mighty port itself, Ephesus died when the harbour silted up, and it was left high and dry. Ephesus's ancient status is reflected in the epic scale of the ruins, which include the Great Theatre, where St Paul addressed the Ephesians in the mid-first century AD, and the vast towering façade of the Library of Celsus, which has been re-erected from the ruins. But for my money what makes Ephesus so fabulous is the sheer beauty of the setting, the vast crumbled fragments of gigantic buildings, and the realisation that, however great man's achievements, in the end all things must pass.

Aphrodisias

Aphrodisias is in Turkey, and until modern excavations, little or nothing was visible. If you can get to Turkey and make your way inland to the site from the coastal port of Izmir, you'll see the magnificent theatre, the odeon, and the extraordinary Temple of Aphrodite which was dismantled and turned inside out so that the columns of a classical temple became the columns between the nave and aisles of a Christian church. Aphrodisias was the centre of a major sculpture industry, exporting its products around the Roman Empire, and some of their work can be seen in the site museum. But the most memorable sight of all is the chariot-racing stadium which has to be the best-preserved in the whole Roman Empire.

Sbeitla

In ancient times, Sbeitla was called Sufetula, and it was in what is now Tunisia in North Africa. Sbeitla was once a fantastically rich Roman province where agriculture and olive groves were in abundance. These days, the Sahara has advanced north, and it's a very different place. Sbeitla is a good day trip from the coast, and you have to drive across the desert to get there. Because the town is so remote, it's escaped the worst ravages of time, and so, amazingly, the temples of its capital are largely intact, surrounded by the tumbled down ruins of the rest of the town which include magnificent mosaics. I like it because it shows that even a minor provincial town could have major public architecture, and it's one of the few places left where you can see reasonably intact Roman buildings.

Piazza Armerina

In Sicily, you can find one of the greatest Roman villas of the Roman Empire, now known locally as Villa Romana del Casale. Built between AD 300 and 320, it includes 3,500 square metres of mosaic flooring alone in an extraordinary complex of rooms, courtyards, porticoes, audience chambers, and baths. Some of the mosaics feature popular rural pastimes like hunting boar and hare, fishing, and even catching animals in North Africa for the circus. No-one knows who owned Piazza Armerina, but it's quite possible an emperor lived there, perhaps Maximian I who 'retired' in 305 (see Chapter 20), or his son Maxentius. It's the climax of villa living, aped by other people with money around the Roman Empire.

Hadrian's Wall

Rome's greatest frontier stretches from Newcastle to Carlisle in northern England. It's quite simply the Roman world's greatest surviving military monument with an array of ruined forts, mile-castles, turrets, ditches, inscriptions, temples, altars, and all set in magnificent wild scenery. The best-preserved sections are in the central sector with the forts of Housesteads and Chesters being two of the best-preserved. Nearby, the hinterland fort of Vindolanda is the source of the Roman writing tablets, still being recovered from ongoing excavations. Great museums at Carlisle and Newcastle store some of the best finds, but the forts at Wallsend and South Shields to the east are the centres, not only of wonderful museums and excavations, but also of pioneering rebuilding. Wallsend has a full-scale set of replica working Roman baths, while South Shields has a rebuilt fort gate, commandant's house, and barracks. There's nowhere else to see anything like that.

Petra

Petra is in Jordan, once part of Roman Syria. Founded in the sixth century BC, Petra wasn't taken over by the Romans until the end of the first century AD. It's a totally spectacular location on the edge of the desert and surrounded by huge sandstone hills which give the place its sensational array of orange, yellow, and red coloured landscape. The stone is easy to carve, and the rich Petrans commissioned the most extraordinary tombs cut into the hills with ornate and beautiful classical façades. Even today, the site is quite a trek to reach, but well worth it. Petra still has to be approached through a narrow cut called the Siq which is just 16 feet (5 metres) wide. The first rock-cut façade to greet the visitor is the *khazneh* ('treasury'), and it's 131 feet (40 metres) high.

Dendara

The Temple of Hathor at Dendara is the finest Egyptian temple to have survived. The reason I'm mentioning it is that parts of the main temple and several of the surrounding temples and other buildings were actually made in Roman times. The 'pharaohs' carved on the walls of the smaller temples are Roman emperors, including Augustus and Trajan, while the hypostyle hall in the big temple was built by Tiberius. On the back wall is Cleopatra with her son by Caesar, Caesarion, so it has great historical significance, too.

It's an epic place to visit, a couple of hours' drive north of Luxor, but well worth it because Dendara sums up the brilliant way the Romans adapted. Realising that Egypt was so steeped in traditions that stretched back thousands of years, the Romans made no effort to impose their own styles of architecture or gods. Instead they 'went native' and posed as Egyptian rulers worshipping Egyptian gods on Egyptian temples, and had their names engraved in hieroglyphs.

Bath

Bath, in Avon (England), was once called *Aquae Sulis* ('the Waters of Sul'). It started life as a natural hot spring, but the Romans made it into a religious, healing, and leisure complex complete with cult temple, massive baths complex, and an array of shops and services to cater for visitors from across the Roman world. People have been doing that in Bath ever since. You can descend to the subterranean galleries where the Roman ground level of the temple precinct is exposed, walk from here past the windows where Roman pilgrims hurled their offerings to the sacred spring, read their curse tablets and dedications to the combination god Sulis-Minerva, and put your hand in the waters of the Roman baths, still hot from the underground spring which bubbles up at around 117 ° Fahrenheit (47.2 ° Celsius) all the time.

Index

● **F** ●

● **G** ●

• S •

Notes

Notes

FOR DUMMIES®

Do Anything. Just Add Dummies

HOME

UK editions

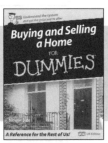

0-7645-7027-7

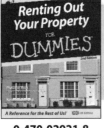

0-470-02921-8

0-7645-7054-4

PERSONAL FINANCE

0-7645-7023-4

0-470-02860-2

0-7645-7039-0

BUSINESS

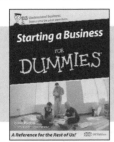

0-7645-7018-8

0-7645-7025-0

0-7645-7026-9

Answering Tough Interview Questions For Dummies
(0-470-01903-4)

Arthritis For Dummies
(0-470-02582-4)

Being the Best Man For Dummies
(0-470-02657-X)

British History For Dummies
(0-470-03536-6)

Building Confidence For Dummies
(0-470-01669-8)

Buying a Home on a Budget For Dummies
(0-7645-7035-8)

Buying a Property in Eastern Europe For Dummies
(0-7645-7047-1)

Children's Health For Dummies
(0-470-02735-5)

Cognitive Behavioural Therapy For Dummies
(0-470-01838-0)

CVs For Dummies
(0-7645-7017-X)

Diabetes For Dummies
(0-7645-7019-6)

Divorce For Dummies
(0-7645-7030-7)

eBay.co.uk For Dummies
(0-7645-7059-5)

European History For Dummies
(0-7645-7060-9)

Gardening For Dummies
(0-470-01843-7)

Genealogy Online For Dummies
(0-7645-7061-7)

Golf For Dummies
(0-470-01811-9)

Hypnotherapy For Dummies
(0-470-01930-1)

Marketing For Dummies
(0-7645-7056-0)

Neuro-linguistic Programming For Dummies
(0-7645-7028-5)

Nutrition For Dummies
(0-7645-7058-7)

Parenting For Dummies
(0-470-02714-2)

Pregnancy For Dummies
(0-7645-7042-0)

Retiring Wealthy For Dummies
(0-470-02632-4)

Rugby Union For Dummies
(0-470-03537-4)

Small Business Employment Law For Dummies
(0-7645-7052-8)

Starting a Business on eBay.co.uk For Dummies
(0-470-02666-9)

Su Doku For Dummies
(0-470-01892-5)

The GL Diet For Dummies
(0-470-02753-3)

Thyroid For Dummies
(0-470-03172-7)

UK Law and Your Rights For Dummies
(0-470-02796-7)

Wills, Probate and Inheritance Tax For Dummies
(0-7645-7055-2)

Winning on Betfair For Dummies
(0-470-02856-4)

FOR DUMMIES®

A world of resources to help you grow

HOBBIES

Poker
0-7645-5232-5

Sewing
0-7645-6847-7

Drawing
0-7645-5476-X

Also available:

Art For Dummies
(0-7645-5104-3)

Aromatherapy For Dummies
(0-7645-5171-X)

Bridge For Dummies
(0-7645-5015-2)

Card Games For Dummies
(0-7645-9910-0)

Chess For Dummies
(0-7645-8404-9)

Improving Your Memory
For Dummies
(0-7645-5435-2)

Massage For Dummies
(0-7645-5172-8)

Meditation For Dummies
(0-471-77774-9)

Photography For Dummies
(0-7645-4116-1)

Quilting For Dummies
(0-7645-9799-X)

EDUCATION

Cooking Basics
0-7645-7206-7

The Koran
0-7645-5581-2

Anatomy & Physiology
0-7645-5422-0

Also available:

Algebra For Dummies
(0-7645-5325-9)

Algebra II For Dummies
(0-471-77581-9)

Astronomy For Dummies
(0-7645-8465-0)

Buddhism For Dummies
(0-7645-5359-3)

Calculus For Dummies
(0-7645-2498-4)

Forensics For Dummies
(0-7645-5580-4)

Islam For Dummies
(0-7645-5503-0)

Philosophy For Dummies
(0-7645-5153-1)

Religion For Dummies
(0-7645-5264-3)

Trigonometry For Dummies
(0-7645-6903-1)

PETS

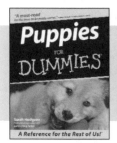

Puppies
0-7645-5255-4

Dog Training
0-7645-8418-9

Cats
0-7645-5275-9

Also available:

Labrador Retrievers
For Dummies
(0-7645-5281-3)

Aquariums For Dummies
(0-7645-5156-6)

Birds For Dummies
(0-7645-5139-6)

Dogs For Dummies
(0-7645-5274-0)

Ferrets For Dummies
(0-7645-5259-7)

Golden Retrievers
For Dummies
(0-7645-5267-8)

Horses For Dummies
(0-7645-9797-3)

Jack Russell Terriers
For Dummies
(0-7645-5268-6)

Puppies Raising & Training
Diary For Dummies
(0-7645-0876-8)